VOLUME 4

THE COLLECTED WORKS OF ARTHUR SELDON

Introducing Market Forces into “Public” Services

THE COLLECTED WORKS OF ARTHUR SELDON

VOLUME 1 The Virtues of Capitalism

VOLUME 2 The State Is Rolling Back

VOLUME 3 Everyman's Dictionary of Economics

VOLUME 4 Introducing Market Forces into "Public" Services

VOLUME 5 Government Failure and Over-Government

VOLUME 6 The Welfare State: Pensions, Health, and Education

VOLUME 7 The IEA, the LSE, and the Influence of Ideas (includes an index to the series)

Arthur Seldon

VOLUME 4

THE COLLECTED WORKS OF ARTHUR SELDON

Introducing Market Forces into "Public" Services

ARTHUR SELDON

Edited and with a New Introduction by Colin Robinson

LIBERTY FUND, Indianapolis

This book is published by Liberty Fund, Inc., a foundation established to encourage study of the ideal of a society of free and responsible individuals.

The cuneiform inscription that serves as our logo and as the design motif for our endpapers is the earliest-known written appearance of the word "freedom" (*amagi*), or "liberty." It is taken from a clay document written about 2300 B.C. in the Sumerian city-state of Lagash.

Printed in the United States of America

09 08 07 06 05 C 5 4 3 2 1
09 08 07 06 05 P 5 4 3 2 1

Library of Congress Cataloging-in-Publication Data
Seldon, Arthur.
Introducing market forces into "public" services / Arthur Seldon; edited and with a new introduction by Colin Robinson.
p. cm.—(collected works of Arthur Seldon; v. 4)
Includes bibliographical references and index.
ISBN 0-86597-545-0 (alk. paper)—ISBN 0-86597-553-1 (pbk.: alk. paper)
1. Finance, Public. 2. Social policy. 3. Welfare state. I. Title. II. Series: Seldon, Arthur. Works. 2004; v. 4.
HJ141 .S376 2005
361'.0068'1—dc22 2004042970

LIBERTY FUND, INC.
8335 Allison Pointe Trail, Suite 300
Indianapolis, Indiana 46250-1684

CONTENTS

INTRODUCTION

Volume 4 of the Collected Works of Arthur Seldon brings together six of Seldon's publications that discuss ways of paying for "public" services other than through general taxation.

One of the features of this volume is that it shows Seldon's prescience, starting in his early days as a professional economist, in foreseeing the dangers of "universalist" provision of services by the state. At a time when most British intellectuals were wholehearted supporters of centralized collectivism, Seldon identified and analyzed the underlying problems of state provision, financed by general taxation rather than specific charges. The problems he foresaw have undermined welfare states almost everywhere.

Throughout the volume, Seldon's main and recurring argument is that nonmarket provision, financed by taxpayers, leads to a fatal disconnection between suppliers and consumers. Suppliers do not depend directly on consumers for payment and therefore have no reason to discover what consumers want, to provide for existing demands, or to innovate to meet the demands of the future. Furthermore, because suppliers do not face any competition, efficiency standards set by rivals do not exist. Consumers see a price of zero at the point of service delivery, and so their demands inevitably expand far beyond what they would have been had they been charged the full cost of the service. In the absence of any price mechanism, the mismatch between supply and demand is not automatically corrected, and thus the state must resort to rationing by a bureaucracy insulated from the market, which, over time, develops a high-handed attitude toward those it is supposed to serve, regarding them as supplicants rather than as valuable customers.

In Britain, the country with which Seldon was most concerned, the reforms that he advocated are, almost forty years after he originally suggested them, tentatively being introduced by the Labour government first elected in 1997. Several years of office appear to have convinced the government that it can no longer simply pour more and more money into "public" services in the hope that they will improve. Grudgingly, Labour has accepted that market forces must play a bigger role and it is very gradually embarking on the necessary reforms, though evidently it has yet to understand and accept the full implications of the Seldon analysis of the benefits of charging.

In the earliest publication in this volume—"Which Way to Welfare?" from *Lloyds Bank Review,* October 1966—Seldon sets out some of the problems of providing "welfare" centrally through the state. He writes of the

> inadequacies, indignities and injustices in all the welfare services, which exhibit increasing demand and flagging supply (p. 3).

The public sector has been inflated and politicians have been diverted from the tasks they should have been performing. The solution, he says, is to create

> the legal and institutional framework within which, where practicable, personal welfare services can be supplied through the market to consumers armed with purchasing power, original or supplemented, sufficient for at least essential purchases (p. 3).

He goes on to explain various ways of creating such markets (for example, by tax rebates, subsidies, cash grants to consumers, or vouchers). These methods are, however, second best: a better way of establishing a market would be through a general reduction in taxation to allow people to pay charges or insurance contributions at market levels. The eventual aim should be that

> It must become more proper and moral for a man to work for himself and his family than to expect others to work for him, unless he cannot help himself (p. 17).

In 1967, the year after "Which Way to Welfare?," the Institute of Economic Affairs published a paper by Seldon entitled *Taxation and Welfare* (Research Monograph 14). It is the second paper in this volume. *Taxation and Welfare* is based on an April 1967 opinion survey carried out jointly by the IEA and the company Mass-Observation. Among the questions asked in the survey were the following: How much tax does the government take from your earnings? How much tax should it take? Should "welfare" spending concentrate on the most needy? and Should the existing welfare system be replaced by one using cash payments or vouchers? The April 1967 survey followed up a number of earlier surveys, starting in 1963, in which the IEA and Mass-

Observation pioneered studies of public attitudes toward state and private welfare provision.

One of the principal findings of the survey was that, contrary to mainstream intellectual opinion at the time, there was no consensus in favor of universal benefits paid by the state and financed through general taxation. Seldon described this result as "unexpected and perhaps . . . remarkable" (p. 56). Almost twice as many of the respondents (65 percent) supported selective benefits, concentrated on the needy, as favored universal benefits (35 percent). Nor was there evidence to support another generally held view of the time—that support for universalism would be strongest among lower-income people.

State welfare through the provision of services in kind, concludes Seldon, has been a "tragic error" (p. 76) and has been "tried and found wanting" (p. 77). High-quality health, education, housing, and similar services will not be provided through taxation; rather, informed purchasers in a market are required. State services in kind should be replaced by

> social benefits in cash, or coupon, for all except the small minority of people . . . incapable of learning choice (p. 77).

In the 1970s, Seldon returned to the argument that a large part of government expenditure is not directed at genuinely "public" goods or services and that markets in the relevant goods and services be established so that consumers can decide for themselves how much they wish to spend on those goods and services. *Catch '76 . . . ?* is an IEA Occasional Paper (number 47), published in 1976, in which Seldon assembled a collection of essays on Britain's then-precarious economic position.

Seldon's own essay in *Catch '76*, "Remove the Financing Flaw in 'Public' Services," reproduced as the third work in this volume of the Collected Works, is notable for a table (p. 86) that lists items of government expenditure and, for each one, shows first the extent to which charges were levied for the goods and services provided by the government, and second a subjective estimate of the extent of private benefit from the government expenditure. For most items the charges are very small. Indeed, they are tiny in relation to the considerable private benefits that Seldon estimates: for the main education services, for example, Seldon puts the private benefit element at 80 to 100 percent, whereas the element of private benefit implied by the proportion of fees and charges to total expenditure is in most cases well under 10 percent. Of course, one can argue about the precise size of the private benefits, but Seldon's purpose in producing the table was to emphasize his point that, though much government expenditure is justified by politicians on the grounds that the goods and services are "public," in most cases the benefits of spending could perfectly well be appropriated privately. Charging for these services is therefore not only possible but also desirable to promote economic efficiency.

Charge, the fourth work in this volume, published in 1977, is a much longer and more detailed analysis of the issues addressed in "Remove the Financing Flaw in 'Public' Services." Seldon was invited to write the book by the publisher Maurice Temple Smith following a letter that Seldon had written to the *Times. Charge* sold well, being reprinted in 1978, the year after first publication.

Early in the book, Seldon quotes approvingly Keynes's remark that governments should concentrate on doing "those things which are not done at all" rather than "things which individuals are doing already" (p. 110). That remark provides the theme for the book, which sets out to demonstrate that a large part of the goods and services provided by British governments are not "public" at all and that charges should be applied to them. The goods and services supplied by government

> do not all have to be organised by government and financed by taxes. Some could be financed by prices. They are not all necessarily in the public interest. Some could be organised outside government. This possibility opens up new vistas of wider choices (p. 131).

Seldon begins by analyzing in some detail, though in simple language, the functions of price—which, as he says, should be considered as a neutral and informative link between buyer and seller rather than as a barrier to purchases. Without price, he points out, the prime means of determining preferences is absent, and so allocation of scarce resources takes place by politicians and bureaucrats who act in a state of ignorance about what consumers want. The machinery of representative democracy is "avoidable and inefficient" where there are private benefits, and it

> unnecessarily but irremediably prejudices lower-income people with little or no social connections, political influence or economic muscle (p. 287).

Seldon separates the main elements of government expenditure into those that are public goods in the economist's sense (of which defense is the main item), those in which some of the benefits are private (for example, roads and public lighting), and those in which most of the benefits are private (such as education, health, and housing) (table B, pp. 136–37). In total, he estimates only about a third of British government expenditure is on goods and services that necessarily have to be financed by taxes (p. 286). Thus, he claims, most state services "yield separable private services that could be more efficiently financed by charges" (p. 286).

Much of the book (part 2) is taken up with detailed analyses of education, medical care, housing, roads, local authority services, public corporations, and other principal items of government expenditure. In these chapters, Seldon shows how government has taken over functions that used to be exercised by the private sector even though, in most cases, there is no "public good" case for it to do so. He explains how charging for such services could be introduced and how consumers and taxpayers would benefit.

In part 3, Seldon confronts the arguments of those who favor state provision and financing. For Seldon, poverty is not an acceptable argument: it is better treated by a reverse income tax. People's supposed "irresponsibility" in making choices is also an invalid argument: they would become more responsible if they were placed in a market. The costs of provision are usually not lower but higher when the state is the supplier. Externality arguments for state provision are generally unsubstantiated. Moreover, Seldon argues that there is no basis for the belief that government control is required to avoid private monopoly: on the contrary, government control perpetuates monopoly and encourages lobbying.

Not long after the publication of *Charge,* in April 1979, the IEA held a seminar to discuss ways of keeping government in check. The seminar was opened by Lord (Lionel) Robbins and addressed by a number of distinguished speakers who analyzed the growth of government and suggested ways of curbing its powers: the proceedings were published by the IEA in 1979 as *The Taming of Government,* Readings 21.

Seldon's contribution to the seminar, "Micro-economic Controls—Disciplining the State by Pricing," is the fifth paper in this volume. In the paper, Seldon begins from the proposition that macroeconomic controls on government are not enough to keep government down to an appropriate size because they will be devised and implemented by politicians and bureaucrats. Following *Charge* and his earlier works on the subject, he puts forward powerful arguments for subjecting state spending to the more objective test of the market: it should price its services and try to sell them in competition with private suppliers. Seldon uses a table similar to that in *Charge* to demonstrate that only around one-third of government spending can reasonably be classified as on "public" goods. Wherever possible, therefore, charges should be imposed on services provided by government. Taxes should be reduced and a negative income tax introduced to help the poor. Seldon summarizes his case for charging as follows:

> The mechanism is quite clear and simple: if you pay directly for something in the market you buy ("demand") less than if you pay indirectly to government through taxes, because you then think its price is nil—that it is "free" (p. 310).

He acknowledges that there are sometimes difficulties in charging (for example, administration costs and lack of information about the right charge). Nevertheless, the drawbacks of not charging are more damaging.

The final paper in this volume is *The Riddle of the Voucher* (IEA Hobart Paperback 21), published in 1986. Its purpose, in Seldon's words, is to study

> the reasons why the education voucher, despite impressive intellectual lineage and distinguished academic advocacy, has so far failed to be applied in British public policy (p. 330).

It reviews the "obstacles, in faulty ideas and vested interests, that obstructed" introduction of the voucher (p. 333).

As earlier papers in this volume make clear, Seldon himself had long advocated charging or vouchers for government services, including education, and British academic economists had since the 1960s also supported education vouchers.[1] Still earlier advocacy of the voucher had come from Milton Friedman.[2]

In the early 1980s, the time seemed ripe for introduction of the voucher in Britain. A reforming government sympathetic to market ideas was in office, led by Margaret (later Lady) Thatcher. Ministers in the Department of Education and Science, especially Sir Keith (later Lord) Joseph, the senior minister who was a well-known advocate of the use of market forces, were known to have been impressed by the intellectual case for vouchers. They had made approving comments about vouchers in political speeches and had been considering in some detail how to introduce vouchers into the education system.

The ministers had gone so far as to invite two education lobbies to comment on ways of overcoming the difficulties envisaged by department of-

1. Notably, A. T. Peacock and J. Wiseman, *Education for Democrats*, IEA Hobart Paper 25, 1964; and E. G. West, *Education and the State*, IEA, 1965, 2d ed. (1970), 3rd ed. (revised and extended), Liberty Fund, 1994.

2. Milton Friedman, "The Role of Government in Education," in *Economics and the Public Interest*, ed. Robert Solo, Rutgers University Press, 1955.

ficials in introducing the voucher. One of these organizations, FEVER (Friends of the Education Voucher Experiment in Representative Regions), in turn invited a number of academics to respond: eleven did so through FEVER, and another three commented separately. Seldon summarizes these academic responses and includes his own in a list of "refutations" in part II of *The Riddle of the Voucher.* Yet, as Seldon explains in 1983, without any specific response from officials to the points made by the academics, the secretary of state for education pronounced the education voucher "dead." Furthermore, even though soon afterward ministers again began to make favorable comments about the voucher, no action followed. The book sets out to solve this "riddle," using three main sources of evidence: documents that passed between the Department of Education and named academics in 1981–82 or that were written in 1983–84, confidential conversations between Seldon and unnamed "knowledgeable individuals in the political process" (p. 333), and records kept by FEVER.

As Seldon points out, the attitude of the Department of Education and Science toward the voucher was essentially defensive, and its objections were completely rejected by the academics, who were "somewhat surprised at the indifferent quality of the argument" (p. 356). He goes on to discuss, with the aid of some academic commentators, the underlying reasons why the voucher was rejected, principally because of its political unacceptability rather than because it was administratively impracticable.

To understand these underlying reasons, says Seldon, the key is public choice theory and, in particular, its emphasis on the power of organized interest groups. Economists should recognize from the episode of the voucher that a good idea will not come to pass "simply because a Government of sympathetic politicians is furnished with the intellectual argument" (p. 391). Powerful interest groups opposed the voucher and overwhelmed the initial instinct of politicians that this was an opportunity to garner a "harvest" of votes from grateful parents.[3]

> The voucher was a challenge to the formidable fortress of paternalism, professional corporatism, monopoly and political authority that had long

3. An insight into the strength of the opposition is provided by a previously unpublished letter from Sir Keith Joseph to Sir Alan Peacock in 1992. Sir Alan, one of the originators of the idea of an education voucher, had been asked by Sir Keith to help counter the opposition of his officials to the introduction of a voucher. Joseph's letter, reproduced in Alan Peacock, "Victory for Vouchers," *Economic Affairs* (autumn 1995), identifies the sources of opposition and says any experiment with vouchers would probably have been deliberately wrecked by some unions and the educational establishment.

> ruled British education. That the ramparts did not fall to the first intellectual assault was almost predictable (p. 389).

Among the interest groups, the civil servants in the Department of Education were in a key position because they would have been in charge of the voucher's introduction. They most likely viewed it as dangerous because it would have transferred influence and control of education away from them and to parents. Ministers, even in a reforming government, were unwilling to antagonize their civil servants: they will often tolerate bureaucratic obstruction of reform proposals because disaffected bureaucrats can undermine ministerial authority. Many teachers also opposed the voucher—those who are "security minded" would have felt threatened by the idea of becoming accountable to parents. So, as frequently happens, it was "producer" interests that combined to seal the fate of the voucher proposal, even though its introduction would have been very much to the advantage of pupils and parents.

There are, says Seldon, important lessons to be learned from the voucher affair that go

> to the roots of British democracy. The politicisation of education has transferred power from *demos* to public "demos" in which the dispersed parent cannot match the marching, banner-carrying teacher (p. 416).

Thus, for Seldon, the ultimate objective must be to depoliticize education, through choice and competition, for the benefit of consumers. One step he advocates to bypass the organized pressure groups is to replace the Department of Education's role as provider of tax-financed schools with a new agency that would distribute vouchers.

The last paper in this volume conveys essentially the same message as the first. The consistency of the message throughout this volume is because, for many years and often as a lone voice, Seldon has maintained that tax-financed government provision of welfare inflates demand, restricts supply, and produces services of inferior quality. Purchasing power should, he says, be restored to people by reductions in taxes and, where necessary, by specific measures such as vouchers. People will then act as consumers, behaving as they do in other markets, and a variety of suppliers will compete to meet their demands. Efficiency in the provision of these services will improve, and, above all, people will regain the incentive to provide for themselves instead of relying on the state.

WHICH WAY TO WELFARE?

Which Way to Welfare?

For more than a century, since before the Forster Education Act of 1870, the philosophy underlying the welfare services—education, health, housing, pensions, libraries and the arts—has been that, where personal income is low or mis-spent, they must be provided by public authority at less than market costs and prices. Professor Walter Hagenbuch's penetrating analysis in this *Review* in 1953[1] showed that the early aim of relieving primary or secondary poverty had developed into an all-embracing universalist philosophy of equal, growing, free benefits for everyone for all time.

The indictment against this philosophy is formidable. It appears to put equality before humanity. It has denied pensioners, large families, neglected children, the mentally sick and others in need. Yet even its equality is spurious, since equal treatment of people in unequal circumstances is inequality. It lies at the root of the inadequacies, indignities and injustices in all the welfare services, which exhibit increasing demand and flagging supply. It has unnecessarily inflated the public sector of the economy, diverted politicians from the essential tasks of government, not least the protection of persons and property, strained our representative institutions.

Attempts by all parties to create humane, effective welfare services without a mechanism for measuring preferences and costs have failed. This article argues that the lasting solution is to create the legal and institutional framework within which, where practicable, personal welfare services can be supplied through the market to consumers armed with purchasing power, original or supplemented, sufficient for at least essential purchases. The small residue, perhaps 1 or 2 per cent, requiring personal care or assistance in kind could then be given the resources they have long been denied.

Professor Hagenbuch's review appeared at about the same time that Mr. Colin Clark's articles (later published under the title *Welfare and Taxation*)

1. "The Rationale of the Social Services," *Lloyds Bank Review,* July, 1953.

pioneered a strategy for transferring welfare from the State to voluntary and private agencies. Together they initiated or crystallized a continuing reconsideration of the universalist welfare policy and philosophy. Yet, in spite of mounting evidence of failure, it persists in the writings of sociologists. One or two, notably Professor Brian Abel-Smith, have indeed recently shown disquiet at the absence of choice by the citizen and at the arrogant power of the public official:

> You wait your turn and are told what you will have. And when shortages of staff generate rudeness from public servants, the customer is seldom in a position to take his custom elsewhere. . . . We have got to get rid of the autocratic frame of mind of some civil servants, local government officers and councillors—even Labour councillors.[2]

Professor Abel-Smith's use of "customer" is rare in sociological writing, which does not normally see that the citizen is not a customer unless he pays for a choice between suppliers competing for his custom. In sociological folklore and political wishful thinking he remains a dependent "beneficiary" beholden to benefactors. To enfranchize the citizen and make him sovereign will require more than "a change in the attitude of all those working in the social services."[3] He must be empowered to reject what does not satisfy. And that he can do only in a market that offers choice.

The Fallacies of Free Welfare

A century of increasing welfare services provided by public authority with no close link, or no link at all, at the point of service, between payment and cost has demonstrated three basic errors: first, its assumptions on the nature of man and his motives; second, the *non sequitur* in the logic of proceeding from the premiss of poverty to public provision; third, the error of supposing that price was no more than a "barrier" to be disguised, distorted or "abolished" by fiat or decree.

The history of free, or partly free, State welfare has substantially vindicated the major precepts and premisses of classical political economy. It has postulated a degree of disinterested benevolence in the givers and of self-less abnegation in the recipients that has never existed anywhere in history except in short periods of emergency, military or civil.

2. *Freedom in the Welfare State,* Fabian Tract 353, 1964.
3. Ibid.

The assumptions, explicit or implicit, on human nature derive from a mystical wishful hoping for a "common purpose," "general good" or "public interest" that misleads its proponents to over-generalize from emergency into normalcy. "The public interest" has no vivid, recognizable, *generally* acceptable meaning in everyday life: human conduct is motivated by the requirements, desires and hopes of the people whom individuals know around them: their families, friends, associates. The error has been to condemn the service of visible, comprehensible purposes as hedonistic self-interest rather than to gear it to mutual satisfaction, which it creates no less effectively because it is indirect and unintentional. Instead, conflicts that individuals cannot resolve have been created—in price and incomes policies, business practice and trade union activity as well as in welfare—between private purposes, which are understood and clear, and social objectives, which are ambiguous and obscure. A man will work harder for "the common good" if his children want food or his wife a new coat, or for a time if Hitler is shelling Dover, than if politicians, who may be culpable, tell him that sterling is under pressure or the gold reserves have lost £37 millions.

Little wonder that politicians down the centuries have conjured crises and emergencies to secure more ready acquiescence in the surrender of private purposes to government discretion. The classical thinkers were wiser. The notion of a universal sharing of goods and services among self-less men received short shrift from Jeremy Bentham:

> The prospects of benevolence and concord, which have seduced so many ardent minds, are . . . chimeras of the imagination. Whence should arise, in the division of labour, the determining motive to choose the most painful? How many frauds would be attempted to throw that burden upon another, from which a man would wish to exempt himself? . . . What an apparatus of penal laws would be required, to replace the gentle liberty of choice and the critical reward of the cares which each one takes for himself. . . .

The doctrine of the primacy of uncomprehended social purpose fastens a guilt complex on the man who serves the people he knows and the purposes he understands. It thus destroys the prime mover of productive effort.

In our day, the philosophers of universal disinterest proliferate among the *literati* as well as among sociologists. Only a few writers with the most penetrating understanding of human nature see through it. Mr. E. M. Forster, whose *A Passage to India* ranks as one of the most perceptive studies of human hope and motive, has punctured its pretences:

> Love is a great force in private life; it is indeed the greatest of all things: but love in public affairs does not work. It has been tried and tried again: by the Christian civilizations of the Middle Ages, and by the French Revolution, a secular movement which reasserted the Brotherhood of Man. And it has always failed. The idea that nations should love one another, or that business concerns or marketing boards should love one another, or that a man in Portugal should love a man in Peru of whom he has never heard—it is absurd, unreal, dangerous. It leads us into perilous and vague sentimentalism. "Love is what is needed" we chant, and then sit back and the world goes on as before . . . we can only love what we know personally. And we cannot know much.

The insight of this passage—the similarity with Bentham is significant—is perhaps not unexpected in a great-grandson of Henry Thornton, author of the essay *Paper Credit of Great Britain* (1802).

Poverty and free welfare

The *non sequitur* is clear. Public provision of welfare has been justified by an appeal to poverty. The incomes of some, or most, people, it is said, are too low to enable them to pay for education or health services or homes or pensions (or books, or music, or art . . .); therefore the State must provide them free or at low prices. Or incomes are enough but many people will not buy them because of ignorance or neglect. These reasons—primary and secondary poverty—were used a hundred years ago to justify State education; they are still deployed today. They are fallacies.

If some incomes are low it does not follow that the State must supply the required purchases for everyone free or at a price below cost. Shortage of private money can be a case for providing State aid in cash so that market prices can be paid: education grants, sickness, unemployment, maternity benefits, family allowances, pensions, national assistance; and even then only if voluntary, flexible organizations cannot supply the missing money better, or if families cannot be encouraged to redistribute income between their members. But it is not a case for supplying universal State education or hospitals or homes free or below cost. Yet a large part—some £3,400 millions out of £6,500 millions of tax and social insurance revenue allocated to State welfare—represents expenditure on goods, services and capital formation.

Nor does secondary poverty necessarily require free or subsidized State welfare in kind. If parents will not pay for the desirable minimum of education, or sick people for medical treatment, or families for homes, or earners for rights to retirement income, logic points in the first place to methods of impelling them to do so by State requirements or standards ensured by inspection. It requires not necessarily State schools but receipt of tuition that satisfies State requirements, not necessarily council housing but housing to council standards. There may be emergency conditions in which State provision—particularly in unpredictable illness or accident—is administratively convenient because there is no time for the market process to work, although, as seen in the NHS casualty services, the State machine is often too cumbersome to respond to emergency. But the welfare services are not designed for a society in permanent crisis, an implication of much sociological writing and political advocacy.

The price barrier

The confusion over the price "barrier" makes easy victims of politicians. The reasoning is *simpliste:* if a price stands between a man and his pension, or a child and school, or a woman and medical treatment, remove the barrier. So is humanity reconciled with political popularity.

But instead of solving the problem, the politician has dispersed or distorted its symptom. Prices have two central—and, as the communist countries are discovering, indispensable—economic functions. They are not only a form of payment by a buyer (and income to a seller): they also ration scarce quantities. If prices are removed or reduced, something or someone else must ration in their place, and these substitutes set in motion a chain of reactions that can reverberate increasingly throughout the economy for decades long after the circumstances that called them into being have disappeared. In education they have lingered at least since 1870, in health services since 1911, in housing since 1915, in pensions since 1925.

Nil or depressed prices swell demand and choke off supply. Demand has to be rationed by officials, often well-intentioned but necessarily less impartial than impersonal prices. Supply has to be provided by public authority out of compulsory levies, which are usually inadequate, so supply is "short." Income deficiencies are alleviated, but in the end those who should benefit most may suffer most, by degeneration into supplicants asking favours. The province of the official and his political employer is enlarged. It will be difficult to reduce except by mounting pressure, perhaps from the children of those originally aided whose income no longer needs supplementing and who want something different from what the State provides: smaller classes, the right to paint a council house purple, doctors with time to explain symptoms, pensions that suit pensioners rather than the Newcastle computer.

The alternative to universal welfare at below-market price is to create markets in which supply responds to individual demand based on personal income, supplemented where necessary by the State. The price barrier should not be destroyed; it should be surmounted.

The Creation of Markets in Welfare: Demand

Most wage-earners and many salary-earners have never had in welfare the sense of buying power they have in consumption. Even where a choice is feasible, it can be exercised only by people with larger incomes, who can both pay taxes for State services they do not use and buy services of their choice in the open market. Millions are financially or psychologically unable to choose between State and private welfare, even when permitted by law.

The financial competence can be created in several ways. First, more income tax can be returned or excused. This method will not, however, substantially influence most wage-earners. Second, notional tax rebates for all could, in principle, be allowed on premiums on insurance policies for school fees, pensions, health services and on mortgage interest. But it is difficult to see that they would quickly enliven interest among those who pay little or no tax. The method required must dramatize the authority of the consumer. He must know the power of making a choice by rejecting unsatisfactory services and selecting the most preferred. Tax rebates of any kind are too remote from the act of choice to convey this power.

A third method is an extension of State or local authority subsidies for suppliers, as now with direct grant schools, universities, hospitals, council housing, Exchequer supplements for retirement pensions. This method reduces school or university fees, hospital charges, rents, etc., below full market cost, or eliminates them, with the familiar effects on demand and supply.

A fourth method is that of cash grants to the consumer rather than the producer—parents rather than schools, patients rather than doctors or hospitals, tenants or buyers of homes rather than councils. This method would make possible full market prices for State and private services, and it would substantially avoid the defects of the other three. But the new buyers would mostly have had little or no experience in making a choice, and guidance, tuition, advice and information might be desirable or essential in the early years.

A fifth alternative might be coupons for specific welfare purchases, or perhaps for a range. An education voucher, for example, could represent the cost of State primary and secondary education, certainly current and perhaps also partly capital; a health voucher could represent the cost of the personal services in the National Health Service, and so on. The vouchers could be taxable, tapered off as incomes rose, and arranged to reward economy and discourage waste.

Ultimately, a sixth method would be best. It would dispense with returns of tax, redistribution of tax revenue, subsidies to producers, cash and vouchers. It is a reduction in taxation so that all could pay charges or insurance contributions at market levels.

Dr. E. G. West has rightly argued in *Education and the State* that vouchers are a transitory phase to market prices paid out of unsupplemented incomes when taxes have been reduced. How long the voucher phase would last turns on economic advance, administrative practicabilities and political timing. But it would seem that returning or redistributing taxation by voucher is an effective way of easing the creation of market pricing and eventual tax reductions.

The experience of other countries is relevant, because it suggests that most of the devices reviewed are both administratively and politically feasible in countries with lower and with higher incomes than in Britain. In education, Australia does not tax income spent on fees, books, uniforms or fares for full-time attendance at a school, college or university or a tutor up to £150 a year; Holland gives university and some other students loans (as well as grants) up to £120 a year. In health services, Norway and New Zealand refund part of the fees paid to doctors; Australia does not tax medical fees or insurance; Switzerland gives subsidies to private insurance organizations. In housing, Germany, France, Denmark, Sweden and Switzerland give (and the Netherlands and Austria are considering) cash grants to tenants and, in most cases, owner-occupiers, varying with income and number of children; Poland is following on similar lines.

The general effect of these devices is to facilitate a choice outside public services and to enable markets to be constructed and market prices to be charged; they create consumers who can go shopping with a choice out of passive recipients who take, with gratitude or resignation, what the State provides.

Measuring potential demand

What demand would there be in Britain if a choice between State and private welfare were available on roughly equal terms? Only suitably devised experiments would yield decisive conclusions and indicate the required administrative mechanics.

In the meantime, a second-best procedure is to construct a hypothetical market by adapting the techniques of opinion polling to market research. In 1963 and in 1965 the Institute of Economic Affairs commissioned Mass Observation to ask a national sample of male married heads of households of working age whether they preferred free State education and health service to the opportunity to buy private education and health services with the aid of vouchers covering part of the cost. (Pensions and housing were omitted because they could not conveniently be covered in the same questionnaire.)[4] The findings have yielded a crude measure of "demand," in the economist's sense of the amounts bought at alternative prices, and of its responsiveness to changes in price and income.

In the 1965 survey, the proportion of the sample using State services was asked whether they would accept a £50 voucher and add £100 to the fees of a day secondary school, and again a £100 voucher and add £50. The findings were that 15 per cent would take the smaller and 30 per cent the larger voucher. And the proportion that would accept each voucher rose successively from 10 and 19 per cent of the "semi-skilled and skilled" group to 23 and 37 per cent of the "upper middle and middle." The occupational groups are defined in terms of occupational status as well as income; this grouping of the relevant criteria is probably better than income alone since the skilled and semi-skilled are less accustomed to buying welfare in the open market than are the lower middle or middle group, even though their incomes, particularly after income tax, may be higher.

For health, vouchers were put at £5 and £7, to which £5 and £3 would have to be added for health insurance of £10 per year per head. Again, the responses were internally consistent in terms of price and socio-occupational group. In total, 23 per cent would take the £5 voucher and 30 per cent the £7

4. The theoretical and practical aspects are reviewed in Harris and Seldon, *Choice in Welfare 1965*, IEA, 1965.

voucher. The proportion taking the £5 voucher rose from 17 to 36 per cent and the £7 voucher from 23 to 47 per cent through the socio-occupational groups.

These market surveys were conducted in 1963 and 1965. (A field survey in early 1966 by the British Market Research Bureau for the British United Provident Association has yielded a broadly comparable result on the health voucher.) It would be premature to draw precise conclusions from them. The purpose is primarily to emphasize the necessity for the "micro-economic" study of individual consumer preferences in response to known prices and costs. The value of market analysis has tended to be neglected in the post-Keynesian fashion for macro-economic studies of "overall" national income, output or "needs" that have proved barren or misleading in the formulation of welfare policy.

This technique of voucher-values was designed to reveal preferences between "free" tax-paid State welfare and private welfare, even at an additional cost to the consumer. If the voucher-values were a higher proportion of school fees or medical insurance costs, the acceptance rate would be even higher than those recorded in the surveys. The transition period between the present financially-biased choice between State and private services, complicated by double payment and tax rebates, and the unbiased choice of a system in which State, local authority and private services charge fees covering full costs might perhaps be based on a compromise cost and pricing structure in which the consumer paid current costs directly in the market and capital costs indirectly through the Exchequer or the council treasurer.

In such circumstances, the voucher could be issued to all parents, potential patients, tenants or occupiers and pensioners to use as purchasing power in the market. The "social divisiveness" charged against the system in which most families with free or subsidized education and health services contrast with small minorities that pay for something different would end. We should all be consumers paying for all our purchases, and if some paid higher school fees, health insurance premiums, rents, mortgage repayments or saved more through pension contributions than others they would no more be regarded as morally different from them than people who spend more on shoes, sherries or shampoos. There would then be some prospect that families spending more on education or medical treatment or on a home would not be derided for indulging in "status symbols," but praised for family concern and providence.

The Creation of Markets in Welfare: Supply

Whatever the efforts made to inhibit independent education or health services, to impede private house-building and home-ownership or to discourage private saving for retirement, they will never be suppressed; and as income rises and social aspirations grow they will be more difficult to resist. However much people may prefer choice and personal service, on the other hand, State welfare will remain because some para-welfare services cannot be supplied through the market or competition makes them more efficient than private services. Both systems will continue as the demand for choice widens with rising incomes, but their rôles will change.

State suppliers

Public expenditure on social services and housing has risen from under £2,000 millions in 1949/50 to just over £6,500 millions in 1965/66. On what principles do politicians provide State welfare?

Beveridge, Keynes and a long line of British economists have discovered that political policy is not based on rational determination of "the common good" but on a wide range of influences, from lofty, long-run principles through Cabinet compromises and official resistances to short-run, sectional pressures. Since the early 1950s, however, new developments in the economic theories of political policy-making and the processes of political choice have been pioneered by young American economists: Professors Kenneth Arrow, Duncan Black, J. M. Buchanan, Anthony Downs, Gordon Tullock and others.

One of the approaches envisages the politician as an entrepreneur devising social policies for his "market" of tax-paying consumers in order to maximize his returns in votes. If politicians insist on furnishing personal services that can be provided in the market and that they cannot suppress by legal prohibitions or fiscal penalty, they act as entrepreneurs in competition with non-political suppliers and they must inform themselves of consumer preferences or go out of business. This is a central dilemma of universalist State welfare that aims to ensure not merely minima but maxima—"the best possible"—for if it tries to provide the maxima practicable for all it will never better the best accessible to some. And the dilemma will be heightened the more rising incomes make people dissatisfied with "the best available to all" and excite them to aspire to the best available to each.

Do the political entrepreneurs know what the consumer-tax-payer wants?

Political elections are not helpful: voters cannot indicate in the polling booth that they would be prepared to pay 5s. a week for smaller classes, or 1d. a week more for better-sprung hospital beds, or 6d. a week on the rates for more frequent refuse collection, or £10 a year for adding life assurance to State pensions. Nor does the "machinery" for "consultation" with statutory or voluntary bodies record individual preferences. The only definitive source is the independent sector. If politicians want to know what their consumers want, or would want if they had a free choice, they must look at the independent schools, the Nuffield Nursing Homes, owner-occupied homes, and not least the variety of pension schemes devised by the pension consultants and a few life offices. State welfare needs private sectors no less than the communist economies will need free world prices so long as they try to manage without markets.

It is odd that the State has rarely used its opinion polling agency, the Social Survey of the Central Office of Information, to engage in market research so that it had information to check its suppositions. Perhaps it would rather not know. For several years there have been rumblings of dissatisfaction, recorded, for example, by the survey commissioned by *Socialist Commentary* after the 1959 general election and in 1963 by *New Society.* The first detailed and systematic survey based on relative costs, that of the IEA and Mass Observation, enquired into opinion on two main alternatives: more taxation for increasing State services or less taxation and the right to contract out. In both 1963 and 1965 just under half for education and more than half for health services and pensions favoured contracting out automatically by income or individually by personal option.

The social philosophy of State welfare—that the State knows better than the citizen and that the citizen prefers State to private welfare—cannot be sustained, because the State does not know what the citizen would choose if he had a choice. It cannot generalize from the ill-informed choices of the financially, socially or mentally exceptional. It cannot appeal to the out-of-date choices before it restricted them 40 or 60 or 100 years ago. It rests on gratuitous political conjecture that professes the public weal but almost certainly defies public sentiment.

Independent suppliers

Despite fiscal and legal discouragement, political hostility or indifference and institutional inhibitions the private sector has shown independent vitality (see table following). Private health insurance had been expected to

Indicators of Expenditure on Private Welfare, 1948–65*

	Health Insurance[1]				Education	Housing		Pensions[5]	
	British United Provident Association, Hospital Service Plan, and Western Provident Association		Hospital Contributory Schemes		Children at preparatory public and other wholly independent schools[3]			Insured occupational schemes and individual policies	
	sub-scribers[2] (m.)	sub-scriptions (£m.)	con-tributors (m.)	total income (£m.)	number (m.)	Owner-occupiers (m.)	Expen-diture[4] (£m.)	members (m.)	premiums (£m.)
1948	0.05	0.13	n.a.	n.a.	n.a.	3.50	562	n.a.	n.a.
1950	0.05	0.20	3.41	2.05	0.51	n.a.	586	n.a.	n.a.
1955	0.26	1.66	3.83	2.74	0.51	n.a.	707	2.33	116
1956	0.30	2.08	3.86	2.90	0.51	"	738	2.59	132
1957	0.34	2.51	3.91	2.98	0.51	"	774	2.92	152
1958	0.37	3.09	3.93	3.03	0.51	"	904	3.21	169
1959	0.41	3.60	3.99	3.11	0.50	5.28	992	3.38	184
1960	0.45	4.21	4.06	3.17	0.50	n.a.	1,042	3.52	201
1961	0.48	4.88	4.07	3.29	0.50	7.07	1,107	4.30	225
1962	0.52	5.63	4.13	3.36	0.50	7.33	1,195	4.37	243
1963	0.56	6.58	4.14	3.44	0.49	7.61	1,311	4.81	253
1964	0.60	7.55	4.07	3.66	0.47	7.90	1,388	4.95	275
1965	0.65	8.59	n.a.	n.a.	0.46	8.04	n.a.	n.a.	n.a.

*In the absence of published or otherwise accessible statistics or estimates of *total* private expenditure, this table assembles information from private and government sources to serve as broad indicators of the general trend of numbers and expenditure (at current prices). I am grateful to Hamish Gray for statistical and general assistance.

[1]There is also health insurance through friendly societies.

[2]Each subscriber covers, on average, more than two persons. The 1965 0.65 million subscriptions covered 1.5 million people.

[3]In 1965 there were also 180,000 children at direct grant schools in the U.K.

[4]Rent paid to private owners (less rates), imputed rent of owner-occupiers and occupiers' expenditure on repairs and improvements.

[5]The members of self-administered occupational schemes rose from 5.37m. in 1952 to 7.05m. in 1963 and contributions from £191m. to £443m.

fade away after the National Health Service was introduced in 1948, but the table shows otherwise. Expenditure on education is difficult to assess; the total number at preparatory, public and other independent schools has remained little changed at half a million, but conceals a falling away in middle-class custom and an increase from families of State-school parents. In all, private education is a small proportion of public: some 6 to 8 per cent in numbers and rather more in expenditure. Health insurance is similarly miniscule: 3 per cent in numbers and 4 or 5 per cent in expenditure. Housing expenditure in the private sector is probably rather more than the total of public expenditure.

More choice and competition would galvanize the private sectors. In education, health insurance, house-purchase financing and pensions, the predominant ethos is professional rather than entrepreneurial. Headmasters, building-society officials and insurance managers tend to be dedicated administrators with a sense of mission rather than alert enterprisers with a sense of urgency. Competitive *élan* is frowned on; marketing is inhibited; new firms are rare. At its worst, the private sector harbours appeasement of State integration in education, lingering complacency in health insurance and restrictive practices in pensions. There are some brilliant exceptions, notably the pension consultants and a handful of life offices which have vitalized the pensions market. There is lately a new stirring in medical insurance and a new class of doctors with a grain of entrepreneurial determination to supplement or abandon the NHS and to find salvation in the market.

Choice within the State and private sectors and between them would in time transform headmasters and administrators into managing directors answerable to boards of directors rather than to boards of governors. Some schools, doctors, hospitals, councils, life insurance offices would lose pupils, patients, tenants, policy holders to others. Pricing would become less governed by precedent, more sensitive to changing supply and demand. There would be new competing suppliers: philanthropic, religious, secular, voluntary, mutual, commercial. And welfare would attract more purchasing power, labour and capital.

Welfare, Consumption and Incomes

Here is the essence. The economic philosophy of State welfare implies that it ensures a higher proportion of national income for welfare than would be spent on it spontaneously. The hypothesis may have been well-founded 100 or 50 years ago. Its truth in the second half of the 20th century is less than self-evident.

There are three main reasons for doubt: empirical, analytical and institutional. First, expenditure on the National Health Service since 1948 has risen very little relative to national income, in contrast to private expenditures in the U.S.A. In Europe, private pensions tend to develop more where State pensions provide least: Holland and Norway contrast with Italy and Sweden. Second, tax-payers will not pay as much for "free" services to be shared by other tax-payers as they would for services for themselves and their families. Conversely, at nil or less than market prices individuals will demand more services privately than they will finance publicly, since they cannot, by reducing personal demands, influence others to reduce theirs. Third, the attitude to taxes and prices differs radically. A tax is seen as a deduction from income; it leaves a sense of loss. A price in the market embodies a disposal of income; it conveys a sense of power. The notion of paying voluntarily to improve services financed by compulsory taxes is less congenial than adding to services bought voluntarily in the market. Compulsion has become virtually a spent force; there remains only persuasion. A massive education campaign on welfare that equalized the balance of advocacy after years of practised advertising for consumption could conceivably rechannel to welfare £1,000 millions or more of the £18,000 millions spent on everyday purchases, many imported, visibly or invisibly.

Even if tax-payers were spontaneously moved to pay voluntarily for improvements in State services, they are prevented by the incubus of inequality. Tax-payers may pay for a swimming bath for a school but not for smaller classes, for television in hospital wards but not for more doctors. Little wonder that non-welfare consumption rises relentlessly, especially since saving among wage-earners does not rise systematically with income. The universalist doctrine that no one may have anything more than anyone else may perplex humanists and moralists; for the economist its significance is that it restricts voluntary expenditure on welfare. State welfare feeds the propensity to consume non-welfare goods and services.

An eccentric doctrine on the relation between national income and welfare expenditure stands the logic of social policy on its head. The informative but inconsequential survey in the August, 1965, *Economic Review* of the National Institute of Economic and Social Research of State services in several countries concluded that Britain was behind some in pensions, even though their incomes were lower. The implication seemed to be that countries should spend more on social services as they grow wealthier or than the less wealthy: that the more individuals can do for themselves, the more must be done for them. Countries with higher living standards tend to have more highly-developed private welfare precisely because their incomes are higher.

The Humane Society

The thirteen years since Professor Hagenbuch wrote have seen radical change in attitudes and opportunities. The means test trauma has succumbed to common humanity and simple arithmetic. Universalism is on the defensive as a principle and a policy. Even if it had no other faults it would fail on the ground of inhumanity: that it denies most help to those with most need. Experience is teaching ministers the resistances to taxation and the limits to public expenditure and therefore to State welfare. The macro-economic approach to welfare is seen to be fallible, not least because of the *débâcle* of the National Plan. Long-term forecasts of aspirations and needs solve no problems; policy based on them crumbles for want of sanction. Market pricing is being studied for land, roads, transport, water, libraries, as an indispensable instrument for registering preferences, allocating resources, ensuring that consumers cover costs, and recruiting purchasing power and capital. "Market forces" are returning to public as well as academic discussion. They are seen not as primeval demons beyond human control, but as men and women serving one another by voluntary exchange. Even the communists no longer fear them. Markets have abolished deficiencies in consumption. They could break social barriers, enfranchize the millions and bring humanity, choice and expansion in welfare.

One essential remains. It must become more proper and moral for a man to work for himself and his family than to expect others to work for him, unless he cannot help himself. This is at once the mainspring of the economy and the tenet of the morality, the economic and the social philosophy, of the humane society.

TAXATION AND WELFARE

A REPORT ON PRIVATE OPINION AND PUBLIC POLICY

SECTION **1**

The Relation Between Opinion and Policy

The interconnections between public opinion and public policy are the study of the political scientist rather than of the economist. The clear subdivision is between policy that leads opinion and policy that follows it. Politicians have been known to claim credit for their wisdom both when they reflect public opinion and when they defy it. The labels "democratic" and "statesmanlike" are commonly appropriated to the two archetypes: the loyal servant of the people and the father who knows best. It was said to be a mark of Franklin Roosevelt's genius that in the Second World War he led American public opinion in the direction it had to go for its good. In Britain recently Mr. Duncan Sandys claimed that public opinion favoured the retention of the death penalty for some offenders and that it should therefore be retained; Sir Geoffrey de Freitas said that public opinion was misinformed and that government policy should not be guided by it.

Paternalism, poverty and welfare

In social welfare the paternalist principle has long held sway. The public must be given what the experts, or social workers, or social administrators, or public officials, or politicians believe they should want. The reasons have mainly been what Seebohm Rowntree called primary and secondary poverty: inadequate or misspent income. People in families would therefore not spend enough on medical care, education, housing, or insurance for maintenance of income in sickness, unemployment or old age. In particular the shortsightedness and irresponsibility of adults would be witnessed on their dependent children. To these two reasons was added a third: that the state or other public authority could provide better welfare than individuals could buy in the market even if they were financially able and spiritually willing to pay for it. Public welfare was comprehensive: by being run on a large scale it could reap economies of large-scale organisation and administration, it could pool risks, and it could ensure preservation of accumulated rights to benefits on a change of employment.

The root fallacies of this approach, which put much of it out of court, are not the subject of this *Monograph.* They are analysed and documented in a growing literature of economic and social dissent from the hitherto conventional and largely unchallenged philosophy of universal "free" state welfare. Suffice it to record the essentials for the convenience of readers who have not yet encountered what may properly be called the liberal counter-revolution in economic thinking.[1] *First,* primary poverty does not require state provision of welfare services in kind. At most it constitutes a case for state *financing* of welfare services for individuals or families with low incomes by transfer payments in purchasing power found from general tax revenues. Primary poverty *per se* requires cash, not necessarily kind. *Second,* neither does secondary poverty require state provision of welfare in kind. It constitutes a case for state *standards* or requirements, such as minimum tuition quanta or school-leaving ages, housing standards, or possibly minimum insurance for medical aid, income maintenance in disability, unemployment or retirement.[2] *Third,* economies of scale of state welfare do not constitute an adequate or conclusive case for state provision of welfare services in kind. They can be reproduced in large measure by voluntary arrangements covering firms or industries and they may be less valuable than the flexibility and variety of individual or small-scale private arrangements. State welfare embodies defects of party political control, resistance to change and entangle-

1. Colin Clark, *Welfare and Taxation,* Catholic Social Guild, 1954; Seldon, *Pensions in a Free Society,* IEA, 1957, *Pensions for Prosperity,* Hobart Paper 4, 1960; A. T. Peacock, "Welfare in the Liberal State," *The Unservile State,* Allen and Unwin, 1957; D. S. Lees, "The Economics of Health Services," *Lloyds Bank Review,* 1960, *Health Through Choice,* Hobart Paper 14, IEA, 1961; A. P. Herbert, *Libraries: Free-for-All?,* Hobart Paper 19, IEA, 1962; Harris and Seldon, *Choice in Welfare,* 1963, 1965; Peacock and Wiseman, *Education for Democrats,* Hobart Paper 25, IEA, 1964; Colin Clark, *Taxmanship,* Hobart Paper 26, IEA, 1964; John Carmichael, *Vacant Possession,* Hobart Paper 28, 1964; John and Sylvia Jewkes, *The Genesis of the British National Health Service,* Blackwell, 1961, and *Value for Money in Medicine,* Blackwell, 1963; A. R. Ilersic, *Relief for Ratepayers,* Hobart Paper 20, IEA, 1963; E. G. West, *Education and the State,* IEA, 1965, and "Dr. Blaug and State Education: A Reply" in *Education: A Framework for Choice,* Readings in Political Economy 1, IEA, 1967; A. R. Prest, *Financing University Education,* Occasional Paper 12, IEA, 1966.

2. If inadequate information among purchasers and imperfect competition among suppliers produce standards that are too low, state standards may be too high if they inhibit choice and competition by proceeding beyond the requirements of safety to satisfy technical ideals; and even safety can be bought at too high a price in the restriction of innovation.

ment with national finances that are avoided or minimised in independent welfare services. Not least, state welfare consumes scarce resources in government machinery that might be better used to supply services—protection of properties and persons, a system of money and banking to lubricate exchange, etc.—that individuals may not be able to organise voluntarily through the market at all, or as well.

Cash or kind?

A less vulnerable case for state welfare rests on the argument for "social benefits" or "externalities": that the community as a whole gains if individuals are provided with more or better education, medical care, housing, pensions than they would pay for in the market. There is also the refinement that it is primarily *visible* deprivation that moves the community to provide welfare and that it is therefore not prepared to transfer large sums of *general* purchasing power to the poor but that it may be willing to provide *specific* aid either in kind or in claims on services in kind, i.e., coupons or vouchers,[3] to remove specific disabilities. Hence, redistribution of income by cash transfers, as through a reverse income tax, is in error. There must be several qualifications to this approach. The provision of social assistance to people who cannot help themselves rests on a more general desire to relieve the disabilities of the poor as such. It requires only evidence of the existence of "invisible" or unobtrusive poverty for the community to provide relief; the essential reason why family allowances in Britain have not been raised as soon as evidence was apparent is that the Government has been tied to the universalist principle which has made it difficult to raise the large sums required for

3. There is a "lack of interest on the part of the public in real income redistribution as such. One must search diligently to find much social 'concern' for the prudent poor whose lives are well ordered and stable . . . that some members of the community are poor does not, of itself, normally impose an external diseconomy on many of the remaining members. What does . . . is the *way* that certain persons behave when they are poor. It is not the low income of the family down the street that bothers most of us; it is that it lives in a dilapidated house and dresses its children in rags that impose on our sensibilities. And we are willing to pay something for the removal of this external effect." (Quoted from MS. of J. M. Buchanan, "What Kind of Redistribution Do We Want?," *Economica*, 1967.) If aid to the "visible" poor were not channelled by taxes through the state and its destination thus made "invisible," more direct aid with specific and definite removal of external diseconomies would be larger. A comparable argument has been deployed by Professor Harry G. Johnson in his Inaugural Lecture, "The Economic Approach to Social Questions," at the London School of Economics, 12 October, 1967.

a universal increase. Of the total of British social benefits of some £7,000 million, a half is provided in the form of cash; and the existence of the remainder in kind is not unambiguously associated with the desire to remove specific disabilities but with general political notions of egalitarianism.

This argument against redistribution in cash is an argument for redistribution in coupon (voucher) or kind. Preferences between cash, vouchers and kind are discussed in Section 6.

These issues, and their many refinements, are debated elsewhere.[4] The debate has yielded discussion of two associated aspects of welfare policies on which this *Monograph* tries to shed modest light. The first is practical: whatever the issues, it has been said, though with less assertiveness more recently, there is little to be gained from discussing alternative policies to all-embracing comprehensive state welfare because in Britain there is no interest in them, there would indeed be general opposition to change, and in any event it is too late or administratively impracticable or politically impossible to reconstruct or dismantle "the welfare state." The Institute's studies in 1963 and 1965,[5] supplemented by several interesting studies since 1960,[6] have created doubt about this supposed obstacle to social change, now increasingly dispelled and recognised as unfounded. The second issue is that of analysing and measuring preferences for services supplied by collective authority without the aid of markets and pricing. Insofar as public policy should reflect private opinion, how do the suppliers of "public services"—in welfare or elsewhere—identify personal preferences?

4. The profuse writings over the years of social administrators, sociologists, political scientists and economists who favour state welfare are well publicised and familiar to students of the social sciences. The more recent liberal writings published by the IEA and others are listed on page 22, n. 1.

5. Ralph Harris and Arthur Seldon, *Choice in Welfare,* 1963, 1965.

6. Discussed by Hamish Gray in *Universal or Selective Social Benefits?,* Research Monograph 8, IEA, 1967, Part II.

SECTION **2**

Opinion on Changes in Taxation and Social Benefits

In April 1967 the Institute collaborated with Mass-Observation in preparing a field study of private opinion on taxation and welfare. M-O addressed one question, with four sub-divisions, and the IEA four further questions to a quota sample of 2,022 people aged 16 to 65, comprising 988 men and 1,034 women in all socio-occupational groups and regions in Great Britain. To distinguish the two sets of questions, the Tables summarising the replies to the M-O questions are labelled A, B, C and D, and the Tables summarising the replies to the IEA questions are labelled I, II, III and IV. The interpretation and inferences are solely the author's.

The first question, in four parts, was devised by M-O to elicit opinion on expected and preferred changes in taxation and social benefits in the April 1967 Budget. The replies are summarised in this Section. The IEA wished to investigate four aspects of the subject; with the technical advice of M-O they devised four questions designed to discover the underlying state of *knowledge* of and *preferences* in policies on welfare and taxation: they asked individual views on public policies rather than on the personal preferences of the respondents. The replies are analysed more fully in Sections 3, 4, 5 and 6. Section 7 discusses the reliability and significance of the findings.

Section 8 assembles the main findings and impressions and discusses the implications for the theoretical study of non-market choices and the practical issue of the "politically possible" scope for social reform. It discusses public opinion on the *direction* of such reform. And it analyses public attitudes to taxation according to the *purposes* to which the tax yield is put; this analysis suggests a possible new aspect from which taxation policies and public finance in general should be studied. Section 9 summarises the conclusions.

Knowledge and preference in taxes and welfare

The M-O question asked:

"In about a week's time the Chancellor is going to give us his budget. Here are some of the things which it is suggested he might change:

(a) Could you tell me whether you think he is *likely* to increase or decrease tax on:
petrol
cigarettes
spirits
income

(b) Do you think he *should* increase or decrease tax on:
petrol
cigarettes
spirits
income

(c) And is the Government *likely* to increase or decrease expenditure on:
education
family allowances
health services
old-age pensions
subsidies for council rents

(d) And do you think the Government *should* increase or decrease expenditure on:
education
family allowances
health services
old-age pensions
subsidies for council rents?"

The responses are summarised in Tables A, B, C and D.

Tables A and B record private expectations of budget changes in taxation and social benefits that were of some interest at the time.

Tables C and D show readings of preferences in changes in taxes and social benefits that are of more lasting interest for the subject of this *Monograph.* There was a strong preference in favour of lower taxes (Table C) on petrol, less strong for cigarettes, almost an equal division of opinion in favour of a

Table A. Expected Tax Changes

Question: In about a week's time, the Chancellor is going to give us his budget. Here are some of the things which it is suggested he might change. Could you tell me whether you think he is *likely* to increase or decrease tax on petrol, cigarettes, spirits, income tax?

Tax Increase or Decrease		Total Sample 2,022	Sex M 988	Sex F 1,034	Age 16–24 414	Age 25–34 396	Age 35–44 426	Age 45–64 786	Socio-Occupational Group: Upper-Middle & Middle 253	Lower-Middle 385	Skilled 823	Semi-Skilled & Unskilled 561
		%	%	%	%	%	%	%	%	%	%	%
Petrol	increase	41	40	42	49	48	38	35	35	42	39	47
	decrease	17	15	20	20	14	17	18	14	15	19	17
Cigarettes	increase	51	46	56	63	58	49	42	40	48	52	57
	decrease	7	5	8	10	6	6	6	4	6	8	6
Spirits	increase	47	46	48	58	48	42	43	38	45	50	49
	decrease	11	9	12	12	11	12	9	7	12	11	10
Income	increase	36	32	41	49	39	34	30	31	35	36	40
	decrease	24	26	23	18	22	27	27	26	28	24	21

Note: The remainder of the sample replied "Don't know" or gave other answers.

Table B. Expected Changes in Expenditure on Social Benefits

Question: Is the Government *likely* to increase or decrease expenditure on education, family allowances, health services, subsidies for council rents, old-age pensions?

Social Benefit Increase or Decrease		Total Sample 2,022	Sex: M 988	Sex: F 1,034	Age: 16–24 414	Age: 25–34 396	Age: 35–44 426	Age: 45–64 786	Socio-Occupational Group: Upper-Middle & Middle 253	Socio-Occupational Group: Lower-Middle 385	Socio-Occupational Group: Skilled 823	Socio-Occupational Group: Semi-Skilled & Unskilled 561
		%	%	%	%	%	%	%	%	%	%	%
Education	increase	80	82	77	83	82	79	77	84	81	80	76
	decrease	8	7	9	5	8	8	9	4	9	8	9
Family Allowances	increase	39	37	41	50	45	35	33	37	41	40	37
	decrease	13	12	13	11	11	13	14	13	13	12	14
NHS	increase	54	59	50	64	57	51	49	53	58	53	52
	decrease	11	9	13	11	10	12	11	8	11	12	12
Subsidies for Council Rents	increase	32	30	34	43	33	31	27	25	30	33	35
	decrease	27	27	26	26	26	28	27	25	28	26	28
Pensions	increase	59	58	59	64	58	59	57	56	58	58	62
	decrease	4	3	4	5	4	4	3	2	4	4	3

Note: The remainder of the sample replied "Don't know" or gave other answers.

Table C. Preferred Tax Changes

Question: Do you think he [the Chancellor] *should* increase or decrease tax on petrol, cigarettes, spirits, income tax?

Tax Increase or Decrease		Total Sample	Sex		Age				Socio-Occupational Group			
			M	F	16–24	25–34	35–44	45–64	Upper-Middle & Middle	Lower-Middle	Skilled	Semi-Skilled & Unskilled
		2,022	988	1,034	414	396	426	786	253	385	823	561
		%	%	%	%	%	%	%	%	%	%	%
Petrol	increase	10	10	10	10	9	11	11	8	11	10	11
	decrease	62	63	60	67	65	59	59	64	62	62	60
Cigarettes	increase	28	26	29	40	29	28	21	36	28	28	23
	decrease	40	40	41	38	41	38	43	28	37	41	48
Spirits	increase	32	29	35	40	35	29	28	28	30	35	32
	decrease	35	37	32	33	33	36	35	35	34	33	38
Income	increase	3	3	3	3	2	5	2	3	3	3	3
	decrease	81	80	81	83	81	78	81	79	80	82	81

Note: The remainder of the sample replied "Don't know" or gave other answers.

Table D. Preferred Changes in Expenditure on Social Benefits

Question: Do you think the Government *should* increase or decrease expenditure on education, family allowances, health services, subsidies for council rents, old-age pensions?

Social Benefit	Increase or Decrease	Total Sample	Sex		Age				Socio-Occupational Group			
			M	F	16–24	25–34	35–44	45–64	Upper-Middle & Middle	Lower-Middle	Skilled	Semi-Skilled & Unskilled
		2,022	988	1,034	414	396	426	786	253	385	823	561
		%	%	%	%	%	%	%	%	%	%	%
Education	increase	70	73	68	77	80	74	60	73	70	70	70
	decrease	16	15	17	11	10	13	23	14	15	17	16
Family Allowances	increase	32	32	33	54	45	27	18	20	24	34	41
	decrease	32	33	32	20	22	34	43	39	34	32	29
NHS	increase	59	60	58	72	66	52	52	60	53	59	61
	decrease	15	14	16	12	12	18	16	15	19	13	13
Subsidies for Council Rents	increase	22	23	20	26	21	19	21	11	16	23	28
	decrease	49	47	51	43	51	51	51	61	58	45	45
Pensions	increase	87	87	88	88	86	86	88	81	87	88	89
	decrease	3	3	3	4	3	4	2	3	3	2	4

Note: The remainder of the sample replied "Don't know" or gave other answers.

decrease and an increase in the tax on spirits, and a massive preference for lower taxes on income. These opinions related to tax rates; if consumption remained unchanged tax yields would vary with tax rates.

There was little difference between the sexes but interesting differences in the four age-groups and in the four socio-occupational groups. Young people were more in favour of cuts in the petrol tax than old people and the "upper-middle and middle" group were much less in favour of cuts in the cigarette tax than the "semi-skilled and unskilled" group. Other differences were less marked.

It is difficult to interpret these results except in the light of the degrees of knowledge of the amounts paid in taxation and of the value of social services received. Some light was thrown on the degree of public knowledge in *Choice in Welfare* 1963 and 1965. Comparable studies in other countries and their significance are discussed by Professor J. M. Buchanan in his latest study of individual choice in collective services (below, Section 8).[1]

Table D shows the results in response to question 1 (d). It suggests that a large proportion of the public favoured more expenditure on retirement pensions (87 per cent) and education (70 per cent), rather less but still a substantial proportion (59 per cent) on health services, there was divided opinion on family allowances, but only a small proportion (22 per cent) for an increase in subsidies for council house rents. Here again there was little difference between the sexes but some interesting differences within the age-groups and the socio-occupational groups.

Not surprisingly, younger people were more in favour of increased expenditure on education and on health services than were the older people but, perhaps more surprisingly, there was little or no difference in the socio-occupational groups. The younger people were emphatically in favour of higher family allowances and the older people almost as emphatically in favour of lower expenditure on family allowances. The "upper-middle and middle" group favoured lower expenditure on family allowances and the "semi-skilled and unskilled" group higher expenditure. The overwhelming vote for higher pensions was shared by both sexes, all four age-groups and all four socio-occupational groups. The clear opinion favouring lower subsidies for council rents was shared by men and women, it was rather stronger among people aged 25 and over than among younger people, and it was more emphatic among the "higher" than among the "lower" socio-occupational groups.

The division of opinion on family allowances may seem surprising in

1. *Public Finance in Democratic Process,* University of North Carolina Press, 1967.

view of the considerable public discussions for several months on child poverty; it may be explicable in terms of the answers to the later question analysed in Table III (page 42).

Significance of the results

The interesting problem in interpreting the significance of opinion on taxes and social benefits is how far it was understood that taxation ultimately pays for social benefits.[2] In a market for consumer goods and services bought and sold by individuals little significance attaches to "opinion" favouring an increased supply of, say, apples, shoes or cars unless two conditions are satisfied. First, it must be related to a price; second, there must be ability and willingness to pay, so that "opinion" or "want" is transformed into effective "demand." In the goods or services supplied by public authority for citizens who pay indirectly by taxation for what they "consume" or from which they "benefit," neither condition is fulfilled. There is often no direct price at the point of supply (education, medical care) or the price is less than the value of the resources consumed (housing, pensions). And even if citizens/taxpayers/consumers/beneficiaries understand that they are paying indirectly by taxation (central, local or social insurance)[3] they cannot relate the value or benefit of the service to the amount they pay. Moreover they cannot as individuals (as they can in markets) affect the amount they consume, or the amount produced, by offering more for it; only if they happen to be one of a very large proportion of the population, usually half or more, or can persuade it to share their attitude, can they influence the amount produced and consumed. Even then they cannot achieve their end by offering to pay more through taxes for themselves but must persuade politicians to raise taxes for everyone.

2. This is a major theme in Professor Buchanan's *Public Finance in Democratic Process,* op. cit. He speaks of "the fragmentation of choice" by separation of decision on collective spending from individual awareness of the cost in taxes, and concludes that surveys "seem to suggest, quite clearly, that individuals do not in general translate meaningfully between the two sides of the fiscal account." For example research at the Survey Research Centre of the University of Michigan in 1960 and 1961 found that 70 per cent of the sample favoured more public spending on help for older people, but only 26 per cent when they were asked the question again "even if taxes must be raised." On help for the needy the percentages were 60 and 26, on education 60 and 41, on hospital and medical care 54 and 25. The second half of these questions goes some way to the IEA attachment of price-tags to its preference questions (discussed in the text).

3. Page 33.

SECTION 3

Knowledge of Taxation

If there seems to be a tenuous link between the "demand" for state welfare exerted by paying taxes and its supply, how much at least do people know of the amounts they pay in taxation?

The four IEA questions began with one on the degree of knowledge of taxation paid by the respondent (or her husband).

> For every £1 which you or your husband earn, how many shillings do you think government *now takes* altogether in taxes on income and the things you buy, rates and National Insurance?[1]

The question was made as simple and explicit as it could be. Everyday discussion suggests that people asked how much tax they pay often think only or mainly of direct income tax and not, or not very clearly, of indirect tax,[2] or rates, or National Insurance contributions. This omission is especially significant for the lower-income groups, who are taxed regressively on their everyday or periodic purchases, who are predominantly tenants (of whom few can have any idea of the rates paid with their rent) rather than owner-occupiers, and among whom uniform National Insurance contributions take a proportionately larger slice of their weekly earnings the lower they are.

1. This is a question on average, not marginal, rates of income taxation, because the interest is in the total amount of taxation paid on individual incomes as a preliminary to later questions on payment for social benefits. A question on marginal tax rates, or supposed marginal rates, would be relevant for a study of disincentives as attempted by Dr. C. V. Brown of the University of Glasgow, *Financial Times*, 24 May, 1967.

2. Recent research by J. Forbes of the University of Virginia into "the propensity to spend publicly out of income" employed the supposition that "indirect taxation tends to generate a fiscal illusion and serves thereby to conceal from the taxpayer-voter the real weight of tax, and hence causes him to support a somewhat higher level of public spending." If British taxation is shifted from earnings to expenditure to reduce disincentives or to make it more like Continental systems, the "fiscal illusion" will be intensified.

The results are shown in Table I. It suggests many conclusions on the degree of knowledge or ignorance of the amount paid in taxation by the taxpayer (or his wife). First, whatever the amount of tax paid by each household (see below), there is a wide range in the proportions of income that taxpayers think they themselves pay within each of the four main socio-occupational groups. Apart from differences in income-tax allowances for children, life assurance, mortgage interest, and in expenditure on taxed purchases, the amount of tax paid by families of similar size within each group can be supposed roughly similar. Yet 54 per cent of the "upper-middle and middle" group thought they paid 10s. or more out of each £ of income, which may be more or less the right order of magnitude, 26 per cent thought they paid less than 10s., in which supposition many were almost certainly wrong, and 14 per cent seemed to have no idea at all. At the other extreme, 37 per cent of the "semi-skilled and unskilled" group thought they paid 10s. or more in the £, in which they were mostly very far out, only 42 per cent thought they paid less than 10s. which was probably true of most of them, and 18 per cent seemed to have no idea at all. These findings may be compared with those of other studies, such as reported by Professor Buchanan in *Public Finance in Democratic Process,* that the lower-income groups tend to over-estimate their tax payments more than do the higher-income groups.

Second, it is unlikely that many, if any, respondents had ever attempted a calculation of the total taxes they paid. Their replies were based on general impressions or guesses, rather than on knowledge. Few people discuss their tax "bill" with their associates and acquaintances as they discuss their grocery, butcher, gas, electricity, telephone, store or garage bills. This inability to compute the figure, and the apathy it engenders, must be disturbing in a political democracy. For the economist its significance is that it renders of doubtful value opinions on welfare policy (or on any collectively-provided services) delivered in reply to questionnaires or in ballot booths. Since most taxpayers pay anything from 6 to 12 shillings on each £ of their income, or 30 to 60 per cent, they can hardly make informed decisions about public policy if they have little knowledge about its cost. It is because of the fundamental principle of economic theory that "demand" for a commodity or service cannot be measured without reference to its price that the *Choice in Welfare* surveys attached prices to their questions. There is no significance in the notion of "desire," "want" or "need" except in terms of the costs of the resources required to satisfy it, which yield a market price. It is difficult to see that the public, even if it were asked, could make intelligent or intelligible decisions about the extent of changes in "public services" or social benefits, or

Table I. Extent of Knowledge of Household Tax Payments

Question: For every £1 which you or your husband earn, how many shillings do you think government *now takes* altogether in taxes on income and the things you buy, rates and National Insurance?

Tax (shillings in each £)	Total Sample	Sex		Age				Socio-Occupational Group			
		M	F	16–24	25–34	35–44	45–64	Upper-Middle & Middle	Lower-Middle	Skilled	Semi-Skilled & Unskilled
	2,022	988	1,034	414	396	426	786	253	385	823	561
	%	%	%	%	%	%	%	%	%	%	%
Up to 2/-	3	3	3	5	3	2	2	0	1	3	5
2/1d. to 3/11d.	4	4	3	7	3	3	2	2	3	4	4
4/- to 5/11d.	12	11	12	16	14	10	9	6	10	13	14
6/- to 7/11d.	12	13	11	9	14	13	12	9	13	13	12
8/- to 9/11d.	9	11	6	6	9	10	9	9	9	9	7
10/- to 10/11d.	20	20	20	17	17	22	22	23	19	19	20
11/- to 14/11d.	12	15	8	8	11	13	13	18	15	11	7
15/- and over	11	14	8	10	13	10	11	13	12	11	10
Don't know	16	8	25	15	14	16	18	14	17	16	18
Others	2	2	3	5	1	1	2	4	1	2	3

indicate its preferences between alternatives, if it does not know the absolute or relative costs it is paying in taxation.

Third, if there is little knowledge of taxes paid, there is probably less knowledge that taxes can be "shifted," i.e., of the incidence as well as of the impact of taxation.

Fourth, the extent of civic illiteracy, probably in all socio-occupational groups, suggests a failure of British education, formal in schools or informal in newspapers, by the political parties, by local and central public authorities, to teach the elementary information without which a western democracy with full adult suffrage cannot form responsible decisions.

Fifth, as indicated, since even a fully informed democracy cannot indicate its preferences without prices, it is desirable to discover them by use of notional prices to elicit hypothetical responses. In this way hypothetical demand schedules showing public readiness to pay for varying amounts at alternative prices can be prepared as a guide both to the state, in yielding a measure of the willingness to pay through taxation, and to independent suppliers as a measure of the alternative prices at which there is probable effective demand.

Sixth, even if all services that could be supplied in response to individual demand were put into the market, civic illiteracy might remain unless services necessarily provided by government, central or local, responded to opinion assembled systematically so that there was a sense of participation in government decisions. The continuing drift of authority from local to national government has intensified indifference. The persistent refusal to use referenda and plebiscites, local, regional or national, stands in marked contrast to practice in other countries. The inescapable impression builds up of a political reluctance to sound public opinion and individual preferences except at infrequent intervals and for authority in the most general terms for the ruling party to do what it wishes.[3]

3. I am indebted to Professor A. T. Peacock for discussion of this conclusion.

SECTION 4

Opinion on the Level of Taxation

So much for knowledge of the extent of taxation. Whatever they know, do taxpayers think they pay too much? too little? And what would they like done with their money?

The second question asked for the IEA was:

> How many shillings do you think they [the Government in the previous question] *should take* out of every £ you/your husband earn?

The replies are shown in Table II. The largest single preference, 22 per cent, was for 5s. to 5s. 11d. A further 37 per cent opted for under 5s. and 22 per cent for 6s. or over. There was little difference between men and women. Forty-three per cent of the "semi-skilled and unskilled" thought the government should take less than 5s. compared with 18 per cent of the "upper-middle and middle" group; the corresponding proportions for 5s. and over were 33 and 61 per cent.

It is easy to dismiss as unremarkable the finding that taxpayers favour lower taxes. Since there was a substantial opinion in favour of higher expenditure on education, health services and pensions (Table D) it must be doubted how far people relate taxes with public services or social benefits, and see one as the "payment" for the other. Nevertheless, the analysis by age and socio-occupational groups suggests that the replies were not irresponsible or capricious. Apart from a small proportion who envisaged taxation at inconceivably low levels, there was logic in the replies. The younger and the lower-paid thought taxation should take less of earnings than did the older and higher paid. And the "bunching" of nearly 40 per cent between 4s. and 7s. 11d. in the £ suggests a substantial "centre" opinion that taxation could be appreciably but not unrealistically lower than its present average of approaching 8s. in the £.

How far this structure of opinions carried with it a recognition that a fall from 8s. to say 6s. in the £ as the average tax would imply a sizeable reduc-

Table II. Public Opinion on the Level of Taxation as a Proportion of Earnings

Question: How many shillings do you think they [the Government] *should take* out of every £1 you/your husband earn?

		Sex		Age				Socio-Occupational Group			
Tax (shillings in each £)	Total Sample 2,022	M 988	F 1,034	16–24 414	25–34 396	35–44 426	45–64 786	Upper-Middle & Middle 253	Lower-Middle 385	Skilled 823	Semi-Skilled & Unskilled 561
	%	%	%	%	%	%	%	%	%	%	%
Up to 2/-	16	14	18	21	22	13	12	5	12	19	19
2/1d. to 3/11d.	14	14	14	14	12	16	14	9	12	14	17
4/- to 4/11d.	7	7	6	5	6	8	7	4	6	7	7
5/- to 5/11d.	22	22	21	22	20	23	22	29	25	20	19
6/- to 7/11d.	10	13	7	7	11	11	11	15	12	10	6
8/- to 9/11d.	4	5	3	3	5	4	4	6	4	3	3
10/- to 10/11d.	7	8	5	6	8	5	8	9	9	7	5
11/- and over	1	3	0	2	2	1	1	2	3	2	1
Don't know	12	8	17	12	11	14	12	15	12	12	11
Others	7	6	9	9	4	6	9	6	6	6	11

tion in the public sector as a whole, or in individual welfare (or other) services or benefits, is the interesting question. The Institute hopes to pursue its inquiries into public knowledge of the relationship between taxation and public services (defence, roads, fire and other) or social benefits. This question in the survey was prompted by a hypothesis suggested by Mr. Colin Clark:[1]

> Can one imagine the results of a social survey which asked people of all classes "How much of your income do you wish to give to the Government?" returning the answer "Just under half"?

The replies in this survey were that nearly 60 per cent thought no more than a third of their income, and 37 per cent less than a quarter. In all, nearly 70 per cent thought less than two-fifths, the present national average of around 8s. in the £. Only 12 per cent thought 8s. or more.

1. "Taxation for Expansion," in *Rebirth of Britain,* Pan Books, 1964.

SECTION 5

Readiness to Pay Taxes in Terms of the Use Made of Tax Revenue

Attitudes to taxation, and in particular "taxable capacity," the limits to the amounts of revenue that can be raised and the proportion of income that can be taxed effectively, are normally discussed in terms of their effect on incentives, effort, enterprise and output. The corresponding resistances are tax avoidance or, in extremes, tax evasion, and the ceilings they set to tax revenue. As total taxation, proportionately to income, grows, tax avoidance and evasion begin earlier in some social classes, no doubt in some age-groups, and certainly in some countries. It is generally thought that they increase in Europe from the northern countries of Scandinavia to the southern countries around the Mediterranean.[1]

Attitudes to government spending and taxation

Analysis of the attitude to taxation *in terms of the uses to which its yield is put* is rare.[2] It could be of considerable interest in the theory and practice of public finance, as well as in the contemporary debate in Great Britain on public attitudes to universal and selective benefits and the use of means tests.

The third question asked for the IEA was:

> Some people think that money collected in taxes should be spent on social benefits for everyone regardless of how much they earn. Others feel that the tax money should be spent on providing social benefits and services for those who need them most. Under which of these two systems do you think you would be more prepared to pay your taxes?

1. Alun G. Davies, *Render Unto Caesar*, Elek, 1965.

2. A quick return to three standard text books, Benham's *Economics* (7th Edition, 1964), Samuelson's *Economics* (4th Edition, 1958) and Alchian & Allen's *University Economics* (2nd Edition, 1967), reveals no reference to the "supply" of tax monies in terms of the use made of them. But it may be that other works have analysed the proposition in theory or embarked on empirical tests.

The choice was thus between paying taxes to be used for what are called "universal" or "selective" benefits.[3] The replies are summarised in Table III. They indicate several conclusions. First, there was almost twice as much readiness to pay taxes if the proceeds were used for selective benefits as there was if they were used for universal benefits. Second, the nearly two-to-one preference for selective benefits was found with almost no variation among both men and women and in all four age-groups between 16 and 65. Third, there was a majority in favour of taxes used to finance selective benefits in all four socio-occupational groups, but with marked variation: from a slight majority in the "upper-middle and middle" group to nearly three-to-one in the "semi-skilled and unskilled" group.

These results are discussed in Section 8. The third is of especial interest. There is a widespread view not only that the opposition to means tests is general in the country as a whole but also that it is particularly intense in the lower-income groups; they are supposed to prefer universal social benefits because they would not wish to be singled out and thereby suffer the stigma of differential treatment. Hence their supposed view that the social benefits must be equal and universal[4] and non-discriminatory. If this representation of public attitudes to the welfare services had been verified and well documented, we should presumably have found a well-defined antipathy to paying taxes for selective benefits in the "semi-skilled and unskilled" groups, and it would have been much more clearly defined than in the "upper" and "middle" groups.

Change in opinion

In June 1966 a survey discussed in an earlier *Research Monograph*[5] found more support for a universal free NHS, subsidised council housing and pension increases among the "semi-skilled and unskilled" than among the "upper-middle and middle" socio-occupational group; there was little difference in the support for universal family allowances. In the April 1967 survey reported in this *Monograph* the finding on attitudes to paying taxes was in the

3. Professor R. M. Titmuss has objected that the choice in social policy is not between universal and selective benefits; he now argues that the structure of social benefits could comprise both. The view is discussed in Section 8, vi.

4. This view has been held by most politicians in all parties and by social administrators who have supported the universalist principle. The recent change in political and sociological opinion is discussed in Section 8.

5. *Universal or Selective Social Benefits?,* Research Monograph 8, 1967.

Table III. Readiness to Pay Taxes Analysed by Use Made of Yield: Universal or Selective Social Benefits

Question: Some people think that money collected in taxes should be spent on social benefits and services for everyone regardless of how much they earn. Others feel that the tax money should be spent on providing social benefits and services for those who need them most. Under which of these two systems do you think you would be more prepared to pay your taxes?

Should be spent on social benefits and services for everyone.

Should be spent on social benefits and services for those who need them most.

	Total Sample	Sex		Age				Socio-Occupational Group			
		M	F	16–24	25–34	35–44	45–64	Upper-Middle & Middle	Lower-Middle	Skilled	Semi-Skilled & Unskilled
	2,022	988	1,034	414	396	426	786	253	385	823	561
	%	%	%	%	%	%	%	%	%	%	%
Universal	35	36	34	35	37	35	33	47	39	33	29
Selective	65	64	65	65	63	64	66	53	61	66	71
Others	1	1	1	0	0	1	1	0	1	0	1

opposite direction. The questions were more general; they followed questions on a wider range of benefits; they referred to attitude to paying taxes rather than to specific social benefits; they were asked a week before a budget when the emphasis was on taxes rather than on benefits; and discussion of the impersonal, income-tax coding as a more acceptable indicator of needs than the conventional, inquisitive means test was more general. Whatever the reasons, the support for taxes to finance universal benefits was 47 per cent in the highest socio-occupational group and 29 per cent in the lowest. More research will be required to establish the reasons for this difference. It would not be illogical for the lower-paid, who would receive the larger social benefits if they were varied with income and needs, to think that their families' gain from the selective principle counted for more than the disadvantage of declaring means. It may be also that the "middle classes" may take a material interest in social benefits on the ground that they should share in them since they pay for them by taxation: many of them use free state education and the free NHS, especially in middle-class areas, even though they could pay fees or insure privately, because they "cannot afford" private services, or because they refuse to "pay twice," or because they derive better service than do the less articulate and less well-connected wage-earners.

SECTION 6

Preferences in the Form of Social Benefits

Throughout the development of British welfare services the debate between those who favour state benefits in kind and those who favour benefits in cash has remained unresolved. The arguments in favour of services in kind have rested on secondary poverty, that cash would be misspent, or perhaps on the view that some people needed personal care because incapable of exercising choice. The arguments in favour of benefits in cash have rested on the significance of increasing choice and independence as a teacher of responsibility and discrimination for people capable of learning by experience.[1]

To discover what the recipients or "beneficiaries," as distinct from the academics, politicians or social administrators, believe, the survey asked:

> Some people have said that rather than give free or part-free benefits, it would be better to give people cash or a voucher for use to buy the services they prefer. Which would you think best?

The voucher option was included as an alternative to cash because it has been discussed increasingly in the last few years as a form of specific rather than generalised purchasing power with which to pay for education, medical care and housing. The voucher in the question was not tied to a named service, but since earlier questions had referred to the four main services—education, medical care, housing, pensions—they would probably have been in the respondents' minds when replying. The principle is familiar to increasing numbers (now probably several million) of salary- and wage-earners in the form of the luncheon voucher.

The replies are summarised in Table IV. The sample divided itself equally between free services in kind and purchasing power in the form of cash or vouchers. There was also no difference between men and women in the

1. A more sophisticated argument in favour of services in kind is referred to on p. 23.

Table IV. Preferences in Social Benefits: Services, Cash, Vouchers

Question: Some people have said that rather than give free or part-free benefits, it would be better to give people cash or a voucher for use to buy the services they prefer. Which would you think best?

Free or partly free services

Cash to buy services they prefer

Voucher to buy services they prefer

	Total	Sex		Age				Socio-Occupational Group			
	Sample	M	F	16–24	25–34	35–44	45–64	Upper-Middle & Middle	Lower-Middle	Skilled	Semi-Skilled & Unskilled
	2,022	988	1,034	414	396	426	786	253	385	823	561
	%	%	%	%	%	%	%	%	%	%	%
Free or partly free services	49	49	49	54	51	47	46	57	51	48	44
Cash	12	11	14	18	13	10	10	7	10	12	16
Vouchers	37	39	36	27	35	42	42	34	37	39	38
Purchasing power (general and specific)	49	50	50	45	48	52	52	41	47	51	54
Don't know, etc.	2	2	1	1	1	2	2	3	2	1	2

preference for free services, but a markedly higher proportion of younger people than older preferred services. And there was a similar difference between the extreme socio-occupational groups: 57 per cent of the "upper-middle and middle" group preferred services contrasted with 44 per cent of the "semi-skilled and unskilled."

Perhaps surprisingly, of those who favoured purchasing power, far more preferred vouchers than cash: about three to one, 37 per cent to 12 per cent. (The preferences are discussed in Section 8.) There was little difference in the sexes: if anything a rather larger proportion of women than men seemed to favour cash and rather more men than women favoured vouchers, but the differences were small and may not be significant. Cash was favoured appreciably more by the younger (16 to 24 group—18 per cent) than the older (45 to 64 group—10 per cent) and by the "semi-skilled and unskilled" (16 per cent) than by the "upper-middle and middle" group (7 per cent). The preferences for vouchers rose from 27 per cent in the 16 to 24 years age-group to 42 per cent in the 35 to 64 group. But there was much less variation in the socio-occupational groups, where the proportion ranged between a third and two-fifths, with a rather higher preference among wage-paid than among salary-paid people.

The question did not ask personal preferences but personal opinion about social policy. That is, it did not ask "Would you prefer services, cash or vouchers *for yourself?*"[2] In a mature, adult democracy, politicians who respect citizens as taxpayers, consumers or beneficiaries as well as electors, will presumably want to know the answers to this question. The sample in this survey were asked for opinions on what was thought best *for people in general.* This question is not open to the criticism that many people are irresponsible and that they will prefer cash to services because they will wish to spend it on everyday consumption goods or pleasurable services rather than medical care, education, housing or other forms of welfare. The three-to-one preference for vouchers over cash in the sample as a whole (varying from 1½ to 5 to one in the age and socio-occupational analysis) may reflect this supposition.[3] The higher vote for vouchers among older than among

2. The alternative forms of questions are discussed by Hamish Gray in Part II of *Universal or Selective Social Benefits?,* Research Monograph 8, 1967.

3. It is true that, although a "welfare voucher" could be earmarked for a named group of welfare services, or a "health" or "housing" voucher more specifically for a single service, it is impossible to ensure that they were not used for other purchases. Like luncheon vouchers they

younger people may also support it.[4] A higher preference for cash over vouchers might have been recorded if individuals in the sample had been asked which they preferred for themselves.

---

could become to a degree generalised purchasing power. The risk would need to be run. The only way to ensure that people receive service is to give them service. It is argued in Section 8, viii, that the balance of argument lies with vouchers and eventually cash.

4. On the other hand, if the general preference for vouchers over cash reflects a general impression that "other people" are considered irresponsible, there are general grounds for supposing that the emphasis of household expenditure on consumption is encouraged by the state provision of free or partly free welfare services (Section 8).

SECTION 7

Reliability and Significance of the Findings

The 1963 and 1965 IEA/M-O surveys represent an effort to apply the techniques of opinion polling and market research to discover preferences between state and independent services and attitudes to the socio-political principles that govern their provision. More specifically, in the *Choice in Welfare* surveys in 1963 and 1965 they were used to construct hypothetical markets for education and medical care[1] by eliciting the response to a voucher with two alternative values. The possible technical limitations and weaknesses of opinion polls, market research and social surveys are familiar to the practitioners and researchers who use them in commerce and academic work, and the search for improved techniques is continuous.[2] But since disbelief or extreme scepticism about the IEA/M-O surveys has been expressed by two eminent politicians of ministerial rank, one in each of the two major parties, and they reflect the doubt with which such surveys have been met from people of a wide range of specialism and philosophy, it is sobering to consider how far the findings are reliable or significant before discussing their relevance for welfare policy.

Objections

Criticism, scepticism, doubt and disbelief are a proper reaction to surveys that cover new ground with untested methods and discover unexpected

1. Housing and pensions were omitted because the method could not readily be applied to the national sample of male, married heads of households aged 21 to 65. A hypothetical market is attempted in a forthcoming IEA study, *Choice in Housing*, by F. G. Pennance and Hamish Gray.

2. The Survey Research Centre directed by Dr. W. A. Belson at the London School of Economics is working, *inter alia*, on the perfection of questionnaires. The Centre is financed largely by industry, a safeguard against influence from government against which academics are increasingly protesting.

findings. Most citizens, taxpayers, consumers or beneficiaries of state welfare or social benefits have rarely, if ever, thought systematically about the relationship between taxation and welfare. Possibly they have never, until recently, thought whether their attitude to paying taxes might vary according to the use made of the proceeds. Very few will have considered that there might be a choice between a state service and cash. And perhaps none will have thought about a voucher in place of both. Therefore, their replies to a stranger confronting them with questions at a time not of their choosing may hardly seem considered, conclusive or decisive. To these reservations are added the familiar suspicion that people are apt to say anything to rid themselves of the unwelcome intruder, or to offer the first reply that sounds plausible, or even to say what they think the questioner expects.

All or most of these objections have substance. It may be held that politicians who found the findings congenial might be less ready to dismiss them. The issue is not whether the method is free from fault but whether the alternatives are preferable. It may be argued, first, that these questions and alternatives should not be put at all; second, that they should be put only after fuller public discussion; third, that they are in practice put in the political process and answered in the ballot box.

Refutations

The first alternative is hardly acceptable in a democracy; let all methods be used: sooner or later the defective ones will reveal themselves. The second objection has substance; but public discussion has been inhibited rather than encouraged by the supposition, common until recently, that no fundamental reform in state welfare was remotely desired or politically possible; it is regrettably the evidence of recent history that policy-makers often wait for a stirring of public debate before they participate in or, hopefully, lead it. British political parties and politicians have for too long neglected their task of civic education and re-education, not least in social policy; some younger spirits in all three parties are recently repairing the omissions of their elders. The third objection is unacceptable: the ballot box caters essentially for majorities, although even they must approve or reject indivisible packages of policy and cannot easily express opinion on individual policies—a procedure that does violence to the principle of the equalisation of marginal utilities as the condition *sine qua non* of the maximisation of total utility or satisfaction. Even worse, minorities up to 49 per cent risk being ignored and must normally tolerate the social order supported by the 51 per cent.

This arrangement may be acceptable for common services that cannot be supplied in a market in response to individual demand: defence against external armies or internal criminals, or for law and order applicable to all citizens as equals, or for a banking and monetary system; it is too crude to provide for individual preferences in medical care, education, housing, insurance for maintenance of income in sickness, unemployment or retirement.[3] In welfare the purpose is not merely to organise the technically most efficient service; attention to personal preference or even idiosyncracy is an indispensable element in judging individual satisfaction and the consumer-effectiveness of expenditure.

The findings of these surveys should be subjected to close scrutiny; their methods should be refined; the results should be tested and re-tested; not least, exaggerated or premature claims should be discounted. But, short of market institutions that enable individuals to declare their preferences in practice, attempts to discover the probable structure of hypothetical demand are a desirable device of social research. And they should be welcomed rather than scouted by policy-makers as an approximate check on politically-decided social policies that may otherwise strain democratic allegiance and institutions if they depart too far from underlying preferences that the ballot box cannot identify. Politicians who conscientiously doubt the accuracy of such social research[4] should provide the machinery better designed to measure private preferences, down to small minorities. If they do not, social researchers will wonder whether their concern is with private preferences or with personal power.

3. A pertinent example was inadvertently provided in a letter to *The Times* from an Enfield Borough Councillor (26 August, 1967) who protested that the Council had done all it could to consult parents on its plans for comprehensive schools and asked what more it could do but satisfy "most" parents. Even if the Council had consulted all local parents in good time, which its critics deny, state education cannot meet the preferences of more than "most" or, even worse, "many" parents; only a market, in which parents pay fees to private and state schools, can do that.

4. The consistency of the 1963 and 1965 *Choice in Welfare* surveys points to their reliability. But a comparison of IEA and other results is equally striking. It "refutes the view that public opinion is obstructing reform of state welfare services. A 'majority' vote (of averaged preferences) in favour of a universalist option was not recorded for any service for which two or more survey results were available." (Gray, *op. cit.*, p. 64.)

SECTION **8**

Implications for Policy

(i) Taxation and social benefits

The findings reported in Tables C and D on preferred changes in taxes and social benefits would seem to reflect barely connected sets of decisions (below, iv). Preferences in tax changes seem to have indicated opinion on the merits and demerits of a change in a tax in isolation, with little conscious reflection on the effects on revenue as a whole and therefore on other taxes or on the amount of revenue available for public expenditure. Conversely, a change upward or downward may have been favoured "on its merits" without conscious regard to the revenue required for higher expenditure or to the reduction in expenditure necessary elsewhere to finance it.

The apparent divorce of taxation from expenditure can hardly conduce to responsible decisions by government or taxpayers. Taxation in Britain is not normally earmarked for specified expenditure. When it has been, as with the Road Fund,[1] the results have not been encouraging. "Raids" on earmarked funds can invariably be rationalised by appeals to financial stringency or emergency. And at the other extreme the attempt to make the National Insurance Fund self-supporting by controlling the incoming flow of contributions and the outgoing flow of benefits has been a telling lesson in political mismanagement tempered by ill-luck: the £1,000 million or so left in the Fund can be hardly more than 3 per cent of the capital sum required to pay sickness, unemployment, pension and other national insurance benefits. There is indeed a good case for recognising that it will never now be possible

1. The Road Fund was created in 1909 to comprise taxes on motorists (petrol and vehicles) and was intended solely for expenditure on new roads and improvements. In 1915 part of it was used by the Exchequer; this "emergency" measure was continued after the war. It was ended as a separate fund in 1936 and abolished in 1955.

to restore the insurance principle[2] and for winding up the Fund[3] to prevent the ghost of national insurance being used as the pretext for raising benefits for contributors who have not paid for an increase (nor indeed for most of current benefits) and who do not need it.

Nevertheless two alternatives present themselves. The first is to make one more effort to heighten public understanding of the relationship between taxation and the social benefits for which it pays and so increase the responsibility with which governments ask for more taxation and taxpayers for more social benefits. A Social Security Tax has been proposed; there may be some merit in a Health Tax to replace the misleading[4] NHS element in the social insurance contribution. An Education Tax could be a more graphic way of bringing home the cost of state education than the figures on the back of the local authority rate bill. Other variations, more or less bizarre, suggest themselves.

The weakness of such proposals is that citizens as taxpayers are expected to act collectively, yet as consumers or beneficiaries of state services they see themselves as individuals. Taxpayers may not welcome an increase even in an earmarked tax that ostensibly pays for a named service if they themselves are not likely to gain from its improvement or expansion. Indeed they may

2. Professor A. T. Peacock has shown that government social insurance was never based on actuarial insurance principles in practice: there were statements of intention, or at least statements described by an American observer as "a stroke of promotional genius." (*The Economics of National Insurance,* Hodge, 1952.)

3. Seldon, *Pensions for Prosperity,* Hobart Paper 4, IEA, 1960. The proposal was that contributors should be offered (as an alternative to a pension reduced to its actuarial value) a lump sum representing the value of their and their employers' contributions, with accumulated interest, to be invested for a minimum period at the discretion of the contributor, a proportion in government stocks. In 1960 the National Insurance Fund would have sufficed for 10 million lump sum repayments of £100 on average. Professors J. M. Buchanan and Colin D. Campbell have proposed that the American social insurance fund be converted into a fully actuarial pension fund by computing the net national debt represented by it, creating Social Security Bonds equal to the computed debt and transferring them to the social insurance fund. Contributors would then have the option of contracting out if they preferred to buy their pension elsewhere; but in any event no one in the state scheme would be compelled to pay in more than the cost of his own pension. The shortfall in revenue represented by payments to current pensioners would be made up from general taxation, thus transferring the burden from existing contributors to the community as a whole (*Wall Street Journal,* 20 December, 1966).

4. Misleading because some people—one-third of the sample of male heads of households in the 1963 *Choice in Welfare* survey (Table II)—are led to think that their contributions

pay an anonymous increase in the petrol or cigarette tax unrelated to a named item of government expenditure with more grace than an earmarked tax for a social benefit that confers no benefit on them as individuals or their families.[5] More generally, collective financing multiplies the scope for rational but irresponsible support by individuals of proposals for increased public expenditure on services for which they themselves are unwilling to pay. Through the political process of the ballot box individuals collectively may be, probably are, paying far more in taxes than they would wish if they could act as individuals.[6]

(ii) Direct and indirect payment

The direct, graphic awareness of cost by direct payment through prices in a market for individual goods or services is not readily re-created in the supply of collective goods. This difficulty itself establishes a strong ground for replacing indirect payment through taxes by direct payment through prices.

There would seem no insuperable obstacle in the way of providing collective goods in return for prices in the form of charges. There are, or have been, charges for some goods or services to cover all or part of their cost—medical prescriptions, school meals, council housing, rail transport, fuel and others. But the scope for charging to reduce queueing and congestion and increase finances and supply remains immense: nursery, primary and secondary school tuition, general practitioner consultations and treatment, medicines, hospital treatment, raising council house rents to current market prices and social insurance contributions to the amounts required to pay for retirement pensions, and others. Charging for roads to reduce congestion and raise funds is under discussion. Charging for other collectively-provided goods and services could bring comparable advantages: water, fire

---

included in the NI stamp (currently 2s. 10½d. per week) pay for the whole of the NHS, whereas they represent only one-sixth of the current cost.

5. This view is reached and amplified by Mr. Douglas Houghton in *Paying for the Social Services*, Occasional Paper 16, IEA, 1967.

6. These and related aspects of the theory of public finance were debated by European economists with insight 60–80 years ago: their writings are assembled in sample by Professors Richard A. Musgrave and Alan T. Peacock in *Classics in the Theory of Public Finance*, Macmillan, 1958, Fourth Impression with new Preface, 1967.

services, libraries, museums and art galleries, refuse-collection, public conveniences,[7] beaches, and others.[8]

(iii) Producer subsidy and consumer financing

The obvious objection that the substitution of charging for hitherto tax-paid ("free" or partly "free") goods or services would create hardship and deprivation among people with low income rests on a simple error. Providing goods or services collectively by public authority free or partly free at the point of collection is only one way of ensuring that people with low income have access to them. Another method would be to give grants to private suppliers, direct grant schools, hospitals, health insurers, and so on, to make them provide free or partly free supplies. This is the method of subsidies to producers, which depresses prices (fees, charges) below market levels.

The third method is to leave prices to settle themselves by competition and to enable people with low income to pay market prices for what are considered minimum amounts of "desirable" or "essential" services in education, medical care, housing, income in sickness, unemployment, retirement. This method requires that the state finances consumers, rather than producers, by purchasing power to supplement original earnings. It is used to a small extent in Britain in education, in family allowances, in sickness, unemployment and retirement benefits, and in supplementary allowances or pensions where earnings or social insurance benefits are inadequate, but hardly anywhere else. It could be used in medical insurance (as it is in Australia, Canada, the USA and elsewhere), in housing (as in Germany, France, Switzerland, Denmark, Sweden, the Netherlands and Poland), and in nursery, primary and secondary education (as it is on a small scale in the USA). Its advantages are that it would create cost-conscious consumers with a

7. There is a significant economic story to be written of the transformation of the "free" but nauseous lavatory at Victoria Station into a priced amenity comparable with the best offered by private enterprise. (The then Chairman of British Railways, who insisted on its reconstruction, proposed a charge of 1s.; his officials fixed it at 6d.) The public is still offered a choice between paying a price and "free" lavatories.

8. The economics of charging for some of these services are discussed in *Essays in the Theory and Practice of Pricing* in Readings in Political Economy, No. 3, IEA, 1967. In Italy art galleries and churches commonly charge for adults but not for children; the beach near Venice that charges at varying rates during the day and in different seasons is better kept than most "free" British beaches.

choice between competing public and private suppliers and re-channel purchasing power away from everyday consumption (and imports) to welfare.

Opinions on "free" services and purchasing power, and on general purchasing power in the form of cash and specialised purchasing power in the form of coupons, tokens, tickets or vouchers, are discussed in viii (page 63).

(iv) Indirect payment and the diffusion of decision

Table D seems to suggest a widespread opinion, in both sexes and all four age-groups and socio-occupational groups, in favour of increased government expenditure on pensions, education and health services. The further researches in the survey show that conclusions drawn on public opinion on state welfare could be misleading.

First, Table C indicates little readiness to pay more taxes. There was an overwhelming (81 per cent) opinion against an increase in income tax, which provides about a half of tax revenue, a clear opinion (62 per cent) against a higher petrol tax, and a clear majority of recorded preferences (40 to 28 per cent) against a higher tax on cigarettes. Opinion on the spirits tax was roughly equal. The general opinion in favour of increased government expenditure on social benefits was not accompanied by a general opinion in favour of higher taxation to pay for them.[9]

Second, Table II confirms that there was a general opinion in favour of lower taxation as a proportion of earnings (with what is known as a "Nelson's column" around 5s. in the £ of earnings, or just over the proportion of national income at factor cost—i.e., less taxes, plus subsidies—above which Mr. Colin Clark has argued[10] there are irresistible tendencies to general inflation).

Third, the opinion in favour of higher expenditure on pensions, education and medical care may have expressed a general sense that standards in these social benefits were too low, but they did not necessarily convey opinion in favour of enlargement of the services as they are now constituted or approval of the principle on which they are based.

That principle is universalism. It is still widely held and asserted, despite

9. It is assumed that opinion on tax *rates* would also apply to total *revenue* from each tax. Opinion in favour of higher expenditure is not incompatible with opinion in favour of *lower* tax rates, but it is not likely that the replies incorporated such sophisticated calculations.

10. "Public Finance and the Value of Money," *Economic Journal*, December 1945. Mr. Clark has elaborated his argument in *Taxmanship*, Hobart Paper 26, IEA, 1964.

exceptions in practice, that pensions, medical care and education should be available to everyone without regard to earnings or capacity to pay and that they should be available without payment at the point of service. The further replies suggest that opinion in favour of increased expenditure does not imply approval of the principle on which it is based.

(v) Universal *or* selective benefits

Table III suggests the contrary. It shows a result that may certainly be described as unexpected and perhaps as remarkable. Contemporary thinking in all schools of social philosophy, at least until recently, has assumed that there is a general "consensus" in favour of the Beveridge principle of universal "social" benefits "as of right." In spite of second thoughts among some academics and politicians, this opinion continues to be repeated with assurance and almost finality in some otherwise well-informed quarters.[11] Yet it would seem that many politicians, academics, trade union leaders and evidently bankers and journalists are out of touch with public opinion.

Table III is significant for two reasons. First, it confirms the findings of IEA and other surveys that there is no general consensus in favour of universalism. There were on the contrary almost twice as many in favour of selective benefits (65 per cent) as of universal benefits (35 per cent). Second, there would seem to be evidence that another widely held view is a superstition. The support for universalism and against selectivity in social benefits is supposed to be especially strong among the lower paid on the ground that they resent being segregated for exceptional treatment.[12] Hence their sup-

11. A recent example is: "In most countries governments have adopted social policies with a decidedly egalitarian bent. It is in this range of expenditure that the steepest escalations in government outlays have occurred. Nor is there much prospect of a reversal of this trend. The welfare state is here to stay." This is not culled from a political or sociological review with *etatist* leanings. It is a presumably dispassionate judgement from the world of finance: *Barclays Bank Review,* May 1967.

12. Examples can be found in three recent Fabian lectures by Professors Brian Abel-Smith, "Labour's Social Plans," R. M. Titmuss, "Choice and the 'Welfare State,'" and Peter Townsend, "Poverty, Socialism and Labour in Power," published in *Socialism and Affluence,* Fabian Society, 1967. A fourth essay by the Rt. Hon. R. H. S. Crossman, Lord President of the Council and Leader of the House of Commons, joined issue with their general approach and showed evidence of the re-thinking that has taken place among Labour politicians since they entered office.

posed bitter opposition to any form of means or income test. The survey found no clear evidence to support this supposition.

The socio-occupational group analysis shows that the third (35 per cent) in favour of paying taxes for universal benefits broke down into almost a half (47 per cent) among the "upper-middle and middle" group and a little over a quarter (29 per cent) among the "semi-skilled and unskilled." And the two-thirds (65 per cent) in favour of selective benefits broke down into just over half (53 per cent) and nearly three-quarters (71 per cent) respectively. These figures question the persistent view that the people most likely to be beneficiaries are most opposed to social benefits unless they are universal. They suggest instead that they are judging social benefits not on doctrinal universalist or egalitarian grounds but on the material ground that people with least should be given most. And it is proper to add the reflection that there is also the ground of humanity; for even the egalitarianism of the universal principle is spurious: equal treatment of people in unequal circumstances is not equality but inequality. It is the supporters of selective benefits who are the true egalitarians.

Two doubts may properly be raised about the wording of the question the replies to which are analysed in Table III. One is that it does not use the words "means test" or "needs test." The decision not to use the words was based on several arguments. First, the words used correctly describe the alternatives in simple language: the use of the words "means test" or "needs test" might have provoked precisely the emotional response that it was essential to avoid if the results were to be an accurate measure of opinion in 1967 as a guide for social policy in the future. Second, the sample was limited to people aged under 65; not many of them would have been adults 35 years ago when the household means test separated families; over half the sample were children, or not yet born, in 1930 or 1935. Third, whether or not there is emotional feeling, it is proper to put the alternatives in words that clearly indicate their meaning: universal social benefits and services are "for everyone"; selective social benefits and services are "for those who need them most." This is the fundamental choice in social policy, and these are the words of plain English in which the debate should be conducted among the people as well as among academics and politicians. Words that conjured up emotions three decades ago would introduce bias into the disputation. Fourth, the words do not seem to strike terror: surveys that have used them[13] find widespread accept-

13. Opinion Research Centre survey on housing, published in the *Sunday Times*, May 1967; the pilot survey for the IEA research study on housing to be published in 1968; Opinion

ance of a means test. Fifth, and this should end the argument once and for all: the form of means test that is being discussed increasingly is an income coding that avoids the objections to the 1930s' household means test.[14]

The second doubt is whether the question should have said "social benefits and services for everyone as of right." "As of right" are words used by Beveridge to describe the spirit of the comprehensive benefits he envisaged. Here again the reply is that we should use language that describes in plain English the situation that is, not aspirations and wishful thinking that may mislead and confuse. The benefits that were supposed to be earned "as of right" by social insurance after 1946 were never fully earned. In Britain social or national insurance has become a charade. There is no parallel between social insurance as it has developed and private insurance. The citizen has a moral right to social assistance if he is in need; and in a sense he has a financial "right" to benefits insofar as he has paid for them by taxation. But they are not the benefits "as of right" envisaged by Beveridge that politicians have intoned for the past decades. And no desirable purpose is served by perpetuating them.

(vi) Universal *and* selective benefits?

It would seem clear that social services and benefits can be supplied either to everyone or only to people identified by a financial measure of income, means or need. State education is either available universally or only to children of parents with income below a stated figure; medical care is available to all social insurance contributors or for payment of a charge that is reimbursed to people below a given income; housing is available at below-market rents either to everyone on a waiting list or at market rents partly reimbursed to people with income below a given level; pensions are paid to everyone aged 60 or 65 or only to those with an income below a stated amount; and so on.

Research Centre survey on attitudes to welfare published in the *Evening Standard,* July 1967. The impact of the words "means test" is discussed in Part II of Hamish Gray's *Universal or Selective Social Benefits?,* Research Monograph 8, IEA, 1967. Research that has been published since the 1963 and 1965 IEA reports indicates that in 1962 there was no majority in favour of universal social benefits and against selective benefits (W. G. Runciman, *Relative Deprivation and Social Justice,* Routledge & Kegan Paul, 1966).

14. Its working is illustrated in "Applying Selectivity in the Social Services," *The Times,* 4 September, 1967.

British social services and benefits are predominantly universal. There are many means tests for individual services and benefits, which are therefore selective.[15] But the distinction in principle is unambiguous; and the overwhelming area of expenditure is on universal benefits. Of £1,350 million spent on education in the latest year only £175 million was paid on a means test, almost none of the £1,250 million spent on the National Health Service, an unknown proportion of the £750 million on housing subsidies and only £300 million of the £2,450 million on social security benefits.[16] All the rest went on services or on transfer payments available for all who otherwise qualified for them by age, residence or other condition that had little or nothing to do with income, means or needs.

Until recently the academic and political debate was clearly between the *principles* of universality and selectivity. The arguments for universality ranged from high moral invocation of "the badge of citizenship"[17] through the avoidance of the stigma of financial segregation to the mundane administrative convenience and simplicity of general distribution: they either accepted abortive benefits as a price of simple administration or tried to mop up some of the waste by taxation. Recently two of the leading academic advocates of universality seem to have changed their minds. Professor Abel-Smith now accepts[18] that "the most obvious remedy is to concentrate help where it is needed and to stop giving it where it is not" but believes it may take a decade to develop the required means tests; and he also accepts the possibility of a negative income tax administered by the Inland Revenue. Professor Titmuss's change of mind has taken a more interesting turn. In his Official War History, *Problems of Social Policy,*[19] he argued eloquently for universalism; he now agrees, in circumlocutory sociological language, that the choice between universality and selectivity is false:

> The challenge that faces us is not the choice between universalism and selective social services. The real challenge resides in the question: what

15. Social benefits that are taxed—family allowances, retirement pensions and several others—are in this sense also selective. See below, vii.

16. Replies to Commons questions put by Mr. John Biffen, April, June, 1967.

17. May it not be that a more appropriate wearer of a badge of citizenship would be the man who rejects a social benefit he cannot conscientiously accept. A telling example was offered by a correspondent to the *Guardian* on 11 May, 1967, who had refused family allowances and risked being taxed on an income from the state he had not received.

18. *Weekend Telegraph,* 25 November, 1966.

19. HMSO, 1950.

> particular infrastructure of universalist services is needed in order to provide a framework of values and opportunity bases within and around which can be developed socially acceptable selective services aiming to discriminate positively, with the minimum risk of stigma, in favour of those whose needs are greatest.[20,21]

In simple English, it is now proper for some services to be universal and for others to be selective. Or is it acceptable for some to be universal (or selective) at some periods in life, or in given circumstances, permanently or temporarily? Whatever the meaning, it is apparently no longer essential to make all services universal in order to respect human dignity. Discrimination, singling out, social divisiveness, segregation by a financial measure, is acceptable in some circumstances, or for some people. Social benefits need no longer be wholly universal, equal without regard to (varying) individual circumstances. The welfare state may now properly comprise universal and selective services; social benefits may now be both equal and unequal.

The academic advocates of unqualified universalism on principle are in an intellectual dilemma from which they cannot escape except by concession of error. If selectivity is morally repugnant there can be no room for selective benefits, even as a superstructure for a substructure of universal benefits. If selectivity is, at last, morally acceptable, there can be no moral reason for insistence on a substructure of wasteful universal benefits. Economic circumstance, intellectual argument and the belated recognition that generalised benefits are inhumane have destroyed the case for universalism. Nor

20. "Welfare State and Welfare Society," an address to the Sixth National Conference on Social Welfare, London, 10 April, 1967.

21. The most recent reformulation is still unavailing. The passage in the above extract has been elaborated for a forthcoming book: " . . . within and around which can be developed acceptable selective services, provided, as social rights, on criteria of the *needs* of specific categories, groups and territorial areas and not dependent on *individual tests of means*." (Italics in the original: *New Statesman*, 15 September, 1967.) But this further attempt to reconcile universality with selectivity is even less satisfactory. The aim is to give benefits to *people* who need. "Categories" or "groups" are no substitute for people. The category "council-house tenant" changes in composition over time: many of them are no longer in need; many people in need are not council tenants. The group "unemployed," or "sick" or "widow," contains many who are not in need. A "territorial area" selected for exceptional assistance contains people who are not in need; and many people who are in need do not live in them. This attempt to salvage the universalist principle but avoid the much-condemned individual identification of individuals in need would combine the worst of both worlds for its sponsor: it would abandon the moral case for universal universalism and still fail to help individuals in need by squandering it on "categories," "groups" and "territorial areas."

should refuge be taken in attempts to pay lip service to both principles, formerly regarded as moral opposites, now joined in an administrative *mariage de convenance.*

The universalist/selectivists have been reduced to their parlous straits by the mounting evidence of inadequacy in tax revenue and misdirection in universal benefits that show no signs of removing the persistent pockets of need among old people, large families, incapacitated and others and of the evident desire of many with rising incomes to provide for themselves education, medical care and housing and pensions better than the state can provide in a centralised, standardised, stagnant service. These are the underlying two socio-economic trends that are making the Beveridge doctrine of universal benefits out of date barely 20 years after they were introduced. They are also provoking a disturbing revolution in thinking among social administrators who can distinguish between human needs and social philosophy. They are causing a rift between the academic universalists and the politicians who have had to change their minds in two years of office. And they will produce social policies in the coming two decades far different from those envisaged by the two main political parties three years ago.

(vii) Selection by taxation or income test?

If it is accepted on all sides that moral principle, or human dignity, or administrative convenience no longer require all social benefits to be universal, how can they best be made selective?

The obvious way is to pay them on a measure of needs, or means, or income. The objections to these tests are discussed above. The conclusion was that the many tests could be replaced by a single automatic indicator of entitlement by the use of income returns and codes. The principle of a reverse income tax seems to have derived from the fertile mind of the late Professor Henry C. Simons of the University of Chicago and has been introduced by Professor Milton Friedman into recent American academic and public discussion. It has been advocated in Britain for some ten years[22] and has recently been discussed by academics and politicians in circles[23] where until

22. *Pensions in a Free Society,* IEA, 1957.

23. They include Professor Abel-Smith, Mr. Houghton and Mr. Christopher Price, MP, the last in *Socialist Commentary,* May 1967. Mr. Houghton discusses administrative aspects in his IEA *Paper.* More recent adherents are Mr. Patrick Gordon Walker and other Labour leaders. The application to social benefits is illustrated in "Applying Selectivity in the Social Services,"

recently means tests were regarded with distaste and as "politically impossible."

The use of the income-tax system to discover entitlement to cash (or coupon?) supplements to original income is designed to remove the two objections to conventional means tests, that they require applicants to initiate a claim and withstand a personal investigation into means, to replace many tests for individual benefits (school meals, university grants, rate rebates, etc.) by one income test, and to reduce the administrative costs of inquiry by an official into means and needs. The method is not a complete solution: it is not satisfactory for the physically or mentally incapable who cannot handle cash and who require personal care; it does not deal with large variations in sizeable items of household expenditure such as rents; and annual or half-year revisions in income codes would not offset marked fluctuations in weekly earnings; it may impair incentives unless appropriately tapered. These difficulties are not insurmountable: the tendency for wages to be paid monthly could be matched by more frequent revision of income codes or reverse tax refunds by income-tax collectors on the lines of tax refunds for payments under covenant. The Inland Revenue is adept at demonstrating difficulties; but it has also found solutions for new problems it had considered insoluble.

But this use of the income-tax system to redistribute purchasing power is more fundamental than the taxation of social benefits (retirement pensions, family allowances, etc.). Taxed benefits are selective in the sense that their net value varies inversely with income. But they are no more than a half-way house, or rather a third-way house for the many (who pay an average tax of 6s. 5d. in the pound). They are not an acceptable substitute for a reverse income tax.

First, taxed benefits are distributed universally. There is no economy in the distributive machinery.

Second, as incomes rise the larger the proportion of taxed benefits returned to the Inland Revenue. A growing part of the government machinery is employed to cancel itself.

Third, even after taxation much remains with taxpayers to inflate expenditure on non-welfare. No government has so far calculated the volume of these abortive benefits.

Fourth, abortive benefits inflate the volume of taxation.

The Times, 4 September, 1967. The latest adherents are Mr. David Marquand, Dr. David Owen and Professor John Mackintosh, "Change Gear," *Socialist Commentary*, October 1967.

Fifth, only some cash benefits are taxed; others are not. And social benefits in kind—nearly half of the total—are not taxed at all.

The taxation of social benefits is a second-best substitute for distribution by means as measured by an income coding.

The objection to a reverse or negative income tax that redistribution of income in cash would not remove visible poverty has been considered on page 23.

(viii) Social benefits in cash or kind?

The surprisingly large preference for cash or coupons (Table IV) suggests that state welfare policy has been developing on unnecessarily restrictive lines. Education, medical care and housing, which take £3,500 million out of £7,000 million of social benefits, are provided on a large and growing scale for everyone who satisfies the relevant non-financial requirements of nationality, residence, age. All three services are short of funds. Yet until recently there was little discussion of an obvious method of enlarging the resources that could be attracted into them.

The solution is gradually to replace services in kind by purchasing power in cash or coupon. In time citizen-consumers would add out of their earnings to buy better quality, as they are now accustomed to doing in everyday or periodic household expenditure. In the field survey for the 1965 *Choice in Welfare* report, 15 per cent of the sample said they would take a £50 voucher for a schoolchild and add £100 to pay secondary school fees of £150 a year. Thirty per cent said they would take a £100 voucher and add £50. In both cases, if each respondent had one child they would add £110 million a year (the crude measure of elasticity of demand, abstracting from the effects on real income, was unity between these distant prices). Twenty-three per cent said they would take a £5 medical voucher for each member of the household and add £5 to pay a health insurance premium of £10 a year. Thirty per cent said they would take a £7 voucher and add £3. If each respondent had a family of four, the amounts added out of earnings would be £45.4 million to the £5 voucher and £35.6 million to the £7 voucher (price elasticity of demand was less than unity).

These would be the initial amounts. In time they could be expected to grow with experience of choice, with competition between schools and between medical services, with the addition of welfare to household budgeting and family decisions, and with rising incomes. This method could effectively tap the £15,000 million or more now spent on everyday or periodic household consumption. It is also the only effective way to encourage people with middling and lower incomes to spend voluntarily on education. The method of taxation seems to have spent itself. If the system of nil-price universal welfare continues it may be half a century before incomes rise enough to enable the 90 or 95 per cent to join the 5 or 10 per cent who can pay for education and medical care out of taxed, unsupplemented income.

The argument that services in kind must continue to be distributed to people who cannot pay is thus in error. Within a short period many more who now accept "free" services with little or no choice could be enabled to pay for services with choice. Nor is it possible to argue that services in kind must be distributed to people who would misspend cash. Earmarked vouchers would largely prevent misspending. In any event, people who misspend will not learn how to spend if they are given services that make no demand on their faculties of judgement, discrimination or responsibility. The use of purchasing power in cash or coupon is itself an indispensable teacher in the process of change from a dependent to an independent society. Only the physically or mentally handicapped who are incapable of learning independence would need to receive services.

The remaining objection[24] would seem to be that services in cash rather than kind would disrupt social cohesion (8(ix)).

(ix) Social divisiveness

Anxiety about "social divisiveness" troubles many otherwise disposed to see the weaknesses and limitations of universal state welfare. It is not difficult to rebut.

In the first place, unless independent schools, doctors and hospitals, owner-occupied homes and private pensions are outlawed, it is a structure

24. A sophisticated theoretical case for distribution of social benefits in kind has been attempted by Mr. Lucien Foldes in "Income Redistribution in Money and Kind," and "A Note on Redistribution," *Economica*, 1967. His analysis has been disputed by Professor J. M. Buchanan in "What Kind of Redistribution Do We Want?," *Economica*, 1967. Mr. Foldes's interesting analytical speculation would need to be clothed with convincing demonstration that it would work in the real world as it appears to do on paper before its relevance for social policy could be judged. Common assumptions about human nature and the political process suggest *a priori* that social benefits in kind determined, controlled and administered by politicians and officials could not readily yield the satisfactions that could be derived from the expenditure of cash (or, in a more limited sense, vouchers) by people informed of the alternatives available in the market.

of state welfare that creates a deep social division between the few who can pay (after tax) and the many who cannot. And the division will tend to deepen as rising incomes enable and encourage more to pay.

Second, social divisiveness in the sense of varying levels of quality in services purchased are an inevitable accompaniment of inequality in income and the institution of the family. If schooling, medical care, housing are equalised, income will be spent on giving children and families other advantages that will be socially divisive. Since even egalitarians do not argue for equality in income, they must show, which they cannot, how inequality in income can be accompanied by equality in expenditure on individual welfare services.[25]

Third, if there is freedom to spend on welfare as well as on non-welfare, the variations in quality will become more numerous but more moderate than the deep rift between state and private education or hospitals. There will be numerous qualities shading into one another, not two between which movement is rare. In time the differences would be reduced with increasing social mobility on the side of demand and competition on the side of supply.

Fourth, cash or coupons can be arranged to reduce social inequalities by being varied with income, family size, and other circumstances.

Fifth, the cash or coupons would remove the arbitrary advantages deriving from social or family origins, connections, or influence. The power to persuade would be replaced by the power of the purse, supplemented by transfer payments until income rose sufficiently to dispense with them. The articulate salary-earner would lose his advantage over the wage-earner, which today is illustrated, within the state sector, by the often painfully visible contrasts between the good primary school in a middle-class suburb or town and the wretched primary or secondary modern in a London or industrial slum.

Sixth, even if conformity and cohesion were desirable, they do not require state organisation. Competing schools, state and private, could be required to teach common subjects at common standards. The merit of diversity would be lost, but cash or coupons would retain competition in supply.[26]

It would be a tragedy if the fallacy of "social divisiveness" were to replace the bogy of the means test as a bar to social reform.

25. Seldon, "Crisis in the Welfare State," *Encounter,* December 1967. The argument on social divisiveness is put by Dr. Mark Blaug and answered by Dr. E. G. West in *Education: A Framework for Choice,* Readings in Political Economy No. 1, IEA, 1967.

26. I am grateful to Professor Buchanan for discussion of this proposition.

(x) Individual choice in collective services

Individuals can make tolerably informed choices between goods and services in markets. Their information is limited, because it is costly to collect, because residual uncertainty is unavoidable, and because they may not know how little they know.[27] Yet individuals buy (and sell) with some knowledge both of the prices of alternatives and of the satisfaction they hope to receive from them.

In the provision of collective goods through the ballot box at nil or perceptibly less than market prices, the individual has relatively much less knowledge. In welfare he cannot readily calculate how much he pays for the education he receives for his children, for the medical care he buys by social insurance and taxation, for the housing subsidy he may receive as a council-house tenant, or for the retirement pension he draws at 65. He may not even know the value of the social benefits he receives. How can he make rational choices between alternative political policies for supplying collective goods? How can he be expected to make rational choices between the alternative services?

Professor Buchanan, a pioneer in the study of individual choices in political decisions, argues[28] the need for research into six essential questions:

1. "How ignorant is the average voter-taxpayer-beneficiary about the fiscal alternatives he confronts?"
2. "How much does he really know about the impact upon him exerted by the various fiscal institutions, existing or potential?"
3. "How much is he obligated to pay in taxes?"
4. "What are the costs of public services he enjoys?"
5. "How much value does he place on the benefits from these services?"
6. "Does he make any effective translation of benefits into tax-costs?"

Professor Buchanan reviews the partial, qualified replies to these questions yielded by researches at the Universities of Virginia, Michigan, Harvard, Cologne, the Institute of Economic Affairs and elsewhere.

The general replies would seem to be: Qu. 1—exceedingly; Qu. 2—not

27. Professor George Stigler's "The Economics of Information" in *Journal of Political Economy,* June 1961, is a seminal analysis.

28. *Public Finance in Democratic Process,* the University of North Carolina Press, 1967. Earlier works by Professor Buchanan are *The Calculus of Consent* (with Professor Gordon Tullock), 1962; *Fiscal Theory and Political Economy,* 1960; *Public Finances,* 1960; *Public Principles of Public Debt,* 1958.

much; Qu. 3—he does not know clearly; Qu. 4—he does not know; Qu. 5—he does not know; Qu. 6—no.

The Institute's work, reported in the *Choice in Welfare* studies, *Universal or Selective Social Benefits?* and this *Monograph,* indirectly throws some light on Professor Buchanan's questions. It is designed primarily to discover preferences between state and independent services; as ancillaries it has studied quantitative knowledge of taxation (as the payment) and of the costs (or "value") of social benefits and general attitudes and attitudes to alternative political policies in social welfare. The research on preferences has attempted to create a hypothetical demand schedule based on two "prices" in the form of the cash that would have to be added to vouchers for secondary schooling and medical care. The findings have made it possible to discern the shape of the demand schedule and thus to arrive at a crude calculation of the price-elasticity of demand. Since replies were elicited in four socio-occupational groups (as used in this *Monograph*), it is also possible to see an outline of the income-elasticity[29] of the demand for secondary schooling and medical care.

Dr. Mark Blaug[30] has objected that one of the parameters of the demand schedule, the "taste" for education at constant prices, varies with the education of parents. This is an unavoidable limitation. The taste for higher standards in schooling and medical care will grow as they become more generally available. Much the same is true in the early years of a new commodity or service. The "taste," in the sense of the readiness to pay, for welfare is sharpened by the experience of choice.

Research into demand schedules for collectively-provided goods has been described as desirable by Professor T. W. Hutchison in a paper[31] on the relationship between the market process and the politically-created framework of laws and institutions in which it has developed in the last two centuries. It is being applied to housing in a forthcoming report on an Institute research study.[32]

(xi) The irrelevance of international comparison

Recent doubts about and dissent from the philosophy of state welfare have provoked efforts to show that the scale of taxation and/or social bene-

29. The responsiveness of demand to changes in income.

30. "Economic Aspects of Vouchers" in *Education: A Framework for Choice,* Readings in Political Economy, No. 1, IEA, 1967.

31. *Markets and the Franchise,* Occasional Paper 10, IEA, 1966.

32. *Choice in Housing,* by F. G. Pennance and Hamish Gray, IEA, 1968.

fits in Britain is more modest than elsewhere. The *Economic Review* of the National Institute of Economic and Social Research has argued[33] from a review of social security in Europe, North America and Australia that social benefits generally were larger abroad even where incomes were lower. *The Times* Business News[34] published two articles by Mr. Peter Jay arguing from OECD statistics that British taxes were not the highest in the world, that they were lower than in many other countries in Europe, and that British government expenditure was not overwhelming its tax revenue. And Professor Abel-Smith, after a similar attempt,[35] sought to allay apprehensions that higher taxation would discourage effort and output by claiming that "such empirical research studies as there are give little support to the supposed general relation between taxation and incentives."

These international comparisons do not advance this discussion very much. They embody an obvious *non sequitur.* Will taxpayers in Britain be willing to pay a higher proportion of their income in taxes by demonstrations (if the figures are accurate) that taxpayers in some other countries pay even more? The reluctance of British taxpayers to pay higher taxes is the main resistance with which British governments have to contend. What matters is not so much international comparisons, interesting though they may be, except at the margin at which people migrate, as the attitudes of taxpayers within each country in terms of recent trends in income and taxation, the degree of conscientiousness in paying taxes, and the taxpayers' valuation of the increase in income (less tax) that can be earned by additional effort.[36] Let us assemble all the evidence we can by "empirical research studies"; only if it demonstrates conclusively that British taxpayers will willingly yield a high and rising proportion of their income to the government for social benefits will the advocates of growing state welfare have established at least the financial feasibility of their case. The evidence assembled in *Choice in Welfare* on attitudes to paying higher taxes in a period of rising incomes lends them doubtful support. The sample in 1965 was asked:

> Suppose incomes continue to rise in the next ten or twenty years, which of these three possible policies would you prefer?

33. "Social Security in Britain and Certain Other Countries," August 1965.

34. 18 and 19 May, 1967.

35. Brian Abel-Smith, "Labour's Social Plans."

36. The habit of weighing the effort against *net* earnings itself suggests that the taxpayer does not regard taxation as the payment for social benefits for which he is prepared to sacrifice consumption (or leisure). Income tax is evidently regarded as a loss, not a gain.

The alternatives were more taxes to pay for better education, health services and pensions or less taxes but private payment for independent services. The question was designed to test the view that economic growth and rising incomes would provide the finance for enlarged state welfare. The replies were: 41, 32 and 34 per cent in favour of higher taxes and more state welfare (education, medical care and pensions respectively), and 48, 59 and 58 per cent in favour of lower taxes and private payment.

The increased interest in international comparisons of taxation and social benefits[37] reflects the perplexity caused by the failure of successive British governments to provide state welfare at rising standards. The central error is to suppose that if other countries raise a higher proportion of their national income in taxation we can, or should, do likewise. It may be true that where national income is higher, more can be raised by taxation for social benefits; but since personal incomes are also higher the state does not need to tax as much because people can by definition provide for themselves. The confusion is between the *capacity* to tax and the *need* to tax for social benefits; as incomes rise the first may grow, but the second diminishes.

(xii) The limits to taxation

That this ceiling to taxation revenues is not far off is testified by two developments. The first is the failure of the government, despite its philosophic adherence to the principle of universal benefits, to raise family allowances for all qualifying children at a cost of £160 million a year, and its search for ways of making the increase selective at a cost of £20 or £30 million by reducing income-tax child allowances. The proposed universal rise in state pensions must be the last, or the last but one. How long and how far other social benefits can be raised universally is the significant question. The second is the discouragement to earn;[38] it is difficult to document but the evidence cannot be denied.[39] The third is the spread of tax evasion. Four tax

37. Further examples and the argument are amplified in "Financing Medical Care," *Medical World Newsletter,* 22 August, 1967.

38. In a letter to *The Times* (21 June, 1967) Mr. Paul Dehn, an internationally recognised film script writer, wrote of the disincentive of the income-tax rates to script writers who could earn up to £100,000 before tax for two scripts in a year (usually paid by the London offices of American companies from dollar sources) but who would be taxed at the top rate on the whole sum. They therefore write only one script, thus depriving the Treasury of large sums both of dollars and of tax revenue.

39. *Ex hypothesi* it is difficult to document the forms and extent of tax avoidance and

specialists, a banker, an investment trust manager, a stockbroker and a tax consultant have testified in *The Times* that "Tax evasion is not respectable, but it is not far from it."[40] This is ominous evidence, confirmed in this survey, that taxation is thought excessive. No international comparisons can gainsay the growing resistance of the British taxpayer to taxes as not a price he is happy to pay for social benefits but an impost he no longer regards as anti-social to evade. The recent amnesty for taxpayers who have invented dependents is a symptom not of political magnanimity but of administrative incapacity; and the savage penalties for omitting to pay TV licence duties is evidence that the bureaucracy is at its wits' end.

Three lines of reasoning support these conclusions. The first is empirical: although incomes will have risen by perhaps 60 to 70 per cent in the nearly 20 years since 1946–48 when the state welfare services as they are now were established, governments of both major parties have failed to find enough tax finance to supply them at the rising standards expected by citizens accustomed to conspicuously rising standards in household and personal consumption. The consumers' sovereignty that characterises conventional consumption[41] contrasts with the common consumer deference in state education, medical care and housing that accompanies their shortages and the consequent resort to rationing by officials: local authority education officers, headmasters, hospital administrators, council housing managers, Ministry of Social Security officials.

The second reason is institutional: the taxpayer's attitude to paying taxes is essentially different from the consumer's attitude to paying prices. A tax is not seen as a payment for a service: it is encountered as a deduction from earnings or an increase in retail costs, an imposition levied by officials which the taxpayer has had little voice in deciding, and which he cannot avoid except by changing his way of life or evade except by risking fines or imprisonment. A price is seen by the consumer as embodying a voluntary decision to buy one commodity or service rather than another that has visible form and that provides immediate satisfaction. Even if it were possible to replace

---

evasion. Professor Titmuss has discussed some forms in his *Income Distribution and Social Change* (Allen & Unwin, 1962), but his studies were limited to the middle- and upper-income groups and largely ignored the lower-income groups.

40. 10 April, 1967.

41. This term is used to refer to food, clothing, smoking, drinking, entertaining, motoring, holidaying, etc.

general by specific taxes earmarked for various services, they will not appear as explicitly within the taxpayer's influence as prices in the market. Patients will pay fees for medical services received more readily than taxes for a state health service.[42] Motorists will pay toll fees for a road more readily than vehicle duties or petrol tax. It cannot therefore be assumed that rising incomes will yield rising tax revenue; for they will bring growing expectations of consumer sovereignty that collectively-organised, centralised, standardised services cannot satisfy.

The third reason is derived from a theoretical principle of public finance: that individuals as taxpayers will not finance and supply as much of a state service as they will demand at nil price as consumers because they have "free rides" in collective services whether they pay taxes or not.[43] However public-spirited or conscientious, they will not discipline their demands since by so doing they cannot influence others to discipline theirs: all they can do is to forgo benefits without discernibly benefiting others.

These reasons to doubt the sanguine expectations of automatic growth in tax revenue and the denial of sociologists that rising taxes discourage work, effort, and enterprise are reflected in the more convincing testimony of academics, practising business men and others qualified to offer judgement. Company chairmen present their experience of disincentives in *Growth through Industry.*[44] Professor G. S. A. Wheatcroft, the specialist in taxation, has argued the politically uncongenial case for a halving of surtax-rates.[45] Mr. Ronald Grierson, a business man appointed by a Labour Government as managing director of the Industrial Reconstruction Corporation, has de-

42. The citizen will pay a social insurance contribution or a social security tax unrelated to specific services less readily than a fee; but he will pay a private insurance premium more readily than a social insurance contribution because he has a choice of insurers, a choice of degrees of insurance and a choice of medical risks to cover. Moreover, because the "deductible," as it is called in North America, or "patient's fraction," as it is called in Australia, requires the patient to pay a proportion of medical bills, and he pays the full bill and claims reimbursement of some 60 to 90 per cent, he is normally made more aware of the full cost of medical care than under national insurance. National and private health insurance are contrasted in "National or Personal Health Service?," *Lancet,* 25 March, 1967 and "Prospects for Private Health Insurance," *British Medical Journal,* 15 July, 1967.

43. This is an abbreviated statement of the "free rider" theorem analysed by Professor R. A. Musgrave, *The Theory of Public Finance,* McGraw-Hill, 1959, and discussed by Professor J. M. Buchanan, *The Inconsistencies of the National Health Service,* Occasional Paper 7, IEA, 1965.

44. Readings in Political Economy No. 2, IEA, 1967.

45. *The Times,* 20 December, 1966.

scribed British taxes on earned income as "By far the biggest obstacle to the dynamic development of industry."[46] Mr. Nicholas Davenport, a financial writer not antagonistic to the government's economic thinking in general, has said "Excepting the French, the British tax system must be the most irritating and disturbing in the world."[47] Mr. Douglas Houghton, a former tax administrator who was a Labour cabinet minister concerned with reconstruction of social security, has said[48] of a doctor[49] who proposed higher taxation to finance urgent improvements in the NHS:

> He probably startles the Treasury when he says that it would require an additional £500 million *a year* (a year!) to give medicine in Britain the relative priority it enjoys in the ruthless capitalism of America. . . . No Chancellor may feel able to face the enormous cost of health services of the higher standard needful in contemporary conditions so long as he has to get the money by compulsory taxes of one kind or another. While people would be willing to pay for better services for themselves, they may not be willing to pay more in taxes for services which are not worth the money price until they as taxpayers actually use them.

Not least Mr. R. H. S. Crossman, who ten years ago prepared the government's proposals for social reconstruction with the aid of Professors Titmuss, Abel-Smith and Townsend, has dismissed as "unrealistic" their claim that government expenditure on social welfare could be enlarged without economic growth:[50]

> . . . there are limits to the amount of redistribution which can be achieved over the shorter term by taxation. . . . I am prepared to assert against our critics that in peacetime the gap between private affluence and public squalor *cannot* be corrected without a fairly rapid rate of economic growth.

Mr. Crossman was presenting realities—the readiness of citizens to pay taxes or accept restrictions in consumption—to confront the philosophical aspirations of his former academic advisers. But he has not gone far enough.

46. *The Times,* 1 April, 1967.

47. *Spectator,* 26 May, 1967.

48. Address to a conference of the Institute of Municipal Treasurers and Accountants, 7 April, 1967, amplified and published as *Paying for the Social Services,* Occasional Paper 16, IEA, 1967.

49. Professor Henry Miller, *Encounter,* April 1967.

50. *Socialism and Affluence.*

He has to demonstrate that growth will bring a readiness to pay more in taxes for expanding and improving collective benefits; he has yet to rebut the view that growth is slow precisely because current taxes, as this survey suggests, are too high.

British tax revenue will not be enlarged by showing that taxation elsewhere is higher than in Britain, but only by showing British taxpayers that they cannot get better value for their money than by paying for state services. That is the unresolved doubt. And it is strengthened rather than removed by the growing capacity of the citizen with rising income to compare and contrast the often insensitive service he receives from the state in education, medical care, housing, pensions with the attentive inquiries and responses from competing suppliers in the market.[51]

The dilemma of the universalists has been seen, to a degree, by leading members and thinkers in the Labour Party such as Mr. Houghton and several younger MPs; in a debate in the Commons on 9 June, 1967, they argued that, since further increases in direct taxation would weaken incentives and in indirect taxation would raise costs and weaken the economy, tax revenue for state welfare would have to be supplemented by purchasing power withdrawn from other forms of taxation and that the method was charges for state services. "Either the social services will not be improved," said Mr. Brian Walden, an economist, in an incisive contribution, "or the universal principle must go." But even this is only a partial recognition of the dilemma. If charges are made for hitherto free state medical care or other services, or if charges are raised, the economic effect is the same as if the prices for private services are reduced, because the gap between the cost of state and private services is narrowed. Charges are economically indistinguishable, except in degree, from tax rebates on the prices paid for private services as in Australia, the USA, Ireland and elsewhere, or as a tax on the notional value of state services in kind would be.[52] Since it is possible to buy privately better education, medical care, housing, than is supplied by the state, charges will induce contracting out to a degree unfavourable and uncontrollable except by draconian measures intolerable in a free society. Once the limits to taxation as a source of revenue for state welfare are recognised, logic, eco-

51. The conclusions and findings reported in this *Monograph* broadly confirm the thesis of Professors J. Wiseman and A. T. Peacock in *The Growth of Public Expenditure in the United Kingdom,* Princeton University Press, 1961, that the limit to expenditure is set not by policy but by revenue, i.e., not by politicians but by taxpayers.

52. "Taxing State Benefits," *Daily Telegraph,* 11 October, 1966.

nomic reasoning and humanity point to a common conclusion: to put welfare to individual choice, to allow state and private services to compete with one another to stimulate expenditure on welfare as a whole, to supplement low incomes by cash (or voucher), and to put quality before equality and concern for the most needy before anxiety about social divisiveness.

(xiii) Private finance for public services

The limitations to tax revenue will raise in an intensifying form questions on the extent and consequences of private finance for public services, which, as in the monopolist archetypal BBC and state schools, provide mediocratic services that avoid the worst but rarely aspire to the best of independent television and education.

All public services are financed by private revenue whether compulsory in taxation (including social insurance) or voluntary in gifts and endowments. Citizens may be supposed to acquiesce in compulsory levies to the extent that they elect, by majority, politicians who impose and enforce them. But not sufficiently. State education and medical care are financed in addition by gifts and subscriptions. State schools have swimming pools financed by subscriptions; universities are partly endowed by private firms and individuals; the National Health Service has research units and hospital wings endowed by industry.

If these additional voluntary monies were designed to dilute political influence in the conduct and development of welfare services, there would be much to be said for them. Their purpose is, *inter alia,* presumably to improve facilities. Their effect is to increase the realm of political influence.

Sooner or later it must be asked whether more good might be done if voluntary monies were used to establish educational or medical institutions independent of the state. The foundation of independent schools, colleges, universities, medical training schools, research institutes, health centres, hospitals could have several main motives. First, and most immediate, they would often provide a better and prompter service: for example, medical care for scarce specialists, from scientists to plasterers, whose time is too valuable to waste in queueing for consultation and treatment. Second, vocational training could often be better carried out independently by industries that better know their requirements than by universities financed through the University Grants Committee. Third, industry could avoid the cumulative errors in government forecasting: independent medical training schools might not necessarily have acted on the view of the 1957 Willink Committee that a surplus of doctors was imminent; independent colleges of science and art would not be subject to fashionable opinion about alleged "national need" for more (or fewer) science (or arts) graduates. Fourth, the standards of politically-controlled universities and hospitals would be raised by competition from independent universities and hospitals. Fifth, the political influence in scholarship, housing and research, described significantly by Professor Edward Shils as "governmentalisation,"[53] would be lessened. Sixth, it would be demonstrated that what Keynes called "decentralised initiative" was capable of organising welfare more effectively than government; and that the case for state welfare, that "private enterprise" has failed, is unfounded.

(xiv) Administrative convenience and ultimate objectives

There are obvious administrative objections to these proposals: the duplication of equipment and buildings; the switch of control away from established, convenient, conventional methods; the disturbance to accepted thinking on the development of education and medical care. They will take time to resolve; but they are secondary relative to the principles of efficiency, specialisation, decentralisation in decision and forecasting, competitive emulation, academic freedom and, not least, the maintenance of initiative independent of the state. What is surprising is that the academic supporters of state welfare overlook its political dangers because they persist in their belief, which history denies, that public officials are *ipso facto* public benefactors, that power will not corrupt nor absolute power corrupt absolutely.[54]

53. *Minerva*, Vol. 1, No. 1, Autumn 1962. Professor H. S. Ferns also lists independence from political influence as one of the several advantages of state aid directed to students who pay near-market university fees rather than to institutions of higher education to charge less than market fees. ("A Radical Proposal for the Universities," *Political Quarterly*, July–September 1967.) Professor Max Beloff has demonstrated the unreality of independence in universities increasingly financed by the state. ("British Universities and the Public Purse," *Minerva*, Summer 1967.)

54. "People who are horrified or amused by the notion of Stalin and his Party colleagues that they could tell Shostakovich what he should compose, are often inadequately aware that the British Ministry of Education and Science is no better qualified to say how a university should be run" (Professor Ferns, "A Radical Proposal for the Universities," p. 280).

SECTION 9

Social Policy in the 1970s

In studying trends in social policy in the long run it is necessary to consider the economic and social movements that underlie the influences that determine policy in the short or middle run. Policy-makers are affected by immediate possibilities and pressures. The easiest road is the one that solves the problems that lie immediately ahead and placates the interests that are most pressing or vocal.

The two underlying long-term economic conditions are the growth in income and the social consequences of the rise in aspirations. The rise in income will make technically possible an expanding state sector in welfare if it yields more tax revenue. But it will also produce a demand for more responsive, varied and flexible services than the state will be able to provide.

Rising income will make increased state welfare financially *possible:* this is the limit of thinking of the advocates of state welfare. The rest is largely wishful thinking. Their difficulty is that rising incomes also make increased state welfare *unnecessary.* And their cross is that the owners of rising incomes will make increased state welfare *undesirable.*

State welfare in the form of services in kind has been in many respects a tragic error. In 1970 it will be 100 years since Forster's Act of 1870, which may be held to mark the beginning of state education. Independent secular or religious schools would in time have made it superfluous.[1] In 1911 the state introduced compulsory state health insurance. Private insurance would have spread faster without it. Since 1915 rent control has produced council housing to supply the homes that would otherwise have been built by private

1. It is a permissible deduction from the new view of the origins of private and state education proffered by Dr. E. G. West in *Education and the State,* IEA, 1965, that the market would have supplied education no less competently than it now supplies entertainment. The Highland Folk Museum in Kingussie displays a document revealing that the Society for the Propagation of Christian Knowledge ran 134 schools founded between 1710 and 1742 for 5,187 boys

builders. In 1925 the state began compulsory social insurance for retirement income. Occupational schemes and personal pensions policies underwritten by insurance would have provided larger and more flexible pensions.

The error in education, medical care and housing was to provide services in kind instead of purchasing power and perhaps standards, and in pensions and income maintenance in ill-health to have made insurance compulsory through the state instead of financially easier by supplying purchasing power and perhaps compulsory for a period through voluntary agencies.

State welfare has been tried and found wanting. It has outlived its day. The state has failed to find enough finance to supply welfare that compares in quality, variety and personal service with the welfare services or the non-welfare consumption supplied by competing independent suppliers. Welfare requires more resources of manpower, equipment, buildings, land. All these are available in the economy, or in the world outside. They can be bought by purchasing power. And of that also there is ample in the economy. But it will not be provided by taxation. In the coming decades only services that recognise consumer sovereignty will command growing resources and purchasing power.

The solution is to replace state services in kind by social benefits in cash, or coupon, for all except the small minority of people physically or otherwise incapable of learning choice. The main obstacle, which this survey suggests the citizen is ready to abandon, is a philosophy that lingers long after economic and social advance have made it a drag on social reform.

---

and 2,618 girls and varying in size from 16 to 252 pupils. In 1837, Charlotte Brontë wrote to her aunt that "they say schools in England are so numerous, competition so great, that without some such step [going to Europe to learn French] towards attaining superiority, we shall probably have a very hard struggle, and may fail in the end" (*The Bronte Letters*, ed. Muriel Spark, Macmillan, 2nd Edition 1966, p. 93).

SELECT BIBLIOGRAPHY

Abel-Smith, Brian, Titmuss, R. M., Townsend, P., and Crossman, R. H. S., *Socialism and Affluence,* Fabian Society, 1967.

Buchanan, J. M., *Public Finance in Democratic Process,* University of North Carolina Press, 1967.

———, "What Kind of Redistribution?" *Economica,* 1967.

Clark, Colin, "Taxation for Expansion" in *Rebirth of Britain,* Pan Books, 1964.

Foldes, L., "Income Redistribution in Money and Kind," and "A Note on Redistribution," *Economica,* 1967.

Harris, Ralph, and Seldon, Arthur, *Choice in Welfare,* IEA, 1963 and 1965.

Houghton, Douglas, *Paying for the Social Services,* Occasional Paper 16, IEA, 1967.

Lees, D. S., "Poor Families and Fiscal Reform," *Lloyds Bank Review,* October 1967.

Musgrave, R. A., and Peacock, A. T. (eds.), *Classics in the Theory of Public Finance,* Macmillan, 4th Edition, 1967.

Peacock, A. T., and Wiseman, J., *The Growth of Public Expenditure in the United Kingdom,* Princeton University Press, 1961.

Pennance, F. G., and Gray, Hamish, *Choice in Housing,* IEA, to be published in 1968.

Runciman, W. G., *Relative Deprivation and Social Justice,* Routledge & Kegan Paul, 1966.

Seldon, Arthur, and Gray, Hamish, *Universal or Selective Social Benefits?,* Research Monograph 8, IEA, 1967.

Titmuss, R. M., *Income Distribution and Social Change,* Allen and Unwin, 1965.

Ware, Martin (ed.), *Is There an Alternative?,* articles reprinted from the *British Medical Journal,* British Medical Association, 1967.

REMOVE THE FINANCING FLAW IN "PUBLIC" SERVICES

Remove the Financing Flaw in "Public" Services

> . . . in the Western world . . . differences about economic policy . . . derive predominantly from differences about the economic consequences of action . . . that in principle can be eliminated by positive economics . . . rather than from fundamental differences in basic values . . .
>
> *The Methodology of Positive Economics* (1952)

If Professor Milton Friedman's classical liberal dictum can be extended to the view that reason and logic will remove differences in economic judgement among men/women of varying basic values, the proposition in positive economics that follows should commend itself to economists and citizens who believe their sympathies to be Tory, Whig, Liberal, Social Democrat, Socialist or even Marxist (*sic:* market-Marxist economists with the ear of their governments in East Europe seem to pay more attention to underlying economics than do some economic advisers of Western governments).

(*a*) Inflation will be difficult to master until government expenditure is disciplined;

(*b*) government expenditure is difficult to discipline because it is increasingly directed not to "public goods" necessarily or preferably financed by taxes but to personal benefits for individuals whose demand would swell without price;

(*c*) therefore, administrative devices in Westminster and Whitehall are not enough and, whatever else is done in 1976, government expenditure must be controlled by pricing identifiable private benefits.

"Public services" and public goods

To begin with a piece of misleading advertising that should carry penalties under a Political Descriptions Act: economic discussion and policy are bemused by the confusion between "public services" and "public goods." This is not the distinction between intangible services (like singing) and tangible goods (like chocolate) but a fundamental distinction between the vast assortment of government goods and services that has waxed and multiplied since the Industrial Revolution, all described seductively as "public services" in common parlance and party political manifestos, and the goods and services that economists delineate very precisely as "public goods."

"Public services" on the hustings are simply goods and services that, for all sorts of reasons—laudable, reprehensible, cynical, or mistily historical—have come to be supplied by government: from defence and street lighting to lavatories and orange juice. The word "public" is question-begging, as it is in "public expenditure," "public monies," "public works" or "public interest." To adapt Abraham Lincoln's tripod of democratic government, "public" services are not *of* (i.e. decided by) the people, *by* the people (who "run" them only very indirectly through "representatives"), or *for* the people (who have no clear way of saying whether they want them or not).

Nevertheless (or therefore) "public" is used gratefully by politicians because it strongly suggests all three. It conveys a flavour of democratic decision, popular control and wholesale beneficence. It is true that some "public services" have to be supplied by government because individuals, or private voluntary groups, could not supply them for themselves—national defence, preventive medicine like treatment of water, street lighting. And others may be supplied more conveniently or cheaply by government, possibly some forms of transport or fuel. But many "public services" as used in everyday language are not "public goods" as defined by economists.

Public goods and private benefits

"Public goods" in economic analysis are very different. They have an essential characteristic that distinguishes them from all others: their conditions of supply are such that their consumers are not "rivals": thus the "consumption" of national defence or street lighting by one individual does not reduce consumption by others. So individuals cannot be excluded from benefiting and cannot be charged individually for their "free ride."[1] For a country to organise its defences, or for a locality to illuminate its streets, the

1. Strictly, even where exclusion is technically possible but not economic because the cost exceeds the revenue, the good is "public."

inhabitants must therefore agree (by majority or other second-best device) to compel themselves to contribute collectively to the cost by taxes paid to a central collecting and controlling agency called "government."

This may be a valid economic justification for socialising goods and services rather than organising them through individual or group demand and supply in the market. But how do "public services" as they have grown in Britain stand up to this rigorous test? How far *must* they be supplied in common and financed by taxes? Are their benefits inseparable among individuals? Or are their consumers rival and excludable? How far therefore *could* they be financed by charging individuals for separable personal benefits?

In Britain so-called "public services" comprise a wide range from (almost) "pure" public goods to predominantly separable individual benefits. The separable private benefits vary from virtually nil in national defence and street lighting (householders who receive more light on their paths and drives from street lamps could, in principle, be charged more in rates or fees than others—or less if they complain of being kept awake by the public "bad" of unavoidable common illumination) to very much, perhaps the whole, in evening classes on arts and crafts. It is fascinating, exciting and encouraging to re-examine the whole structure of British government services and judge the relative proportions of unavoidably common services and separable individual services.

Governmental goods and services in kind in 1974 cost some £25 billion out of £74 billion of Gross National Product at factor cost (excluding taxes but including subsidies), or 35 per cent. The Table (pp. 86–87) shows the services for which the element of payment by price was accessible at the time of writing in the 16 main categories of local services from educational to environmental, with expenditure for the most recent year in column 1 and income from fees and charges in column 2. If the fees and charges reflected the effort of the authorities to charge for personal benefits (which they do not[2]), the element of personal benefit would be as shown in column 3. There is a wide

2. "Public" services have been created and are supplied at nil price or less than cost for "social" or political reasons: poverty, irresponsibility in individuals which was supposed to justify paternalism, equality, and social ("external") benefits, such as the notion that all gain by requiring individuals to read and write. None of these reasons made less than market pricing or government organisation imperative: inability to pay could have been removed by a reverse income tax, and common values encouraged by government standards. Inability to pay may be the *result* of taxation levied for "free" benefits.

Government Expenditure and Private Benefits, England and Wales

	(1) Expenditure 1973–74 (to nearest £m.)	(2) Income from fees and charges 1973–74 † (£m.)	(3) Element of private benefit implied by the proportion of fees and charges to expenditure § (col. 1 ÷ col. 2)	(4) Impression of element of private benefit (%)	(5) Notional gross income from pricing based on private benefit ‡ (col. 4) (£m.)
1. Education					
Nursery	10	*	—	80–100	9
Primary	839	9	1	80–100	755
Secondary	1,073	34	3	80–100	966
Special	131	15	11	?	?
Further—Polytechnics, etc.	127	10	8	80–100	114
Colleges of Art	17	1	7	80–100	15
Agricultural	10	2	16	100	10
Other Major	294	28	9	80–100	264
Evening Institutes	22	4	19	100	22
Teacher Training	127	3	2	80–100	114
School Health	46	*	1	40–60	23
Youth Service: Recreation and Physical Training	29	*	2	60–80	20
Adult Recreation, etc.	13	*	6	100	13
School Meals, Milk, etc.	294	5	2	60–80	206
2. Libraries	95	5	6	80–100	85
3. Museums, Art Galleries	11	*	3	80–100	10
4. Health					
Health Centres	9	*	8	50–70	5
Midwifery	18	*	1	40–60	9
Home Nursing	35	*	0	40–60	17
Vaccination, Immunisation	4	*	0	20–40	1
Ambulance	62	1	2	40–60	31
Family Planning	6	*	2	60–80	4

5. Personal Social					
Children's Residential Homes	83	13	16	10–30	17
Homes for Elderly	139	47	33	40–60	70
Home Helps	55	3	5	40–60	28
Meals in the Home	6	*	14	40–60	3
6. Police	535	12	2	30–50	214
7. Fire	123	2	2	30–50	49
8. Justice	56	1	2	30–50	22
9. Sewerage	242	13	6	60–80	169
10. Refuse	167	7	4	100	167
11. Baths (Swimming and Washing) and Laundries	49	11	22	80–100	44
12. Land Drainage, Smallholdings, Pest Control, etc.	46	3	8	20–40	14
13. Roads, Lighting, Parking, etc.	33	19	60	100	33
14. Youth Employment	10	*	0	40–60	5
15. Sheltered Employment and Workshops	8	*	7	?	?
16. Environment					
Parks and Open Spaces	134	10	8	20–40	40
Prevention of Air Pollution	6	*	0	10–30	1
Public Conveniences	20	*	2	100	20
Town and Country Planning	116	5	4	70–90	93
River Pollution Prevention	4	*	0	10–30	1
Allotments	2	*	23	100	2
Private Street and Other Works	20	10	51	100	20
Registration of Births, etc.	6	2	36	70–90	5

Source: Local Government Financial Statistics, England and Wales, 1973–74, Department of the Environment, HMSO, December 1975.

* Less than £1 million (col. 2).

† Including payments between local authorities.

§ Percentages rounded after calculations based on columns (1) and (2) to first decimal place.

‡ Column (5) shows the notional gross revenue derived by multiplying expenditures in column (1) by the proportions in column (4) (or by the middle point in ranges). In practice the net revenue would be reduced by a) the reverse income tax, b) the nominal value of vouchers for education, health or other services, c) the reduced demand (except in compulsory services like education).

spread from nil to some 60 per cent (for car-parking) and 50 (for private street or other local authority "works"), but a clustering around 5 to 10 per cent and with several in the 20's and 30's.

This spread may make social or political sense, but it makes no economic sense. Since social and political objectives require the optimum use of resources, which economists and citizens of all schools of philosophy must see in logic, the method of payment should vary according to how far "public services" are public goods or separable personal benefits. The distinction is not rigid in practice. In a sense no activity is purely individual, and everyone is affected by (almost) everything everyone else does: everything has "external" effects on others, welcome or unwelcome. But public policy does not rest on perfectionist demarcations, and common sense as well as economic reasoning indicate the distinction clearly enough for policy.

To provoke thought on a neglected subject, an effort to suggest the element of private benefit is made in column 4. This is a first subjective impression and no doubt many readers will differ. The important purpose is to begin the task of thinking afresh on a long-evaded but central aspect of economic policy.

How much for private benefits?

The proportions may seem high but it should be emphasised that they are *not based on ability to pay* (or paternalism, or other "social" reasons) but *solely on the element of private benefit.* They also reflect the view that social benefits are, in practice, often less important than they appear in the conventional textbooks: they are less extensive, more difficult to identify, more costly to measure, are often taken into account in private reckoning as risks and uncertainties weighed up and allowed for,[3] and are arguably removable by revising property rights.[4]

The sense of shock will be diminished if three parts of the argument are borne in mind. First, inability to pay is not a reason for supplying govern-

3. Some of the external effects for which the conventional textbooks propose compensation by tax or subsidy are more properly dealt with in the economic theory of risk and uncertainty which individuals have in mind and discount in their dealings with others. A man who buys a house with good neighbours, amenities and views knows he may lose them: he has, in the jargon, "internalised" the externalities.

4. Economists still do not sufficiently allow for the work of Professor R. H. Coase. In a forthcoming Hobart Paper, Professor Steven Cheung argues that very little is left of the economic theory of social costs or externalities.

ment services at a nil or low price, and is therefore not an obstacle to charging, because it could be removed by topping up low incomes. Second, the proposal is that a beginning be made with new or higher charges in 1976, or with closing the wide gap between 1973–74 proportions and a realistic assessment of private benefit, perhaps by a three- to seven-year scale of annual increases. Third, a structure of charging private market prices would make possible tax reductions to leave the purchasing power in private pockets or vouchers with which to pay the charges.

The scope for charging

The scope for charging differs.[5] If it is argued that education yields external benefits for the community at large, it nevertheless has substantial private benefits. A five-year period of phasing school charges would be facilitated by reductions in general taxes, by education tax allowances as in Australia, or perhaps most effectively by an earmarked voucher. The only education item with large social benefit is school health services.

The services of public lending libraries are very largely if not wholly private. If the literati understood pricing they would see it as a more satisfactory method of recompensing them than public lending rights.

Charging for museums and art galleries is common in Europe. No economist can applaud the Conservatives' tepid approach to it, and even less the Labour Party's abandonment of it. What was at fault was not the principle of charging but the small charge and the argument it gave the vested interests that the administrative costs made charging uneconomic.

Health services seem to have a large element of common benefits, but all give individuals personal benefits. A charge for ambulances may seem hard-faced, but not where they are used when individuals can arrange private transport[6] and pay for it by insurance. What is more "private" than family planning? It has an external benefit since very large families might burden others. But on that score everything is public and nothing is private.

The National Health Service itself (not in the Table) provides further scope for charging. The proportion of the NHS financed by charges has

5. Oral evidence on the general principles of, and the scope for, charging was presented, with Ralph Harris, to the Layfield Committee on Local Government Finance at its request and is being published as an Appendix to its Report.

6. "As an active member of a busy casualty unit, especially late at night, I would . . . charge £5 for any non-essential ambulance calls."—Letter to a national newspaper, 1 November, 1975.

fallen somewhat from 5 to 4 per cent in the last year or two. Economists of all hues must recognise the veritable economic hodge-podge that comprises the NHS: from preventive measures that are almost pure public goods to eminently personal aspects of bed and board, choice of surgeon, convenience of location, timing of surgery, etc. Ten years ago Lord (then Douglas) Houghton thought hospital charges of £5 or £10 per week should be considered. Health insurance vouchers that could be topped up are an alternative.

The official description "personal social services" reveals the confusion. Home helps and home meals are largely personal benefits, as are some of the others. (Charging, to repeat, is being judged in terms of common and personal benefits, not of capacity to pay.)

The element of personal benefits in police services is certainly larger than is commonly supposed. Convoying heavy loads, attendance at private sports and other events, advice on theft precautions are clearly personal services for which charges would be appropriate. Some personal fire services could also be priced.

Justice may seem a common good but in practice is often a personal service for which individuals could therefore pay. The legal aid scheme is designed to deal with inability to pay: it could be otiose with a reverse income tax.

In sewerage it may be easier to make a case for charging since the Courts have ruled that households not on main drainage should not be required to pay for it.

Charging seems to be easiest in refuse collection. It would encourage householders to burn combustibles, sort out paper or other re-cyclicable materials, and pay only for the rest to be removed. Charging would thus *reduce* the resources used in government services. And if garden fires intensified the external nuisance of smoke, no doubt a non-smoking incinerator would soon be invented.

Baths, for washing or swimming, and laundries offer a clear and large element of personal services. In sports amenities, low charges represent redistribution of income from wage-earners who use them less to the middle-incomes that use them more.

Drainage and flood prevention are more beneficial to some than to others. And if this argument seems to be directed at large land-owners and large farmers, it applies equally to smallholders.

Car parking is one of the few government services where current charges seem to represent anywhere near the personal benefit. Even so, parkers paid only 60 per cent of expenditure in 1973–4 for what is a wholly personal benefit. (Postscript, pp. 92–93.)

A charge for youth employment services seems a burden on youth or the low incomes they earn, but 40–60 per cent may seem not unrealistic as a measure of personal benefits.

Finally, the environmental services seem most difficult of all, since they would seem to be a clear case of common benefits. But exclusion is clearly feasible in some. Parks and some open spaces can have gates. Charges for pollution have been argued cogently; pollution prevention may benefit some more than others. Public conveniences are private conveniences! (and the 5p makes the British Rail convenience at Victoria a pleasant contrast to the noisome lavatory at Charing Cross). Town and Country planning permissions could be auctioned, as the late Professor Frederick G. Pennance urged. Allotments seem a wholly personal benefit. So, clearly, are the officially self-confessed "*private*" street and other works (for which beneficiaries paid in 1973–4 only *half* at the expense of their fellow rate- or tax-payers). And even registration of births, etc., is a private benefit for which people might pay more.

Charges would reduce government expenditure in three ways. They would yield income inaccessible to government through taxation or rates (or national insurance). They would reduce costs by increasing the efficiency of the resources used in government services. And they would reduce the outlay on services for which the demand was reduced.

Three half-truths

Charges would deal with three half-truths, or half-myths, in recent commentary on government expenditure. One is "Spending is out of control" (*The Times,* 19 December, 1975). This is true to the extent that the government services yield private benefits that are supplied below the market price so that demand is inflated. Charging would remove the inflation.

Secondly, it has been argued "For the social services the next few years will be a difficult period" (Mr. Harold Wilson, 10 December, 1975). This will be true only if the Government persists in financing private benefits by taxes. There is no shortage of money in Britain for welfare—as would be evident if people could pay in the ways they preferred. Large sums might be transferred from consumption to welfare.

And, thirdly, the question-begging challenge "What would *you* cut?"

(*Hansard,* every other day), which politicians in government direct at politicians in opposition, would be seen as the half-truth it is. Governments that want to reduce government expenditure have to "cut" it only on common services that cannot be priced. The large and increasing elements of private benefits can be left to be "cut" by their consumers, who would know better where *they* prefer to "cut," since charges would tell them the extent of the other purchases they would have to sacrifice. There would, to this extent, be no need for political bargaining in emergency Cabinet meetings with tension between the Treasury and spending Departments or the threats of resignation from Ministers "defending" sacrosanct "public" services.

The control of government expenditure has been defective on two counts, and the February White Paper will show that the Bourbons in Westminster and Whitehall have learned nothing, or not much. It is still macro-economic, and it is still paternalistic. The treatment required is micro-economic charging so that *individuals* will do the "cutting" that governments have shirked. It is a long-range treatment that deals with fundamentals; all the more reason to make a beginning in 1976.

Postscript: In Place of Price

The latest official document on the financing of government services, Department of the Environment Circular 129/75, HMSO, January 1976, offers "advice" and "guidance" to local authorities on restraining expenditure to help the Government fight inflation. In places it reads more like exhortation and admonition. The advice seems naive (if not impertinent) unless it is supposed that local government is incompetent, extravagant or callous.

The only general advice on pricing is in the environmental services, where local authorities are told not to permit "those services which ought to be self-financing to run at a loss" (they are not named), and in transport, where the advice is to raise parking charges to meet a larger proportion of costs. Otherwise, apart from higher bus fares and rents, there is silence on the scope for new or higher charges.

The result is that much of the reasoning—that unavoidable new commitments for demographic or other reasons must be off-set by economies through increased efficiency or reductions in services—embodies *non sequiturs.* Charges, the alternative that could maintain services, and/or avoid higher rates and/or taxes, are ignored. It is not true that the public must choose between poorer services and higher taxes.

Economists should remind politicians and the public of the three functions of price: a method of rationing scarce resources, a method of determining income, and a source of information available in no other way. Perhaps the lack of understanding reflects the dominance of neo-Keynesian macro-economic thinking.

It must remain puzzling that charges continue to be largely ignored in political, public and even academic discussion, where economists often seem to forget that demand is a function of price.

The restraint of government expenditure will be needlessly difficult without charging, which would: (1) raise revenue not available through taxes or rates (nor national insurance); (2) prevent a run-down of "public" services; (3) release revenue to improve the pure or near-pure public goods (security, law and order, environmental, public health, etc.).

CHARGE

For every man,
and perhaps even more for every woman,
unrepresented by political "representatives,"
to help them see
how they can run their lives,
themselves,
at last.

ACKNOWLEDGEMENTS

I am grateful to Charles Rowley, Professor of Economics at the University of Newcastle, for scrutinising the theoretical passages on the nature of public goods; to Ralph Harris, General Director of the Institute of Economic Affairs, for detailed comments and, more generally, for twenty years of stimulating partnership that has refined my thinking; to Stephen Haseler, of the City of London Polytechnic and the GLC, for criticisms on an early draft; to John Mills, Deputy Leader of Camden Council, for reading several chapters and pulling no Fabian punches; to Sudha Shenoy, a young leader in Britain of the revived Austrian School of Economics, for Whiggish suggestions on sharpening the argument; and to scores of IEA authors from whom I have learned much down the years. None would accept all I say; some would differ mildly, several sharply.

I am also indebted to Marjorie Seldon for judgement on how people might react to several proposals and for specific suggestions; and to Maurice Temple Smith for general advice, astringent opinion and discerning editing.

Not least, I should like to thank Michael Solly for acting as literary longstop; Ken Smith for prompt discovery of elusive references; and Joan Roffey for good humour in transcribing tired longhand into pleasing typescript.

I have written this book as a personal venture. My views are not necessarily shared by anyone associated with the IEA.

“Take what you want,” said God,
“and pay for it.”

PART 1

Populism and Prices

CHAPTER 1

Pundits, Politicians and People

Our world has largely been shaped by the thinking of scholars, academics, experts, specialists, writers, teachers—the "pundits." For years, decades, centuries, they have debated among themselves and influenced the actions and policies of leaders and statesmen.

This direct influence of paternalist ideas on action was inevitable and possibly desirable up to about a century ago when ordinary people lacked the knowledge or the resources to participate in the formation of policy. But the pundits have continued to talk to one another, mostly far over the heads of the people, for a century in which there has been increasing education and enlightenment, understanding and responsibility. Under their advice the politicians have created institutions and services—from schools, transport and hospitals to libraries, nurseries and abattoirs—for the good (they said) of the people. They have also created electoral machinery—"representative democracy"—to enable the people to show their approval or disapproval.

But something has gone wrong. The machinery—Parliament, the ballot box, representative democracy—has never worked effectively. The machinery of representation does not represent individual members of the public but the organised groups that claim to speak for them. As a result the institutions have increasingly diverged from the wishes or preferences of the people as individuals. Some of them—such as law and defence—were necessary and desirable when they were created down the centuries, and in principle remain so. Others—many or most of the nationalised industries, welfare services and local government amenities—should never have been created, but are still seen as necessary, or as sanctified by time, long after the conditions that once seemed to justify them have passed into history.

The central position from which this book starts is this: how can we decide what services the government ought to provide, and how can we make them fit more closely the needs and wishes of the ordinary people for whom they are supposed to be provided?

At present, the only or main control on government services is political, through the institutions of representative democracy. This device is necessary (though faulty) for the institutions and services that *only* government can provide: but it is far too crude for all the personal services, from medical care and housing to car-parking, that could be provided in response to individual preferences. It is crude because the ballot box does not record and is not geared for supplying individual requirements. Despite that decisive disqualification, government is still unnecessarily used for a vast range of institutions supplying personal services that individuals could provide themselves.

Resistance to reform

What services should government provide? How should we pay for them? How much of what government now provides could and should be provided outside government?

The only way to discover the answers to these questions is to establish machinery to record individual preferences and test new mechanisms outside government. We could then see which services do not have to be provided by government. But the pundits still largely advise, and the politicians still endlessly create, government institutions "for the good of the people." Their reputable reasons are that they continue to think that *all* the institutions they happen to have created in the last century are in principle still for the good of the people, or that they see no other way of adapting them to individual preferences except by variations within the existing arrangements (because "we must start from here"). The less reputable—though understandable—reason is self-interested resistance to change by government employees whose jobs would be at risk. Too much time is therefore spent patching up government services (for which the public is forced to pay) instead of questioning their justification or very existence, and far too little on making room for new services for which the public would pay voluntarily. The cosy corner of politicians, bureaucrats and pundits resists change.

Even so, new ideas are coming to the fore as old ones are refined or discarded, and it is possible to see some politicians adopting new thinking as the changing abilities and attitudes of individual citizens make new institutions more timely or urgent—and therefore electorally more rewarding. But the resistance to reform from intellectual conviction and self-interest slows down adaptation to new conditions. It may be that the general public will have to participate more directly in the debate without the mediation (or barrier) of "representatives." To do so, it will need to understand what is at stake and indicate its readiness for change, or, better still, its anxiety for early reform. It does not have to burden itself with detail; but it must know the general principles.

The people must lead their leaders

This book is an effort to clarify for the general reader the debate between the pundits. It rests on a core of economic thinking that economists have been evolving and developing for two centuries—the notion of "public goods." They are still refining the idea and they draw different conclusions for policy from it. My interpretation of it is that the central truth is simple enough and its implication for policy clear enough for people in all schools of democratic political sympathy to accept and apply in practice. Moreover, I believe it resolves a difference of outlook that has deeply but unnecessarily divided the British people.

Public support for reform may have to assert itself all the more strongly in a representative democracy, where government yields to pressure from organised interests that stand to lose from change. Not only is there no machinery in representative democracy for asserting individual preferences over much of the services of contemporary government; the sizeable number of government employees who provide them invariably prevail over the much larger number who use and pay for them. It may be that the providers of government services are too powerful to be made subject to the sovereignty of the mass of consumers. In that event the outcome will be either a period of possibly benign paternalism or acquiescent conformity (such as in Sweden, at least until 1976) or a refusal to accept bureaucratic encroachment on personal and family lives. The resistance to taxation by avoidance (legal), evasion (illegal), power bloc organisation (the self-employed) and emigration does not indicate that the process of encroachment can continue much longer without provoking the very tension and social divisiveness that government services are supposed to prevent.

It may be that some of our leaders think further (or even existing) encroachment is generally desired. I do not recognise this as the preference of ordinary people. That is why I address this book to them. They could have much more say, informed by more knowledge of the world created for them. Politicians and pundits are welcome as eavesdroppers; some of them may see that there is a good case for creating effective machinery to record private preferences where "representative" democracy is ineffective. In that sense the argument is not about philosophical value-judgements of ultimate right and wrong, but about the task of devising tools for the people to use themselves. This task has been largely neglected by all three British political parties for a century.

The unnecessary divide

This book questions conventional beliefs over a wide range of human activity, public and private. Some readers will find it startling, others common sense. But as it follows questioning and criticism with constructive proposals for reform, readers who persevere with the argument to the end will judge it better.

The central argument is derived from the main principles of economics, which are not difficult to grasp and which, once understood, make simple and clear what once seemed complex and difficult. Many of the basic truths of economics are refined common sense, though some may strike newcomers as surprising.

The book is written for three classes of readers. First, I intend it for everyone, in every walk of life, interested in himself, his causes and his country. It has a bearing on the way we run the family and the household as well as industry and government. Its second market is the general reader who wonders what economists are saying that can shed light on the issues of the day. The third market is the newcomer to economics at school or university who wants an unconventional entrée into the heart of economic thinking to accompany formal text-books.

In the first market I shall be writing perhaps even more for women than for men. They are rather more numerous; but also they may respond more sensitively to the central theme than men. They are often less sentimental and more experienced in ensuring daily "micro-economic" value for their money in shopping for themselves and for their families. They may see the good sense of what I shall be saying sooner than more politically-minded men whose seduction by (wrong) ideas and ideals in "macro-economic" national affairs has, I would say, made possible the massive errors in public policy (and social policy in particular) of the last century, especially in the thirty years since World War II. It is man in the mass who can be most easily misled into applauding policies he would ridicule at home with his wife and family: and that is as true of xenophobic Conservatives as of class-obsessed trade unionists. Macro-man at mass factory meetings, mass marches or mass General Elections is seldom a good advertisement for humanity. Macro-woman has her moments. Both are better in micro-quantities.

Readers who want to know what economists are saying and debating will find the central issues discussed without jargon, or at least with the few necessary technical words explained in plain English. The man and woman who finishes this book will, I think, make more sense of—and take with a larger pinch of salt—"what the papers say" as well as "what the politicians preach." It will help them understand the great debates of our day—how much income should be left to individuals to spend as they wish and how much should be taken by the state and spent for them; how much production must be left to or controlled by the state; how people can best pay for it; how much influence they can exert over it; how much choice families and households can exercise over their lives; how far our lives must be run by officials and politicians; and ultimately what bearing all this has on the choices between capitalism and communism or between social democracy and liberalism.

Students of economics will find the central principles applied to the real world in which they live and in which the issues and policies of the day will continue to be debated.

The reader does not require formal training to understand the essence of economics. Many non-economists grasp it intuitively better than some graduates in economics.

But you must be ready for some very unconventional and unfashionable thinking, and even more for unorthodox and provocative conclusions for public policy. This thinking will be quite different from what you have come to expect in the last ten years from every political party, from Conservative to Communist, and from every newspaper, from *The Times* to the *Morning Star.* But it is thinking that will have to be recognised and absorbed in the next twenty or thirty years if the liberal character and temper of British society is to be preserved. In this time the parties may have regrouped themselves and the newspapers may be replaced by other kinds of publication that belatedly reflect the thinking they have ignored for decades.

The conclusions for policy will apply to the whole range of human action, from the privacy of the family to the more public activity of government. I shall argue that almost every institution is run less effectively than it could be, with adverse effects on living standards and personal freedom, because it ignores a device that has been condemned in error by almost every school of thought for a century. Often the motives have been of the best; though they have also disguised other objectives far less worthy. At their best the inspiration has been the paternalist notion that people in authority, with a wider and longer view than the individual, could make better use of resources. At their worst, and more often, the impetus has been the authoritarian urge to win and exercise power in public life over other people who are thought incapable of choosing for themselves—or even of *learning* to choose, which is to take an even more scornful view of them. This paternalism suffuses British society. Pundits in politics, academia, the press and the pulpit *know* how the citizen should live, and they fight among themselves for the power to compel him, directly in politics or indirectly through influence on politicians.

These people have used plausible excuses for giving government more and more power to run society and provide people with their requirements. Their arguments have been mainly five. *Poverty:* some people, they said, could not provide essentials for themselves and their families out of their own means ("primary poverty"). *Irresponsibility:* the associated argument was that some people with enough means would be too foolish, short-sighted or callous to provide essentials for themselves or their families ("secondary poverty"). *Economy:* it was more efficient for government to provide basic essentials on a large scale for many people and without duplication. *Social (or "external") benefits:* individuals or families would not engage at all, or sufficiently, in activities that benefited third parties, so government had to tax the people to provide the services, or provide them on a larger scale than individuals left to themselves. *Monopoly:* some essentials were most economically produced on such a large scale that only a small number of producers (perhaps only one) was likely, and that would give them power to exploit their fellows. These arguments, or pretexts, are examined later, together with a more recent sixth applying to the so-called basic national services: that government control and financing were desirable or necessary for management of the economy.

Public and private goods

All schools of thought have long agreed that some goods and services have to be provided by government. But in Britain and other Western countries government does far more. In Britain, it directly *produces* with its own employees about a third of the entire national output of goods and services. It *controls* or *influences* far more. It takes a further fifth of national income from individuals and firms and is supposed to redistribute it in cash, although, as we shall see, in large part it goes back to the same individuals. And it regulates and restricts much of the two-thirds of production run by private

Table A. Government by the People? Or by unrepresentative minorities since the Second World War

			Conservative*			Labour			Liberal		
General Election	Electorate (million)	Votes Cast (million)	Votes Won (million)	% of Votes Cast	% of Electorate	Votes Won (million)	% of Votes Cast	% of Electorate	Votes Won (million)	% of Votes Cast	% of Electorate
1945	32.84	24.98	9.96	39.87	30.33	11.99	48.00	36.50	2.25	9.00	6.85
1950	34.27	28.77	12.50	43.45	36.48	13.30	46.23	38.81	2.62	9.11	7.65
1951	34.63	28.60	13.72	47.97	39.61	13.95	48.78	40.28	0.73	2.55	2.11
1955	34.86	26.76	13.31	49.74	38.18	12.41	46.38	35.60	0.72	2.69	2.07
1959	35.40	27.86	13.75	49.35	38.84	12.22	43.86	34.52	1.64	5.88	4.64
1964	35.90	27.66	11.98	43.31	33.37	12.21	44.14	34.01	3.10	11.21	8.63
1966	35.96	27.26	11.42	41.89	31.76	13.06	47.91	36.32	2.33	8.55	6.48
1970	39.34	28.34	13.15	46.40	33.43	12.18	42.24	30.96	2.12	7.48	5.39
1974 (Feb)	39.75	31.33	11.96	38.17	30.09	11.65	37.18	29.31	6.06	19.34	15.26
1974 (Oct)	40.08	29.19	10.46	35.83	26.09	11.47	39.29	28.62	5.35	18.33	13.35

*Including Conservative allies

individuals and firms in order to ensure safety and other standards, or for more obscure or questionable reasons.

The third of the output of goods and services produced directly by government (national, regional or local) covers a wide range, from nuclear defence through police to adult evening classes in basket weaving. Some of them are what economists call public goods that must be produced collectively, by government, or not at all. The remainder could be produced by individuals or firms and offered on the market, so that consumers could choose between competing suppliers. The distinction between public and other goods is central to the argument of this book because public goods must be paid for by taxes and other goods can be paid for by charges.

Public goods have characteristics that distinguish them from other goods. They are necessarily provided for large groups of people in their catchment area. They are thus supplied jointly or collectively rather than separately to individuals or small groups. They require general agreement (ideally unanimous, but in the real, imperfect world only majority, or even minority) to pay jointly, that is, they require voluntary collective arrangements to coerce one another and also individuals who do not want the services at all but who cannot help benefiting from them. They are non-rival in the sense that, if they are used by more individuals, they can still be used by others—until a stage of full capacity and over-crowding; in other words, additional consumers can be serviced with no additional cost. Public goods thus render external benefits to third parties in the area who are not parties to the agreement. But the essential characteristic of public goods is that they cannot be refused to people who refuse to pay, and who would otherwise have a "free ride" if they were not required to pay. Public goods, to be produced at all, cannot therefore be produced in response to individual specification in the market: they must be financed collectively by the method known as taxation. Their benefits are provided to all the individuals in the catchment area, but the benefits cannot be paid for separately by individuals because they are inseparable, indivisible and indiscriminate.

All goods have some public qualities (a private house across the road may please you by its architecture or offend you by the colour of its front door). And all public goods yield private benefits (there is no more personal benefit than having your life saved by the armed forces). So there are no "pure" or entirely public or private goods.

Most goods can be made by individuals or firms for other individuals or firms who will pay for them directly (food, clothing, books, homes, motorcars and personal services of all types). But if people who refuse to pay for a commodity or service cannot be excluded, so that they have a "free ride," no private person or company would produce it even though all or most individuals want it produced. This, then, is the characteristic that requires goods to be produced collectively by government for the people as a whole. All other goods are in this sense not "public" and do not have to be produced collectively or paid for by taxes.

The archetypal public good is defence—national against external enemies and local against internal. Law itself is a public good from which all benefit jointly—or a public bad from which all suffer. Protection against contagious disease is another public good. A not obvious but important one is the production of knowledge and information. In these and other goods and services it is impossible to keep out people who will not pay. Anti-aircraft guns defend all people and property in the city against bombing. Police patrols or anti-malarial treatment of water protect everyone in the area.

Then there are goods and services from which people who refused to contribute could be excluded, but only at a cost that would make exclusion not worth the candle. Putting a high fence round a national park and posting ticket collectors on all the roads and paths entering it might cost more than would be raised in entrance fees.

I must add at once that, although government is the only method of producing public goods, it is a very imperfect solution, because it has no mechanism for measuring individual preferences in the kind and scale of public goods that people want. Government can use only the crude instrument of general elections every few years in which people are asked to vote for two or three parties each advocating 34, 57 or 86 varieties of policies. The party elected may—probably does—spend too much or too little on some services it provides, but voters cannot indicate their approval or disapproval of expenditure on, say, defence, overseas aid, commercial attachés, ante-natal clinics or allotments.

Not least, although people must agree collectively to tax themselves to pay for public goods, they will not all put the value on them that is represented by their taxes. A person who opposes fluoridation must nevertheless pay for it in his rates or taxes if a majority agree it should be provided; and it is virtually impossible to go further and compensate people who object to public goods or who suffer from them (like those who are kept awake by street lighting).

Despite these objections, public goods must be produced by government or not at all, because some people will refuse to pay unless they are coerced by representative political democracy. If government confined itself to what are in this sense public goods it would be accepted as necessary. But does it? Are all the "public" services, as they are beguilingly called, really public goods at all?

Keynes and the classics on public goods

The proper province of government has been a central concern of economists for two hundred years or more. Adam Smith, the founder of economics as a science, laid down the general principle that, apart from external defence and internal law and order, the state must also provide services that

> can never be for the interest of any individual, or small number of individuals, to erect and maintain: because the profit can never repay the expense to any individual or small number of individuals though it may frequently do much more than repay it to a great society.[1]

Under this heading the classical economists who followed Adam Smith developed a list of state functions: some kinds of money, tax collection, some education, welfare services, relief of some kinds of poverty, roads, bridges, canals, harbours.

Over twenty years ago[2] Lord Robbins, perhaps the most influential British liberal economist of our day, showed that J. M. Keynes, who was supposed to have destroyed classical economics and who still, thirty years after his death, dominates thinking in government, some British universities and the press, said much the same as Adam Smith. Keynes's formulation in a celebrated tract, *The End of Laissez Faire,* ran

> The most important Agenda of the state relate not to those activities which private individuals are already fulfilling but to those functions which fall outside the sphere of the individual, to those decisions which are made by no one if the state does not make them. The important thing for government is not to do things which individuals are doing already and to do them a little better or a little worse: but to do those things which are not done at all.[3]

1. Smith, A., *The Wealth of Nations* (1776), J. M. Dent.
2. Robbins, Lord, *The Theory of Economic Policy in English Classical Political Economy,* Macmillan, 1952.
3. Keynes, J. M., *The End of Laissez Faire,* The Hogarth Press, 1926; *Collected Writings,* Macmillan, 1972.

Keynes's formulation is quite clear. The state should provide only those functions or services that individuals *could not* provide for themselves, that is public goods that cannot be refused to free riders who refuse to pay. Since Keynes is still usually claimed as a destroyer of classical economic philosophy in his best-known (1936) book, *The General Theory of Employment, Interest and Money*,[4] I should recall that Keynes reprimanded some of his followers as "sour and silly" shortly before he died in 1946,[5] that no one knows what he would be saying in 1977, that some economists argue his post-war followers, or at least some who claim his name as "Keynesians," have misrepresented him, and his writings only a few years after *The General Theory* in 1938–9 suggest his name has been misappropriated. The Keynesians have usually ignored Keynes's declaration that he was not replacing but perfecting the classical system of thought and policy.

In his newest book,[6] the latest in a succession of works that should delight readers with their classical prose as well as their classical liberalism, Lord Robbins added a further guide to the scope for state action. It is "to govern well, govern little," attributed to the eighteenth-century Marquis d'Argenson, a predecessor of early French economists whose crude thinking Adam Smith refined in his classic *The Wealth of Nations*. This warning to governments to keep off the people's grass, said Robbins, would have been respected by the British classical economists for two reasons, both very central to this book. First, the government that developed under two centuries of state control, called the mercantile system, was inefficient and corrupt, as all government sooner or later tends to become. Second, the controls wielded by eighteenth-century government in England were harmful or superfluous; they either made no difference or, if they did, it was for the worse. And although the classical economists made a reasoned and subtle case for the state to provide defence and other services, *the case was not that the state would provide them satisfactorily but that no one else would provide them at all*. The classical formula was thus the same as Keynes's: public goods. In short, the state was tolerated not as a desirable or efficient instrument, which a hundred years of Fabian and conservative paternalism has taught generations of teachers, but as *a necessary evil*. That is, efficient or not, corrupt or not, government *has* to produce public goods that individuals want but could not

4. Keynes, J. M., *The General Theory of Employment, Interest and Money*, Macmillan, 1936.
5. Keynes, J. M., "The Balance of Payments of the United States," *Economic Journal*, 1946.
6. Robbins, Lord, *Political Economy Past and Present*, Macmillan, 1976.

produce individually for one another. The notion of public goods thus provides a necessary but "second-best" justification for the state.

So far so clear. The classics and the moderns agree that some functions should be performed by the state because there is no other way. And we shall see later that state activity also has defects of its own—a concentration of power, high taxation, rationing by bureaucracy to replace the guideline of price—that must be weighed in the balance against the state doing anything unless its advantages over private action clearly and substantially exceed these defects. We shall also see that the advocates of government provision surprisingly overlook these incidental disadvantages of government activity.

Professor F. A. Hayek has lately questioned one of the functions of government that economists have accepted for two hundred years, that of providing money. He argues[7] that government has never provided a reliable, stable money: government-controlled money has stimulated inflation, economic instability (boom and slump), "public" expenditure and economic nationalism. It was least harmful when controlled by the gold standard, but the best solution is to take money out of government hands and have it provided by competing private suppliers whose self-interest it would be to limit the supply in order to maintain the value.

A creaking hinge

The public goods formula for state action is thus a creaking hinge. It seems to be clear, at least as a principle, that, where individuals cannot be made to pay directly for a service they want, they must be compelled to pay by taxation or not have it provided at all. But it does not follow that government in practice will perform its function so as to achieve that purpose satisfactorily because it has severe defects of its own. And since people cannot indicate their opinion by making or withholding individual payment, we cannot even know whether people really want the public goods they are supposed to vote for by electing a party into office, or whether they want them to continue or discontinue once created.

Moreover, most of the "government" sector in present-day Britain consists of goods and services that are not "public goods." They are produced by government, or so it is claimed, for the five main reasons I have described as "plausible," by which I mean superficially persuasive but not really decisive. In

7. Hayek, F. A., *Denationalisation of Money,* IEA, 1976.

other words, *most present-day British "public" services do not have to be produced by government.* They could be produced by individuals, firms, voluntary organisations, cooperatives and other variants of *private* activity, catering directly to individual preferences.

Even those who believe that government should go on supplying these things still face a further and crucial question: is it best to continue financing them by taxes, the *collective* method, or by a method which links *individual* payment to *individual* benefit? This is the ground over which the battle rages. This book offers a solution that could commend itself to people who think themselves wide apart or even in opposite camps.

CHAPTER 2

Price: Barrier or Missing Link?

The great debate that has torn the British in two for a century has been over what is, at bottom, a simple error in reasoning. It lies at the root of unnecessarily big government, unnecessarily high taxation, avoidably large bureaucracies, and of their converse—unnecessarily restricted liberties, narrowed choices, discouragements to work and save.

The most common error lies deep in British social history and political thinking. It is buried in this familiar argument:

1 all people should have the minimum essentials for civilised living;
2 incomes are sometimes too low to pay for them;
3 therefore they should be provided free by the state.

This is the reasoning that has produced the apparently compassionate cry that a civilised society should not allow price to come between people and the essentials of life. Price was a "barrier" to be destroyed. Lord Beveridge, in his famous 1942 report that inspired the post-war Labour-Liberal-Conservative welfare state, condemned it as an "economic" barrier. The late Professor R. M. Titmuss, who influenced governmental and academic thinking on welfare policy in the 1950s and 1960s, inveighed against it as a "price" barrier. A Minister of Health in the late 1960s, Mr. Kenneth Robinson, later Chairman of the London Transport Executive, denounced it as a "financial" barrier.

It is a misunderstanding of the function of price to think of it as a barrier between a would-be buyer and a service. Price is a neutral symptom of the deep-lying conditions in which we live: an imperfect world in which we have insufficient resources for everything we should like to do. We must therefore allocate those resources among numerous alternative uses. In this task we require a sign, or measure, or signal that tells us where resources are best used. We can then shift them from where they are used less well to where they are used better. Despite all the heat worked up about it as a "barrier," price is *a tool that mankind cannot do without.* Before we go any further we must understand it and its qualities.

Price is neutral

Price is the sign, or measure, or signal that emerges spontaneously if people who want services talk terms to people who can supply them. Both groups can benefit by exchanging goods or services in a "market" where people who want them are in contact with people who can supply them. In modern communities we exchange services for money, but money is only a convenient intermediary which simplifies agreement on prices. Ultimately we all exchange services: we give our services as butchers, bakers, builders, miners, railwaymen, engineers, teachers or doctors to others who give us their services as grocers, tailors, actors, writers, publishers, hoteliers or pilots. And price describes the terms on which we exchange, swap, trade, buy, sell and borrow—or, in short, serve one another. It is unique information created only by people coming together to exchange in the light of their unique knowledge of their affairs. The structure of prices is called the price "system" and the whole social structure is called a market economy.

Price is useful

Price is not merely the fulcrum around which the market system turns. It is also the method of indicating the relative importance or "value" of resources in alternative uses and the method of allocating resources to the best uses. People will pay more for something they value more than something else. This is not a perfect measure of the value of putting resources to different uses, but other methods are even more imperfect. In the popular catch-phrase, the price system is the worst in the world except all the others.

Price is pacific

In allocating labour, equipment, buildings, land and so on to the best uses, pricing automatically excludes other uses. Where this excluding function is not performed by market prices, and people differ about how to decide which uses are the best and which shall be excluded, they argue and debate and, in political democracies, organise political parties to gain power and compel minorities (or even majorities) to accept their way of deciding.

They also, in Fascist and Communist societies, fight and kill one another. Pricing is a peaceful way of resolving argument and conflict.

This is true of families as well as nations. In the family, friction between a high-taxed father and growing children over the unrestrained use of the "free" telephone, hot water, light, heat or petrol is removed if they pay for it (out of earnings or even pocket money), because every single act of paying reminds them of the sacrifices they are making and induces them to think twice. Without pricing, the hard-pressed father has to go on reminding his forgetful offspring, and becomes stricter and less popular if they persistently ignore his reminders. With pricing the reminders appear spontaneously, without the personal appearance of an admonishing father. Pricing obviates instructions, commands, compulsion, sanctions, friction, disaffection, estrangement. Father does not have to demand "cuts" in the use of services; the offspring make the "cuts" in the light of knowledge of the cost to them of over-use.

Replace "father" by "government" and "offspring" by "consumers": the parallel is essentially complete. Churchill's "Jaw, jaw; not war, war" is more likely if individuals in different countries haggle over prices than if their governments negotiate international deals or spheres of influence in which their peoples may trade, or raise barriers, enforced by law and arms, against trade.

Price is knowledge

Without price there is no guide to relative costs or values or the sacrifices required to obtain desired goods or services. Prices are imperfect guides because of monopoly, inequality in resources or information, and for other reasons; but without them buyers and sellers are blind. The absence of price in public goods, where price is impracticable, requires them to be controlled by government, that is, individual politicians and officials who must decide when to extend or contract them, or more fundamentally when to continue or discontinue them. But, in the absence of price, government must use even more crude indicators of the value of resources in different uses. In public goods government control is an unavoidable second best to pricing.

Price is non-authoritarian

If prices are not allowed to emerge spontaneously, the alternative is to apportion and allocate resources by authority vested in the state and working through officials. This, essentially, is the method used in the "directed" or non-market economies in Eastern Europe and China and in some other countries in Asia and Africa. It is also the method used in Western democracies in services where the price "barrier" is abolished, as in the British National Health Service, and state education and local government services supplied "free" with no price charged to each "customer." *The alternative to allocation by price is thus allocation ("rationing") by government.* We must choose between the two. We cannot avoid rationing by pretending we have abolished price by supplying goods and services "free."

Price is a teacher

By creating and imparting information, price teaches care in comparing values, caution in making purchases, forethought in using services and resources, and husbandry and economy in managing money and household, business and national budgeting. Contrast the thoughtless use made of unpriced services (telephone, heating, the firm's stationery or the NHS) with the thoughtful shopping in the supermarket.

There is no third choice in the world as it is other than rationing by price or by direction. The way out for the people who like neither is to escape from reality by imagining that humans are selfless or resources infinite, so that rationing is unnecessary. There can be many individual or group acts of selfless giving in a free society, but we are not living in a world where everyone will give enough to everyone else, where most people will permanently make an effort without reward. Until that day comes, the Utopians are not helping the poor by their dreams.

If politicians were always benevolent and officials all-wise and fully informed about people's wishes, they could conceivably arrive at better terms for exchange and better rationing of resources than would be produced by prices arising from spontaneous exchange between individuals (or families, households, voluntary groups and associations, partnerships, firms, companies). But politicians have their own objectives to pursue—power, prestige, wealth, ideology—and once they obtain power they do not let it go easily. In directed economies the parties not in power, even where not suppressed, do not have much of a chance to replace the party that is in power. Even in market economies where government, as in Britain, controls a large part of activity, the parties have become skilled at staying in power by altering the general tempo of economic activity between General Elections and engineering changes in employment and inflation so that they win electoral praise for high employment and avoid blame for high inflation.

Still more importantly, officials cannot possibly know all the information that is in the heads or records of millions of people about which services they want and which they can supply. Some economists have argued that prices can be used in societies where the government owns and controls resources and that computers would enable the central authority to set prices and make decisions on the allocation of resources more efficiently than a market system.[1] To some extent pricing is used in Hungary, Yugoslavia and other Communist countries. But by the time all the prices are collected by the central authority and the orders to switch resources have been transmitted and put into effect by the hundreds of thousands of managers of factories, offices, dockyards, mines, railways, universities, schools, warehouses and so on, the wants of the millions of individuals and techniques of production have changed. In such a system the use of resources in practice lags behind people's wishes and preferences. Even worse, authority is tempted to modify these preferences, reinterpret them in a way that suits itself, or ignore them. In time, perhaps, people may protest; but, short of civil war, their power to see that their preferences are respected is much weaker than in a market system where suppliers of services who do not satisfy them can be abandoned for others who do.

In a market system the control over the use of resources, and over those who own or manage them, arises from *choice* between *competing* suppliers. Where choice and competition are impracticable or uneconomic (that is, in public goods) other controls are required. Even then the problems and tensions of rationing remain in the political market, where they may take more violent means to resolve. Economists distinguish the private market, where goods and services are produced, allocated and exchanged by personal decisions guided by price, from the political market, in which people decide collectively the production and allocation of public goods, and the charity market, in which individuals separately or collectively allocate gifts. The private market has been studied intensively for two hundred years or more, the political market with the same intensity only for some twenty years, and the charity market only for some ten years.[2]

1. Lange, O., "The Computer and the Market," in Feinstein, C., *Capitalism, Socialism, and Economic Growth,* C.U.P., 1967.

2. Johnson, D. B., "The Charity Market: Theory and Practice," in *The Economics of Charity,* IEA, 1973; Perlman, M., "The Economics of Politics," in *The Vote Motive,* IEA, 1976; and Tullock, G., *The Vote Motive,* IEA, 1976.

Price is unavoidable

Price is (except in public goods) ultimately unavoidable. It is like a plant that grows through all the obstacles in its way. It cannot be suppressed by law because it is a symptom of the urge of people, everywhere, to come together as buyers and sellers. Even if the state could inspect every human activity and every home, prices would emerge. In directed economies, in wartime Fascist Germany and peacetime Communist countries, something of the sort was and is attempted: officials are employed, or people enthusiastic for the regime are encouraged, to watch for and report outbreaks of unofficial pricing. Even in countries such as Britain attempts are sometimes made (especially in war but also in peace, as in the Price Code and incomes policies) to suppress unofficial free pricing. And again people are encouraged to watch out for "offenders." Yet the most rigidly directed economies find it expedient to turn a blind eye to spontaneous pricing when, as periodically in Russia, authority thinks its official centralised allocations have gone too far and are discouraging production by weakening the urge of people to serve one another as buyers and sellers. If they are forbidden by the state and its "law," they come together in "black" (or "grey") markets, which save the system from seizure by economic arthritis. In Russia, although it claims to be a centrally planned state with no individuals making money out of private activity, there is spontaneous pricing in agriculture, house-building, medical services and other activities difficult to control from the centre.[3] In Britain, and other countries in Europe, the suppression of spontaneous pricing of labour in "incomes policies" is, after a year or so, increasingly evaded by reclassifying an employee to justify a higher rate of pay, by premature promotion, by creating other forms of payment like fringe benefits, and so on. And in the government services, pricing breaks out in bribes and corruption. It cannot be prevented merely by passing laws against it. Pricing is mightier than government.

So pricing is neutral, useful, pacific, informative, a teacher, non-authoritarian and irrepressible. Politicians, sociologists and others who denounce it as a barrier are therefore uncomprehending and futile. It should be understood and welcomed as an indicator of relative wants and relative scarcities. It conveys *knowledge* that makes the use of resources better informed and therefore more efficient; and, whatever methods are evolved in

3. Miller, M., *Rise of the Russian Consumer,* IEA, 1965.

non-market, directed economies, they are all essential to replace the *information* that a price system supplies. To denounce price as a barrier is to blame it for reflecting the underlying scarcity of resources.

The missing link

We can go further than that. A price is better thought of not as a barrier but as its opposite—a *link* between buyer and seller. If it is irrepressible, it is better brought out into the open and made as serviceable an instrument as it can be in achieving the best use of resources. And this means refining it, rather than trying to suppress it: *making as much rather than as little use of it as possible* to yield information on relative valuations and costs, so that we are aware of the alternatives we forego in using resources for, say, hospitals rather than housing, swimming pools rather than police, Concordes rather than motor-cars. The central theme of this book, indeed, is that the absence of prices as landmarks, benchmarks, bearings and signposts causes confusion, distortion and waste, and their restoration wherever possible is essential in making the best use of resources, whatever their use—consumption, investment, charity or anything else.

This conclusion is clearly illustrated from three elemental services whose prices we in Britain have been increasingly trying to suppress: education since 1870, housing since 1915, medical care since 1948. How to use price as much as possible in all three is discussed in Chapters 4, 5 and 6, and in other services in Chapters 7, 8 and 9.

The mighty "margin"

Economic reasoning can shed light on how pricing helps in making decisions that affect vast resources.

In the real world—whether in government, industry or the family, in spending, saving or indeed giving—the decision is not between the *whole* of one product or service and another. A government has to decide between a *little* more expenditure on, say, hospitals at the expense of a decrease in expenditure on, say, housing, or between higher farming subsidies (to save rural seats) and lower commuter fares (to win suburban seats). A local authority has to choose between spending more on swimming pools at the expense of more on police. A family that wants to spend more on its home has to spend less on holidays. Anyone who wants to spend more altogether has to save less (or borrow more). A charity or a philanthropist who wants to give more to an old people's home has less to give to an orphanage. Choices at the margin have to be made in all three markets—private, political, charity. There is no escape in wishful thinking, denouncing wicked capitalists, indulging compassion or assuming that scarcity has been replaced by superabundance.

These increases and decreases are the "margins" that economists analyse in the "law of diminishing marginal utility," which explains how expenditure is apportioned among all the uses to which it can be put. The economic law that emerges is that utility derived from all the items is maximised when it cannot be further enlarged by switching marginal expenditure from some items to others, that is, when the marginal utility of expenditure on all the items is equalised. Thus a government maximises its utility (political, economic or other) from its total expenditure when the last, marginal, million pounds applied to, say, medical research yields no more and no less utility than if it were applied to law and order or the EEC. The special difficulty about all government expenditure, whether on public goods or non-public goods, is that utility cannot easily be measured unless there are prices. A firm maximises the utility (or productivity in this case) from its total expenditure on resources when the marginal ("last") thousand pounds spent on equipment yields no more and no less utility than if it were applied to wages or salaries. Measurement of utility is easier here because the firm loses money if it makes the wrong decision, so it can be assumed that by trial and error it will, in a competitive market, have to learn to make the right decisions. And a family maximises the satisfaction from its total household budget when it equalises its marginal expenditure on food, clothing, drinking, smoking, gambling, entertaining, and even within each category on different kinds of food, clothing, drinking and so on.

The all-important opportunity cost

A perhaps unexpected conclusion is that there is nothing inherently good or bad in any of these goods or services. Although we are accustomed to think of education, medical care, housing and other (usually "public") services as necessarily good and of many forms of (usually private) expenditure, such as entertaining, drinking, motoring, gambling or adornment as bad, or at least as self-indulgent, there is no substance in this distinction at all. What matters is the marginal expenditure on each category and how much utility, satisfaction or productivity it could have yielded if it had been spent on something else. It is possible for another million pounds spent by government on "good" things such as the National Health Service or Council housing to reflect less satisfaction than it would if spent on sports centres or defence or road signs, which may not seem such obviously "good things." And a hundred pounds more on warm clothing or even good books may yield a family less satisfaction than if it were spent on motoring, bingo or fancy footwear. What matters is the alternatives that are foregone—what economists call opportunity costs, one of the most illuminating ideas in economics.

Marginal utility in all government goods and services must be assessed, however crudely, and opportunity cost must still be estimated, however roughly, for government to make decisions. When reductions of £100 million in expenditure on defence are called for, it is implied that the country as a whole, or the people, will derive more satisfaction or utility if the money is spent on, say, education, parks and pleasure grounds, or overseas aid. That may be; but government judgement is based on no specific, real information at all, such as that provided by prices and the real personal opinions and valuations of individual men and women. In practice it is based on hunch, the spurious accuracy of estimates, guesswork, prejudice and calculation of political advantage. Price in open markets is usually more or less imperfect, but in its absence the way is open to decide the use of resources by much more imperfect political influences. Price, at least, reflects the opinions and wishes of the many in the market on how *they* wish to use their resources; in its absence, decisions are taken by the few who gain power in government and who use price not as much as possible but as little as they can by bringing under their control, as "public" services, a widening range of activities in which there are no prices at all.

Price is fundamental

Not the least essential characteristic of price is that, without it, "demand" and "supply" are meaningless. This notion is at first difficult to master. The non-economist is apt to think of the "demand" for a commodity or service as reflecting a natural state of "need," a self-evident quantity that requires no explanation. In a world without scarcity, and therefore without opportunity cost (so that using more resources to produce, say, fish would not withdraw resources from producing meat), that would be so. We can also properly talk of "need" in the sense of a minimum quantity of basic essentials like food or medical care that it is thought no human being should lack. In a Western economy that sense is also permissible, and if a minority of people lack these needs they can and should be provided by others. But in general "demand" is related to price: the lower the price, the larger the demand, because the less the opportunity costs of other things that are sacrificed. And the lower the price of something, the less of it is supplied, because resources can yield more elsewhere.

The mistaken idea that people have absolute "needs" originates in the notion that some goods are "essential" and must be obtained whatever the price. This may be true of some things inside narrow price-ranges within which demand is absolutely "inelastic." The demand for milk used in fixed proportions with tea may be inelastic: it does not alter with a change in price (unless the rise is so large that milk is given up).

But the availability of substitutes (made of different quality materials, etc.) makes demand elastic, and it falls perceptibly as price rises. Thus the "need" for a hospital bed is not fixed. If its cost rises, the individual may prefer a cheaper ward in order to keep up other purchases; and the NHS will similarly reduce quality to keep costs down, as by closing wards or casualty departments. Even in the gruesome example of coffins the demand is not fixed: we all die only once and demand only one; but if they are expensive (that is, require a large sacrifice of other things) cheaper woods or other materials can be used, or *in extremis* shrouds, as prepared for the expected victims of the London blitz. "Public" services also should be, and have to be, modified as costs change; otherwise the public is being unnecessarily burdened by being compelled to sacrifice alternatives it values more. The danger is that the modifications will be delayed because the government fears unpopularity and loss of parliamentary seats as well as because of compassion for people who would suffer. (This is what has happened in Britain over the cuts in government expenditure that have been under debate in recent years.)

The essential is to grasp that there are not enough resources to satisfy all "needs," that the use of resources cannot therefore be governed by what are considered "needs," but must be based on demand backed by purchasing power to indicate the value that people place on various commodities and the sacrifice of other goods they are prepared to make; and that demand is not fixed but varies with price—and is indeed meaningless without reference to price. There is no such thing as "the demand for" good housing, or hospital beds or teacher-training places, any more than there is a fixed demand for Eccles cakes, toffee apples or tripe and onions. The demand varies with the price. And that is true in Moscow, Warsaw, East Berlin and Peking as well as in Stockholm, Paris, Washington and London. There are no free health services, universities, convalescent homes, bus rides, cinema shows or anything else anywhere.[4]

No such thing as a free health service

If the price of a service is suppressed it must be paid for in some other way. In a society where income and wealth are widely unequal, it may be possible to remove part of the income and wealth from people who have more ("the rich") to provide services "free" to people with little income and no wealth who could not pay the price ("the poor"). This is the main one of the pretexts used in extending "free" local government services in the past century, free state education since 1870, in providing partly "free" (subsidised) housing to several millions since 1915, and in creating the "free" National Health Service in 1948.

The tragic result is that, as incomes have become more equal, the effects have changed. A transfer of payment from rich to poor made sense. A transfer away from taxpayers with middling (and even less than average) income and back to themselves as *users* of "free" state services—or even to the better-off, as in higher education and sports amenities—makes nonsense (Part 2). The more they have realised this truth, the more reluctant people have become to pay at all (as taxpayers) even for services they otherwise regard as desirable. And this means that the quality of the social services and benefits they receive is lower than they *could* pay for, and might *want* to pay for in ways they themselves could decide. The "welfare state" has made us cut off our noses to spite our faces.

This is a most unwelcome—and unexpected—development. And not much help is obtained from restating the case for price-less (or partly "free") services as transferring payment from people at the times of life when they have more income and wealth to the times when they have less. People as taxpayers stubbornly refuse to see this subtle distinction. And if this is what they want to do, they do not have to do it through the state. They simply do not like paying taxes at *any* times of their lives. They object not to the tax-rates, the tax-base or the tax-locale (central taxes, national insurance, VAT, local rates) but to the tax-take. They simply are fed up with someone else spending their money for them.

Why? This obstinacy seems puzzling. It may appear especially mulish

4. Dolan, E. G., *TANSTAAFL (There Ain't No Such Thing As A Free Lunch)*, Holt, Rinehart & Winston (NY), 1971.

when the tax payments are made for services that seem obviously desirable like education, medical care, housing, transport, fire protection, refuse collection, and so on. Some perplexed people refuse to believe it. "I have long believed," said a former Minister, "that if the people understand what they get for their taxes they are less likely to argue against them." (Mr. Eric Heffer, *The Times,* 12 March 1976.) It is impossible to demonstrate that he is wrong, but until he proves he is right his opinion sounds like wishful thinking. It is not a view he can claim to be true until it is proved false. Governments of all parties have since the war asked the people to pay higher taxes for more or better social benefits for all and sundry. Increasing tax avoidance and evasion show they would rather not. And politicians of all parties are at last accepting the evidence.

Why will people pay less in taxes for "free" services than they could pay, and might prefer to pay, in other ways? Why are "free" British state welfare services less good than priced welfare services might be?

Paying by charges or taxes

The solution is not difficult to see. It requires only an unsentimental, though not unworthy, view of human nature—the reactions of men as husbands, women as wives, and both as parents. It can be wrapped up in jargon as economic theory but it can be put in plain English: *ordinary people will pay more for a service if they can see their families will benefit than they will in taxes for a service in which they can see no benefit for higher tax-payment.*

It is this realistic reading of human nature that reveals the inappropriateness of taxes as the method of paying for personal welfare services. It is not a theory or a hunch, or a cynical view of human selfishness. It is a description which realistically captures, without illusion or humbug, the attitude of ordinary men and women all over the world, under all economic systems, capitalist, socialist or communist. And it is what the exceptional politician of perception and integrity sees, and says, when he tries in the real world to run social policies based on the unworldly assumption that men and women are far-seeing saints. In 1967, after two and a half years as Minister coordinating the social services, Mr. Douglas (now Lord) Houghton said:

> While people would be willing to pay for better health services for themselves, they may not be willing to pay more in taxes as a kind of insurance premium which may bear no relation to the services they receive.[5]

5. Houghton, Lord, *Paying for the Social Services,* IEA, 1967, 1968.

And in 1969, after two years as Minister for Social Services, the late Richard Crossman, who was too much of a scholar to blur the truth as he found it, signed a White Paper on National Superannuation which said:

> . . . people are prepared to subscribe more in a contribution for their own personal or family security than they would be willing to pay in taxation devoted to a wide variety of different purposes.

Self-interest and selfishness

The British are not callous or ungenerous: they pay taxes willingly to help people who, through old age, disability or other causes, cannot help themselves;[6] and they work for and give money to good causes, their neighbours in trouble, the local hospital or school, the old people's home, their church. But they object to helping people who can help themselves. Where there are two ways of paying for a service (taxes and prices) and one way (taxes) gives no benefit to themselves, they prefer to pay in ways (prices) that do.

That is hardly surprising. It is, however, disappointing to many who hoped that people would willingly go on paying in taxes for communal causes. That is the assumption behind the welfare state common in all political parties. But it requires a decision by each man or woman to put the benefits to his family second to the consequences to others, including strangers of whom he may not approve. That degree of self-sacrifice may be expected from uncommon individuals, or in wartime or other crises. But why should we suppose that people would be better human beings if they put causes they do not know before causes they do? Because we have confused self-interest with selfishness.

The better arrangement is to avoid the conflict between a man's family and outside interests and try to guide him to serve the general interest, which he cannot know, by serving his family or personal causes, which he does know. He is moved to serve his personal or local causes not by selfishness but by knowledge.

The apparently simple question, whether to pay by market prices or to suppress them and pay by taxes, thus raises deep philosophic issues. But the question must be answered by citizens and their representatives in a democracy; and it must be answered all the sooner if an error in reasoning

6. Seldon, A., *Taxation and Welfare,* IEA, 1967.

is preventing people from paying as much as they could and would, and therefore producing services that are inferior to those they wish to have. When the services include education, health, housing and other basic services, we must give the matter urgent thought, and reverse policies shown to be undesirable.

The reigning error

Happily such reconsideration has begun. At long last, after years of irresponsible over-spending by Conservative and Labour governments, both central and local, anxiety about government expenditure and the urgency of making cuts spread to people in almost all schools of thought and all the major political parties. But the right solution will not be adopted until all these groups and sub-groups recognise a fundamental flaw in British thinking on social policy.

The error lies in the three-stage argument at the beginning of this chapter.

1. All people should have the minimum essentials for civilised living;
2. their incomes are sometimes too low to pay for them;
3. therefore they should be provided free by the state, and not only to people with low incomes but to everyone.

The first stage is accepted by everyone. The second is self-evident. The fatal flaw lies in the third stage. It simply does not follow from the first two.

We may differ about the meaning of minimum. We may differ about how often incomes are too low, and about the cause; whether the low incomes are unavoidable and what can be done to make them large enough. But what should not have been accepted—certainly after World War II—is the conclusion that the state therefore had to supply services wholly free, or partly free at prices reduced by subsidies. This error has misled all British governments for a century to create a vast unnecessary structure of free education, almost wholly free medical care, partly free housing; free libraries, museums, art galleries; free "personal" social services such as home helps and meals in the home; free or largely free local health services such as health centres, midwifery, home nursing, vaccination and immunisation, ambulances and family planning; (almost) free police and fire services; free sewerage; free recreational and sports facilities; free roads, partly free (subsidised) parking; free employment agencies (now called Job Centres); free environmental services—parks, public conveniences, town and country planning, allotments; subsidised private street works, etc., etc. Much of this structure was unnecessary; it is increasingly undesirable; and it can be changed.

Abe Lincoln didn't live here

All the services that happen to have been taken over by government, local or national, are described as "public." This is a highly misleading term. It can mean, first, that they are, in Abraham Lincoln's words, "of" the people (that is, decided by them), run "by" the people, or "for" (the benefit of) the people. None of these claims is self-evident. Second, it can mean that all these services are "public" in the sense that they differ in a fundamental way from "private" services. This claim is not true either.

Of the people?

Which "public services" arise out of public wishes?

There is no systematic mechanism in Britain for recording public opinion on any single "public" service. When did anyone in Britain have the opportunity to record a vote for or against the National Health Service? or Council housing? or public libraries? or public golf courses? Apart from the referendum on the Common Market in June 1975 no one has ever been able to say "Yes" or "No" to any single political question. Your opinion is sought through your representatives—in Parliament or Councils—on twenty, thirty or ninety issues at once. But that is a very imperfect second best. It means that everyone must accept (or at least pay for) the "public" services supported by the political party or group with the largest number of votes. If there are more than two groups, one group can compel the *majority* of us to accept what the group with the largest *minority* wants to do. That has been the situation in Britain for many years. In October 1974 the group elected was supported by less than two in five of those who bothered to vote (or not much more than one in four of all citizens with votes). Indeed, since the war no government of any party has had a majority of the votes cast, still less of the votes that could have been cast (Table A).

There is, then, no way in which any one "public" service can be isolated and supported or opposed. We must support or oppose all the proposals offered by each party or group. And this means that if a proposal for, say, the National Health Service is made by *all* groups, we have no choice at all: no way of opposing it or escaping from it once it is implemented—except by emigrating, which some people have preferred. Moreover, if the representatives take it into their heads after they have reached Parliament or the Council to make another service public—say, theatres, or fire insurance, or medicines, or tourism, or banking or bingo—there is nothing we can do about it. In this way they can depart a long way from the wishes of the *real* public who are the sovereign people with the power (on paper) to decide what we think should or should not be made "public": for it is we who benefit or suffer, and not least, it is we who pay.

Any idea should, of course, have a chance of being tried *at the expense of private individuals,* but the British political system gives individual political activists the chance to foist a new "public" service on the public, at *its* expense, and on a national scale which destroys for years and years the chance to reverse it if it fails.

By the people?

Are the "public" services run by the people? On paper the people are represented by MPs and local Councillors who reflect their opinions. In practice the reality is very different. Representatives may be opinionated, self-willed autocrats who say one thing on party platforms or in election addresses and do another after being elected. Even if they were all upright, conscientious servants of the people, they are not elected as spokesmen on this, that and the other, but as men who in principle reflect the general approach of the people and apply it to unforeseeable circumstances as they emerge. And even though they must represent their electors on collective services, such as protection against world or internal disorder, they cannot represent each individual elector in a personal service.

This is the basic weakness of controlling education, medical care or many other services, through "representatives." Ministers and politicians know first-hand from their party officials, stalwarts and activists what they think individuals in the party, or even outside it, think about public goods, but they cannot know their private feelings and wishes as husbands and wives, parents and children, in personal services. No representative in, say, education can represent hundreds of parents, who know the characters and temperaments, the feelings and anxieties, of their children better than anyone else. Much the same applies to most of the personal benefits in the public services. It is unrealistic to suppose that politicians (even if saints) and officials (even if geniuses) can know as much as millions of men and women who have to adapt themselves to unforeseen, changing conditions. And politicians are not saints, nor officials geniuses.

Even when politicians and officials do their best to provide good schools, hospitals and so on, the man whose wife is not comfortable in the hospital ward or the parent whose child is not happy in the school cannot change conditions except by the lengthy business of persuading hundreds or thousands or millions of other husbands and parents, a task which daunts most, especially the inarticulate. Such services are therefore innately impersonal, unresponsive and conservative; they are bureaucratic rather than democratic. They bend to political muscle, personal connections, social influence, individual pressure or bullying. What ordinary, quiet, uninfluential people want is a method by which they themselves, by private *individual* action, can influence conditions quietly and without confrontation, voice-raising, marches, public meetings, petitions, deputations or any other kind of public fuss. What they want is simply a means of exit to another hospital or school. Such methods are available (Chapters 4 to 9), but they are not made part of the machinery of "public" services in Britain. Politicians on the hustings claim it serves the public, but in real life it dissuades or stops the people from trying something else if they are dissatisfied.

For the people?

Are public services run for the people? It is again impossible to tell, for by definition public services cannot be compared with alternatives, which on the contrary may be outlawed—as in transport, fuel, postal services, etc. If government were really efficient in satisfying the people, it would provide easy ways for them to try alternative services, so that it would be clear for all to see beyond dispute whether the people preferred public to alternative services. But this is precisely what government does not do. Politicians characteristically abhor competition; unlike nature they prefer a vacuum.

So we must take with a large pinch of salt the notion that "public" services are necessarily in the public interest. Simply calling them public, or talking about public accountability through Parliament or the local Council, is not enough.

"Externalities" and "free rides"

The previous chapter discussed the characteristic which marks off what are truly public goods from those that are really private services in disguise—that public goods have to be supplied for everyone or no one and cannot be withheld from people who choose to take a "free ride." This special characteristic of public goods makes it necessary (or at least desirable) to organise them through government and to finance them by taxes—in short to nationalise (or municipalise) them.

The difference is clear enough in principle but it may be difficult to work in practice, because many goods and services shed benefits to outsiders or third parties who cannot (technically or economically) be charged for them. In this sense almost every human activity yields what economists call "external benefits." A man who plants sweet-smelling flowers benefits his neighbours, and if he wears button-holes he may please both friends and strangers; but he could not charge them fees to help him pay for his seeds. If we all considered the feelings of neighbours and strangers we should increase happiness all round. But it does not follow that we should transform all private individuals into public services, or even regulate all private activities by political devices. For we might lose the other benefits of individual choice, variety and initiative if we had government subsidies and inspectors to ensure that everyone's garden grew flowers that pleased all neighbours. There could be no end to that process of maximising externalities. We should all be living in one another's pockets. So in practice public goods are confined to those whose external benefits are clearly and considerably larger than the costs and defects of state control, and where there is no economic method of financing them except by taxes.

In practice "public services" has become a political term, almost an advertising or public relations label, used for all the services that have gradually, down the years since the mid-nineteenth century, been gathered together under government for all sorts of reasons, willy-nilly. It conveys the impression that they must all be organised by government and that they are all necessarily in the public interest. That is a myth. They need not be. And they are not.

Charging for choice

They do not all have to be organised by government and financed by taxes. Some could be financed by prices. They are not all necessarily in the public interest. Some could be organised outside government. This possibility opens up new vistas of wider choices for users of services, competition between suppliers, and a wider variety of methods of payment.

If services now supplied by government can and should be financed by prices—charges, fees, etc.—the chances are that people who pay prices will want the same feeling of personal choice that they now have in purchasing family and household goods and services—food, clothing, furniture, books and newspapers, motoring, holidaying, and so on. They will look around for suppliers who can give them the choice that national or local government cannot, or does not. That is where the old thinking—that only the state can or should supply what are now called "public services"—will have to give way to "new thinking"—that a service should be provided by *any* supplier, state or private, who can supply it in the form that most pleases the customer. But that is a long and exciting story that must wait for Part II. If the main purpose is to satisfy people as individuals a lot of established myths and charades will have to be abandoned. Not least of them is the notion that government introduces a new service only when it is required by the people and ends it when it is no longer wanted. The myth that "public" services are necessarily a good thing has made them seem sacrosanct; they must not be touched whatever new requirements arise, or whatever new circumstances are brought by technical and social change. No one may say a word against "free" public baths and wash houses that go back to 1846, or "free" public libraries that go back to 1850, or "free" refuse collection that goes back to 1875—despite the enormous changes in the last century and a half. Yet, for public men who represent the people, to refuse to change anything when circumstances change is itself a public dis-service.

CHAPTER 3

Private "Public" Services

The great debate has at last begun over how to cut inflated government expenditure. But it will not be resolved as long as it continues to ignore the extent to which "public" services are not public goods at all but yield private benefits that could and should be paid for by price. And it will not be resolved so long as we think only of rearranging the government machinery by which cuts are made from on high by politicians.

This debate will not lead to the right solution so long as people who at long last joined it, tardily, like the late Mr. Anthony Crosland, argue that cuts in government expenditure may be desirable as a temporary necessity to fight off inflation (by increasing production and shifting resources into industrial investment and exports) but are not based on a permanent principle.[1]

What is at stake is very much a permanent principle. It is the true principle, perhaps new to politicians but not to economists, that public goods should be financed by public methods (taxes) but private benefits where possible by private methods (prices). And it must replace the false notion that any activity or function that government has happened to gather to itself for a rag-bag of reasons, good or bad, still valid or wildly out of date, sensible or nonsensical, shall all be christened "public" services and financed by taxes whether or not this is the way to efficiency, economy, equity, choice or democracy.

A permanent principle

Shedding the old principle will not be easy for men and women in all schools of thought and parties, Conservative, Liberal or Labour. The debate

1. Crosland, A., "The Long-term Future of Public Expenditure," Fabian Lecture, *Guardian*, 24 March 1976.

will be abortive unless Social Democrats like Mr. Roy Jenkins recognise the new principle. Others like Mr. David Marquand[2] and Professor Lord Vaizey[3] seem to have done so, or at least moved towards it. Paternalistic Liberals and Tories, no less than paternalistic Labourites, will have to abandon the wrong principle and accept the true one. It is a permanent principle because government expenditure is in large part wrongly financed by taxes, and therefore will not be cut as it should be—by informed consumers rather than by uninformed politicians—until it is financed by charges. No insuperable technical or political obstacles stand in the way. The adoption of the true principle could transform and reinvigorate British society in a decade. That is the solution for which this book argues.

In 1974 the total national output of goods and services was around £75 billion (a billion in this book is a thousand million). The figure is growing—because of inflation rather than economic efficiency—but we are more concerned about the *proportions* in which it is divided between public goods and private benefits, which will remain much the same until policy is changed from taxing to pricing. About £25 billion, or a third, was produced directly by government (national, regional or local), by government employees and equipment in government offices, factories, mines, quarries, generating stations, ordnance depots, barracks, railways, buses, coaches, abattoirs, schools, hospitals, universities, more offices, job centres, libraries, museums, art galleries, health centres, ambulances, children's residential homes, homes for the elderly, prisons, police stations, fire stations, law courts, sewage farms, water reservoirs, refuse vans, swimming and washing baths, town halls, roads, parks, car parks, tennis courts, golf courses, theatres and yet more offices.

In addition to the third of the total national output directly produced by government, it also decides the disposal of a further fifth of the national income. This part is returned in cash, in family allowances, grants of various kinds, pensions and so on, for people to spend as they wish (subject, even then, to taxes on their purchases). Government thus directly controls the production and the distribution of a third of the national output and then indirectly decides who shall receive a further fifth of national purchasing power. In this sense it controls over half the national economy. And in so far as taxes have the same effect on production, incentives, costs of collection, avoidance, evasion and so on whether they are returned in goods and ser-

2. Marquand, D., "A Social Democratic View," in *The Dilemmas of Government Expenditure*, IEA, 1976.

3. Vaizey, Lord, "The Roulette of Public Spending," *New Statesman*, Feb. 1976.

vices or in money, it is correct to think of the government controlling over half, not one-third, of the national product.

Public goods proper

For readers who like to think in figures, the tables that follow show the broad orders of magnitude at a glance. Table B arranges all the main items of government expenditure into five broad groups, not rigidly defined but overlapping at the edges. Group I contains the more or less "pure" public goods which yield common benefits to all, and which cannot be separately organised by each person, family or household. This group accounts for about 15 per cent of total government expenditure and 8 per cent of GNP. It is essentially the hard core of unavoidable government functions. Even here one or two of the smaller items, such as land drainage or law courts, may contain private benefits that could be separated and charged for.

Public services with some separable private benefits

Group II contains services familiarly supplied by local or regional (county) government, usually without charge, but containing some benefits that are or could be rendered to individuals and financed by charging. Roads, police, fire and other services are discussed in later chapters. This group accounts for about 14 per cent of government expenditure (8 per cent of GNP). The "public corporations" are included here because transport and fuel are sometimes regarded as "social services" that should not charge prices that will cover costs but should be financed partly by taxes. Mr. Sidney Weighall, the General Secretary of the National Union of Railwaymen, has vividly maintained that the railways should no more be expected to pay for themselves than aircraft carriers. He saw no difference. The difference is that aircraft carriers are public goods; railways are not.

Separable private benefits

Group III contains services that have also been supplied by local, regional or national government, some for a century or more, some for only a quarter of a century, but which largely comprise separable benefits. It may be surprising to say this of education and medical care, although it is obviously true of housing. Unfortunately, although "housing" is a clear enough description of houses or flats or other forms of living space, "education" is a technical term that covers a wide range of services from public goods to

Table B. Where Our Money Goes: Government expenditure in 1974 (millions)

	Total expenditure (£)	Proportion of total government expenditure (£41,600)	Proportion of gross national product (£74,000)
I *Public goods with inseparable benefits (charging impracticable or uneconomic)*			
Military defence	4,221	10	6
Civil defence	14	*	*
External relations (embassies, missions, EEC, etc.)	654	2	1
Parliament & law courts	221	1	*
Prisons	149	*	*
Public health	101	*	*
Land drainage & coast protection	69	*	*
Finance & tax collection	496	1	1
Other government services	166	*	*
	6,091	15	8
II *Public goods with some separable benefits (charging partly practicable)*			
Government (central & local) and "public" corporation current & capital expenditure	2,429	6	3
Roads and public lighting	1,195	3	2
Research	326	1	*
Parks, pleasure grounds, etc.	265	1	*
Local government services ("misc")	700	2	1
Police	706	2	1
Fire services	169	*	*
Records, registration, surveys	38	*	*
	5,828	14	8
III *Substantially or wholly separable benefits (charging substantially practicable)*			
Education	4,864	12	7
National Health Service	3,819	9	5
Personal social services	677	2	1
School meals, milk & welfare foods	282	1	*
Employment service	268	1	*

Table B (continued)

	Total expenditure (£)	Proportion of total government expenditure (£41,600)	Proportion of gross national product (£74,000)
Libraries, museums & art galleries	222	1	*
Housing	3,942	9	5
Water, sewage, refuse disposal	730	2	1
Transport & communications	1,894	5	3
	16,698	40	22
IV *Subsidies, grants, pensions and other (mostly) cash disbursements*			
Agriculture, forestry, fishing, food	1,049	3	1
Cash benefits for social insurance, etc.	6,845	16	9
Miscellaneous subsidies, grants, lending, etc., to private/personal sector	1,363	3	2
	9,257	22	13
V *Interest on National Debt*	3,732	9	6
TOTAL GOVERNMENT EXPENDITURE	41,606	100	56

Source: The figures are from the National Income Blue Book, 1974. The classification into groups is mine.
*Less than one per cent

purely personal benefits. So does "the National Health Service" which I shall argue (Chapter 5) is a dog's breakfast of a term that is both too wide and too narrow to describe the services designed to maintain or restore health. Group III accounts for about 40 per cent of government expenditure, and 22 per cent of GNP.

Cash raised in taxes and returned

Group IV contains tax monies paid back in cash benefits to taxpayers, often the very same people: about 22 per cent of government expenditure. These are the "transfer payments."

National Debt interest is shown separately as Group V.

Public corporations?

The "public" corporations are mostly the familiar nationalised industries, the Post Office, coal, electricity, gas, airways, railways and buses—housing and new towns. At this point we may again note the repeated use of the misleading term "public." This is a political term that does not indicate a real economic distinction. Neither general reasoning nor experience supports the insinuation that public corporations are necessarily "in the public interest," in contrast with private industry which it is implied, is not in the public interest because it works for private profit. There is a confusion here between purpose and result. It may be the *intention* of Parliament that public corporations shall work only for the public interest. It does not follow that the intention is fulfilled in practice. But more than that: whether or not their intention matters morally to the real "public" (the users and consumers of nationalised fuel and transport) what certainly does matter to them is the *result*—whether they receive good value for their (private) money. Obversely, whether or not private capitalists work only for personal profit, what matters to the user of privately-produced food, clothing, homes, books, entertainment, motoring, etc., is the result: good value or not. And, in this result, the question whether government producers are financed by prices from customers or by taxes from politicians is very much one that should be, but is hardly ever, asked.

Since the late 1960s these "public" industries and services have been required to cover their costs, though not necessarily in every single year. In practice we know that the railways, air, steel and others are constantly asking for government grants (taken from the taxpayer) or loans to cover losses. And even if, in any one year, one of them has covered its costs as a whole, there is internal "cross-subsidising" of some services by others. For some years the telephones have been subsidising the parcels services, the Inter-City train traveller has been subsidising the outer commuter working in London, and so on. How much sense does that make?

Private benefits: public money

To discuss the extent to which government services could be paid for by prices, I have shown in Table C the expenditure on local government services for the latest year available, and the income drawn in fees, charges and sales. (Later figures will show much the same story until charges are made or raised.) I have then calculated how much of the total expenditure is financed

Table C. How Much We Pay for Local Government Services by Charges and by Taxes

	Expenditure (£ million)	Income from fees & charges and sales[1] (£ million)	Charges etc. as % of expenditure	Remainder paid by taxes[2] (%)
1 *"Rate fund" services (current expenditure)*				
Education:				
Nursery	10	*	*	100
Primary	839	9	1	99
Secondary	1,073	35	3	97
Special	131	15	11	89
Further:				
Polytechnics & regional colleges	127	12	9	91
Colleges of art	17	1	8	92
Agricultural	10	2	18	82
Other major colleges, etc.	294	36	12	88
Evening institutes	22	4	19	81
Other	206	72	35	65
Teacher training	127	4	3	97
School health	46	*	1	99
Recreation & social & physical training				
Youth	29	1	2	98
Adults, etc.	13	1	7	93
Other education services	6	*	6	94
School meals, milk, etc.	294	100	34	66
Libraries	95	5	6	94
Museums and art galleries	11	1	5	95
Health:				
Health centres	9	1	8	92
Mother/children clinics, etc.	22	1	6	94
Midwifery	18	*	1	99
Visitors	21	*	*	100
Home nursing	35	*	*	100
Vaccination & immunisation	4	*	*	100
Ambulance	62	1	2	98
Prevention of illness	15	*	3	97
Family Planning	6	1	1	99
Personal social services				
Residential care	249	66	26	74

Table C (continued)

	Expenditure (£ million)	Income from fees & charges and sales[1] (£ million)	Charges etc. as % of expenditure	Remainder paid by taxes[2] (%)
Day care—day nurseries (incl. play groups)	15	2	12	88
Community care:				
Home helps (incl. laundry)	55	3	5	95
Meals in the home	6	1	18	82
Other	37	1	2	98
Police	530	19	4	96
Fire	123	2	2	98
Justice (courts, petty sessions, probation)	56	1	2	98
Sewerage	242	15	6	94
Refuse	167	11	7	93
Baths (swimming & washing) & laundries	49	13	26	74
Land drainage, flood prevention	33	1	4	96
Smallholdings	6	1	12	88
Sea fisheries, pest control, etc.	7	2	27	63
Roads: Highways	471	12	3	97
Public lighting	48	1	2	98
Vehicle parking	33	20	60	40
Youth employment	10	*	*	100
Sheltered employment and workshops	8	3	41	59
Environment				
Parks and open spaces	131	11	8	92
National and countryside parks	4	*	1	99
Town & country planning	115	5	4	96
Housing (other than below—2)	282	18	6	94
Public conveniences	20	*	2	98
Air pollution prevention	6	*	*	100
Other health measures	46	2	5	95
River pollution prevention	4	*	*	100
Allotments	2	*	23	77
Private street, etc., works	20	10	51	49
Registration of births, etc.	6	2	35	65
Civil defence	2	*	1	99
Coast protection	5	*	*	100

Table C (continued)

	Expenditure (£ million)	Income from fees & charges and sales[1] (£ million)	Charges etc. as % of expenditure	Remainder paid by taxes[2] (%)
2 *Housing (current expenditure "revenue account")*	1,231	740	60	40
3 *"Trading services"*				
Water	208	174	84	16
Passenger transport	90	76	84	16
Cemeteries & crematoria	20	7	35	65
Fishing harbours	0.4	0.2	61	39
Other ports & piers	14	12	88	12
Civic restaurants	4	4	88	12
Markets horticultural	3	1	39	61
others	15	8	55	45
Slaughterhouses	6	3	55	45
Aerodromes	20	12	63	37
Industrial estates	11	2	20	80
District heating schemes	0.5	0.4	83	17
Corporation estates	31	4	15	85

Source of figures: *Local Government Financial Statistics, England and Wales, 1973–4*, HMSO, 1975.

*Less than £1 million or one per cent

[1] Sales are of miscellaneous used vehicles and equipment, publications, agricultural produce, waste paper, etc.

[2] The true balance of expenditure paid by the taxpayer (and ratepayer) is in some items higher than shown in the last column because the figures for income from fees and charges include sums paid by local authorities in other areas, not by direct private consumers or users (for example, fees for children at boarding schools).

from prices paid by the users of the services and how much by the ratepayer and taxpayer, who may use them little or not at all.

These official figures will, I imagine, shock some readers. The most surprising item is that only half of the expenditure on what is openly and officially called *private* "street and other works" is evidently paid for by charges levied on the people for whom the work is done; the rest is paid for by taxes extracted from other people who do not benefit from the work, at least directly and obviously (further discussed below). Then again car-parking, a convenience for the individual motorist, drew less than two-thirds of its expenditure from charges; the rest was paid by local taxpayers who did not park, who may indeed not own cars, or who may prefer to keep cars out of their shopping areas or even altogether out of their towns, suburbs or villages. And so on: homes for the elderly had a third of their costs paid by charges, allotments less than a quarter, swimming and washing baths and laundries just over a fifth. In each of the rest the proportion was under a fifth, in many under a tenth, and in some (including the largest, such as education and health) 5 per cent or less. These are averages for the country as a whole. For individual local authorities the gap between expenditure and charges in car-parking, sports facilities, housing and other services may be even more.

Externalities and absurdities

In some of these services it could be argued, and is argued by some economists, sociologists and politicians, that the benefit was not only personal to the user but spilled over to other people, so that it was right for part, most, or all of the cost to be borne by third parties, or by people in general on their rates or taxes. In principle that argument is right: perhaps passers-by are pleased by the private "street and other works" as they pass by and don't snap at their children when they reach home. The benefits of car-parking spill over to pedestrian shoppers who have fewer cars to avoid in the streets, to shopkeepers whose sales may rise, to out-of-town car-borne shoppers attracted by free or subsidised car-parking, to ratepayers in general whose rates are lower than they otherwise would be because shopkeepers' rates are higher, to enthusiasts for clean buildings because shopkeepers paint their shop-fronts more frequently, to the local church, old people's homes and hospitals which receive more gifts from better-off traders, and so on without end.

This line of reasoning—that individual activity affects the community by its "externalities"—is strongly argued by sociologists who tend to see all life as communal and by politicians who naturally rather like to think that the state could run human activity better than short-sighted, blinkered individuals could do for themselves. But all the same it reduces logic to absurdity. It ends with the conclusion that *everything* we do—from eating and drinking to queuing and waiting—affects everybody else, that nothing we do is personal or private, and therefore *every* activity should be financed by taxes and directed by government officials. This, of course, is the recipe for the all-in, comprehensive, totalitarian society. No country that hoped to maintain any personal liberties could go as far as that, even if some efficiency in using resources was lost by maintaining individual decisions.

But more than that. Even if the externality argument made sense it would merely show that the liberty to make individual decisions has costs, *not that the costs are too high to pay.* This is the key to understanding the fallacy of the argument that supposed or conjectured externalities—like the social good that it is thought will be done by university graduates—are sufficient to make the case for subsidising the producer (students in this case) at the expense of everyone else who is supposed to benefit. In conception we may all do (unintended) good to everyone else, but it produces no basis for policy. The externalities would have to be measured much more precisely by an army of calculators, estimators, assessors and adjudicators; a vast structure of subsidies from everyone to everyone else would have to be calculated by more officials; still more officials would have to be recruited to pay them; more taxes would have to be raised to finance them; and more tax-gatherers would be required to collect the taxes. There would be fewer of us left to produce the income and wealth to yield the subsidies and the taxes, and we should all end up leaning on one another. In short, even if the externalities could be identified and measured, the cost of transferring the subsidies from everyone to everyone else would in the end exceed the benefits.

We can go even further than that. Individual initiative that does not need official permission also has external benefits—in stimulating innovation, change, abandonment of old attitudes and institutions, economic advance. Progress might be largely stillborn if innovation were closely regulated even by a benevolent state, as it was in the guild system of mediaeval England, as it now is by authoritarian states in Eastern Europe, Asia and Africa, and as some politicians would like in Britain today. This totalitarian policy would throw out the baby with the bath water. Rather than try to calculate all the remote and indefinable public benefits that could flow from private action, we must work the other way round and assess what proportion of "public" services consists of separable benefits to particular individuals who could be identified and who could be made to pay for them.

This is sometimes a very difficult task. No one knows the exclusive, separable personal benefit in a "public" service for which individuals would pay rather than go without. The reason is simply that they have never had to pay for it: there has been no "market." The only way to find out is by the characteristically British method of trial and error. And, to begin the process of thinking in this unknown territory, it is a refreshing exercise to start from scratch and consider each service to see how far it yields personal benefits that could be paid for in prices. We can then discuss how much should remain paid for by taxes.

We are leaving aside for the moment the plausible reasons why many activities have been made "public" services—poverty, irresponsibility, economy, monopoly—and also the less reputable reasons like political aggrandisement and civil-service empire-building. (They are discussed in Chapters 10 to 12.) Here we consider only the extent to which "public" services yield separable personal benefits for which people could pay.

How far are "public" services public goods?

"Public" services are supplied by three agencies: central government, the public corporations and local government. ("Agencies" is a good word: it reminds us that, at least on paper, they are not authorities over the people, but their "agents": not independent principals but employees.) In practice public services are run by politicians who go their own way and civil servants whose power as disobedient servants was vividly suggested by the late Richard Crossman's account of Departments that generated their own policies, consulted opposite numbers in other Departments to thwart difficult Ministers, and behaved like an independent authority of able, well-intentioned but still irresponsible autocrats who act as judge and jury on what is administratively practicable, and who, without much knowledge of public wishes at all, offer advice on what is "politically possible."[4]

The agency that supplies the largest element of real public goods like defence is the central government (Group I, Table B). But it also supplies a surprisingly high proportion of separable private benefits (Groups II and III).

Defence

Defence against external enemies is clear enough. There is no known way of making people pay for it by private fees, or at least no way that is economic. Even if it were possible to calculate the risks from destruction of life, liberty or property from aerial attack or invasion in different locations, and the value of individual lives, liberty and property saved by efficient defence, it is impossible to confine defence to people who pay. And for such services, at least for the foreseeable future, all must agree to pay collectively by taxes, though individuals may supplement collective provision (below). Perhaps one day, if technical development makes the defence of small groups pos-

4. Crossman, R. H. S., *Inside View: Three Lectures on Prime Ministerial Government*, Jonathan Cape, 1972.

sible, "fees" may become practicable, as some brighter younger American economists persist in discussing.[5]

Civil defence

Much the same goes for civil defence, since the damage caused by modern nuclear weapons is widespread. Even so, people will supplement whatever defences they finance jointly through taxes by coming together and combining in small groups to reduce (by blast-proofing, laying in stores, etc.) loss of life and damage to possessions from localised weapons or warfare. And no government can stop them, even though they do so unequally.

External relations

External relations seem a clear case of a public good that benefits all citizens (or, if they are not conducted wisely, a public bad from which all suffer). The benefit may not be equal but it is not easily separable or traceable to individuals or local groups and so cannot be paid for by charging. Even so, services to individuals or firms may be.

Parliament

Parliament is another public good (or bad). Its law-making affects us all; and we cannot easily be charged as individuals for the benefits we have had from (or compensated for the harm done by) the externalities of nineteenth- and twentieth-century politicians or governments. Shakespeare knew about externalities when he said: "The evil that men do lives after them, the good is oft interred with their bones."

Justice

The law courts seem another obvious public good that must be paid for by taxes. Yet the settlement of disputes over agreements and contracts does not have to be done by government officials. It is possible to conceive of private arbitration and even courts, strange though that may sound. Some American economists are ahead of us[6] in developing these ideas.

5. Friedman, D., *The Machinery of Freedom,* Harper & Row (NY), 1973; Rothbard, M. N., *Man, Economy and State,* Van Nostrand (USA), 1962; Rothbard, M. N., *Power and Market,* Institute for Human Studies (USA), 1970; and Rothbard, M. N., *For a New Liberty,* Collier-Macmillan (NY), 1973.

6. Friedman, D., *The Machinery of Freedom.*

Prisons

Prisons are another obvious public good that cannot be paid for by pricing (though prisoners could pay for their keep by working, and perhaps compensate people they have wronged). It does not follow that prisons are best conducted by government officials; but that—the whole question of the difference between government and private management, even of public goods—is a subject for a separate book.

Public health

These are the environmental and preventive activities (such as treating polluted water and other sources of infection, or supervising disease-carrying overseas visitors) that benefit us all. Even here we can be charged for some, like inoculations. (A common mistake is to suppose that *all* health services are public.)

Public goods with some separable private services

So much for the main public goods in Group I. All the direct government services in Group II—roads, research, parks and pleasure grounds, "miscellaneous local government services" (perhaps sports and recreational facilities are tucked away here: they are not shown separately), police and fire services—have services supplied jointly. But equally obviously they all render, or could render, services that are individual and separable, though possibly to a lesser extent. And to this extent they could be financed by charges.

The reader accustomed to thinking of them as public services may be surprised, but I would ask him or her to recall that charging is being advocated because it is a better method of financing some services than is taxing. The scope for pricing local government services is discussed in Chapters 7 and 8.

The public corporations provide services like fuel, transport and telephones, that could be financed largely or wholly by charging but often are not. They are discussed in Chapter 9.

Public services with substantially separable private benefits

No less is this true of the welfare or social services in Group III.

Education

There are clearly personal separable services in education. In Australia the parents of one child in four pay fees. In Britain fees are paid for one child in twenty in addition to taxes for state education that some parents prefer not to use. This is not solely because of higher income but partly from preference; not all fee-payers are wealthy. In Australia parents who want to pay fees have been helped by being allowed to deduct fees, fares and other school costs from taxable income.

Health

In medical care also charges are conceivable, feasible and practicable, as has been seen in prescription, appliance and other charges in Britain, and as is clear from the practice of every other English-speaking and West European country, none of which has followed Britain in financing health services (almost wholly) by taxes. They use a variety of charges financed by a mixture of social and private insurance, and a mixture of voluntary insurance with compulsory insurance for basic and major ("catastrophic") health risks.

Personal social services

Personal social services (the official description) hardly require further argument: they are separable by definition. The confusion here has been between poverty and medical incapacity. Poverty is not a reason for "free" supply: people with low income can be enabled to pay by "topping up" their income. Neither is incapacity a reason for "free" supply, but for "topping up" the low incomes of incapacitated people. Here an important principle in social policy is much misunderstood. We help people not because they are old, or disabled, or widowed, or for any other physical or social deficiency, but where old age, disability or some other handicap prevents them from earning enough to pay. By no means all the old or incapacitated or widowed are poor; and the more help they receive the less is left for those who are.

Other public services with private benefits

Employment services, libraries, museums and the arts, sports and recreational amenities, housing, water, sewage, refuse disposal, transport: there is no technical obstacle in the way of supplying these personal separable services and financing them at least partly if not largely by charges. Then why are charges not used? What are the obstacles? That is the subject of Part 3. But before that we discuss possible methods of charging and the advantages of doing so in Part 2.

PART 2

You Pays Your Taxes, But You Gets No Choice

CHAPTER 4

Education: Paying for Consumer Power

One of the most important elements in the vast structure of so-called public services that, like Topsy, has "just growed" for a hundred years or more is education. State education has been created according to policies decided by central government, executed largely by local government, and financed by both with little heed to the preferences of mothers and fathers. Little wonder that politicians (Conservative as well as Labour), officials and teachers point to the incapacity of parents, and even lack of interest in education, as reasons for resisting efforts to give them more influence and authority in the curricula and conduct of British schools. Circular reasoning could hardly be more evident: parents cannot choose schools; therefore we will continue with the system that discourages them from learning how to choose.

In 1977 there is still little sign that the education pundits see the inconsistency in their claim that state paternalism must continue for ever more. They can hardly concede that family paternalism would not have tolerated the recent deterioration in tax-financed state schools and standards recognised, at long last, by a Labour Prime Minister. Good teachers will privately agree; their trade union officials and politicians will blithely talk of raising standards by continuing the old attitude of keeping parents out by not encouraging them into state schools. If parents had paid fees they would have made a fuss long before now.

Since 1870 education has increasingly been supplied more or less "free" by the state. To put it more honestly, it has been paid for increasingly by more and more of us through rates and taxes rather than by prices. Why? Were taxes the only way of paying for it? Are they now the best way?

This will be a fairly long chapter because it discusses general principles—in particular the objections to charging, choice and competition—that apply also to other public services. The following chapters on health, housing and others are accordingly shorter.

Not public goods

Most of us in Britain have never paid for education—directly. But as the lengthening list and rising costs of "free" goods and services require more taxes to be paid by people with middling and lower incomes as the wealthier are taxed to the limit, more and more of us are coming to know that payment must be made in the end by no one but ourselves. (The figures come in Chapter 10.)

But perhaps there is no other way? Perhaps, whether paying by taxes is the best way or not, it is the only *practicable* way and we must accept it whatever its disadvantages? That is not true. All forms of formal education, from nursery to adult, can be supplied to individuals separately, so they can be financed individually, as is informal education by books, lectures, visits to museums, travel and so on. They are predominantly not *public* goods in the sense that they cannot be refused to people who refuse to pay; they provide separable private services. They may have beneficial external effects in the sense that we all benefit from living with fellow-citizens who can read and write. That is a case for encouraging people to buy education by giving them cash (or vouchers) and possibly for setting school-leaving ages, but not for universal government control and tax financing of "free" schools.

Education is not supplied to individuals, or families, and paid for by prices (fees) instead of taxes because of the errors of intellectuals; the lack of vision of politicians; the empire-building pressures of officials; the resistance of teachers to change. And it is not sufficient for politicians, officials or teachers to reply that, whether my argument is right or not, we "cannot turn back the clock," or we "must start from here." These are little more than the alarmed reactions of people who fear change, who are finding reasons for rationalising their prejudices, who have probably never thought of better methods of financing, and who are putting themselves before the public who pay them. There is nothing impracticable in changing the financing of much or most of education from taxes to prices. The one requirement is sufficient public understanding of the issues, on which individual parents, who ultimately pay the teachers, have never had a chance to give their opinion in a way effective enough to change policy. Once the change is demanded, it could be introduced. The obstacles are man-made and removable by public pressure.

The reigning error

The errors go back to 1870. For many decades, since the early 1800s and even earlier, education had been spreading without government organisation or collective payment by taxes. The first state subsidy to (*private*) education came in 1833. Even from what we should now regard as tiny incomes, parents were finding the few pennies a week to send children to "voluntary" schools (as parents are now doing in low-income developing countries in Africa and Asia). The schools expanded from rather under half a million children in 1818, not long after the Napoleonic wars, to over one and a quarter million in 1834, and they could not all have been the children of the rich. Parents were helped to pay the fees by church and lay organisations.

Education developed in the nineteenth century much more than was generally thought until recently. We used to be taught that it was so meagre as barely to exist and was generally harsh and inhumane. Some teachers using out-of-date text-books still teach this history. They taught (and some still teach) that it was not until the state stepped in by the famous "Forster" Elementary Education Act of 1870 (so named after W. E. Forster, the Liberal Minister in charge of education under Gladstone) that education developed substantially and systematically. But in 1965 an economist turned historian, Professor E. G. West, in a book at first regarded as notorious but now seen as a classic, *Education and the State*,[1] questioned the conventional reading of history. By a pertinacious study of the documents, he found the evidence that stunned and angered some historians. The sources, he insisted, had not been studied or had been misread. This is a fascinating story in historical detective work, and the debate among the economic historians continues. In further writings, especially in *Education and the Industrial Revolution*,[2] Professor West persists with his findings.

Briefly, it seems that even by 1851 two out of three million working-class children were receiving some kind of daily instruction. It was, of course, short and inadequate by our present-day standards—only four, five or six years, ending around the age of ten. But it was spreading, and by 1870 more children were at school for more years than earlier, and were increasingly leaving later. Moreover, this schooling was entirely voluntary and almost entirely paid for by fees. Even where there was assistance from other sources (private, church or state grants) parents provided most of the money. The

1. West, E. G., *Education and the State*, IEA, 1965, 1970.
2. West, E. G., *Education and the Industrial Revolution*, Batsford, 1975.

old myths linger in school histories, in fiction and in politics, but Professor West's evidence stands.

British parents in the nineteenth century

Are we surprised? Commonsense and an elementary understanding of human nature should have made us doubt the view that it was not till Forster's Act created "board schools" that "a national system of education" (the supposed purpose of the 1870 Act) was developing. What seems to have happened was that too much attention was paid to the spectacular writings of the social novelists such as Dickens, Mrs. Gaskell and Disraeli who, like journalists and newspapers down the ages and round the world, attract attention by reporting and dramatising the exceptional rather than the general: it may be true, but it is not typical, and it makes bad history. Dotheboys Hall was a fictional creation based on a visit to a Yorkshire school in a cold winter in the late 1830s. Dickens, aged twenty-five or twenty-six, went with a false name and wrote up the school in *Nicholas Nickleby* in 1838. (A school history text-book published in 1965 still cites Dotheboys Hall as evidence of conditions in British schools.) Another economist and historian, Professor Mark Blaug, has found that, at least until very recently, conventional British histories of education largely ignored the evidence on the spread of literacy in the nineteenth century before the coming of state education in 1870. Yet school attendance and literacy in 1850 in England, *almost wholly privately-financed*, exceeded that in the world as a whole a century later.[3]

This neglect of the historical evidence probably reflects a perhaps unconscious sympathy with the massive critique of nineteenth-century industrialism taught for a century by historians from Arnold Toynbee in the 1880s, through influential social reformers like Sidney and Beatrice Webb and historians J. L. and Barbara Hammond, to such present-day historians as Professor E. J. Hobsbawm of Birkbeck College and E. P. Thompson. The neglect of the historical evidence on the spread of private education may be repaired more quickly as the long-held but erroneous view of the effects of industrialism on social conditions is also questioned by its critics, notably Dr. Max Hartwell of Oxford and other historians. (Dickens's "pious fraud" at Dotheboys Hall and its aftermath are recounted by Professor West in *Education*

3. Blaug, M., "The Economics of Education in English Classical Political Economy," in *Essays on Adam Smith*, University of Glasgow, 1976.

and the Industrial Revolution.[4] Dr. Hartwell and other historians write in *The Long Debate on Poverty.*[5] Readers who have unwittingly accepted the social novels of Charlotte Brontë, Charles Dickens, Benjamin Disraeli, Elizabeth Gaskell, Charles and Henry Kingsley, Charles Reade, Frances Trollope and other writers of fiction as social history will find these two books as exciting as detective stories.

But the neglect of the nineteenth-century evidence on literacy and spreading education paid for mainly by parents has done its work. The myth remains, stubborn and hard to dislodge, that education did not evolve spontaneously in response to parents' concern to educate their children but had to wait until politicians took it into their heads to tax parents in order to supply it "free."

Again I ask: why should we be surprised that parents, even a hundred or more years ago, wanted to educate their children? The question is of more than historical interest. For it points to two questions that are central to policy on education in the 1970s. First, if our grandparents and great-grandparents were sufficiently concerned about education to sacrifice the fees from their small incomes, are not we as parents today likely to be even more concerned about the education of our children? Second, if we (or at least 95 per cent of us) do not show that concern to the extent of dipping into our pockets, what is stopping us?

British parents in the twentieth century

These are the two most important questions we can ask about education. They are far more fundamental even than the one that seems to dominate discussion on education: whether all children shall be compulsorily channelled into standardised comprehensive schooling. The two questions are more fundamental because, until they are understood and answered to the satisfaction of parents, it is futile to discuss a form of education which *assumes* that parents have accepted educationists, officials or politicians as the ultimate arbiters of their children's education.

The answer to the first question must be that parents in the twentieth century would be even more concerned about education than their forebears were in the nineteenth. They would therefore be even more prepared

4. West, E. G., *Education and the Industrial Revolution.*

5. Hartwell, M., "The Consequences for the Poor of the Industrial Revolution," in *The Long Debate on Poverty,* IEA, 1972, 1974.

to dig into their pockets. And, since their real incomes are five to six times larger, their pockets are five or six times deeper, the fees they would have to dig out (or the premiums on insurance policies or instalments on credit schemes to stretch the fees out over longer periods) would be impressively large. *Moreover, they would probably in total be larger than the sums they pay for education through their taxes.* In other words, we should now, as individual families and as a country, be spending *more* on education than we do. And the gap reflects the wishes of parents that are thwarted by state education.

Parents who pay, moreover, would not only add resources beyond those that can be raised in taxes. They would also expect their money to be used more effectively by paying more attention to the way it was being spent by the schools. Asian parents from the backward rural districts of India visit their children's schools in Britain to monitor their progress because they paid fees at village schools and saw education as an investment. That is how paying stimulates parents' interest. And that is why non-paying in Britain has made some British parents uninterested in the education even of their own children.

A tax is a loss of income; a price is a disposal of income

Would parents really pay more in charges than in taxes? The reasoning again is based on common sense refined by economic observation, most recently confirmed by the increasing indifference to the "social wage" (which even shrewd but wishful-thinking politicians like Mr. Denis Healey used to think as recently as a year ago should reduce the pressure for inflationary wage settlements). There is a clear, rational and predictable distinction between the attitudes to paying taxes and to paying prices. A tax is felt as a forced extraction of resources; it is seen as a reduction of purchasing power; it conveys a sense of *loss,* once tolerated but increasingly resented. A price is seen as a voluntary act of using personal resources; it is seen as an exchange of purchasing power for a desired commodity or service; it conveys a sense of *gain,* since voluntary exchange is a game in which both sides win. (Unless both buyer and seller stand to gain from an act of sale, they will not take part.) The difference is that in a free exchange *both* sides are willing; in tax-payments normal taxpayers are unwilling because they see nothing in return.

This proposition on the difference between paying by taxes and charges may seem self-evident, even trite. When I argued it in 1965[6] it seemed obvious, certainly not original. Yet it ran contrary to the assumption underlying British social policy since then, and the whole thinking behind the welfare state which seemed to suppose that people would want to pay more in *taxes* so that everyone else could obtain social benefits—the source of the "social wage" fallacy. Trite or not, it explains much that has gone wrong with social policy in Britain—with the whole of the welfare state—and it is the key to how social services in particular and "public" services in general will have to be financed in the future. For it shows that if we are forced to pay by taxes instead of by prices we shall have less—of education, or anything else—than we should like to have and are able and willing to pay for. Payment by taxes—the financial mechanism of state education and the welfare state—prevents us from doing as much in welfare as we wish and can.

This is essentially the nub of truth in the views reached by Houghton and Crossman. Their diagnosis of the deficiency in finances was the same as here, though their solution was to graduate the social insurance contributions and offer larger *state* benefits to people who paid more. The outcome would then depend on whether people saw the contributions as taxes or prices. This truth also seemed to emerge from studies I had worked on with Ralph Harris at the Institute of Economic Affairs in 1963, 1965 and 1970 discussed in Chapter 10.[7] And it is also confirmed by Professor West's conclusion after ten years of research that by jumping on "the galloping horse" of fee-paid education in 1870 the state did not urge it on but probably slowed it down.

Parents would pay more in school fees than they save in taxes

So much for the first fundamental question. If, then, parents would by now be spending more on education in fees than they are paying for it in taxes, the answer to the second question (Why are they not?) must be the very taxes they have to pay to enable the state to provide education "free." Although people prefer to pay by service-related prices rather than by unrelated taxes, they are naturally reluctant to "pay double" for private services after being taxed to pay for the "public" services. As a result, the total spending on education (or health care, etc.) is kept down.

6. Seldon, A., "Which Way to Welfare," *Lloyds Bank Review,* 1965; and *Taxation and Welfare,* IEA, 1967.

7. Harris, R. (with Seldon, A.), *Choice in Welfare,* 1963, 1965, 1970, IEA, 1971.

This is the answer to two pretexts for state education: that many people could not pay the fees, and that, even if they could, they would spend their money on less worthy purposes. The first is circular reasoning: it is the state that makes people unable to pay fees. With a reverse tax to top up the low incomes the money would go direct from the parent to the school rather than through Whitehall or the town hall. Moreover, the bureaucracy would not cream off its upkeep en route. Not least, the money would go further because schools paid by parents would be more efficient in using resources to satisfy them: the dissatisfied customers' choice of going to competing schools would keep them on their toes much more than Parent-Teacher Associations, Parent Governors or other second-best substitutes.

The second pretext for state education—that parents who could pay fees would not—is also weak. No doubt some would not. But this again is circular reasoning. If parents in the twentieth century would neglect their children's education more than parents in the nineteenth, that must be because they have never had to give much thought to it while it was being supplied "free" by the state. The part of their minds that would have developed a stronger desire to educate their children has atrophied by neglect. It may take time to nurse it back to vigour as the method of payment changes from taxes to fees. Parents who require legally compulsory school-leaving ages to keep their children at school will need less compulsion as, in time, they learn the value of paying for education.

If, moreover, it were thought that returned taxes would not be spent on education they could, of course, be earmarked by being put in the form of a coupon or voucher that could be used only to pay school fees. The principle is essentially the same as the luncheon voucher, a paternalistic device in earmarked purchasing power designed to ensure that employees eat a sustaining meal. The education voucher would be a half-way house to the eventual policy of leaving income with taxpayers to use for education (Appendix 1). It could gradually be replaced by lower taxes, perhaps over twenty years, as the readiness of parents to buy education was strengthened by increasing knowledge of its benefits. And, as a final safeguard, a school-leaving age could be used as a long-stop for the dwindling minority of parents tempted to waste their vouchers by withdrawing their children early. Parental irresponsibility is an undeserved and insulting reflection on the good sense of working-class parents. It is no objection to changing from taxing to pricing in financing education.

How the education voucher would work

How would the education voucher work in practice? Its value could be calculated as the average cost of each child at a state school, or the average obtained by dividing state expenditure by *all* children, which would give a slightly lower figure because about 5 per cent are in private schools. It would be about £300 a year for primary schools, £450 for secondary schools and £800 for sixth forms; and 5 per cent less if it included all children. It is a form of purchasing power that can be used only for the named purpose and, just as a luncheon voucher can be used to buy lunch at a restaurant of the voucher-holder's choice, so the fundamental principle is that the education voucher would be used to pay for education at any school of the parent's choice.

So much is clear in principle. In practice how the voucher would work would vary with local circumstances. The only experiment in the world so far was for several years in a school district in California. Conditions in some respects were different from those in Britain but parents found a new interest in education by being able to choose between schools (and also between "mini-schools" in some of them). Here in Britain we must wait to see whether Kent County Council or any other local government will introduce an experiment.

Yet the general outline is clear enough. The secret of the voucher—the source of new "parent power" it would bring—is that it puts parents into the circulation of the money for education. It makes them the new source of finance for schools. As the system of state education developed, state schools looked to their local education authority for money, and it in turn looked to the central government. Parents have not come into the financial circulation at all. No headmaster or teacher thinks of being paid by parents; and no parent thinks he is paying his children's headmaster or teacher. The link between customer and supplier is completely broken. The voucher would restore the link by giving the parent purchasing power and thus change him (her) from a recipient of "free" education to a customer who pays for it with money. A voucher book could be issued each year with three vouchers, one for each term. The parent would take it to the school, to pay for education for a term; the headmaster would send the voucher to the local education authority, which would give him money in return.

The whole outlook of the school would thus change. Instead of looking to local politicians and officials as the source of its money for salaries, books, materials and so on, it would look to parents. It would thus want to know more and become much more aware of their opinions and preferences. The headmasters and teachers would, of course, retain the authority they acquire from their experience in teaching. A parent would, of course, still be *guided* by them. But no longer *directed.* The ultimate decision would be in the hands of parents, who would look for information and advice wherever they wished. Schools would be inclined to give much more information to parents, to welcome them into the work of the school, and to consult them on the reactions of their children to the school's teaching.

Teachers would remain the technical experts, but the respect they would win from parents would come from the quality of their advice and teaching, not from their status as employees of the local monopoly education authority. And in time the chances are that they would find more satisfaction in teaching children whose parents had chosen their school than in teaching children who were virtually captive customers who were stopped by teachers, officials, zoning or other devices from going where they preferred.

Strengthening and equalising choices

The range of choice would, of course, depend on the nature of the area. There would be more choice in towns and cities than in the country. But that is not an argument against having any choice in the towns at all, unless there is a virtue in the argument of the misanthrope that nobody should have anything unless everybody can have it. If you prefer to live in the country you may have a choice of only one church, cinema, garage or grocer. That is not a reason for not living in the country. It is your choice. It is certainly not a reason for making everyone who lives in a town or city have a choice of one church (what a row that would cause!), or one cinema, or one garage, or one grocer, or for putting all churches, etc., under state control.

All sorts of variants of the voucher idea can be envisaged. It can be taxed so that it has effectively less value for the family with more income than the family with less income. It can be confined to state schools but better extended to private schools to increase competition by comparison between them. Families can be allowed to top it up so that it can be used at schools whose fees are more than the cost of state schooling (though some are less). Or it can be available only for private schools prepared to accept it and not require topping up.[8]

8. Maynard, A., *Experiment with Choice in Education,* IEA, 1975.

The voucher idea has spread fast in the last year or two, and is also being discussed in Australia. The objections to it are fairly predictable. Some teachers may feel it would disrupt schooling, Labour Councillors that it would stop the onward march of comprehensivisation, some Liberals that they cannot see how it would work, and some Conservatives that parents cannot be expected to choose schools. All these objections are questionable. They prejudge the whole matter by all allowing apprehensions to replace evidence. If they have some validity the evidence would emerge only if the idea was tried out in practice. None of the objectors has much of a case against *experiments* to see how the voucher would work, so that their doubts and objections can be tested. They may be well-founded. But no one knows. What we do know is that keeping parents out of schools has failed to produce good education.

Whatever the objections in theory and the obstructions from politicians, bureaucrats or union officials in practice, the central significance of the voucher that is more important than all else is that it is a device—probably the only practical one under present circumstances—of giving ordinary people, not least the lower-paid working man and his wife, the same chance of having a say in education as the middle-class man who can pay fees, or the more monied man who can move home to escape a bad state school in the hope of being near a better state school, or anyone of whatever social class and income who can make a fuss and get his way by sheer persistence, nuisance-making or bullying. This, of course, is not a criticism of people who pay fees for private schools or who move homes to give their children a chance of better state education; on the contrary they should be praised for sacrificing other things for their children. Neither is it true that they are necessarily the more wealthy: it is a calumny on working-class parents to suppose they do not care about education, or would not care more if they had the opportunity. The essence of the voucher is that it would enable working-class parents to be able to make the choices of those with more money who now pay fees or move their homes. In this sense it is egalitarian. And, moreover, like charging in general, it is *educational:* it would in time *teach* parents how to choose schools. That is the retort to middle-class people in all parties who claim that parents cannot be trusted to choose. If nineteenth-century parents showed they cared about education it is unhistorical to suppose that twentieth-century parents do not, or would not if they could. The boot is on the other foot: it is those who talk like this who are perpetuating a system in which parents will never learn care or choice.

Elusive externalities of education

A third pretext for tax-paid state education is that it benefits society as well as individual families and children, that children "belong" to society as well as to their parents: school should therefore be tax-paid whether parents and children wish it or not.

This is an elusive argument. As discussed earlier, virtually every activity has externalities, beneficial or harmful. But, although strenuous efforts have been made to measure them, they often end in the mist of guesswork. Education was said to be a good thing for society in the nineteenth century because it would reduce crime or other anti-social behaviour. The chain of cause and effect is not clear, but in any event no one can show with conviction *how much* crime was avoided for *how much* expenditure. That is the relevant calculation. It is not enough to say "education will reduce crime." That is much too vague. It is the reduction in crime *at the margin* that must be calculated, compared and equated, for resources can be used in many other ways that people may prefer. A reduction in crime, even if certain, can be bought at too high a price in hospitals, housing, or pensions. And the onus of evidence is on those who make the claim. In any event, some forms of education, especially where parents are virtually excluded, may stimulate disrespect for people and property (would parents tolerate arson?), and other activities, like church-going, may reduce it.

The externalities argument is used much too loosely to justify untold public expenditure on anything that takes the reformer's fancy or captures the passing fashion. We should ask for more evidence than vague assertions from enthusiasts who want tax-money for their bright ideas but who will not put in their own. We should be especially on our guard when the expenditure is on a large scale and irreversible not least because among the opportunity costs are the piecemeal expenditures that have to be foregone on small-scale or local experiments to discover possible improvements in existing practices and institutions.

Are politicians better than parents?

Not least, we may recall that the "children belong to society" argument, or the "government should save children from their parents" argument, has been used by tyrants down the ages, and in our own day in Fascist and Communist countries, to mould society to suit themselves, not the long-term interests of the children or their parents. The Hitler Youth was a short-lived nightmare; its Communist counterparts are continuing present-day realities. If the choice in the control of children and education is to lie between parents and politicians, there can be little doubt which a civilised society will prefer. Parents may go wrong, but they can be guided and advised; politicians can do much good but also much evil, and when they go wrong they are usually out of control except by civil war. Payment by taxes gives parents little say: perhaps that is why politicians (and teachers' union officials) like it. And that is why parents should want to pay by prices.

The argument for paying fees rather than taxes applies to all forms of education. Fees for nursery schools to increase the number of nursery places were commended by several members of the 1966 Plowden Committee.[9] Primary and secondary schools could be paid for by fees facilitated or encouraged by tax refunds or rebates, or by vouchers. Further and higher (university) education fees could be facilitated by tax refunds and loans. So could fees for teacher training and adult education.

No parent can obtain better education by paying higher taxes

To replace (or, in the early stages, supplement) tax finance by prices we must contemplate a structure of school fees. Before we go further into it we should deal with two objections.

First, why pay fees when we already pay taxes? The reply is simply that taxes are not enough. If you as an individual parent want to pay more in taxes, no doubt the Inland Revenue or the local Council will welcome voluntary contributions, but your child will not receive better education. And if you think income tax or rates (or any other tax) should be raised for everyone, you are free to persuade the millions of other taxpayers to pay more in taxes than they are asked, or to petition Parliament to raise taxes for everyone. You will not have an easy task. Nor will you be popular. Even if you succeeded, education would remain "free," no one would know what it cost, and still the advantages of individual pricing—consumer authority—would be lost.

Second, is it wrong to have to pay for a service you must use by law? This odd argument has been used for decades for "public" services other than education. Is it really true that anything made compulsory by "the community" (a euphemism for Parliament, representative or unrepresentative)

9. Plowden Report, *Children and Their Primary Schools,* HMSO, 1967.

should be paid for by "the community," that is, by taxes? "The community" lays down a myriad of regulations for people as individuals or in groups (families, firms, voluntary associations, schools, etc.) to observe and pay for. It is compulsory for industrial buildings to have safety precautions, for firms to calculate PAYE deductions, for public houses to have separate lavatories for men and women, for hotels to have fire escapes, for motorists to have third party insurance. Does "the community" therefore pay all these costs? Or should we insist that because, say, motor insurance is compulsory, it must be supplied by government, even if the motorist believes he could get higher cover or a lower premium from a private company?

What is wrong is not to pay in prices for a compulsory service but the very opposite: for *it is inefficient to pay in taxes for a service that need not be supplied by government.* If education (of a specified kind or amount) is considered desirable by general agreement of citizens, government need go no further than to lay down standards—examinations, or other methods of checking on education imparted and acquired, school-leaving ages, and so on. What is improper is to oblige people to pay in taxes for compulsory service *unnecessarily* supplied by government without choice: and that is true of most so-called "public" services because they are not public goods.

Events will increasingly enforce attention to charging, but public opinion has yet to make itself effective. When the Government in 1976 was urgently considering cuts in its expenditure, a proposal from the Treasury for a £10 a year fee for state schools was quickly rejected as "politically impossible," without anyone asking the people if they would rather send their children to deteriorating schools. Thus are decisions made by the pundits, not by the people.

—but he can by paying prices

Whatever the differences of opinion about its quality, many people think that state education is short of resources and should have more. Others argue that it wastes a lot and may have too much. My argument is that, if taxes are not yielding enough to reflect family preferences, some other source of revenue must be found, and that the only new source is fees—or preferably topping up a voucher, which would be better than fees at least in the early stages because it would give all parents of children in state schools the new dimension of choice for which they would be prepared to pay something (Appendix 1).

The other facile solution—less spending on defence—is question-begging. To argue that the community would gain by diverting expenditure from defence to education requires knowledge about the value of marginal expenditure on defence which educationists cannot usually claim. As explained above, the choice is not between "defence" (bad) and "education" (good) *as a whole* but between additional (marginal) expenditure on one switched to it from the other. The National Union of Teachers is not an authoritative (or disinterested) witness on that judgement.

Would not fees for state schools reverse the tendency of a century? turn back the clock? go back to the bad old days? No. It would be a resumption of the natural wish of parents to educate their children. If the alternative to deteriorating education is higher taxes that people do not want to pay, the only way out is individual pricing in one form or another. Fees or vouchers would continue a trend that a century of "free" schooling has interrupted, but which would have continued if the politicians had encouraged it rather than denounced it as immoral.

This is the shock that will have to be absorbed if British education is not to deteriorate further. In the short run, for perhaps twenty years, revenue from fees allied to vouchers is the best way to avoid larger classes or ageing equipment and all the other symptoms of financial stringency and official rationing of resources. But I am also proposing that pricing be built into British education as a long-term principle, on the general grounds that financing education by pricing is superior.

Resources for education

The proposal is that education costs—from nursery school to further and higher education—should be covered by fees, most of which would be paid by the device of the voucher, with a small proportion (say 10 per cent) being "topped up" by the parents. With primary school costs at £300 a year for each pupil, parents could pay £30 a year, to top up a £270 voucher. With secondary school costs at £450 a year, parents would receive a £405 voucher, requiring £45 a year. Sixth-form costs are around £800 a year—voucher £720, topping up £80. A family with one child of each type could have three vouchers worth £1,395, requiring them to add £155, a small price for the influence and choice in education that state school parents have never had. Low-income parents could have 95 per cent or 100 per cent vouchers.

Let us begin with nursery education, recommended 44 years ago in the dark days of 1933 by the Hadow Report and again 33 years ago in the famous Butler Education Act of 1944. By 1966, 33 years after the Hadow Report and

22 years after the 1944 Act, "nothing effective" had been done, said a Note of Reservation to *Children and Their Primary Schools,*[10] the 1967 Plowden Report of the Central Advisory Council for Education (England), which courageously recommended nursery fees. This Note was signed by a distinguished group of academic and public people: Lady Plowden (the Chairman—or Chairwoman—of the Council), Professor A. J. (now Sir Alfred) Ayer, the Oxford philosopher, Dr. I. C. R. Byatt, Reader in Economics at the London School of Economics and later Under Secretary (Economics) at the Treasury, Professor D. V. Donnison, then Professor of Social Administration at the London School of Economics and later Chairman of the Supplementary Benefits Commission, Mr. E. W. Hawkins, Director, Language Teaching Centre, University of York, Mr. Tim Raison, MP, the former Conservative Shadow Minister for Local Government, Brigadier L. L. Thwaytes, Vice-Chairman, West Sussex County Council, and Dr. Michael Young, a former Director of Labour (Party) Research, of *Which?* fame, later Chairman of the National Consumer Council (appointed by Mrs. Shirley Williams in 1975). Their intelligent Note raises several fundamental issues in the financing of nursery education that also apply to education generally. It is examined here in detail to see how the assumptions behind it typify the kind of establishment thinking that any radical change will have to confront in education or anywhere else.

First, it said the reason why nothing much has been done by government since 1933 was "Quite simply there have not been enough resources, in teachers or buildings." This remark is characteristic of the confusion of thought on "public" services in general that has for a century made them public disservices and thwarted public preferences. It is the central error in the thinking of the pundits who have advised government and misled the public into denying itself services it wanted and could have paid for. There could have been—and were—resources for teachers and buildings. The trouble has been that they were misrouted elsewhere. The tragedy was that the state could not gather them *by taxation.* Parents had increasingly adequate purchasing power for nursery places but only a tiny minority thought of paying fees. (Local authorities would not always license nursery schools.) The vast majority did nothing about nursery places not because they had no resources (at least for a contribution) but because they simply did not think,

10. Plowden Report, *Children and Their Primary Schools.*

or know, that nursery places were something—like dancing lessons, or music training, or sports coaching—they could pay for.

Equality means waiting for the slowest

The essential error in this reasoning of the pundits is that in a democracy where government scrupulously reflects public wishes, the state has to wait until a decisive number of voters are prepared to pay for nursery places in taxes before *any* parent can have a nursery place. In democracy as it is operated in practice, parents have to wait until government thinks it is politically safe to compel *all* parents as taxpayers to pay for the nursery places wanted by *some.*

But in this system, in which consumers are represented by government, no individual parent can obtain a nursery place by paying more in taxes—however much he or she is prepared to sacrifice other expenditure regarded as less important for the family. This is the end result of the view that some services, like education, should be equally available to all. Right or wrong, it has consequences that have rarely been discussed in Britain. By transferring decisions from the parent to politicians it reduces the total amount of resources channelled to these services. Parents who would be the earliest to pay for nursery places do not pay by fees and are not required to spend anything in taxes until a large number of other parents are also demanding them. But others who would follow once they had been shown what could be done have no information to guide them; so they are less likely to demand a "public" service, and meanwhile they too spend nothing in fees.

The myopia fallacy

The eight signatories of the Plowden Note of Reservation proposed, rather tentatively and timidly, "a parental contribution" to the costs of nursery education. They argued that the contribution would be for the benefit of children whose parents could not pay it as well as of children whose parents could. Without it, nursery education could not be extended at all, and the children of parents who did not pay would be no better off. With the new fee there would be new nursery schools or classes that could be attended by children of poorer parents both in "educational priority" areas and others. Charging the parents who were richer (and/or had smaller families) would thus help parents who were poorer (and/or had larger families).

This reasoning is, of course, correct; but there is another fundamental error in the thinking that has dominated British social policy. If we are never to do anything in education (or medical care or anything else) unless it can be provided *immediately* for all, whatever their income, size of family or other circumstances, we shall be prevented from developing policy in ways that would help the most unfavoured families *eventually.* The argument for equality as deployed by egalitarians sometimes seems to have no dimension of *time.* Not everything can be done at once for everybody everywhere. The signatories knew that nursery schools would develop spontaneously in some districts sooner and faster than in others, but they did not seem to understand that gradual piecemeal development can be an advantage, not a defect. It enables those that come later to benefit from the mistakes of those that came earlier. And if they came earlier because local parents' incomes were higher (or, often overlooked, because they preferred education to other spending out of middling or lower incomes, as farm and town labourers did in the nineteenth century) they could confer the benefits of that experience on the poorer or the more conservative who came later. This externality of the rich (or of the not rich but loving) parent is usually overlooked, especially by sociologists who have approached social policy from the poverty end and who have put equality before the long-term interests of the poor.

Through the voucher to equality

In any event, the poorest and largest families can be helped to pay by making them less poor by general cash grants or by earmarked nursery grants in the form of a voucher. The Plowden minority, instead, favoured remission of fees, and then, in fear that some poorer or larger families would be too proud to accept remission and so would deny their children nursery education, they admonished them to remember that many parents, including the poorest, accepted state support for university education. "If in universities," they asked, "why not in nursery schools?"

This obstacle of pride would disappear if parents received vouchers, or even an additional nursery-school component on the family allowance (which hardly any parent, however rich, rejects). All parents would then pay the charge without social differentiation, with no exemptions as a source of social divisiveness, with more dignity for the poorer, and with no lack of take-up. There would be the added advantage that poor parents would feel they were paying on an equal footing with all other parents, not receiving a free gift for which they should be grateful. It would, far more than remissions, give them not only an equal voice with all other parents but also a voice made effective by the power of exit—to withdraw their child to another nursery school if dissatisfied.

Affluence and externalities

In urging the charge, the Plowden minority said they recognised that "in public services benefits and contributions to cost cannot, and should not, be precisely equated. Public services exist where one cannot, and should not, try to [equate them]." They went on to give two very revealing grounds for arguing that nursery education was, perhaps, not nowadays a public service. First, people would not pay taxes to provide it, for themselves or for others. Second, parents were (in 1966) "more affluent [and] more interested in education."

The first reason seems to suggest that people become more unwilling to pay taxes for public services at a time when they are becoming more affluent. That notion conflicts with the theory taught by the leaders of British social thought, from the Fabians in the 1880s through the Beveridge-Liberals to the paternalistic Butler-Conservatives. What becomes of the theory of the "social wage" in state benefits in kind like education that people will, we have long been assured, readily pay for? The second reason destroys two of the ancillary arguments for making a service public: that people could not pay (primary poverty) or would not pay even when they could (secondary poverty). "Today," said the Plowden minority, "*they are for the most part able and willing to contribute.*" (My italics.) That is the most profound sentence in the Note by these eight eminent academics and public people. If people can and will pay for a service there is no reason on grounds of poverty or irresponsibility for making it public and paying for it by taxes.

Fees for nursery education are practicable and could be economic. They are paid voluntarily in Britain on a small scale and in varying degrees in Western countries and Communist countries (including Russia). In Britain they are opposed by out-of-date conservative Tories, Liberals and Fabians.

Other forms of education

If this reasoning—that people are increasingly able and willing to pay—applies to nursery education, why should it not apply to other forms of education? They are also short of resources, and it has evidently been found impossible to supply enough out of taxation. People resist higher taxes no less for primary, secondary, further, higher, adult, teacher training, recreational, physical training, or any other form of education. They simply do not like paying higher taxes. Perhaps once they may have resented higher taxes less for purposes they approved, such as retirement pensions,[11] but there is no knowing that their taxes will go to these causes. Even national insurance contributions are not earmarked for stated benefits, and there is no assurance that hard-pressed governments will reserve incoming monies for intended destinations. But if they are able and willing to pay for nursery education they are willing, and could be made able, by vouchers and lower taxes for all and reverse taxes for some, to pay for other kinds of education.

There is no shortage of money in Britain for as good education as the people want. How much there is in total and where it would come from are discussed in Chapter 10. Paying for education by fees from parents is financially possible, even though most have never thought of doing it and 95 per cent have never done it.

By 1978 or 1980, the cost of educating a child in a state primary school may be around £350 a year, in a secondary school around £600 a year, and in the sixth form £1,000. These fees could be reached in three, five or seven years, beginning with a nominal amount in the first year, rising by annual increments, and assisted by vouchers, tax refunds or tax allowances, by transfers of expenditure from other goods and services, for people with little or no income by a reverse income tax, and by earning to pay for something really worthwhile for the first time. There would be no hardship or injustice. There would be no disruption if the change took place over a period. But the transition should not be unnecessarily long. It should be short enough to encourage every family to give education the thought it has never had in planning the household budget.

Charging for choice

The transition would be eased by making education a better product than it has been in the past and so "worth paying for." The most effective way would be to supply the ingredient that is missing in tax-paid (in contrast to fee-paid) education: choice, and the influence and authority that go with it. The transition to full fee-paying by all parents would be eased if the new dimension of choice were created and made effective by returning taxes in the

11. Seldon, A., *Taxation and Welfare*, IEA, 1967; and Seldon, A. (with Gray, H.), *Universal or Selective Social Benefits*, IEA, 1967.

physical form of a document empowering the parent to pay for education wherever he found it to his liking. This is the education voucher.

Further and other education

Table C in Chapter 3 indicates the other main forms of education provided by local government, and now financed by local rates and national taxes transferred to local government.

Higher (university) education is financed mainly (about 90 per cent) by central government through the University Grants Committee.

The special schools are essentially for handicapped children and young people, who are not necessarily poor. Whether they should continue to be paid for by taxes turns on the role assigned to the family. If a handicapped child is regarded as the responsibility of the family, the parents should pay if they can, or be enabled to pay if they cannot. If the child is regarded as a responsibility of society, its cost should be paid by taxes.

None of further education is compulsory, so there is not even that pretext for financing it by taxes. The same applies to other education services, and to school food.

University students pay on average 10 per cent of their fees, often with assistance from local government. These fees could be raised to cover costs with the assistance over five years of loans and vouchers. The independent University College of Buckingham is the first pioneer for centuries in fee-paid higher education.

Overseas students are no exception. If it is decided for political reasons that Britain benefits by educating them, whether they are rich or poor, and whether their government will pay or not, they could be given vouchers to pay fees. To decide the value of the voucher, the external benefit (to Britain) would have to be measured, a difficult task that might yield estimates varying from substantial amounts to nil. (Detriments would have to be assessed as well as benefits.) But the hard-pressed British taxpayer should require something more than vague assertions of intangible externalities to support large claims on tax revenue. For the opportunity costs in higher pensions for older people with little other income, or in more money for the police, or for under-five play groups, must be weighed in the balance.

CHAPTER 5

Medical Care: Making the Payment Fit the Case

Few of us under forty-five remember paying for medical care directly. Yet few health services are public goods, in the sense used in this book. Preventive measures benefit everyone in the area whether they pay or not, so charging is impracticable or uneconomic; but hospital treatment is private, family doctor services are essentially personal, most local authority services are separable and personal—health centres, midwifery, health visitors, home nursing, ambulance, family planning.

There are some "catastrophic" risks (such as major surgery or crippling diseases) against which it is very costly to insure, and people may fatalistically prefer to run the risks rather than reduce their living standards by insuring against a rare disease or an accident that may never happen. It is possible for individuals or for society as a whole to pay too much to restore health after disasters.

This reasoning may sound harsh, but it is people who ignore the "opportunity costs"—the enormous sacrifice in education, housing, or pensions or everyday consumption required for total health—who are (unwittingly) callous. People make better judgements as individuals than in the mass. No individual man (or woman) thinks health must be secured at *all* costs: he (or she) would otherwise never cross the road, or smoke, or swim, or fly, or eat without a food taster. It is only the National Health Service—a mass, make-believe, macro-artifact—that teaches the myth that the best health can be preserved or restored "free" for all. In practice it does not do what it preaches: it has to ration kidney machines, for example, and so condemns some patients to death. (And it is a bit of a fraud as a supposedly comprehensive "National" "Health" Service. It is both too all-embracing, since it comprises private benefits as well as public goods, and not all-embracing enough, since it does not supply all the services required for good health—the right food and other requisites.)

In the real world there are unavoidable or accepted risks to health, and treating ill-health uses resources. The costs can mostly be covered by insurance, and people with low incomes can be enabled to insure by a reverse income tax or by having their premiums paid on a sliding scale by government, as has been done in Australia. Catastrophic risks can be collectively tax-paid, as war damage was from 1939 to 1945. Most Western industrialised countries have mixtures of social and private, compulsory and voluntary, insurance. The result is that they channel more resources per head to medical care than we in Britain, who for the most part (95 per cent) are allowed to pay only by taxation. In Europe, North America, Australasia 6½ to 8 per cent of the Gross National Product goes to medical care; in Britain it is barely 5½ per cent. The higher figure indicates the advantages of diversifying sources of finance. Perhaps even more important, it reflects the preferences of the people who pay. This is the reply to defenders of the British system, which relies mainly on one source, who say that resources, even if less in Britain, are used more efficiently than in other countries. The reply is that, whatever the relative efficiency of the British state system, which is debatable, it does not allow people to pay in the ways they prefer. It is imposed on the people by politicians, officials and "experts" who claim they know better. They have not been able to escape from it because all the political parties have supported it.

That is why we in Britain—and only we in Britain among Western industrialised countries—have a "National Health Service." The reason asserted for making people pay by taxes is that it removes the price barrier, so that everyone can have the treatment he "needs" without worrying about paying. This may be the reason that moved the early enthusiasts for the NHS, like Aneurin Bevan in 1946, but it is still being repeated by his followers today, thirty years later, when social conditions have changed beyond recognition so that many can pay, directly out of pocket or by insurance, and when, in any event, the methods of dealing with poverty have been transformed and it is no longer an insurmountable barrier to medical care.

Not a public good: instant equality

The real, main motive for replacing prices by taxes in 1946, and for persisting with taxes despite the social and economic changes of the intervening thirty years, has nothing to do with medical care as a public good. Nor is the motive basically the desire to deal with poverty: that idea appeals to compassionate enthusiasts, but at the bottom it is a politician's rationalisation. The motive may have a tenuous connection with irresponsibility—by replacing the supposedly callous parent or relative and the amateur patient by the informed and kindly state. It may use externalities as a supporting pretext, though there are other methods for dealing with social benefits of medical care than abolishing pricing. It claims to have something to do with economy by avoiding duplication in medical services or insurance financing, though the NHS bureaucracy burdens medical care with delays and piles up administrative costs. And the NHS monopoly has no internal generator of efficiency.

The central motive for maintaining state medicine in the face of economic change is rather the anxiety of impatient reformers who want to establish instant equality; they dislike the reverse income tax because they think paying for medical care is "obscene," and they cannot wait for incomes to be equalised as social mobility spreads the opportunity to learn and to earn.

Rationing health care

What stands in the way of equality of access to medical care (or anything else) is inequality of income. This inequality produces unequal *demand* for medical care, and it is tempting to take the short cut of making income irrelevant and equalising the *supply* by announcing that it is available "free" without limit to all comers. This is called abolishing "rationing by the purse." It has externalities: it makes politicians important and creates jobs for bureaucrats.

But it does not abolish rationing. Since there is no price to apportion supply between the various demands, there must be rationing by other means. In the National Health Service medical care is rationed above all by time. "First come, first served" sounds fair but it favours the fleet of foot, the loud in voice. People and patients who are rich in time receive more or better medical care than those who are poor in time. The more individuals can wait and queue, the more attention or the better treatment they receive. So the work-evading worker or the self-centred housewife has better access to the National Health Service and gets more out of it than the conscientious worker or the selfless housewife. What sort of equality is that?

The other rationing devices, no less arbitrary, are influence (if you know your doctor or hospital official you are treated better than if you don't), literacy (the middle classes who speak the same language as the doctor do better than the working classes), cunning (those of any class who know how to "work" the system do better than those who resignedly accept it), sex-attraction (which favours women), blackmail (of doctors who will not readily sign certificates), and other arbitrary influences like political status which ensures earlier treatment for Ministers than for the taxpayers they are supposed to serve.

The irony of rationing under the National Health Service, which its enthusiasts will not face, is that these differences are even more objectionable than differences in income, which at least to some degree reflect differences in value to the community. For differences in influence and bully-power are even more difficult to reduce or remove. Favouritism is more widespread in the National Health Service than we like to admit, as it is in other "free" systems in Russia, Hungary, Poland and Bulgaria. The NHS has not abolished inequality: it has driven inequality underground and made it more difficult to correct.

The strongest argument against the NHS and its replacement of pricing by taxing is that it prevents us from channeling as much resources to medical care as we wish. Evidence from other countries seems to show that tax-financing reduces the funds for salaries, equipment and buildings for health centres and hospitals. Americans and others who return to their countries with praise of the National Health Service speak of their experience with it in emergency. People in their countries are not told (because tourists do not stay long enough to find out) of the months or years waiting for "cold" surgery or "elective" (optional) treatments that may turn "hot" and imperative in the waiting. There is almost no discussion in Britain of the central reason why doctors emigrate and patients wait, surgeons lament inadequate equipment, research languishes, casualty departments are closed, wards are short of nurses. The central reason is that, since people and patients do not pay directly by fees but indirectly by taxes, the decisions are made by the politicians, guided and advised by officials, who can impose their notions of the good and the bad. And the "good" notion for thirty years has been that price stands in the way of equality of access and shall therefore be banned *even if the resources channelled to medical care are less than they otherwise would be.* That is the truth that no amount of repeated assertion that "the National Health Service is the envy of the world" can suppress.

Paying by pricing (through insurance) can be restored. The choice is between the "planned," tidy, tax-financed National Health Service with less resources and a priced system with more resources, organised and financed by diverse methods. The obstacles are not technical but political: if we showed we preferred better medical care for all to less medical care (endured in the name of equality but still unequal in practice, whatever the objective), the politicians and the officials would have to find the way. The essential is that the red herring of equality shall be recognised and abandoned. Here as elsewhere it has barred the way to better service for all.

More resources for medical care

The extent to which better medical care could be available for all is indicated by the additional resources that would be assembled if we could pay by prices (based on insurance). We should then be spending, in all, in my judgement, something of the order of 6½ to 7½ per cent of the GNP, as they do in Europe and Australasia (even more is spent in North America). If we take the mid-way point of 7 per cent, we should be spending £7,000 million on medical care, not the barely £5,500 million that is all the state can extract in taxes for the National Health Service—or more than 25 per cent as much. The additional £1,500 million could go on higher pay for doctors, nurses and non-medical staff, better equipment, more pain-killing or life-saving medicines and machines, more new buildings and, not least, in ridding the poorest and the less articulate of the queuing and the waiting, the subservience and the obsequiousness that go with the tax-financing of medical care.

The medical services that should remain financed wholly or largely by taxes are those that are public goods with inseparable private benefits. They are the environmental and preventive services, largely local, shown in Table C of Chapter 3. The remainder of medical care yields separable benefits that can in principle be paid for by pricing (charges for goods, fees for services). When the third or fourth crisis in NHS finances came in 1967, 17,000 family doctors had signed un-dated letters of resignation (as self-employed they do not strike). The British Medical Association appointed a panel of ten doctors and two independent laymen to draw up a new structure of financing medical care in the event of a breakdown in the NHS. The Chairman was Dr. Ivor M. Jones, a general practitioner of outstanding ability, dialectical skill and negotiating power. The panel spent two years, 1968 and 1969, studying the weaknesses of tax-financing in Britain and the wider varieties of financing used in almost every other Western country, as well as the methods used in the Communist countries, to see what could be learned. (The Western countries were Australia, Austria, France, Germany, Iceland, Luxembourg, the Netherlands, Belgium, New Zealand, Norway, Sweden, Switzerland and the USA.) It reported in April 1970, but by then the government had granted terms the doctors considered acceptable, and the 600-page report, *Health Services Financing*, was pigeon-holed (and cold-shouldered) by the BMA hierarchs, perhaps because it had become an embarrassing reminder of earlier friction with a government with which the doctors had come to terms. But five years later, in 1975, the fifth or sixth crisis in the long history of chronic financial deficiency came when the swollen government spending made possible by three years of mounting overseas borrowing was cut back. This contraction, combined with the apparent determination of the Government to increase the tax-financing from 95 to 100 per cent and squeeze out private medicine, brought stronger action from the doctors than ever before, including unprecedented working to rule and strikes.

Hitherto the hope of doctors had been that they would be able to persuade a strong Minister, Labour or Conservative, to squeeze more for the NHS out of the Chancellor of the Exchequer in the Cabinet room. Sir Keith Joseph is said to have succeeded with Mr. Anthony (now Lord) Barber in 1971 or 1972. Mrs. Barbara Castle is also supposed to have had some success in 1974 and 1975. But since late 1975 cuts have been the order of the day, even for the "essential" NHS. Some senior doctors then began to wonder whether the NHS would ever find as much money for medical care as they thought it should and could have. Apart from some flirting with the fond hope, which has long attracted doctors, that government would give them the money through a Health Corporation or some such mechanism and let them spend it as their medical judgement told them and without political intervention, they returned to the argument of the Ivor Jones report as indicating the alternative to tax-financing in their evidence to yet another Royal Commission in 1976.

Like the agreed unanimous reports of all committees, the Ivor Jones Report was a compromise, but it was the first attempt since the foundation of the NHS to document a new financing mechanism in place of almost total reliance on taxation. Because the doctors, some with reluctance, were at last prepared to contemplate a change from taxing to pricing, as one of the independents I signed the report although I did not agree with its proposed division of health services between tax-financed and price-financed (based on insurance). (There was a puzzling BMA prejudice in favour of "free" drugs.) It would have clarified the argument if I had put my list in a minority Note. But the central principle was established, and worked out in some detail, that tax-financing was not suitable for all medical services.

The sole criterion for obligatory tax-financing is whether a service is a public good with inseparable private benefits. Other reasons—inequality in income, efficiency, monopoly, etc.—may make taxing desirable but have to be proved. On this principle, hospitals, general practitioners and dental and ophthalmic surgeons and local authorities can be paid by fees (which can mostly be insured). Drugs and appliances, too, could mostly be covered by insurance. It is true that half of the 450,000 hospital beds are occupied by long-term chronic cases of old and mental patients, who are not all poor but whom it may be administratively simplest to finance by taxes. Severe or "catastrophic" acute cases, such as polio, or heart disease, or kidney failure or major accidents may require heavy expenses that are difficult to insure. These also may best be paid by taxes if they cannot be covered by state-assisted insurance.

Evolving a refined structure of charging

In all, a much more refined financing mechanism is required than taxation, both to minimise the deterrent effect to patients of fees or insurance costs and to use price as a reminder to them and to doctors and nurses that medical care uses scarce resources that could be applied elsewhere. Other countries such as Australia and the USA have gradually evolved and refined mixtures of voluntary and compulsory, state and private insurance, co-insurance or "patient's fractions" (where the patient bears a proportion of charges shared with the insurer) and deductibles (where the patient bears the first slice of the charge), state assistance for low-income people to enable them to insure along with everyone else, and so on. These mixtures are not as tidy as tax-financing, which is what politicians and bureaucrats prefer, but for patients their very advantage is that they are all more varied and flexible, as they should be in financing the wide range of services, from emergency treatment for heart failure to optional surgery for varicose veins, that in Britain are bundled together and described, grandly but simplistically, as "the National Health Service"—a name no scientist or patient or economist concerned with individual circumstances would have given it, but which comes naturally from an administrator or a planner excited by organising services for large numbers.

The main triumph of the mixed systems overseas is that they maximise the resources for medical care, which the NHS does not. More accurately, they approach nearer to the *optimum* amount, in the sense that they enable people to say how much they want to spend on medical care at the expense of all the other goods and services they could have. These mixed systems create no false hopes and no myths. They show what the vast range of medical services cost, and they allow people to pay in the ways they prefer. They have created no Nirvana, or mirage of "the best medical care for everyone," which we in Britain have been misled into thinking was not only possible but what the NHS was giving us in our everyday lives, but which it has not given, does not give, and cannot ever give.

Here again the voucher could be used to ease the transition from taxation to charging. In medical care it would cover not fees, as in education, but insurance costs, or a proportion of them. Topping up the voucher out of pocket would be the source of additional finance for medical care. The IEA surveys again showed impressive interest in health vouchers in all social classes (Appendix 1). More than a third of the highest incomes and (even more surprising) more than a quarter of the lowest incomes said they would make up a two-thirds voucher if they could insure privately. These proportions would grow once the system started.

CHAPTER 6

Homes: Ending the Rent-Tie

A third of us (or more) have never paid for our homes—directly. For increasing millions, housing is another long-standing "public service" that is not a public good. It can be supplied separately to individuals and therefore paid for directly by prices (rents, or mortgage repayments, or purchase money). Yet it remains paid by taxes, in part or large part for millions. In all, taxes have paid around 40 per cent of Council rents (Table C).

Indictment of house-financing by taxation

Restricting rents began in 1915 with the aim of limiting the rising costs of living in wartime. As a short-term measure it might have been convenient, but it has now lasted over sixty years. It has spread to 6 million households in government-owned homes and 4½ million in private homes. It has dried up private investment in house-building to let. It has entangled local government in owning houses and building them, sometimes by costly direct labour. It has forced central government to provide large subsidies. It has brought rationing by official rules, favouritism by officialdom, personal frustrations, political bribery and bureaucratic bullying, the corruption of government officials and local government, the spilling over of rent controls to privately-owned homes. It has intensified immobility of labour penalised by losing rent subsidies if it moves house. It has created the vested interest of direct (building) labour. It has manufactured a large constituency of rent-favoured yet degraded tenants, and made politicians more concerned with how tenants will vote at the next election than with the efficient use of resources in home-building and maintenance. With the best of intentions rent restrictions have had the worst of results: in intensifying shortages of homes, worsening dilapidations of existing structures, destroying the incentives to build, and ignoring people's preferences. More perhaps than any other social policy, British housing displays the abject failure of political sensitivity to public circumstances and preferences that is the disagreeable reality behind the facade of "public" service.

None of this was unavoidable. It has happened not because rent control was the only way to deal with rising rents or low incomes but because it was the politicians' easiest way to public favour by being seen to be protecting the poor in general and the tenant in particular against inflation or "landlordism," the declamation of the demagogue down the decades. Politicians in all democratic countries display the same anxieties to be seen to be up and doing: rent restriction has been their favoured instrument in Europe, North America and Australasia. And always it has the same results.[1]

Political difficulty of removing tax-finance

Even when politicians come to see the results of tax-finance on housing, and are appalled, as they gradually are becoming in Britain, they encounter the same difficulties in ridding the country of the cause. Even when it is removed (as largely in Australia, though it lingered in New South Wales), the memory of it and the fear of it returning continue to deter the building of homes to let and so perpetuate its results long after it is discarded. Austria, the USA, France, Britain and Sweden tell much the same story. In all of them (and some others) valiant, painful efforts have been made by a few brave or more sensitive spirits among the politicians to thaw out the ice of frozen rents, as in the British Rent Act of 1957 (for which one of the Conservative intellectuals, Enoch Powell, should be praised). The 1965 Act re-froze the ice by extending controls. The 1972 Housing Finance Act tried to rethaw the ice by replacing subsidised rents with rent allowances (cash) for private tenants and rent rebates for Council tenants, but was obstructed by political demagoguery. The 1974 Housing, Rents and Subsidies Act, which froze the ice on rents for furnished flats, has dried up their supply.

Politicians in all parties who saw the case for thawing out rents have defended their inaction with the excuse that rents could not be raised to cover costs as long as there was a scarcity of housing. This is putting the cart before the horse. There is always a scarcity of housing, as there is of everything else, otherwise there would be no prices. Charging less than "economic" (market) rents itself creates shortages by swelling demand and choking off supply. A rise in rents nearer to current housing costs was a necessary pre-condition for diminishing the scarcity and removing the shortage by increasing the number of homes built. The real obstacle to an increase in building for let-

1. Friedman, M. (with others), *Verdict on Rent Control*, IEA, 1972.

ting was the lack of faith that the politicians would raise official rents nearer to housing costs, or that, having raised them and abolished rent controls, they would not be tempted to restore them for electoral reasons.

Whenever an opponent of reform obstructs it by admonishing us to "face the facts," to "start from here" and begin with the undesirable policies and practices we wish to reform, we should reply that to reform the present we must understand not only how it began but also what could, or would, have happened in its place. There are still some Bourbons (in all parties and none—like Shelter) who have said that the fault with rent control is that it is not strict or extensive enough. They have had their way; in 1974 it was extended from unfurnished to furnished rooms; students who want furnished rooms are learning first hand of the difficulties of families who have long wanted unfurnished flats or houses but found they had vanished.

The long leap in restoring market prices

To the more intelligent but conservative-minded, and to the timid in all parties who say that rent restriction is unfortunate or dreadful but has come to stay, and all that can be done is to remove its worst effects by making rents a little more flexible, we must reply that if you are surrounded by a swamp a short step is futile: the only hope is a giant leap.

A long leap is now the only hope of escape from the bog of rent control. It will become possible when the people understand what would have happened if rent control had been nipped in the bud in 1919 after the First World War before it had sunk its roots, before it had frightened off people who would otherwise have continued the pre-1914 development of investment in home-building to let, so that in 1919 local government had to be required by the Housing and Town Planning Act to build the first of the Council houses that now house more than one family in three. The alternative that would have developed since 1919 is home-ownership. By now we should have had not the 50 per cent of households it recently reached in Britain (9 million home-owners out of 18 million households) but the 67 per cent as in the USA or 75 per cent as in Australia. Three to five million rent-paying tenants in Council or private houses or flats would be owner-occupiers. When the public understands that this is the perfectly practicable alternative, ways will be found by politicians and officials, and we shall hear less of "difficulties" and "facing facts." When a politician "faces the facts" of electoral opinion, voters' displeasure or ballot box rejection, he finds ways to act.

The only fundamental solution to the politicians' failure to stop the (partial) financing of housing by taxes is to replace them by prices, that is by rents. The only long-run solution to the evils created by lingering tolerance of restrictions on rents is to remove the restrictions. The only lasting solution is to let people pay for their homes by prices, by allowing rents to rise to the amounts agreed between suppliers of homes to let and people who want them. This is the only way of allowing people to decide whether they want to continue as tenants or to own their homes. Since in time more (perhaps most) tenants of rent-restricted Council or private homes would move to ownership, Councils could at last move out of owning and building homes into which they should never have been misled by central government, and private owners would put their rented houses and flats into good repair and build more for people who preferred hiring to owning their homes.

Here again the voucher could be used, initially to help low-income families and then rent-restricted tenants generally, both Council and private, to rent or buy homes of their choice. In Australia a Housing Assistance Voucher Experiment is enabling tenants in "public" housing estates to escape to other areas and to private housing.

The argument that subsidies to purchasers of homes should be removed in parallel with subsidies to tenants raises wider issues. Removing the tax allowance on mortgage interest would logically require the removal of all fiscal encouragement to long-term saving, as in life assurance and pensions. To avoid biasing the choice between tenancy and ownership, all subsidies should be removed. If it were desired to encourage home ownership in all income groups, the objection to the (income) tax rebate on mortgage interest is that, by definition, it varies directly with income, so that the man with higher income who buys a larger house with a larger mortgage receives a larger subsidy than the man with lower income who buys a smaller house with a smaller mortgage. But that is a consequence of progressive taxation. If income taxation were more proportional, the objection would be weakened. If the tax assistance were varied indirectly with income, as it could be in a housing voucher, the objection would have changed its ground.

Second-best solutions

Raising rents to cover costs is the best long-term solution. All others are second-best. It is the measure of the long years of political neglect that second-best solutions should have to be sought. They all have the flavour of short-cuts—from selling Council houses to occupying tenants at a privileged price to ease them out, to giving Council houses away in order to get tenants off ratepayers' backs. They are best used as means of hastening the long-term solution. A package of policies, comprising the long-term solution and short- and medium-term cuts in tune with it could be:

1. All rents, Council and private, to rise by annual instalments to cover housing costs in four years;
2. between 1977 and 1980 local authorities to be empowered to offer tenants first claim on Council houses to be sold by auction[2] either (a) individually to occupier-buyers (existing tenants or others) or (b) in parcels to home-renovators for improvement and re-sale to individual occupier-buyers in the open market;
3. tenants under forty-five with income below a stated sum to be offered matching finance of £1 for £1 found for the deposit on a home; half to be repaid in seven years;
4. tenants of forty-five and over with income below the stated sum to be given half of the deposit; a quarter to be repaid in five years; pensioners with no other income to be left in occupation for life, without succession;
5. from 1977 to 1980 rent subsidies to be made mobile to remove the penalty on mobility.[3]

Tenants would by these measures be enabled to make informed decisions on renting or owning, staying put or moving, and be given incentives to change to larger or smaller homes, and so on. Millions have never made these decisions, or have not made them for years, so that many are in the wrong homes and places, and are using methods of payment that no longer reflect their underlying preferences. In this way people would sort themselves out and end by living in homes that suited them better; they would no longer be tied to their houses or flats by outdated subsidies, they would make better use of the stock of homes, and they would have an effective mechanism (rent-price) for indicating what sort of homes they wanted.

In housing, as elsewhere, charging rather than taxing, when the results of both are explained, is what the people would prefer. It is not public opinion but political punditry that stands in the way.

2. Pennance, F. G., "Introduction," *Verdict on Rent Control,* IEA, 1972.
3. Pennance, F. G. (with Gray, H.), *Choice in Housing,* IEA, 1968.

CHAPTER 7

From Reading to Rubbish

There could be no more decisive demonstration of the argument for changing to the maximum possible extent from taxing to pricing "public" services than the talk-in between the political and bureaucratic pundits far over the heads of the populace on PESC, PAR, PEC, and PAC (below). The score in debating points has swung this way and that. The outcome is still in doubt. The pundits on both (or all) sides seem to be enjoying it. There is hardly a ratepayer or taxpayer in sight.

Here is Mr. Roland Freeman (Conservative), formerly finance chairman (a sort of local Chancellor of the Exchequer) of the Inner London Education Authority (ILEA) and later of the Greater London Council (GLC), doing battle with Lord Diamond (Labour), former Chief Secretary of the Treasury. Lord Diamond had said that "public" (my quotation marks) expenditure programmes had "built-in driving power so that if they were not stopped they would consume nearly all, or all or more than all, the resources regarded as appropriate."[1] Mr. Freeman retorted with three ways that, he claimed, could yield "a rich harvest of economies": abandoning instead of merely postponing capital projects in "public" services, a ruthless pruning of programmes to slim down fat instead of "the sporadic" forays of PAR, and, "most revolutionary" of all, cutting the number of administrators which Lord Diamond had said could not be done.[2]

There was some reference to the restive taxpayer, but neither thought of letting *him* (or, perhaps more effectively, *her*) make the decisions of what, where and when to cut, which is impossible as long as they pay compulsorily by taxes. PESC, PAR, PEC and PAC are machinery and instruments devised, debated and deployed by the politicians and the pundits that the public pays for but has never (well, hardly ever) heard of. PESC is the Pub-

1. Diamond, Lord, *Public Expenditure in Practice,* Allen & Unwin, 1975.
2. Freeman, Roland, *Municipal Review,* April 1976.

lic Expenditure Survey Committee created in 1971 to produce five-year plans, which Cabinets hardly take seriously because decisions are usually made hastily, under pressure from interests not bothered by well-laid five-year plans, by Ministers more concerned with elections than with avoiding over-spending (which in any event, the Opposition may have to contend with two or three years later when their turn comes in Government). PAR is Programme Analysis and Review, created in 1970, that investigates suspected excessive expenditures but spasmodically and often too late. PEC is the (public) Expenditure Committee of MPs that examines estimates of "public" (i.e. government) expenditure, in particular to see how the policies they imply can be carried out more economically; it has power to investigate but not to require government to heed it if Ministers think its recommendations politically inconvenient, as they usually have done. And PAC is the Public Accounts Committee of the House of Commons (fifteen members, Chairman usually from the Opposition), the main job of which is to see whether the money granted by Parliament has been overspent or misspent by the Department to which it was granted. If money has been overspent the PAC reports on whether there is objection to the shortfall being met by an Excess Vote. It investigates possible waste of public money brought to its attention by the Comptroller and Auditor General. A Treasury Minister is a member but hardly ever attends. (The public, whose money it investigates, is not allowed in.)

Much of this machinery has been ineffectual. It requires action by politicians. But Labour politicians, the Socialists among them rather than the Social Democrats, do not believe that government expenditure can ever be excessive. And Conservatives, with a handful of exceptions, would temperamentally rather avoid announcing "cuts" in the hope that economic growth will make them unnecessary. PESC, PAR, PEC and PAC are macro-economic machines for dramatising and identifying "cuts" that government will defer as long as it can. *What is wanted is micro-economic machinery that will enable each man and woman to make the cuts themselves in the privacy of their homes.* For that purpose they must know the savings they could make by cutting out marginal bits of services here and there after comparing them and discussing them with wives, husbands, children. The information they must have can be given only by telling them costs and charges.

Macro-ignorance and micro-knowledge

How many of us know the cost of a year in a nursery or secondary school? or in an evening institute or teacher training college? of borrowing a book for a fortnight? of a visit to an art gallery? a week of home nursing or a three-mile trip in an ambulance? a home help for a week? a meal on wheels? a visit from a police patrol to investigate a burglary? two fire-engines and crew to douse a chimney fire? a four-day court hearing to settle a neighbour's boundary dispute? removing 500 gallons of sewage? or half a ton of refuse? an hour at a swimming pool? the use of an allotment for a season? an hour's car-parking? the use of 50 miles of main road?

These and others you will recognise as the so-called "rate-fund" services of local authorities that are supposed to be provided free (wholly or largely) out of the rates. Is it not arrogant of government to think it can cut intensely *personal* services without asking any of us what effects cuts of varying sizes would have in millions of our homes? And are we not likely to make cuts more readily if we make them ourselves so that we can minimise the inconvenience, discomfort or pain?

That is not all. Suppose some of us, or many of us, decide we should prefer to make no cuts at all, or only in the services we feel we could most easily sacrifice. Then we have several courses of possible action in maintaining the services we value highly. First, we could reduce expenditure on private consumption goods like everyday household purchases. Second, we could reduce new savings. Third, we could draw on existing savings. Fourth, and not least, we could try to earn more to keep up our expenditures on services we felt we would rather not sacrifice at all. None of these four "feedback" reactions, which could yield large new funds for education (through fees), medical services (through insurance), roads (through tolls), etc., is likely if the government finds it can defer cuts no longer because of lack of revenue from taxes (or for home and overseas loans) and makes wide-sweeping "cuts," in which none of us has any say at all as individuals. And this, of course is what has happened more than once recently in existing or projected nursery schooling, school, university and polytechnic building, hospitals, roads, police civilians, fire services, research and training, libraries, environmental services, etc. As usual, capital expenditure figured largely because it does not reduce services immediately and is therefore politically less unpopular for hard-pressed governments than cutting current expenditure. This kind of political motivation in the supply of public services may make them inherently inefficient. I am here assuming they continue to be supplied by government and discussing only the method of payment: by macro-taxes or micro-prices.

To make possible this better-informed decentralised structure of micro-decisions, we must therefore know relative costs and prices. We can then pay the charge if we prefer to go on receiving a service, which itself will cause us to think twice or encourage us to find ways of going without, or doing it—or part of it—ourselves, or finding cheaper suppliers, public or private.

"Do-it-yourself" cutting

A glance down Tables B and C will stimulate the reader to think how he and she and the family and household would react in several kinds of circumstance if people were allowed to react *separately,* micro-economically, according to individual, personal, family decisions instead of being part of a mass or a herd responding powerlessly to macro-economic decisions made by uninformed government. These circumstances are basically two. The *first* is a crisis period, such as since 1970, of over-spending by local and central government that has to end because the borrowing that bolsters it cannot go on till Kingdom come. The *second* is the more fundamental long run in which, at last, we elect a government to treat us like sensible people and recognise our ability to decide which goods and services we can largely judge and select for ourselves.

In the recent period of over-spending, by both Conservative and Labour governments, the two alternatives we have been proffered by politicians are higher taxes or deteriorating "public" services. This is how the two Prime Ministers of 1976, Sir Harold Wilson and Mr. James Callaghan, spoke. That is what the newspapers, with few exceptions, said. It is not true. There is a way to maintain the public (and social) services, or at least those that the people want to maintain, without continually raising taxes. It is to pay for them by charges. Payment by charges would also indirectly make them more efficient by encouraging competing suppliers outside government.

Consider the macro-economic action of the politician, and ponder its clumsiness. A circular from the Department of the Environment to local authorities in December 1975 offered "advice" and "guidance" on restraining expenditure to help the central government fight inflation. The general theme was that there could be no improvements in public services and that new commitments made unavoidable by changes in birth-rates, etc., must be compensated for by reductions in services or by economies elsewhere. In April 1976 the government White Paper on Government Expenditure repeated that "any increases in individual services, whether for demographic or other reasons, must be offset by levels of provision in other services." It then listed reductions in government expenditure on housing, environmental services, police and firemen, education and libraries, and social services for several years to 1980. It made them seem mostly tolerable pauses on a road of steady progress onward and upward. But let us examine three examples: pre-school facilities for the under-fives, libraries and water.

Penalising the pre-school child

A member of the Merseyside County Council and of the Association of Metropolitan Authorities Social Services Committee, although trying to put the best face on things, was moved to say:

> the public expenditure cuts are painful . . . At first sight, the cuts . . . in nursery education for the pre-school child in particular . . . are horrific . . . virtual standstill on all new work . . . a far cry from our cherished dream of making top quality provision available for all children in these vital years of their lives . . . the backlog of shabby schools still in use . . . no solace either from day care centres [where] the cuts will mean capital expenditure must be halted . . . places available hardly measure up to waiting lists for priority cases, let alone contribute to general demand from such as working mothers.[3]

There followed a learned argument in favour of some services against others, which meant little more than that social workers were caught up in fashions that might not last but (for reasons that might be abandoned before long) created pressure for government to spend here rather than there.

Fewer books for "public" libraries

There was also a shock in store for libraries.

> . . . libraries are being forced to reduce services to a level that may do permanent damage . . . [They] are having to cope with budget cuts of between 15 and 30 per cent at a time when they need an *increase* of more than 15 per cent just to cope with inflation, or 40 per cent to meet the average rise in the price of books over a year ago . . . Buckinghamshire over the past year has spent only £65,000 compared with £291,000 the year before. [Sunday newspaper]

As a result of the cuts, libraries were buying fewer books and appealing for gifts, or cutting hours by closing on Saturday afternoon, the busy session; the waiting time for "popular" books is sometimes two years; choice, especially

3. Simey, M., *Municipal Review*, April, 1976.

in fiction, is severely restricted; publishers were becoming reluctant to publish new fiction writers. A Library Association spokesman warned the government: "we are not prepared to see library budgets cut by up to 30 per cent when other services are cut by only 10 per cent." The implied threat—writing to rule? down pens?—was not elaborated.

A Society of Authors spokesman weighed in with: "The local library is the most used neighbourhood amenity. Each year our libraries make 600,000,000 lendings. To cut back on this is a bad policy both culturally and economically."

Moreover the (Labour) Government could be breaking the law (passed incidentally by its own party as recently as 1964): the Libraries and Museums Act makes it a duty of public libraries to provide a comprehensive and efficient service, which the Department of Education has defined as 1,000 books for 4,000 residents. Buckingham (500,000 readers) will be spending only a quarter of its required quota, Surrey only a half. Other counties are evidently also facing cultural deprivation, in the fashionable sociological jargon.

Water, water, everywhere short

There was an even more scarifying story about water. Britain has periodic droughts; quite rightly equipment is not geared to deal with the exceptional season but with the normal. So periodically the natural scientist suggests *technical* solutions. Desalination of sea water has been a spectacular favourite; a national water "grid" has had its champions.

Meanwhile in 1976 Wales might have to cut off supplies to industry, said a serious newspaper, London might have to ban "even garden hoses," and in Wessex a water official tried praying on a Botswana rainmaker's mat. The typically technical solution of the eventual water "grid," begun in 1974 by creating ten water authorities for England and Wales, was bravely carting water from surplus to drought areas (an expensive business, as the brewers discovered a century ago when they established local breweries).

When the dry summer of 1975 was followed by the dry winter of 1975–6 and the parched summer of 1976, farmers were apprehensive of water rationing, which could mean meagre salad, vegetable and hay crops. The Wessex water authority bought four 4,000-gallon beer tankers, had 1,000 standpipes ready for rationing, and was spending £1 million to take water from rivers and cart it around the region. Garden hoses were banned in some areas; new boreholes were sunk. There was urgent talk of importing water—and perhaps paying for it with North Sea oil.

The cause of the troubles

These three examples of public services supplied "free" illustrate the central issues. Pre-school nurseries for the under-fives reflect the common view of social workers that parents are incompetent, require guidance, or should have somewhere to deposit their young children while at work. Libraries were established over a century ago to provide the working masses with easy access to literature. Water was supplied free when English towns developed.

None of these three is a public good with inseparable private benefits. Charges would yield income to increase facilities for the under-fives, or prevent the run-down of libraries, or make people think twice about using and wasting water. In all three cases, none of the discussion seemed to acknowledge that there was any other solution than transferring public expenditure from other services (which the claimant was not competent to judge), or presumably raising taxes even higher. Paying by price was simply in no one's mind—the social workers', the librarians', the authors', the water engineers', the administrators'.

But observe the essential differences between paying by taxes and by prices. In the first, no one may have under-five facilities, all must have deteriorating library services, all must suffer the consequences of drought unless we *all* agree *collectively* to pay more in taxes (or, in practice, unless politicians, who control the means of payment and make the decisions, judge that we all—or a majority, or a muscular minority—agree). This method permits the most conservative-minded and the most stick-in-the-mud authority to stultify the most adventurous individual or firm, anxious to discover new ways to improve on old methods. In contrast, paying by price not only enables the uncommon, unconventional, inventive individual to propose new methods and solutions; it also taps resources that are not reachable by taxes where no one may move unless everyone moves, or can be compelled to pay.

We have examined the basic services of education, health and housing. Suppose we re-examine every other "public" service organised by government and financed by taxes (wholly or largely) and ask: "Why should this service be run by government? Why should it be paid by taxes? Was there ever good reason? If so, is it still applicable? Has social or economic change made it inapplicable? Are there other ways of paying for it? Are they better?"

Let us now, then, re-examine afresh the wide range of services that we have come to regard as the natural function of government, national, regional or local, and see how many can be better paid for, wholly or largely, by price (charges, fees, etc.). As an introduction let us briefly recapitulate the origin, nature and functions of price.

Real and artificial prices

Prices are the rates at which goods and services exchange for one another. We are not confined to barter (as in schoolboy "swapping" or bilateral deals of goods between countries). We use money (which is anything that is generally accepted in exchange for objects or services) so that we do not have to take what the buyer of our goods has to offer but can take money and use it to pay for something else he does not have but which we prefer. Prices are thus usually expressed in the form of money. As such they create crucial information that enables us all to know what the goods or services we have to offer will bring in exchange for all other goods and services, so that by comparing prices we can finally make the exchange that bring us the goods and services that give us most satisfaction.

Without this information we should be plunging about (almost) blind. Look what happens in capitalist firms or communist countries with no spontaneous pricing. Firms that have no internal prices try to reconstruct them by creating "transfer" prices for raw materials or half-finished goods passing between departments (as in Unilever and Shell in Britain) or, in the last resort, "hive off" departments to work as separate firms which then buy and sell among themselves (like General Motors in the USA). Communist countries with no internal prices that reflect the real underlying value of goods and services passing from industry to industry or plant to plant have tried two substitutes. They have used prices in the outside capitalist world as broad guides to the value of agricultural products, raw materials or manufactured goods. And internally they have tried to restore the advantages of pricing by ordering their plant managers to produce up to the point at which the cost of the last unit ("marginal cost") equals the price. Here in Britain we have similar problems of knowing how much to produce of tax-financed goods and services supplied without price ("free") or with a subsidised price lower than what would emerge as the market price. ("Need," whatever that means, is not much of a guide, because when something is available free "need" can expand inordinately, almost without limit.)

Price that emerges spontaneously from voluntary exchange is not perfect. It may be impaired by lack of knowledge, distorted by monopoly on one side or the other, imperfect because of externalities. But there is no purpose in contrasting imperfect price in the real world with perfect price in a non-existent world. The only choice we have is between imperfect spontaneous price in voluntary exchange in the real world and its only alternative in the real world. The only alternative is price fixed by government, and the verdict of reason and history is that it is even more imperfect, or no price at all, which is even worse.

Prices laid down by government may or may not reflect real, underlying, spontaneous values. Ideally government can be thought to have access to all the information—political, environmental, etc., as well as commercial—and this should enable it to take into account the externalities in deciding where resources are to be used. Whether government that on paper *can* adopt this wider, long-term, disinterested and entirely public-spirited approach *will* do so in practice in the political world of short-term electoral and day-to-day pressures is widely *assumed,* without any reasoning or evidence at all, by people temperamentally favourable to government action.

The main defect of voluntary exchange pricing is usually said to be that it is paid out of earnings or wealth, so that people with more can pay for more, and people with little or none may have to go without unless they are helped. Until unequal earnings are seen as the reward of unequal merit, unequal access to services will be regarded as unjust. And it is true that, like an indirect tax on a purchase, price is regressive: it takes a larger slice out of a smaller income.

But this view, especially common among people concerned about social and welfare services, confuses price as emerging from the interplay of supply and demand with inadequacy of demand. *The solution is not to abolish price but to ensure adequacy of demand.* For, as was argued in Chapter 2, price also has unique characteristics. It is not a barrier, but a link. It is *desirable* as a measure of strength of desire, even though imperfect. It is *superior* as a method of rationing to other methods because it is more easily corrected for inequality. It is a more *humane* way of conducting human affairs than authoritarian commands or military force. It is *unique* as a source of information. It is therefore a *teacher* of care, forethought, husbandry. And it is *irrepressible* even if driven underground.

How far, then, must the existing "public" services be financed by taxes and how far can they be financed by prices? Let us go through the familiar services and begin with what many people would regard as an extreme example: the police.

Police: public goods and private services

Protection against law-breakers, like burglars, is the job of the tax-paid police. But it does not follow that all their services must be paid for by taxes.

Some of them, like general patrols by police-car or policemen on foot, are public goods (or, where they are corrupt, public bads). Others, like advice on theft prevention, carrying money, storing valuables, convoying heavy loads, maintaining order at sports or social events, and others are separable personal or private services for which the police are or could be paid by fees. The county police forces have probably been understaffed for many years (although it is difficult to tell without pricing); and if tax revenue does not suffice to finance public order and safety it would be no more than good sense to draw on new sources of money to maintain and improve them. But it may be more than that: it may be essential.

> Wherever you live, if you took a short stroll from your home and were attacked, what chance would there be that your call of "Police, police!" would be answered? In most cases none at all.

This is the view of Henry Cecil, the author and a County Court judge for twenty-eight years (*Daily Telegraph Magazine,* April 1976). But that may be what people want if they prefer sports palaces or municipal theatres for their money (rates and taxes). If they want better police his solution is not original or helpful:

> Why then at a time of rising crime are there not enough policemen? . . . because Parliament, while allocating funds for all sorts of frills, will not provide the pay to make a policeman's career attractive to recruits.

But a County Court judge is no judge of the competing claims on tax revenue of more policemen or of "frills," which politicians may think more important for the welfare or happiness of the people, or for their own popularity. If it is desired to prevent or detect lawlessness, the task that requires solution is that of raising more money for the police. No individual taxes are earmarked for individual "police funds," and people in general will not readily pay taxes for better police service from which they personally (or as families or households) may not benefit. Those who think they run little risk of burglary or other crimes will not see why they should pay for police to protect others whose risks are higher. But many people would pay more if they saw a direct personal benefit. That is precisely why there has been the development of "private police" like Securicor, Group 4, and others to supply the *private* benefits of police protection.

The truth that Crossman saw in Welfare Services—that individual payment was not linked with individual services—applies to the police and everything else, even if conventionally regarded as "public" services.

The important question is whether the police are providing, or are especially equipped to provide, direct personal benefits for which they could make charges to supplement the inadequate funds they are allotted out of taxation. They could then have more income out of which to raise pay, improve equipment and make their services generally more efficient. The assumption is that more funds will be spent efficiently, which they would tend to be if there were competition from private suppliers of personal police services.

General police patrols seem in principle to be a typical public good from which all in the patrol area benefit, from which they cannot be excluded, and for which they cannot be charged. But patrols benefit homes or buildings not according to their size (roughly reflected in their rates) but according to the value of the property (and life) protected. These values are reflected more accurately by insurance cover.[4] Police charges could therefore be made to reflect the varying value of patrol services to individuals or firms in the area according to the lives or property at risk. Whether the services responded efficiently to varying demands would remain to be seen. It may be that competition from private police services would be desirable as a stimulant and a basis for comparison as well as to supply additional services the public would not want from the public service.

The scope for charging is much larger. The police render, or could render, a wider range of services than is commonly supposed. In a quixotic reversal of political roles, a Labour MP Mr. Arthur Lewis proposed in 1971 (through a parliamentary question) that if the police charged for security services the shortage of manpower could be reduced. The Conservative Home Office spokesman replied that the Government did not think the police should "go into business." In spite of this obscurantist cavalier-Tory reply, the real public interest in a strong and efficient police force should override fusty notions about the impropriety of police "going into business."

The decisive considerations are the citizens' *demand* for security and other police services (in the economic sense: the amount they will pay for) and the ability of the police to *supply* them. And here the police are clearly equipped to offer services—convoying, guarding, advice, etc.—for which individuals or firms will pay. Chief constables are empowered by law to provide services at sporting events for fees, but in practice they raise a tiny fraction of police income from such services. This lack of development may itself reflect the shortage of policemen, in which event there is a vicious circle

4. Carter, R. L., *Theft in the Market*, IEA, 1974.

that can be broken only by Chief Constables becoming more entrepreneurial and making their services widely available and generally known. But that is difficult to envisage as long as they think they can fall back on taxes, which many must now begin to doubt.

No merit in public non-service

The police are schooled to think of themselves as public servants, "giving," not selling, their services. This feeling may give them the sense of satisfaction in providing a "public" service rather than engaging in sordid commercial selling. And this satisfaction is evidently common among government officials, teachers, social workers, doctors (or is it that they would rather not be paid directly—and judged—by their customers?). But if the obverse of this coin is chronic deficiency of equipment and manpower because of dependence on tax finance, the satisfaction must be tempered by the ironic *failure* to give the public the service it wants. A service that is "free" but not available (or inferior) is nothing to boast about because it is not serving the public. Public employees who are *not* supplying debatably public goods—university and school teachers, doctors, nurses and many others who are suffering from the shortage of public (tax) funds—must feel even less satisfaction when they reflect that people would be prepared to pay for their services personally rather than go without. "Public servants" can hardly enjoy the prestige of their role if the method by which they are financed prevents them from serving the public when and where it wants them.

There may also be the reluctance of Chief Constables to draw income from fees for services unless a breach of the public peace is probable. This is the traditional view of the quintessential police function, which is another pure public good. But there is an awkward consequence for upholders of this view. If using police to attend demonstrations or marches of political extremists, student sit-ins, public protest meetings and strike picketing reduces manpower for other services and increases the danger to individuals from personal after-dark muggings, burglaries or trespassing, people will want to spend more on personal and private protection for themselves, their families and their homes, shops, offices, factories or other possessions where they feel they may derive direct visible benefit. They will spend more (privately) on safes, door locks, double glazing, alarm systems, stout walking sticks (perhaps fitted with weapons), guard dogs, private security services; and they will spend more on insurance as the long-stop if these measures fail to prevent loss, injury or damage. The public is thus forced into additional private expenditure because the public service for which they have paid taxes is not serving them efficiently, *because* it is paid for in taxes. Politicians who make policy on the police, and Chief Constables who execute it, will see that these measures in private protection are a consequence of the police concentration on collective protection—"public peace."

The policeman's dilemma

The police, therefore, have no monopoly of protective or security services, and will not have a monopoly unless government, to protect the public service, suppresses or excludes private effort by individuals to protect themselves, as it has done in education or medical care. This is the dilemma the police cannot ignore. If the police indulge a superior opposition to charging, they must not be surprised to see more development of private security services. Individuals exposed to personal or private risks will hardly listen to admonitions that protection and security are the functions of the public police forces. And, once they look to private services, the role of the public police will be further invaded, and there will be diminishing scope to develop the services of guarding, convoying, advice, etc., in which they could successfully compete with private services. The police must therefore compete with private services or face further contraction.

The police forces may thus have to develop services for which they could charge fees. "Charging" the criminal may seem even more bizarre than charging by the crime-preventer. But there is no more case for free board and lodging in prison or detention centre than in hospital or school. And, as elsewhere, by restoring the awareness of cost, it would deter some lawbreakers by inducing them to "think twice." Larger fines for more offences and charges for detention would provide a fund for compensating victims. Fines could also be an alternative to detention, thus reducing government expenditure on over-crowded prisons, detention centres, etc., as well as increasing its income.

Personal fire services

This general reasoning—that public services that yield separable private benefits face a financing dilemma because they cannot escape private competition—applies to other services. Fire services are largely neglected as a source of income from charging. As with the police, charging seems to suggest a return to seventeenth- and eighteenth-century conditions when individuals made arrangements with suppliers to protect specified individuals or buildings. Some fire services, like general police patrolling, are public goods. Like diseases, fires can be contagious; people who do not pay for fire brigades in the hope of enjoying "free rides" (or free fire-dousing) would thus be paid for by others who feared their neighbours' fires would spread.

But other fire services in the twentieth century are not public goods. Private security patrols protect life and property against fire as well as against injury, theft or damage. Evidently the demand for protection and security against fire is also, like that for police services, not being met, in quantity or quality, or both, by the public service.

Again the economic truth is that tax-financed fire services are not monopolies but are in competition with private services. Charging for existing services according to the service rendered to individuals, at home or at work, and extending services for which charges could be made, would seem to be desirable developments, although the charges would be crude until there were competitors for comparison. The alternative is to concede fatalistically that public fire services are unavoidably inefficient and try to forbid or prevent individuals from spending privately to protect their homes, cars, or places of work from fire. That would, no doubt, be resented even more by the populace than preventing or outlawing private expenditures on measures against personal injury, theft or damage, or on education or medical care.

Charges could be not only a reinforcement of tax revenue but a more accurate method of relating payment to prospective benefit. Fire services are financed in part by rates, which vary broadly with the size of home ("hereditament"), and partly by general taxes, which are broadly proportional to income. But neither rates nor taxes are a close measure of fire risks.[5] Here again a better measure could be the values (of buildings, possessions and possibly lives) covered by insurance. Thatched houses would thus pay more than tiled, and wooden factories than brick.

The advantage of paying the contribution to the upkeep of fire brigades in a charge rather than a general tax (rate) is that it would reduce the calls on the fire services because the charge would be varied to allow for fire precautions taken by each home occupier, shop-owner, etc. Like price generally, it would act as a deterrent to avoidable demand. Rates and taxes unconnected

5. Carter, R. L., "Pricing and the Risk of Fire," in *The Theory and Practice of Pricing*, IEA, 1967.

with the degree of precaution taken by individual ratepayers have no such "feedback" effect on efficiency and cost.

Fire brigades could therefore be financed partly by rates and taxes to reflect the variation in individual risk and benefit. They could then have not only the prospect of more revenue from new private suppliers, but also, if they remain under-financed, more competition to fill the deficiency. Unless private self-help is outlawed, which is hardly credible, the police (and the doctors') dilemma re-appears.

Refuse collection

Refuse collection also has an element of public good in removing the externalities of noxious smell or nuisance, or risk of disease but it is separable and chargeable.[6] It is financed by charges in several countries. Street refuse is a public bad and its collection and disposal a public good. The earliest public scavengers seem to have been employed by the City of London in the early fourteenth century. The growth of towns in the first half of the nineteenth century strengthened the argument that removal of refuse would improve sanitation and health.

Politics rears its head even in rubbish. Industrial waste is charged for, though its collection is partly a public good; but it is politically safe to do so because the ultimate incidence of the charge (on consumers, suppliers, shareholders, workers) is difficult to trace. Yet the collection of home refuse is also both a private as well as a public good. Public nuisance laws may suffice to induce individuals to burn or remove refuse to avoid legal penalty. If those who hope for a "free ride" allow refuse to accumulate, it may pay their neighbours to have it removed to avoid the spread of dirt and disease. This is the best case for refuse collection to be paid by taxation, but it is not strong. Social and technical change can alter public goods. It can hardly be argued that most people in Britain today would risk the health of their families—or even of their neighbours—by failing to remove rotting refuse. Domestic refuse collection is largely a separable private benefit that can be financed by charging. Its advantages are again those of price rather than tax; paying a charge varying with the quantity of refuse would encourage householders to sort refuse into the combustible, the re-usable and the disposable.

6. Shenoy, Sudha, "Pricing for Refuse Removal," in *The Theory and Practice of Pricing*, IEA, 1967.

Domestic or garden fires could burn the rest; glass, metal and paper would be saved for recycling; and the labour and resources (vehicles, land) used in disposing of useless refuse would be reduced. The advantages seem clear.

Refuse collection from homes in some countries on the Continent is paid for by charges. In the USA financing methods vary from municipal "free" (tax-paid) collection to individual charges paid to private refuse-collectors at the extremes, with a lump sum paid by the local government to a private contractor in between. A recent survey of 2,000 cities covering a quarter of the population (210 million) found[7] that on average local government costs for a twice-a-week curbside collection were 69 per cent higher than those of private firms on contract. Sixty-one per cent of the population were served by municipal collection (mainly in the larger cities); 63 per cent of the cities (mostly the smaller) have only private collection.

The "information" function of pricing is illustrated by the comparison of collection costs in cities of varying size and for municipal and private collectors. In a city with 60,000 people, the cost of weekly municipal collection was 22 per cent higher than private contract for curbside collection and 35 per cent higher for back garden collection. The cost per household fell markedly with size of city up to 30,000 population and more gradually for cities up to 50,000, beyond which (and up to 700,000) costs were more or less unchanged. This information could be used by smaller cities (if there were an inherent inducement to economy) to reduce costs by joining together for refuse collection (municipal or private contract) and by larger cities to divide themselves into districts of about 50,000 and change from municipal to private collection. Individual charging was more costly than payment by lump sum on contract largely because of individual "billing," but the survey did not investigate the effects of refuse-sorting by householders on the amount or value of refuse collected. Two hints of these effects were that 51 per cent of cities with municipal service had at least twice-weekly collections, about double the 26 per cent of cities with other systems; and in cities with municipal collections they were twice-weekly in 51 per cent where households have no choice but only in 33 per cent where they have. Competitive refuse-collection and charging thus seemed to reduce waste and increase efficiency.

Mounting refuse is a mark of industrial development and the rising living standards it brings in goods packaged for hygiene, durability and ease of

7. Savas, E. S., "Solid Waste Collection and Disposal," Graduate School of Business, of Columbia University, 1972.

handling. Some private companies offer inducements to their customers to return containers, such as empty bottles, but inducements are rarely offered by local government to retain, clean and return used materials. That is a small symptom of the big difference between competition and monopoly. Periodic generalised macro-appeals or exhortations from Ministers are not as effective as the direct, personal micro-inducements of pricing, whether as payment for "empties" or charges for unloading unsorted rubbish. Here as elsewhere the tax-financed service is crude and insensitive. Charges could raise revenue for improved services and reduce the avoidable refuse that need not be collected by municipalities and dumped into expensive or unsightly tips. And it would induce efficiency by stimulating comparison by competition. Here again Britain is behind other countries in North America and Europe.

CHAPTER 8

From Roads to Deck Chairs

Charging for roads could help to improve the use of existing roads, gather more revenue for better roads, and even ultimately reduce costs by threatening competition from private toll-roads. Motorists can pay indirectly by road licence duty, petrol tax and purchase taxes on vehicles and accessories and valued-added tax on services, but these payments are only crudely related to the use of roads by individual motorists, so there is no incentive to think twice by road-users, or to provide the roads they would pay for. A motorist on a "free" road is less thoughtful of the mounting costs than a taxi passenger with a meter staring at him and ominously clicking every quarter-mile. Nor has the motorist any idea of the cost of roads per Mini-mile (or Rolls-mile) even though he is sending up the tax bill against himself. And no individual motorist can make known his personal objection to unsatisfactory roads by withdrawing his custom. Protests on his behalf by the AA, the RAC or other motorist organisations acting macro-economically for millions are a second- or seventh-best substitute. What is required is a method of direct pricing that reflects the wear, tear, congestion and other costs that individual motorists inflict on the roads and on other road users, and that induces road-suppliers to supply better roads at minimum cost.

The solution is to reproduce the taxi-meter: the micro-economic pricing device. No precise calculation may be possible because of the large element of overhead costs that have to be incurred for general maintenance whether an individual motorist uses the road or not, and because costs imposed on third-parties by congestion, etc., (externalities) cannot easily be calculated. But there are some direct (marginal) costs that can be attributed to motorists for each unit of road used. Economists debate whether road-pricing should cover only marginal costs or also a share of overhead costs included in full, long-term average costs. But it seems that almost any price is better than no price at all, without which the motorist and road supplier are driving and building financially blind. The meter as the solution was examined and recommended over ten years ago.[1] It could be the size of a small book and form part of the number plate. It would clearly cause motorists to rethink the amount and timing of their road use: the charge could be varied to encourage them to shift from peak to non-peak hours, crowded to uncrowded days, congested to uncongested roads. And it would induce road suppliers to look to their costs.

Street lighting

What about road lighting—in towns or on motorways? In towns it is a public good. It is true that street lighting falls more on paths and drives near lamps, but the cost of "policing," recording, billing, etc., would probably exceed the income from individual charges. Street lighting is also a possible example of a public "bad"—to people disturbed by light shining into bedrooms—and in principle would require a reverse charge. Many government-controlled activities create public "bads"—the noise of RAF aircraft on flightpaths, the noise from motorways, the pollution of air and water by ordnance factories, the traffic dislocation caused by Government receptions to VIP (or not-so-important politicians), and so on.

Car parking

Meters are used increasingly for parking on the street or in car-parks. But the charges for local government car-parks do not generally cover costs (Table C). Municipalities and Councillors or officials that appeal to external benefits shared by all citizens—for example, attraction of visitors—should be required to replace vague assertions of "benefits to the town" by calculations of *how much* benefit goes to *whom* (shopkeepers? restaurateurs? cinemas? betting-shops?) and show why those who benefit should be subsidised by widows without cars, pensioners, the lame and the halt who do not. They should be required to show why parking charges should not cover the total costs incurred by taxpayers. They do not because ratepayers passively accept their rate burdens and few Councillors do their job of representing their electors.

1. *Road Pricing: The Economic and Technical Possibilities* (Smeed Committee), HMSO, 1964.

Is research a public good?

Government-financed research in medicine, armaments, etc., seems to be a public good that bestows its benefits to all and sundry without favour, because no one can be excluded physically or charged economically. Yet the economic analysis of research (that is, the production of information and knowledge) suggests a more refined approach.

The argument for financing research collectively by taxes is that it would not be undertaken by individuals because it cannot be charged for. Industry spends large sums on research to improve its products, methods, use of materials, and manpower, and "charges" for it in the selling prices of its products. In so doing it showers externalities on everyone for many years ahead. The brain-scanner, which photographs "slices" of the head and may benefit everyone for all time, was evolved by EMI after years of research. This is another example of the untold, incalculable, unintended externalities that are produced every day all over the world. It generally suffices for their immediate costs to be covered to ensure they are produced. Economists debate whether the basic source of innovation—the restless, inventive spirit of men and women—requires to be stimulated or rewarded by patents, copyrights or other exclusive rights to charge.[2] And rather shallow social scientists have claimed that the divergence that innovation opens up between private and social benefit destroys the argument for allowing individual researchers, inventors, scientists, etc., to pursue their genius; we should instead, it seems, direct them by officials who will calculate the incalculable by seeing the unseeable externalities. How far, then, is knowledge and information produced by "pure" research—with no specific purpose but to explore the unknown—a public good that must be tax-financed because its beneficiaries cannot be charged?

No doubt there are such uncovenanted spin-offs from the advanced techniques used on atomic reactors, Concorde, the Rolls-Royce RB 211 engine, the vertical take-off Harrier, computers and others. But the possibility of such externalities cannot be used to justify technical monstrosities such as giant aircraft or underwater mechanical brontosauri that might never cover their costs, especially if their opportunity costs in alternative use of resources

2. Plant, Sir A., "The Economic Theory Concerning Patents for Inventions," *Economica*, 1934; "The Economic Aspects of Copyright in Books," *Economica*, 1934; and *The New Commerce in Ideas and Intellectual Property*, The Athlone Press, 1953.

thereby lost are taken into account—the improved living conditions, health care, help for pensioners and others who cannot help themselves, the arts, shorter working weeks to leave more leisure for reading and reflection. Enthusiasts for technical wonders can justify untold expenditure on the ground that externalities are *possible* that may benefit someone somewhere sometime. They can succeed more easily in their often euphoric but unsupported claims if the expenditure is public and the taxpayer who pays for it does not know enough to ask questions before it becomes politically irreversible (his "representatives" in Parliament were no match for the informed officials and did not stop the Concorde extravaganza before it was too late). But that does not make government research and development a public good for which British taxpayers should pay.

First, if anyone anywhere may benefit some day, the money should come from taxpayers everywhere; so our government must induce other governments in every continent to contribute to the costs (to "internalise" the externality on a world scale).[3] Second, it is dangerous to finance research and knowledge and scholarship from one source, political or private, because the unforeseen and unsought results may displease or damage the sponsor. So the sources of finance must be diversified: this is the strength of the privately-financed University College of Buckingham and of the Institute of Economic Affairs in contrast to state universities or research institutes that are almost wholly or very largely government-financed. Third, the political tax-financed sponsorship of research is more dangerous to its independence and objectivity than private sponsorship because political abuse (like the effort to direct scientists towards or away from an electorally sensitive subject) is more difficult to correct than abuse of private sponsorship.

The argument is thus for facilitating multiple sponsorship (by tax concessions for private research grants, as in the USA) rather than for tax-financing to encourage the externalities of government research. Because of the political popularity of giving public money for evidently "good causes" or prestigious projects such as space and medical research, and the large claims made for them that are difficult to disprove by comparing costs and results, there has probably been too much tax-financed government-sponsored and too little privately-sponsored research. The externalities from tax-financing are likely to have been over-stated and the externali-

3. Tullock, G., *Private Wants, Public Means,* Basic Books (NY), 1970.

ties from private pricing (charges built into the selling prices of industrial products) under-developed.

Research is substantially a public good with potentially wide but unknowable externalities; but exclusive tax-financing of it is inferior to widespread price-financing encouraged by tax concessions. Private sponsors would be more sceptical of unsupported claims and more likely to require evidence of fruitful yields in terms of opportunity costs. When a physicist or sociologist asks for tax-money for research he should say "If you give me the monetary value of a hospital or a school I *may* discover a new antibiotic or social habit, but your supporters are certain to lose their hospital or school." And let the tax-paying public decide.

Personal social services

The official description "personal social services" seems to be a contribution to confusion. It reflects the vagueness of government language. "Social" means, if anything, shared; but "personal" must mean not shared. Can anything be both?

The term is used for a range of services provided by local authorities to help people handicapped by age, incapacity, family difficulties, etc.—day nurseries, meals on wheels, home helps, and many more. Although they may yield external benefits they are not public goods in the essential economic sense because they can be—and are—given to individuals, and those who refuse to pay can be excluded. But the services are provided wholly or largely free. And here the term betrays a confusion that has fogged thinking about social policy in Britain for decades.

There is no dispute that people who cannot help themselves should be helped by those who can. That is common ground, and there is no excuse for the Child Poverty Action Group, Age Concern, or Shelter, or social workers or politicians to claim a corner in compassion. I argued earlier that we do not help people because they are old or disabled or widowed but because their age, disablement or widowhood prevents them helping themselves. That is why it has been such a tragic, callous mistake to make help available to all pensioners (millions of whom are well enough off), all the disabled (some of whom are well off) and all widows (some of whom are rich). The only criterion of entitlement to public help should be capacity for self-help, for which we use earnings as a broad measure. The balance of people who could help themselves but do not are the awkward squad of spongers who bring other recipients of help under suspicion.

Apart from the awkward squad, the criterion for social help should be, in practice, whether there is a shortage of earnings (or other income). If so, the case for help is made. But it does not follow that help should be given in kind—which means "free." Where there is physical or mental incapacity, help in kind may be best, or even necessary. Elsewhere it may be better to give cash—for all the reasons why it is better to provide services for a price rather than free. Help in kind teaches nothing and acclimatises its recipients to go on receiving it. Cash educates by its information, by teaching discrimination in choosing between alternatives, and by giving the recipient the status and dignity of the customer who pays in contrast to the supplicant who receives.

It must now be time, after decades of experience, to consider whether any of the help given by local authority "personal social services" in kind could not be replaced by cash. The main ones are "residential care," "day care" (day nurseries, including play groups), "community care" home helps, meals in the home. For some of these services there is a small charge. Cash grants or topping up incomes to enable recipients to pay the charge would remove the sense of indebtedness. The benefit to the recipient is often clear enough. The obstruction would come from public employees who would lose their jobs or even voluntary workers who would lose their power.

There is probably even more argument for cash grants or reverse taxes to enable beneficiaries to pay for, or to pay the full cost of, local authority health services—health centres, mother/child clinics, midwifery, health visitors, home nursing, ambulances and possibly though less clearly family planning because of its externalities. In some circumstances a free or low-charge service may produce higher quality from dedicated social workers, nurses, etc., who would prefer to be paid by the local authority than by the "client" and thus feel they were "giving" the service rather than selling it. But their feelings should come after those of their clients, who may prefer to pay as customers rather than receive as beneficiaries or supplicants.

Books, pictures, the arts

Free libraries, museums and art galleries are long overdue for payment by fees to cover part if not total costs. All are short of funds, though the suppliers and supporters of art and culture appear to prefer to importune politicians than to accept payment from their customers. Perhaps they think politicians can be persuaded to part with others' money more easily than customers with their own. But they must accept the consequences—battling it out in the press, Parliament and the Cabinet room where the outcome is more arbitrary than if the revenue of museums and art galleries were in part dependent on their popularity with the public. Even worse, as the doctors are finding at last; if you accept money from politicians you must also accept influence or control. And if you escape it, the politicians are not doing their duty by the public whose money they are giving away without anyone accounting for it.

Art and culture have widely dispersed externalities, but they are not public goods in the essential sense: they can be refused to people who refuse to pay. There may be room for paternalism and some tax-subsidy to bring some works of art to the public; how much is for the advocates to prove in terms of the alternatives sacrificed (like higher pensions for old people with low incomes). And it does not follow that there should be no charges at all. Countries like Holland, Italy and others that habitually charge have not killed off interest in art: their museums and art galleries seem to be used more generally than museums and art galleries in Britain. The relationship between price and demand may indeed be the opposite: I might have enjoyed the Constable exhibition at the Tate Gallery even more if I had paid £1 than I did at the free viewing shepherded by a Trustee.

At public libraries a 25p charge (cheap enough) for 600 million borrowings would yield around £150 million a year. This sum could fall to around £120 million if allowance were made for 10 per cent of borrowings by low-income pensioners and a further 10 per cent by children of low-income parents. Both groups could be excused payment by a certificate (as on the buses). Better still, they could be given earmarked purchasing power (a library voucher) or culture supplements with reverse taxes, so that they could pay along with everyone else, thus avoiding the nightmare of the sociologists—social divisiveness. This calculation supposes that borrowings do not fall away; but, if they do, they could hardly have been important to the borrowers.

Authors would be better advised to look for revenue from library charges than from government subsidies, and they should no more object to payment of fees by library borrowers than to payment of prices by book buyers.[4] In practice good writers would probably find it easier to get money out of readers than out of the government. They would certainly run no risk of political pressure. It is the library officials who are likely to obstruct charges, as administratively impracticable. They have no authority for obstructing them on poverty or other grounds: that would be special pleading.

4. Harris, R., in *Libraries: Free for All?*, IEA, 1962.

Information on jobs

Employment services may produce social (external) gains but they are not a public good necessarily financed by taxes. There is little clear thinking on the proportions in which job-finding should be paid for, perhaps through insurance by the three parties involved: the government (to represent the externalities), employers and employees. The retraining and other activities of the Manpower Commission are a public good with externalities that government supplies in the effort to offset the effects of its public bads like housing subsidies that discourage changing homes. Labour mobility is unavoidable in Britain with its large dependence on overseas customers. On average people change their jobs four or five times in a working life. A million people change jobs each month. But still too many people will not move from their districts—and still fewer from their homes. Subsidies tied to housing must be blamed in part; trade union power to induce government to subsidise a failing firm is another culprit; and the Benn view that firms fail because of poor management and can be saved by worker control aided by a subsidy is a possible third. No wonder government is now having to try harder to encourage men to change jobs. But still it does not follow that employment or deployment services should be "free."

As with other government services, "free" but passive government employment exchanges have been increasingly deserted in favour of priced but alert private agencies. One reason for the desertion is the lack of funds to increase the efficiency of the exchanges and the lack of incentive for the managers to improve them. Charges would help in both.[5]

Until recent years the employment exchanges were used mostly by wage-paid manual employees and were offering little competition to the private agencies and their specialised skills in placing salaried, professional, secretarial and nursing staffs. The employment exchanges have belatedly improved their own staffs and premises but will have to do more to compete for salaried clients. Competition from the private agencies has galvanised government to supplement its employment exchanges by more business-like Job Centres, although charges may be necessary to convey the spirit of a skilled service designed for individual clients rather than a social service for national insurance beneficiaries. And again the intention of government to remove competition by licensing and restricting the private agencies is suppressing a symptom (under the pretext of anxiety to prevent the agencies'

5. Fulop, Christina, *Markets for Employment*, IEA, 1971.

over-activity in encouraging mobility) that will reappear in other forms unless the government service is improved. And that is unlikely on the required scale as long as it remains a "social" service given free (for taxes) and fails to transform itself into a personal service sold for fees.

The doubt remains whether a service managed by state officials and bureaucratic procedures can change its nature. At least charging would give it the best opportunity of discovering its potentialities. In that event it would also have to segregate its "social" functions of paying unemployment and other social benefits.

Water and sewage

Charges for delivering water to industry and for collecting sewage may seem more familiar. Malvern has long had a metered supply of water. And a House of Lords decision has required local authorities to return a proportion of rates to ratepayers not on main drainage. Charging for both these services would have the advantages of information, economy, consumer alertness, cost consciousness, potential competition; it seems hardly necessary to argue it further. The opposition to charging is based not so much on reasoning as on inertia and conservatism.

School meals, "welfare" foods

Charging the full cost of school meals, milk and welfare is more controversial because it is in the "social" sphere where it is thought that some parents are destitute, irresponsible or ignorant. Even if these accusations were well-founded about enough parents to justify free meals, etc., for the children of all parents, including most who are not destitute, irresponsible or ignorant, this policy would not remove the supposed shortcomings. Free or subsidised meals do not teach parents to be less destitute, less irresponsible or less ignorant. A gradual change to cash, or in the early stages to vouchers for meals, milk and welfare foods, would restore or create the sense of responsibility for a child's well-being, not least by putting parents with cash or vouchers on the same economic footing as parents who paid.

Sports and recreation

There remains a wide range of sports and recreation facilities and amenities—from swimming (and washing) baths to "free" beaches.

Government baths for washing and baths for swimming have been paid for by rates (and taxes) for over a century.[6] They originated in the Public Health Acts of the 1850s and 1860s which authorised local authorities to provide them out of taxes. The main impulse was the hope of improving personal hygiene as a safeguard against contagion or infection in the growing cities with primitive sanitation and drainage. Poverty—the inability to pay—was a supporting reason. Insofar as everyone benefited by cleanliness in everyone else, so that the benefit was inseparable, such amenities contained an element of public goods. With generally low incomes it was easy to argue for financing through rates and taxes, though it was (indirect) taxes themselves that partly made people too poor to pay—the same circular reasoning as in the argument for free education.

Gradually baths were followed by other amenities and facilities. A century after the Public Health Acts local authorities are still providing "free" (or with charges that do not cover costs so that they are wholly or partly financed by taxes) a wide range of amenities from children's play gardens to golf courses. The whole structure was formalised in 1965 when control passed from the Department of Education and Science to the Sports Council, with nine regional councils to make grants to local activities. In 1972 the task was given to the local authorities.

The supposition implied in the emerging political creation of sports and recreation facilities as a function of government is that people would not wish to play or watch sport unless stimulated by government; or that, if they did, they would not be able to pay to attract resources from other activities. Here as elsewhere, these and other of the five ancillary reasons—that government would build on a large scale and therefore more cheaply, etc.—have been called in to justify a growing structure of "public" services for which people must pay by taxes. In 1971 the Sports Council estimated that some £300 million to £400 million would be required in tax funds in the ten years to 1981 for indoor swimming pools and sports centres, for golf courses, and for other facilities. It said there was "a need for local authorities to take the initiative on an increasing scale to provide sports facilities for the community."[7] In 1973 a Select Committee of the House of Lords showed its concern by proposing that the new District Councils in the reorganisation of local government should have a Recreation Department and a Chief Executive. This proposal had in principle been anticipated by the Durham and Teesside

6. Jenkins, A., "Leisure Amenities and Local Authorities" (Ms), IEA, 1975.
7. Sports Council, *Sport in the Seventies,* 1971.

Authority, which had established a Department of Arts and Recreation "to co-ordinate and combine leisure activities," and had "co-ordinated" and "combined" theatres and libraries with playing fields and sports centres. An early product was Thornaby Pavilion, said to be "a unique approach to leisure . . . a place to practise one's interests in a social setting."

Sport, recreation, leisure amenities are, like health and education, commonly thought to be clearly desirable "good things." Especially if their tax-costs, and, even more, their opportunity costs in roads or police manning, etc., are overlooked, they must be a tempting way for local politicians to combine "doing good" with enhancing their chances of returning to office at municipal elections (to go on doing more good). Here the economist, like the doctor who identifies over-indulgence as a cause of obesity and prescribes commonsense avoidance of fattening foods as its cure, is apt to attract dislike for pointing to the link between cause and result. The economist also has to add a dash of clear thinking that is the essence of economic theorising. If sport and recreation are "good things" in themselves, there is no limit to the lengths that local government should go in providing them. Twenty thousand pounds is then well spent on a wave-making machine for Nottingham Council's municipal swimming pool: better than still water, it would teach Nottingham children to cope with the currents of the real sea. Still better, imported sharks would teach them to resist the dangers of the deep. And so on, *ad infinitum.* The costs to the balance of payments would be remote from the ratepayer's and taxpayer's attention, and no politician would disturb the euphoria by emphasising it.

These examples may seem grotesque. On the contrary, they are logical extensions of the view that people should swim in realistic conditions, that swimming is a public good from which all may benefit by the increase in potential life-savers, and that it is therefore proper for government to encourage swimming by providing it partly free. They also illustrate the grotesqueries that could follow as more services are financed communally by taxes without the individual awareness of cost that comes with charging, and therefore without calculation or even recognition of opportunity costs. The concept of externalities as used by economists is carefully defined as uncovenanted effects on third parties. When used loosely and vaguely by politicians and sociologists it can appear to justify unending use of resources on activities that would reduce living standards by yielding benefits that the people—for whom, after all, they are intended—have not said they want at the costs that would be entailed. The Sports Council said in 1973 that sports centres are desirable "to avert social and medical ills." So are eating and sleeping: that is no reason for supplying food and water-beds on the rates. The economist is not satisfied with only one side of the account; he wants to know, or rather he says the people must know, the other side before investment in Sports Centres can be justified. And they cannot know unless there are charges to indicate costs and the alternatives sacrificed.

I rather like the idea that people who lightly claim public money for this, that or the other good cause should have a personal stake and pay a penalty if the benefit does not materialise.

There is not much time to lose. By 1974, 265 sports centres were open or being built in England and Wales; by 1981, 815 will have been built if the Sports Council has its way. So far the shortfall between expenditure and revenue has been commonly between £50 and £100 million. (In 1973–4 it was £88,000 in Guildford, £231,000 in Bracknell.)

The poor benefit less than the rich

Much the same is true in general principle of other "public" sports and recreational facilities. An irony is that the "social" justification of a century ago has been turned on its head. These "public" services were then supposed to have been provided by government because they were a way to transfer income from the rich (who paid the taxes) to the poor (who enjoyed the bathing and the swimming). It seems that now, a century later, half of the adults who use the sport facilities regularly (twice or thrice a month) come from the upper and middling income groups; a third of swimmers from the highest income groups.[8] Another study found that only a quarter were 19 years of age and younger (mostly in table tennis, trampoline and judo); two-thirds were aged 20 to 40 (mostly squash, badminton, sauna).

A charge, of course, reduces demand by acting as a "barrier," as the priceless sociologists like to put it, or more correctly as a reminder of the resources used in production by the supplier and the alternatives forgone by the buyer. How much it will deter demand is measured by the "elasticity." Some people will be deterred strongly: they prefer something else. Others may not be deterred very much, if at all: they want to pay the higher price and sacrifice the alternative. How much higher charges would diminish the use of sports facilities is for experience to reveal. In squash it seems that the higher charges at sports centres do not discourage users.[9] The reason may be the relatively

8. Jenkins, "Leisure Amenities and Local Authorities."
9. Ibid.

high income of squash-players or the popularity of the game that stimulated the wide development of private courts charging prices that cover the full costs, so that squash-players are accustomed to pay them. And this strong demand has evidently enabled sports centres to charge prices around double those for badminton, basketball, cricket (nets), five-a-side football and golf.

But the ratepayers continue to pay heavily for public swimming pools. In 1974–5 local ratepayers, whether they used the pools or not, paid around £50 million; swimmers paid about £15 million. The Sports Council judged in 1972 that 411 indoor pools were "required" in England by 1981 (including replacing a third of old pools, many built before 1900) at a capital cost of £58 million. Few pools cover their costs (including interest on loans). The loss ranges up to a quarter of a million pounds per pool.[10] If state schools had to cover their costs they would soon find ways to make their pools pay. (They too are subsidised by ratepayers under the heading of education.)

Charges for a "public" service are sometimes varied according to ability to pay. This variation is confusing to supplier and buyer because it obscures the information conveyed by price, which is that a stated amount of resources has been used, whether by poor pensioner or rich pop-singer. It is therefore better to vary the element of *topping up* so that everyone can pay the *same* price. (This is also the argument against varying prescription charges with income.) In some circumstances it may nevertheless be administratively simpler to vary the price. Two out of three users of new pools (built since 1960) are children. Half of the adults are "skilled manual workers" but a third come from the highest incomes. Between half and two-thirds go as families.[11] Only one in twenty go professionally; the other nineteen go for recreation. (The pools at Bletchley and Heringthorpe Leisure Centres have artificial palm trees as well as wave machines.) It may be that cunning (but concealed) calculations have divined that the externalities of swimming are especially high and that swimmers are more worthy or deserving of tax-subsidies than other pleasure-seekers. But none of these wholesome, health-giving recreations is a public good that cannot be refused to people who refuse to pay; and all yield private benefits that should not be subsidised by people who cannot or do not enjoy them.

10. Ibid.
11. Ibid.

Parks and open spaces

Parks and open spaces may be public goods because, although individuals can be excluded, the cost of collecting entrance fees may exceed the income. The cost to taxpayers in 1975–6 was over £100 million. If admission charges are uneconomic, income could perhaps be drawn from park-users in other ways. In North Yorkshire the persistence of a principled Councillor (Chapter 12) has persuaded the Council to provide more informative guides to the Yorkshire dales and to charge for them, thus changing an expenditure borne by ratepayers generally into a surplus. The leaflets were also used more considerately rather than forming litter. (Predictably the reform was opposed by the bureaucracy.)

For sports and recreation generally, charges would increase income and so provide the resources for improved services and, moreover, help to indicate more precisely which services the public wanted. They are used by one in four of the population, mostly by people with higher incomes. In evidence to the Layfield Committee on local government, Mr. Alan Jenkins, an economist with specialised knowledge of the sports industry, judged that charges could be raised by an average of 25p at sports centres and swimming pools.[12] This would mean doubling or even trebling them, and would close the wide gap between costs and charges. The higher charges would help to take the facilities out of politics and enable the managers to adapt them more closely to public preferences without the arbitrary fluctuations in policies and funds produced by the party pendulum. Not least, they would avoid the tragicomic use (as in medical care, education, etc.) of nil or low charges (squash 10p instead of 60p) in the vain hope of making a service available to all and ending by making it available to none—except at lower standards because tax-funds fail to fill the gap between cost and income.

Seaside facilities

Recreational facilities in seaside resorts also show the scope for improvement by charging, or by charging nearer cost. The range is from beach charges and boat licences to deck chair and cabin fees.[13] Like museum and

12. Ibid.

13. Peppiatt, W. D., "Pricing of Seaside Facilities," in *The Theory and Practice of Pricing*, IEA, 1967.

art gallery charges, they are common in Holland, Italy and other countries on the Continent, whose tourists in Britain often find lower standards for which the low (or nil) charge is no compensation since they would rather pay for something better. The closer comparison by British and overseas holidaymakers with other countries (and the competition from them) is itself a reason for charging for facilities in Britain to raise revenue for improvement. Only the natives suffer from indifferent refuse collection in Ruislip or ill-stocked libraries in Lowestoft, but the balance of payments suffers if overseas tourists are repelled by rubbish-strewn beaches or poor boating facilities.

Here again, as elsewhere, there are errors and attitudes that obstruct reform. The notion that beaches are "public" property that should be provided "free" dies hard. It overlooks their scarcity: good beaches are not merely spaces lapped by the tide but also with comfortable surfaces, patrolled by beach-keepers, periodically tidied, protected from high wind, facing south, near hotels or caravan sites—but not so near as to attract over-crowding and the inevitable and irksome, time-wasting rationing device of queuing. If price is not used they will tend to be unkempt, and crowded. Like other "public" services, they will end up "free" but undesirable, because they will not offer the quality that people want, can pay for and are accustomed to in services for which they are pleased to pay elsewhere. Again, the fallacy that a public service paid for by taxes is somehow intrinsically better than a private service sold for a price obstructs clear thinking. Charging would encourage beach suppliers to meet the users' requirements, perhaps by inducing local authorities to farm them out to private, competitive beach amenity specialists rather than leave them to be run by town hall officials.

Of 3,000 miles of British coastline, only a third is beach owned by local authorities, of which about a half is commonly preferred by holidaymakers. Since there are no charges (for people on foot), rationing is enforced by "first come, first served," as in the NHS or public libraries, or by queuing, as with public conveniences, or by subterfuge and black markets, like crossing the palm of the deck-chair attendant, as with Council housing. The moral question is whether these forms of rationing are less objectionable than charging. The public can be guided to less frequented beaches by paternalistic placing of beach shops, cafes, car-parks and other amenities, but there is still rationing: there is no escaping scarcity.

The virtue of the tax-paid system, which forces most people into a quality of beach that is either higher or, more generally, lower than they would prefer, is not readily clear. What is clear is that British beaches offer no choices between lower-quality free beaches and higher-quality priced beaches; and the one quality offered is lower than available in countries with charges. Yet charges for deck chairs and wind-breaks, or for storing and launching boats, are administratively simple. Differential charges for chalets and huts provoke no bureaucratic barrier. People with their own chairs or tents can be charged for use of the space they occupy. Since these are not characteristically bureaucratic services, they might be made to yield revenue by the sale of franchises or concessions to private firms.

It may not be apparent to the casual or even periodic user that beaches are not natural features but require maintenance of sea walls, groynes, promenades, shelters and so on. If the income is inadequate (or used inefficiently), maintenance can be postponed, but with gradual deterioration and inconvenience (or danger) to the public.

Boating is an increasingly popular sport that could not have been foreseen a century ago, and there is no reason why errors and attitudes must persist when conditions change. Speed-boats, usually carried by trailer and sometimes launched from beaches, compete for space and cause congestion. They could yield increasing revenue in launching and mooring fees. Fishing rights carry charges, but often low or nominal.

Piers and harbours, like car-parking, can be said to attract visitors whose purchasing power benefits local traders, and it may be argued that their charges should therefore not have to cover their costs. The probability is that the external benefits are over-estimated, so local ratepayers are over-taxed and users under-charged. Direct charges are more likely to provoke protest if they are raised or seem high, but ratepayers can rarely argue back at Councillors who speak vaguely about the importance of providing "public" services that attract visitors, although many of these Councillors are shopkeepers or hoteliers. Such claims are rarely accompanied by statistics that can be challenged. Local traders who benefit personally from visitors should pay for the public services that attract them.

Seaside entertainment provided by local authorities is another public service it is tempting to justify as attracting visitors and thus properly paid for by uncomplaining ratepayers. Here the reluctance to raise charges nearer costs can create a vicious circle. Low charges bring inadequate revenue which is met by reducing outlays. Falling quality then reduces revenue further. Higher charges could be the way to improve quality and raise revenue to cover costs.

Decorative illuminations seem to be an obvious public good from which non-payers cannot be excluded and which should therefore be financed by the rates. Scarborough has charged for its Wonderland Display but all visitors to Blackpool can see its illuminations. Bands can be heard over a wide radius at Folkestone, Bournemouth and Colwyn Bay, but charges can be made to enter the "stands" for better hearing. (That these patrons may often be pensioners is not a reason for low charges that subsidise affluent pensioners and non-pensioners but for vouchers or reverse taxes to top up the low incomes of non-affluent pensioners.)

A close observer, W. D. Peppiatt—a school-teacher of economics who is also a Councillor in Thanet,[14] has concluded that conventional seaside charging is inadequate on five main grounds: the revenue falls short of costs; it does not efficiently equate supply and demand; revenue from local rates or government grants is insufficient for capital outlays; congestion in the short peak season alternates with under-use during the rest of the year; seasides have failed to provide the sophisticated services expected both by British holidaymakers accustomed to higher standards abroad and by overseas tourists bringing their currencies to succour the ailing balance of payments. The ultimate solution is charges as the alternative to further support from rates or taxes. Otherwise British seasides may deteriorate progressively, as is seen by occasional abandonment of facilities such as the West Pier at Brighton, or the increase in private provision, as in the new Marina also at Brighton. There has been a lopsided persistence in older amenities (such as entertainments) because they do not require much capital expenditure and a failure to develop new facilities that do (boat moorings, etc.).

This imbalance of supplies and demands is a not unexpected result of failure to use price to equate them. Charges nearer costs would help to right the imbalance. Higher launching fees and mooring charges and perhaps an annual boat fee would yield revenue to improve harbours. New (or higher) charges varying with beach amenities would reduce congestion and enable beaches to be cleaned and patrolled.

In a word, there has been little logic about the haphazard mixture of rates, taxes and charges that have financed—or failed to finance—the varied services of the British seaside. It is the outcome of outdated conditions, chance, expediency, habit, tradition, prejudice, error and conservatism. And much the same is true of all or most of the other "public" services. They are all hallowed by time, sanctified by usage; and if that is how we want them so we shall have them. But indulgence in this mixed bag of nostalgia demands a high cost: the neglect of facilities the public would prefer and would enjoy if it were allowed to pay charges instead of being confined to the outdated method of taxes.

14. Peppiatt, "Pricing of Seaside Facilities."

CHAPTER 9

From Coal to Clean Air

The last five chapters reviewed activities that, for a century, government has increasingly argued are "public" or social services which should not be sold commercially as in a market but should be provided wholly or largely "free." This chapter discusses more summarily services that government provides usually not as public or social services but as trading or commercial services; and the question is whether the charges should cover cost. Some are supplied by local government, others through organisations that used to be known as "public utilities" and in recent years as "public corporations."

Local government trading services

The local government services are a mixed bag from restaurants to crematoria. To see how far they are, in practice, supplied as trading services that cover their costs and stand on their own feet rather than on the ratepayers' corns, I listed them earlier in Table C and showed their cost (expenditure) and receipts from fees, charges and sales. We saw that incomes were much higher as percentages of cost (government expenditure) than for the "social" services, national and local. Some were in the eighties but others lagged far behind. Before we ask why taxpayers have to pay even for trading services, let us recall from Table C what they are and how much is still found by taxes.

If the official statistics mean what they say, it would seem that in a recent year we were paying in taxes not only for public (or social) services but also, in large part, for "trading" services that local government sells in return for payment, as in private industry. Municipal aerodromes cost £20 million (in 1973–4) but drew only £12 million in charges and left ratepayers and taxpayers to find the rest—£8 million. Horticultural markets cost £3 million but drew only £1 million in charges, leaving £2 million to ratepayers and taxpayers. Slaughterhouses cost £6 million, earned £3 million and received £3 million from the rates and taxes. And so on.

Should taxpayers pay for private benefits?

None of these services is a public good in the sense that it cannot be denied to individuals who will not pay. Indeed there were charges for all of them. There must be reasons why the charges do not cover costs.

As we have seen, it is easy to argue that a local government service, such as an aerodrome, benefits the town as a whole and should therefore be financed partly by local taxpayers. That argument could justify every town impoverishing its people to supply visitors with free transport, entertainment, restaurants and hotels, *ad infinitum,* for imponderable benefits. Politically powerful groups like officials, contractors who hope for contracts, or organised employees may benefit, but the town, its government and its taxpayers have to consider whether the subsidy to visitors could be used better in other ways. If these subsidies to local trading services with undefined and uncalculated externalities continue, it may be simply that local taxpayers have not noticed them, because the cost to each taxpayer is small and tucked away in total expenditure figures that he cannot investigate, or because his elected representatives in the town hall have failed to represent him.

Whatever the reasons, the not generally known and surprising truth seems to be that slaughterhouses, markets, cemeteries, corporation estates, industrial estates, ports and piers, etc., are evidently paid for in part by local ratepayers who do not use them. Do they know? Do their representatives tell them? Is that what they want? Is it too difficult or costly to find out for themselves? Are there remedies? Or is the empire-building by local Councillors and officials too powerful?

If it is thought these services should be subsidised by ratepayers, they should not be classified as "trading" services. And if local government is careless in running trading services inefficiently, so that charges do not cover costs, perhaps they should have them run by more efficient managers. In the meantime it is not difficult to see why rates are high. It has evidently been too easy to load the costs on to ratepayers, who are many, so that the cost per head is small (and will be concealed in the rate demand notice). Although local taxes have been rising for a century, ratepayers do not examine their rate demands as closely as their butchers', bakers' or garage bills. If they did, and were shocked, they cannot individually escape paying rates except by moving or emigrating. Their collective revolt of recent years, and their continuing passive resistance by late payment, was provoked by the dramatic increase in the nominal number of pounds demanded due to inflation, not by reading the rate demand notice and asking whether local services were worth the rate bill. In any event, to judge value for money, ratepayers would have to know the value of services and costs to them individually, which would require full charging.

The official statistics suggest that if charges for local government trading services covered their costs, rates and taxes in 1973–4 could have been reduced by about £500 million (item 3, fourth column of figures in Table C, assuming overhead costs were accurately allocated to individual services).

Public corporations

Trading services supplied on a national scale by public corporations are more familiar because they are larger, and they have been the focus of political controversy by being nationalised. (One of them, indeed—steel—has been denationalised and renationalised, and another—the Post Office—changed from a government department to a supposedly independent corporation.) Also, they impinge on daily lives more than little-noticed slaughterhouses, which seem to have come down from the distant past, or the aerodromes that Councillors may, like the politicians of developing countries who build air-strips, regard as prestigious symbols of status.

Whether public services should be paid for collectively by taxes or individually by charges is the central controversy over the running and financing of the public corporations producing fuel, transport, steel, broadcasting and other communications. They accounted for 16 per cent of the GNP and 8 per cent of the labour force in 1974, and since then we must add British Leyland and other undertakings "taken over" by government. They are described variously as Councils, Boards, Corporations, Executives, Authorities, Groups, even Companies. Ideally they should be free of political control, so that they can concentrate on efficiency in adapting themselves to changes in technology and consumer preferences in market conditions. For various reasons—at best because they have high degrees of monopoly, arguably because they can be used in macro-economic management to keep the official price index down, at worst because they can be used by government in its electoral tactics of creating jobs and buying votes—they are supervised by Ministers "in the public interest." Their orders from government have varied from injunctions to act commercially and cover costs to requests, sometimes backed by subsidies, to keep their prices down in the hope of limiting the inflationary rises in the cost of living, especially for people with low incomes, and persuading trade unions to restrain their wage demands in operating incomes policies.

Beyond these diverse tactical government objectives there is the overriding philosophic question whether the corporations are selling their products at a price to cover costs or supplying them as social services, for which prices are secondary, irrelevant or objectionable, as has been argued for rail and bus transport. Before he resigned from the British Railways Board, Sir Richard Marsh indicated fairly plainly that it was difficult for him (or anyone else) to run the railways effectively if the government did not know its own mind, or changed it unpredictably between the two philosophies—tactically to meet current economic problems like inflation or strategically to meet the changing balance of power in the governing political party.

The central theme of this book is thus at the heart of the dispute over the role and function of the government-supervised (if not government-directed) industries that supply the basic commodities of fuel and steel, the basic services of transport and communications, and the jugular vein of an open society, broadcasting.

Monopoly and externality

There are two complex issues affecting charging. First, the public corporations run industries in which, it is argued, there is a large element of heavy investment and equipment. This makes very large units, which can offer the economies of scale, necessary for efficiency (which may be true, as in steel, but not always). There cannot therefore be many producing organisations, so there is the possibility and danger of monopoly. Second, these industries are said to have large externalities so that they should not be run commercially to cover costs but should reflect wider social repercussions.

Recent governments have therefore evolved the policy that their prices should be equated with marginal costs: the direct costs of producing the "last" unit, not the full average costs which include an allocation of overhead costs. Other economists have argued[1] that this is an artificial application of the pricing policy that emerges spontaneously in competitive markets where firms try to maximise the surplus of revenue over costs, i.e. their profits. Since the public corporation industries are not necessarily monopolies but could operate in competitive markets if restrictions on competition from new forms of fuel, transport and communication were removed, the better policy would be to remove these obstacles and to leave them to make the charges required to maximise their profits by covering their costs.

1. Polanyi, G., *Comparative Returns from Investment in Nationalised Industries,* IEA, 1968; and *Contrasts in Nationalised Transport since 1947,* IEA, 1968.

Second, if charges are to be decided or guided by analyses of external or social costs and benefits, estimates of the benefits to third parties would be required. But, as indicated earlier, these estimates are in practice very crude and little more than rough and arbitrary guesses. There is really no convincing way of measuring external benefits (or detriments) imposed on third parties except by confronting them with a series of prices and seeing how they react in the real world. The Victoria line in London reduces congestion on the roads, but the value of the easier movement from avoiding delay could be discovered only by finding how much travellers would pay for, say, faster buses. So again it would seem better to leave the corporations, like private firms, to charge what they think necessary to maximise their profits, but in as competitive a market as possible.

If this procedure left some people with inadequate transport, and it was thought desirable that they should remain where they are rather than move, they could be given individual grants so that they could pay the charges. Again as before, the special assistance is better given on the demand side, at the expense of the country as a whole, than on the supply side by fares too low to cover costs and therefore at the expense of the industry.

More simply, the supply of transport in, say, rural areas where public transport is inadequate or expensive, could be increased by allowing car-owners to charge for lifts or private coach-owners to compete with nationalised road and rail transport. This solution would require little more than the removal of restrictions on competition. These restrictions are made by man—politicians and bureaucrats, not by nature. Many commuters could travel more cheaply by private coach than by nationalised train. And competition would turn the railways from devising fare increases to internal cost reductions.

Finance by charging in competitive conditions

There is thus no difference in principle between charging in public corporations and in industry in general. And basically the reason is that public corporations are operating increasingly, and could be made to operate even more, in competitive conditions.

Unfortunately the official statistics conceal rather than reveal how far charges cover costs. There are direct subsidies in the form of money transferred to pay costs (British Rail has received around £500 million a year and in 1968 wrote off £1,250 million of capital as a dead loss). There are also indirect subsidies in the form of protection from competition, both from inside Britain (restrictions on Laker Airways, road hauliers, etc.) and from outside (tariffs on imported oil and coal). The discouragement of competition has probably bloated costs, so that the subsidy is larger than it otherwise would be. The Post Office, for example, has continued postal services long after they were uneconomic. Without the effective discouragement of bankruptcy to prove them wrong, public corporations can find imposing social reasons for continuing services they cannot make pay by charging to cover costs.

What is clear is that these deficits might have been less if the corporations had been left to adjust their prices to their costs and if costs had been exposed to more competitive conditions. Government policy could then have been directed, first, to preventing costs from being inflated by removing the obstacles to competition rather than consolidating them and, second, confining assistance to individuals, such as pensioners, who would have suffered hardship from paying, say, the whole cost of their fuel and transport. A general directive that the corporations must also cover their costs without subsidy might have helped to prevent those costs from being pushed up by trade unions, which under the present system are in a dominating bargaining position in wage negotiation and in obstructing the pruning of uneconomic railway lines and stations, coalpits, bus routes, etc. Governments are not as effective in restraining these extravaganzas as the prospect of having to close down because competitors are more efficient.

Allowing the corporations to vary their charges in a more competitive environment, and with selective assistance for the low-income consumers, could thus have avoided many of the wastes, excesses and distortions in these basic industries and services. Some government attention would still be required, because for a time some of the services provided might be able to make their charges higher than their costs because of a degree of monopoly. But the monopoly has been crumbling in all of them—fuel, transport, steel, communications and broadcasting—and it would have crumbled even faster if competition had been welcomed rather than discouraged or suppressed. In broadcasting—"pay-TV," in postal services—private carriers, in transport—toll roads, in fuel—North Sea oil, and in steel and coal—imports: these are examples of potential competition that has been inhibited or held at bay. Until competition is allowed it cannot be argued that the corporations have an *unavoidably* high degree of monopoly such that they cannot be allowed to vary their charges without political control. More competition would by now have reduced costs in all of them. It would have induced the Post Office to mechanise sorting, cut out twice-daily or weekend delivery (or better still require higher charges). It would have compelled British Rail to cut its 11,000 miles to the 6,000 or 7,000 used by passengers prepared to pay enough in fares without expecting others to pay part of their fares in taxes. More flexible fares could have evened out the daily, weekly and seasonal fluctuations in travel instead of intensifying them. In fuel, more competition would have pruned staffs, galvanised selling techniques and improved sensitivity to consumer requirements. If not, the public corporations would gradually have been replaced by private firms providing better services at lower cost. (Professor Milton Friedman says his son, David Friedman, has discovered that government services usually cost twice as much as private competitive services).[2]

Not least, all the corporations would benefit in their capital-raising by being provided with a trading framework in which their more competitive (more commercial, less political) charging would more quickly identify which of their activities were profitable, in growing demand, and should be expanded, and which were in declining demand, making losses, and should be shut down. But as long as the public corporations can look to politicians and taxes to make up for low charges they can hardly be expected to put the public first.

The conclusion is that, as elsewhere, charging should be used as much, not as little, as possible, to cover costs.

Paying for the environment

There remain government services that create the environment for human activity, and government measures to optimise the use of the environment (air, water, etc.) in human activity.

Insofar as environmental and preventive services are public goods, such as measures to contain contagious or infectious diseases, they should be financed by taxes, since everyone benefits by everyone else being treated, including those who refuse to take part or to pay. Even here, however, there is room for a charge. Individuals who are treated would benefit even if others were not; and if it was thought that some individuals would be foolhardy and put both themselves and others at risk, preventive measures could be required by law if enough citizens (a majority? two-thirds? three-quarters? 95 per cent with a veto by 5 per cent?) agreed.[3]

Coast and bird protection, conservation of areas of natural beauty by national or countryside parks, preservation of buildings of historic interest,

2. Friedman, M., *From Galbraith to Economic Freedom*, IEA, 1977.
3. Tullock, G., *The Vote Motive*, IEA, 1976.

safeguarding of works of art and the preservation of civilised life itself may be substantially public goods that would not be produced at all unless produced for all and paid for collectively by taxes. They yield benefits to everyone in the area; increased use by some does not reduce use by others; they cannot be refused to individuals; charges cannot be levied.

At least, so say people who would like to see these activities paid for by others. But not everyone is a bird-watcher, a visitor to stately homes or a fresh-air fiend. The argument, here as elsewhere, can easily be overdone, and the opportunity costs conveniently overlooked. Culture is a good to be preserved, but should the uncultured pay for the cultured? Should working-class soccer fans pay for middle-class opera-goers? And what about the opportunity costs? How many museums for how many hospitals?

Moreover, amenities are not all necessarily best provided without direct charge to anyone. Especially where congestion is possible or likely, as in beaches or stately homes, charges may be practicable and advantageous. A flexible method might be *voluntary* charging such as at the Chicago Art Institute, which is "free" but which suggests donations that individuals may care to make. But compulsory partial charging is better.

Even where "free rides" are unavoidable and charging is impracticable, tax-financing and "free" provision embodies the defect that there is no sensitive indicator of the *scale* on which public goods should be protected, conserved or safeguarded. Do we spend too little tax-money on coast protection or on bird sanctuaries, or too much? Do we spend too much on the Tate Gallery, or too little? Is there a tragic loss of Tudor mansions, or a surfeit? The scope for error, favouritism, corruption that is inherent in the political method of control of free public goods may make it the second best. An even better instrument might be one in which individuals could indicate the strengths of their personal preferences through pricing. Referenda are again a possible method. In a Virginia county recently the people voted against a new (tax-financed) courthouse. Referenda are frequent in Swiss cantons. Town meetings are another possibility, reminiscent of the direct democracies of the Greek city states.

Finally, parts of the environment may require protection, not from neglect but from over-use. Here there are several main elements in the argument.[4] The environment is partly unprotected where it is unappropriated by any owner and thus *really* free (no quotation marks): no one owns it, so

4. Beckerman, W., *Pricing for Pollution*, IEA, 1975.

no one ensures that it is not despoiled. Again, the purpose is not to prevent all pollution but to optimise it, where a little of the environment (clean air, water, etc.) can be used to make a lot of goods and services to raise living standards. Further, the environment is polluted by government as well as by private industry, and in communist as well as in capitalist countries. Not least, the better method of protection may be not by outright prohibition but by charges to reveal preferences and discourage over-use (pollution) and to stimulate the search for methods to reduce both. Pricing the environment can thus be a more effective way of protecting it than direct government regulation or prohibition, which provides no measure of the cost of the environment used or polluted, and no incentive to reduce its pollution.

Charging for the environment is the means of conserving it. There is thus a case for charging even where it might be thought least applicable.

Resistance to reform

If the advantages of charging are so plain, why are charges absent or inadequate? The answer must be that there are no incentives to charge to cover costs, or that there are incentives *not* to charge to cover costs. Charging puts the suppliers—politicians and bureaucrats—face to face with the customers who feel the power of people who pay, who know they pay, and who know how much they pay. Politicians and bureaucrats have a more comfortable (because less demanding) and more powerful (because less accountable) life when the customers are more distant, less informed and less well-placed to complain—that is, when they pay by taxes. Resources can then be used more as politicians and bureaucrats think fit, and less as the awkward paymaster-customers want. That is why we must expect politicians and bureaucrats to prefer indirect payment by taxes, to look askance at direct payment by charges, and to do what they can to resist it. They are not selfless paragons. They are men with personal interests—from families to philosophies—to serve. That does not make them morally worse than the rest of us, but it means we cannot assume that they are necessarily better. They erect a real, formidable resistance to reform. They have a direct, personal interest in keeping the government, that is, the tax-paid sector, as large as possible. This means they support the inefficient use of resources in all public services that are not public goods. The arguments they use to defend their position are the subject of the next part of this book.

PART 3

Objections Overruled

CHAPTER **10**

Socially Undesirable

This and the following two chapters will consider the three main objections to charging directly for the separable private benefits in public services. This chapter discusses the view that it is socially unacceptable.

The social objections are of five main kinds:

First, people and their needs come before paying and prices. Mankind is more important than money; adequate health, decent housing, good education and other essentials are man's birthright, which it is objectionable and obscene to submit to commercial calculus.

Second, poor people cannot pay charges.

Third, some people who could pay would not pay for good housing, health, etc., because they preferred less important things.

Fourth, charging might in time require people to choose between different suppliers, political and/or commercial, who would persuade them against their best interests.

Fifth, charging would be socially divisive. Each individual (family) would think of himself (itself) rather than of society; in contrast, sharing in public services for which we all pay by taxation is socially cohesive.

Compassion and cost

The social objections to charging—particularly that the poor cannot pay—are the most difficult to discuss rationally because they are advanced for emotional as well as logical reasons. It is easy for the opponents of charging to make themselves seem to be on the side of the angels: compassionate, caring, concerned for the poor, the halt, the lame, the sick, the blind, the fatherless, the deserted, the neglected, the bashed and in general the downtrodden, the under-privileged and the disadvantaged. Conversely it is easy to make the advocates of charging appear cold, callous, unfeeling, hard-hearted. The late Professor Richard M. Titmuss, a leader of the post-war thinking that favoured "free" social services, commonly made his adversaries appear to be not only wrong but also immoral. He, and two other writers nearest to him, Professor Peter Townsend and (rather less so) Professor Brian Abel-Smith, wrote in the cadences of compassion, almost as spokesmen for the underdog, and often with more than a hint that their adversaries were more interested in economic systems, or even commercial interests, than in people, especially the poor.

As a participant in the post-war controversy with the senior trio of welfare sociologists, Titmuss, Townsend and Abel-Smith, I often sensed the accusation of callousness. I always thought they were doing no service to clear thinking to obscure it with emotional speculation about motive, but I tried to see whether there was substance in their emotionalism. Such writers seem to think that economists who analyse social policies in terms of their costs and prices, supply and demand, profit and loss, must put people and their needs second. The characteristic sociological feeling is that the economist's study of (or emphasis on) costs and payment is commercial, materialistic, mercenary, grubby. (I use sociological to mean relating to society or groups, mostly large groups, rather than to individuals: "pensioners" rather than George Baker, retired bookkeeper, bookbinder, bookseller, bookmaker. . . . In this sense sociology is a macro-study and makes the same mistakes as macro-economics that forgets its micro-economic components.)

This paternalistic disdain for the choices of ordinary men in the market can be rationalised as compassion. And there may be the view that the economist is hard-hearted in his persistence with the fundamental and unavoidable truth that people must pay in one way or another for what they receive. This, of course, is a simple error of transferring to the economist the frustration or anger that should be directed at the scarcities of the world. It is about as sensible as blaming the meteorologist for drought (or flood). And it may have been prompted by the witch-doctor pretensions of some economists to make rain by schemes for abolishing unemployment in a world of change, preventing inflation so long as the supply of money is controlled by politicians, achieving equality in a world of diverse human abilities, or annihilating poverty in a world of scarcity.

The truth is the opposite of the sociologists' complaint. To begin with the "wicked motive" bogey: there is an obvious fallacy here. An argument is not wrong because interests indirectly or unintentionally benefit; probably all ideas benefit some interests. In any event, consequences matter more to people affected than motives. But more important: in his method of analysis, the economist who never loses sight of the realities underlying costs and prices, supply and demand, profit and loss does more good for people as individuals than the sociologist who discusses policy in terms of "the pensioners," "the sick," "the disadvantaged." The economist must analyse the benefits and the costs to *individuals.* The sociologist (Titmuss was the arch-exponent of this approach) is forever talking about *groups*—sometimes enormous like "the pensioners" (8½ million) or "Council tenants" (6 million), very large like "hospital patients" (450,000) or "deserted wives" (650,000), or less large like one-parent families with four or more children (about 50,000)—in all of which the individual person is submerged and out of sight.

Economists who believe that social policies must be built up on the subjective evaluations and judgements of individuals are more compassionate than sociologists who believe, sincerely or arrogantly, that they can judge what people "need" by their physical, mental or legal characteristics ("old," "sub-normal," "deserted") which may have little to do with their income, circumstances, or requirements and therefore with their "needs."

In studying costs, the economist, moreover, is being more concerned about humanity than is the sociologist who sees the "needs" of a group and calls for state action to satisfy them whatever the cost and *without reference to needs elsewhere of other groups.* Cost includes opportunity cost: no economist would advocate satisfying one set of needs in, say, housing unless the opportunities foregone showed that the resources called for could not be better used in health, pensions or elsewhere. It is the sociologist who is being callous when he calls for more help for this, that or the other group without counting the cost. His motives do not help the deserving; his consequences harm them.

Helping the poor to pay

The second objection is more specific: people simply cannot afford to pay for education or any of the other services supplied by local and central government. How can the poor, or even the average earner, afford to pay school fees, doctors' bills, high rents, library charges, ambulance fares, refuse collection costs, water charges, full-cost parking charges, etc., etc.? This objection seems to be decisive. Yet on examination it has very little substance.

In the first place, the very term "cannot afford" is question-begging. Whatever our income, there is always something we cannot afford. But that means only we are spending our money on other things because we prefer them. The poor man who says he can't afford better shoes for his children means that he and his wife would rather buy more food for them. The middle-income man who says he can't afford a holiday means he would rather keep up his smoking or motoring. The rich man who says he can't afford a boat is saying he prefers a Rolls. No one can have enough of everything. We all "cannot afford" something.

But do we in the 1970s really prefer the things on which we spend our money (or what is left after tax) to the things supplied for us by the politicians and officials who use our taxes? Do we really prefer spending on clothes, cars, cosmetics to spending on education, health and housing? Broadly our public services often seem shabby and scrimped in contrast to the private services, which are more to our taste and in which we take more pride. That is what the eloquent American phrase-maker Professor J. K. Galbraith meant when he popularised "private affluence, public squalor." But he misunderstood the reasons for the difference, and therefore drew the wrong conclusions for policy. He was condemning ordinary people for spending too much on their personal pleasures and individual indulgences and too little on the much more important public services. He therefore condemned commercial enterprise (run, of course, by the very same ordinary people) for pandering to their profligacies, and he condemned the very same ordinary people for not paying enough in taxes for better public services.

Like social reformers down the decades, he took the easy path of writing for a human species as yet unknown, not for the people of his day. Human nature can change, and may become more saintly in the future. But we must design institutions for man as he is now. Nineteen seventy-seven man evidently prefers to spend his money himself than have it spent for him by others, whatever their pretence that they yearn to serve him. What he spends on himself is called private goods; what others spend it on is called public services. The commonsense conclusion—which Professor Galbraith did not see—is that we should let people spend more of their money themselves so that further squalor (in, say, education) is turned into private affluence (better schools) because they would spend more on education, etc., by diverting money from entertainment, etc. What matters is not who supplies the services or what they are called (public or private) but that they are supplied at all, that they suit us, and that they use our resources efficiently. There is no virtue in public services divorced from individual circumstances, preferences, even idiosyncrasies, at which superior people turn up their toffee noses.

In any event, if it is true that the income of 5, 10 or 15 per cent of the people is too low to pay charges because they have little or no expenditure to divert from entertainment, etc., it does not follow that the only way to provide them with public services is to supply the services free, both to them and to all the other 85, 90 or 95 per cent. The 5 to 15 per cent could be put in the same position as the 85 to 95 per cent by topping up their incomes with a reverse income tax.[1] They, too, could then be on the way to afford to pay.

Who pays now?

To say that the British cannot afford to pay for education, etc., is simply not true. Who else has paid for British public services except the British? It is only in the last few years that sheikhs and other rich creditors have lent us masses of money we could not earn for ourselves to enable us to keep our public services going: in the past the British were a nation of overseas lenders, not borrowers.

The British have *as a nation* long paid for their public services. In the past, the richest families helped to pay for the poorer (though the poor always paid for themselves through indirect taxes more than is usually recognised).

Today, the truth which no politician shouts from the roof-tops is that, except at the extremes of income, *the British family is increasingly paying for its own public services.* As we shall see, a very large part of the taxes paid by households is simply returned to them in a vast, wasteful shifting of coals to Newcastle. This little acknowledged but vitally important truth lies at the centre of the whole argument and we shall examine it in some detail.

Macro-taxes

First, let us grasp the huge macro-economic total of taxes. In 1974, to enable government to supply us with entirely or partly free goods of nearly £42 billion, income tax took £7 billion out of wages and salaries, not far short of £3 billion in tax on companies, £2¾ billion from employees and nearly £2 billion from employers in national insurance, and £3 billion in rates, and a lot of other taxes—surtax, taxes on capital, death duties, and others bringing in several billion more. In all, £11½ billion came from direct taxes on individuals, £10 billion from indirect taxes, and other taxes on companies; the rest was raised by borrowing.

We might then glance down the depressing list of taxes levied on purchases:

1. Polanyi, G. (and others), *Policy for Poverty,* IEA, 1970.

Table D. Tax-as-You-Buy
(1974; the figures are much higher now)

Purchase	Tax £million
Beer	592
Spirits	626
Wines, cider & perry	154
Tobacco	1,462
Clothing	376
Motor cars and cycles	231
Furniture & floor coverings	97
Chemists' goods	65
Recreational goods	113
Petrol and oil	852
Travel	72
Entertainment and recreation	59
Etc., etc.	

These indirect taxes are less obvious to the people who pay them than are direct assaults on the pay-slip in the form of PAYE, but even the direct taxes do not necessarily affect people in the way they think. There is an important distinction between where taxes initially land and where they finally end up: the difference between what economists call impact and incidence. Taxes imposed on industry, whether giant companies or self-employed one-man firms, on their purchases, sales, earnings or capital, may, if the demand for their products is strong (inelastic), be passed on to others—customers, suppliers or employees. So government does not know where such taxes end up. To this extent its taxation policies may be shooting wide of the mark and its claim to superior wisdom is empty. It taxes the baker on his petrol, but the tax may ultimately be paid by the pensioner or widow who buys the bread. So much for all-wise, all-knowing government and its scientific policies. In much of its financing it is almost as blind as a bat.

Micro-taxes

So total "macro" tax figures are not sufficiently illuminating to the individual taxpayer. What is required is "micro" information on taxes paid by individuals or families. Much more interesting—exciting or dismaying—than the total taxes are the official figures of taxes paid by each household, particularly whether it pays more in taxes than it receives in benefits, or less. Fortunately the government Central Statistical Office (CSO) has assembled such figures since the early 1960s,[2] though they are hardly known to ordinary people, for whom this book is primarily written.

The statistics have been based on a sample of households in which members aged sixteen and over are asked by the Department of Employment for details of income (including government benefits in cash and kind), taxes paid and purchases over fourteen days (to assess taxes paid on them indirectly). The main purpose has been to yield information on expenditure to adjust the "weights" in the index of retail prices. (Over the years there has been falling expenditure on bread and more on Scotch salmon, less on lard and more on butter, and so on.) The number of households studied in 1974 was 6,695—lower than usual because of the two General Elections in February and October. The information is collected for each household rather than for each family or individual person because all the occupants of a house or flat share, to some extent, in housing, fuel, lighting, food and perhaps other items, so it would be difficult to separate the taxes on pooled purchases of, or subsidies on, food, rent, rates, etc., paid or received by each family or individual.

The survey thus covered taxes paid by (or for) each household—taxes on income, national insurance contributions, taxes on purchases (cars and drink, VAT on other goods and services), local rates, and taxes on what are called "intermediate products," such as local rates on industrial property and employers' national insurance contributions attributable to each household. These taxes (£21.42 billion) paid for just over half of the £41.61 billion of government expenditure. The other taxes that could not be attributed to separate households—mainly corporation tax and capital taxes—covered about 20 per cent of government expenditure. A further 13 per cent of expenditure was covered by trading income (rents, interests, etc.). The remaining 15 per cent was the gap between government expenditure and the revenue it raised in taxes, etc. (This is the measure of government overspending, misleadingly called in official documents the public sector borrowing requirement (PSBR), which rather implies that the government can spend as much as it likes and simply plug the gap by borrowing.) The taxes not allocated to households were thus a little under 30 per cent.

2. Nissel, M., and Perez, J., "Effects of Taxes and Benefits on Households," *Economic Trends*, Feb. 1976.

Social benefits

On the government expenditure side the survey covered the services that the CSO officials said could be allocated to single households. Benefits in cash were obvious and easy. Subsidies on housing and food could be calculated from the information on expenditure supplied by each household. The benefits in kind—state education, the NHS, school meals, milk and welfare foods—could also be estimated as averages according to the number of children in the household and the average use of health services, etc., in the country as a whole. In all, the allocated benefits accounted for 37½ per cent of total government expenditure, or £15.62 out of £41.61 billion expenditure. In this sense, we may note, these public services are officially acknowledged as providing *private* benefits rather than being public goods proper. Moreover, only the *cost* of the benefits could be allocated, and these, the survey admits, "may bear little relation to the value which the household would itself put on these services." In short the official document was saying that where there are no charges freely paid by users there is ignorance. Government costs ("inputs") are not necessarily indicators of value ("outputs").

Other government services, said the officials, were not allocated. Here we are in the thick of the argument of this book. First, defence (the archetypal public good and the largest single item, 12 per cent of government expenditure including external relations) and tax collection and other administrative costs "are not generally thought of as conferring benefits of a kind which can be allocated to individual households." The officials could hardly be expected to add that if public services were financed by pricing as *much* as possible (not as *little* as convenient for politicians and public officials not anxious to see their domain diminished), tax collection and administrative costs would be much smaller.

Then again, expenditure on regional support and industrial development, such as investment grants, research and roads (about 8½ per cent), was not allocated to households because, said the officials, although they influence the general weight of taxation as well as jobs and therefore incomes, "there is, at least at present, no practical way of estimating these effects on individual households."[3] But there is a way of calculating the personal benefit from roads (by the black box for long-distance roads, Chapter 8); and the economic argument for regional policy is very shaky[4] and much of this expenditure should not have been incurred at all.

3. Nissel and Perez, "Effects of Taxes and Benefits on Households."
4. West, E. G. (and others), *Regional Policy for Ever?*, IEA, 1973.

What are misleadingly called "environmental and protective services"—refuse collection, museums, libraries, parks, fire services, police, water, sewage, etc. (8.9 per cent)—were also not allocated because, continued the officials, "not enough is known about the extent to which each is used" (by each household). This is precisely, as argued in Chapters 7 and 8, the group of local government services in which a large element of pricing could be introduced; and it would make plain the extent of private benefit, not only to each household, but also for each family and even each individual.

Finally, capital expenditure on the social services and public corporations was also not allocated (11.6 per cent). Households derive current benefits from past capital expenditure on schools, hospitals, etc., "but to value them," persisted the officials, "requires more information than is presently available." Here again, pricing, facilitated by the new dimension of choice conveyed by education, health and housing vouchers, could identify the personal family and household benefit (Chapters 4, 5 and 6). These unallocated benefits in the Family Expenditure Surveys accounted in 1974 for 62½ per cent of all government expenditure, yet a large part of them are private benefits.

A final comment on the official (or, at least, these officials'[5]) opinion, half true and half false: "If this analysis were trying to estimate [the] effects [of allocated expenditure such as education and medical care] on the welfare of households, they should perhaps be measured in terms of the values placed upon them by the households themselves." This is fundamentally true: only the user of a service can in the end know its value for him. Economists who hold this view have long adhered to the subjective theory of value, which derives from the Austrian School of economists, and which Professor (Lord) Robbins once explained graphically as "nothing is valuable but thinking makes it so." Unfortunately the official judgement concluded that there was "no practicable way" of measuring the values placed on services by households. This is not true: there certainly is such a way, and there is no insuperable technical obstacle to measurement. The only obstacles are intellectual confusion, political conservatism, civil service obstruction, and trade union defence of vested interests. The way is charging.

Each kind of household's loss or gain

The important question is: what was the net effect on each household of this industrious governmental activity in moving money out of households

5. Nissel and Perez, "Effects of Taxes and Benefits on Households."

in taxes and shifting benefits back in cash (insurance benefits, family allowances, pensions, etc.) and in kind (education, health and other services)? Who gains or loses in this vast game of swings and roundabouts?

To illustrate the net result, figures for eight families varying in size and income are shown in Table E(ii) with the detail of each main tax and benefit for the year 1974. Not surprisingly, since benefits often go to individuals rather than the family as a unit (family allowances and education for each child), the larger households received higher value in benefits than smaller households. So, within each income group, households with two adults and three children or three adults and four children received more in benefits than a household with two adults and two children. What is more surprising is that a wide range of households of middling size and income ended not much better off if their original income was relatively low, and not much worse off if their original income was relatively high. (Later figures will show much the same result.)

Table E(i) shows the gains and losses for each of the ten groups analysed by size of household. On balance only the sole adult and the household with four children gain; all the other groups lose. But the gains and losses are mostly within 20 per cent of original income. And in total, all groups together "lose" 10 per cent of original income, of which a large part is the cost of erecting and running the swings and roundabouts. Personal incomes in 1974 were £75 billion, so the running costs of the tax/benefits game may be up to £7½ billion.

The figures for each group of households within a given income and size are not as reliable as the figures for the sample as a whole. So the smaller the size- or income-group the less useful the averages and estimates that emerged. It is convenient to show the figures in tabular form, but the argument can be followed in words here. Readers will find it instructive to keep a record of their own household figures for a fortnight and compare them with the average for their range of income and size (kind) of household. They will teach you a lot you did not know about the half (on average) of your income you have not thought about much because it is spent for you by others.

These figures are the best available statistics for measuring taxes and benefits. In spite of their incompleteness and limitations[6] the figures are used by the government statisticians to give "a comprehensible picture of the impact of government expenditure and taxation on individual households in

6. Peacock, A. T. (with Shannon, R.), "The Welfare State and the Redistribution of Income," in *Westminster Bank Review,* 1968.

Table E. The Swings and Roundabouts, 1974
(i) Total original and final income after paying taxes and adding benefits for 10 groups of household by size

Households		Average Income (£)		Result	
Size	Number	Original	Final	Gain (%)	Loss (%)
1 adult	1,255	931	1,103	18	—
2 adults	2,113	2,479	2,100	—	15
2 adults, 1 child	607	3,097	2,455	—	21
2 adults, 2 children	808	3,293	2,857	—	13
2 adults, 3 children	334	3,385	3,296	—	3
2 adults, 4 children	117	3,275	3,700	13	—
3 adults	510	3,914	3,052	—	22
3 adults, 1 child	199	4,216	3,686	—	13
3 adults, 2 children	116	3,844	3,723	—	3
4 adults	153	5,342	4,324	—	19
All households in sample	6,212	2,719	2,448	—	10

different circumstances."[7] What emerges is evidence that the "can't afford" argument is very suspect. The figures suggest massive movements of tax-money (half of income on average, much more in many households) out of homes in Wapping, Worcester, Wolverhampton and Wigtown to Whitehall and town hall, passing a massive opposite movement of money (family allowances, etc.) and services from Whitehall or town hall to Wapping, Worcester, Wolverhampton and Wigtown.

This intriguing dénouement which, to repeat, few politicians mention, still less emphasise, raises the fascinating question: "If large numbers of us are paying for our own benefits, more or less, why do we have them controlled by people in government offices? Why can't we buy them ourselves?"

Billions of taxes are returned

The more the edifice of taxes and benefits is examined the more it shows that we have all evidently been the victims of a political hoax (which would long ago have been denounced as an obscene swindle if it had been the work of "the capitalists"). For it shows that, when governments say that they must

7. Nissel and Perez, "Effects of Taxes and Benefits on Households."

Table E. The Swings and Roundabouts, 1974

(ii) Average original income and final income (£ per year) after paying all taxes and adding all benefits for eight types of household

		Retired	Non-retired	Retired and non-retired					
		1 adult	2 adults 0 children	2 adults 1 child	2 adults 2 children	2 adults 2 children	2 adults 3 children	2 adults 3 children	2 adults 1 child
Number of households		579	229	74	76	118	64	64	26
Original income	range	under 381	3099–3749	1749–2115	1749–2115	2116–2560	2561–3098	3099–3749	over 5490
	average	88	3403	1960	1957	2366	2829	3399	8943
Add benefits									
(i) direct in cash									
family allowance		—	—	—	45	45	98	99	—
retirement & old age pension		444	36	—	—	—	—	—	—
widow's pension		14	13	21	—	—	—	—	—
disablement and war disability pension		8	1	5	—	3	—	—	—
invalidity pension & allowance		4	1	10	21	2	—	—	—
unemployment benefit		—	5	4	7	6	—	5	—
sickness & industrial injury benefit		—	13	27	13	11	22	5	—
family income supplement		—	—	—	1	—	3	—	—
supplementary benefit		116	1	—	—	10	—	—	—
maternity benefit		—	1	19	7	6	2	3	4
death grant		1	—	—	—	—	—	1	—
redundancy payment		—	1	—	—	1	—	—	—
other cash benefits		3	—	—	—	—	—	—	—
(ii) indirect (subsidies)									
housing		73	43	44	61	34	78	37	12
food		9	16	20	25	27	34	34	21

(iii) direct in kind								
education	—	15	96	268	308	561	570	137
NHS	108	110	209	191	189	192	201	139
welfare foods	—	—	6	19	14	27	34	7
Total benefits	780	256	461	658	656	1017	989	322
Original income plus all benefits	868	3659	2421	2615	3022	3846	4388	9265
Deduct taxes								
(i) direct								
income tax and surtax	3	561	195	150	229	320	364	2145
NI contributions (employees')	—	154	98	99	117	135	144	172
(ii) indirect								
local rates	48	80	60	66	67	78	83	135
on purchases[1]	43	381	264	273	301	321	407	603
on other items[2]	30	128	96	97	115	130	138	274
Total taxes	124	1304	713	685	829	984	1136	3329
Final income	744	2356	1708	1930	2194	2862	3251	5936
Net result of all taxes and benefits	+656	−1047	−254	−27	−172	+32	−148	−3007

(*Note:* totals may not add up to the sum of items because individual figures are estimated to nearest whole numbers.)

Source: Abstracted from Table 3, *Economic Trends,* Government Statistical Service, HMSO, February, 1976

[1] Customs and Excise duties on beer, wines, spirits, tobacco, oil, betting, etc.; VAT; motor vehicle duties; driving licences, television licences, stamp duties.

[2] These are rates and taxes on goods and services used in the production of goods and services bought by consumers. They include local rates on commercial and industry property, vehicle licences, customs and excise duties on hydrocarbon oils, import duties, stamp duties, employers' NI, NHS and redundancy contributions.

supply this, that or the other because we the people "cannot afford" to pay for them ourselves, *it is they who have made us incapable of paying.* This confidence trick has gone back over a century (Professor West showed it was true of working people and their indirect taxes in the 1870s and earlier[8]) but we have only in recent years had the figures to show how wide-ranging it is in our day.

Take the first of the eight kinds of households (Table E.ii): the retired person living alone (probably a widow whose husband died a few years after he retired). Such households in the sample had an original income (perhaps from the husband's occupational, trade union or other pension or her small earnings) of £88 on average. The retirement pension, supplementary benefit and benefits in kind yielded £780. Total £868. Even at this low standard of living, rates and indirect taxes reduced the final income to £744. But at least the mighty machinery of benefit and taxes raised income from a derisory £88 (average) to £744.

At the other income extreme of the eight households the largest original income recorded was a group with over £5,490 a year. Here there were too few households with two adults and one child for very close calculations. Their average income was £8,943. They received only £6 in cash benefits but £316 in benefits in kind (untaxed and therefore worth much more: I argued some years ago[9] that they should be taxed) raising their gross figure to £9,265. This was reduced by £3,329 paid in taxes, mostly income tax. The final net income of £5,936 was thus £3,007 less than the original average income for the group. The mighty machine of taxes and benefits had redistributed income away from the upper end of the income range.

The extremes of family size are also affected by the tax-benefit machine. The household in the more or less middling income group of £3,099 to £3,749 with an average of £3,403 was left substantially worse off. Such households in the sample had no children under eighteen (perhaps because couples could not have children, or where the children had married). They received £256 in benefits but paid £1,304 in taxes, ending £1,047 worse off at £2,356. Whether you regard it as redistributing income (though such households are hardly rich) or as taking from childless couples or from parents who had brought up a family, again the massive machine had worked.

But what of the typical family households in the middle, with more or less

8. West, E. G., *Education and the State,* IEA, 1965, 1970; and *Education and the Industrial Revolution,* Batsford, 1975.

9. Seldon, A., "Taxing Social Benefits," *Daily Telegraph,* 1968.

average incomes and numbers of children? Apart from the extremes of income, and in families with two or three children, the tax-benefit machine left much less of a mark. Households of two adults and two children in the income range £1,749 to £2,115, an average of £1,957 a year, much less than the national average, received £658 in benefits but paid out £685 in taxes. Their final income was thus £27 less than they started with. A lot of activity for a little result: a third of income taken in taxes, and put back in benefits, less a slice for the officials who assess and collect taxes, return benefits in cash and run benefits in kind. Net result: final income down by 1.38 per cent. And against this they lose influence over the £478 of benefits in kind.

Households of the same size but with rather more income (an average of £2,366) ended up £172 worse off than they started after receiving £656 in benefits and paying £831 in taxes. Shifting 28 per cent of their income in and 35 per cent out left them 7.27 per cent worse off.

Or take two rather larger types of household: two adults and three children in the income range £2,561 to £3,098. They had an average original income of £2,829. After a lot of heaving and shoving, with £1,017 in benefits and £984 in taxes, they finished £32 better off. Again a mouse (plus 1.13 per cent) out of a mountain (a third in and out).

In the higher income range of £3,099 to £3,749, households with an average original income of £3,399 ended £148 worse off (4.35 per cent) after receiving £989 in benefits and paying £1,136 in taxes (again around a third in and out).

Finally, households of two adults and one child in the income range £1,749 to £2,115—markedly less than the national wage—started with an average of £1,960, received £461 in benefits, paid out a surprising £713 in taxes and ended £254 worse off. More than a third was moved out, less than a third was moved back: result, the household was left 12.96 per cent worse off. (It lost more because of its small size than it gained because of its low income.)

Two main conclusions follow. The first is that all this activity in raising taxes and returning benefits seems to have only a balancing effect in altering the final distribution of income in most households. There must be a better way of arranging this relatively small amount of true redistribution without heaving and shoving such vast amounts of taxes and benefits to and fro. Many more households would then no longer be "too poor to pay," and the excuse for providing "free" services would have evaporated. They could be made customers who paid charges for choice.

The second is that the persistence with raising taxes to finance the increasing element of private benefit in public services is driving taxes further down the income scale. Households with barely average incomes are being taxed, and even those receiving state benefits have to pay part of them back. This is not only coals to Newcastle; if the official figures are about right, it looks more like a vicious circle of benefits in Bedlam. The state treats its citizens as intelligent enough to elect legislators, competent enough to live daily lives without poisoning or killing themselves; yet, in thus depriving them of the power to dispose of their incomes, it questions their humanity, their competence, their responsibility and integrity. It mocks their intelligence most by telling millions they are too poor to pay when it is the state itself that makes many of them poor.

How much taxation is "abortive"?

How far is the state itself, by taxation, making people unable to pay for its benefits? How much British taxation is "abortive" in the sense that it could be left with taxpayers to enable them to pay in the first place? How much goes back in cash or kind *to the very same households whence it came?*

In the USA, Professor Friedman has estimated that only about a third of the billions of dollars spent on social benefits in the mid-1960s was required to make the lowest incomes up to the minimum income regarded as the poverty line so that poverty in this sense was wiped out. Two-thirds, it would seem, need not have been raised for this redistributive purpose and was "abortive."

The British statistics do not make this calculation. Yet it is one of the most important that could have emerged from them, even if the benefits statistics account for only three-eighths of government expenditure and taxes allocated cover only rather over half of government expenditure. Moreover, what is important for individual decision-making is not the total macro-figure for the country as a whole but the micro-finances of each family or household. The figures for each of the 6,695 households in the sample are not available, but I have calculated them for the 6,051 in each of the 69 groups large enough for separate figures to be available (those with over 10 in each group). This is a first rough approximation because the figures were averages for each group. The results are shown in Table F.

The 6,051 households paid just over £7 million in taxes and received rather over £3¼ million in benefits (the totals of the last two columns). In all therefore 46 per cent, or not far short of half, of the taxes were refunded in benefits *to the very same households.* This calculation applies only to the taxes that could be traced to households. We do not know how much of the taxes not analysed by the government statisticians were eventually returned to the households from which they came. I would expect that probably much more than half and possibly as much as two-thirds or three-quarters of all British taxes are raised unnecessarily and wastefully in this way. This is a measure of the enormous sums that could be left with people to use, or to learn to use in time, to buy goods and services now supplied by government.

The figures available provide, at least, the most reasonably reliable figures measuring the swings and roundabouts of taxes and benefits. As pricing is spread to other benefits, and it becomes possible to trace other taxes to households, we shall be able to make a more complete assessment of the extent of abortive taxation and unnecessary government. This in itself is a powerful case for charging to yield the *information* we cannot collect in any other way for government policy to make sense because it would then be based on knowledge rather than politicised judgement or guesswork.

The figures have been calculated to show the average taxes paid by households in each of the 69 groups and the average value of the benefits they received. It is then possible to calculate the percentages of taxes returned by the state in benefits. Where taxes were less than benefits, all the taxes, 100 per cent, can be regarded as being returned; where taxes exceed benefits, less than 100 per cent. Thus, in the 1974 households of a sole adult, the group with original income up to £1,748 had, on average, all their taxes returned. The groups with the highest income, £1,749 to £2,560 (there were some with higher income but too few to yield averages), paid more in taxes than they received in benefits, which were 74 per cent of their taxes. Within each group, household figures would have varied because of differences in expenditure (and therefore indirect taxes), tax allowance (for dependents, life assurance, mortgage interest) and so on.

Of the 6,051 households, 2,068, or over a third, had all their taxes returned in benefits, and could possibly not have been taxed at all (subject to the qualifications below). A further 486 households had 80 to 99 per cent returned; 517 had 60 to 79 per cent returned; 1,062 had 40 to 59 per cent; and the remainder, 1,918, had less than 40 per cent. They could all therefore have been taxed either very little or much less than they were, and some—those with the lowest incomes or most children—almost not at all.

How much, in money, of taxes could be left with families—or not levied in the first place? The calculations suggest that, on average, that is for all families in the country as a whole, the proportion of taxes that are now levied to pay for "the social wage" but that could be left with families is not less than half. I have argued that it is probably higher. But even at half it would mean

Table F. Abortive Taxation, or Coals to Newcastle: a first approximation by averages for groups of households, 1974

Households			Average for each group of households				Total taxes	
Composition	number	Original income £	taxes paid £	benefits received £	taxes returned in benefits £	%	paid	returned
1 adult (retired)	579	under 381	125	781	125	100	72,375	72,375
	46	381–556	183	633	183	100	8,418	8,418
	38	557–815	286	631	286	100	10,868	10,868
	27	816–1,193	424	553	424	100	11,448	11,448
	20	1,194–1,748	542	635	542	100	10,840	10,840
	14	1,749–2,560	781	578	578	74	10,934	8,092
2 adults (retired)	340	under 381	225	1,241	225	100	76,500	76,500
	73	301–556	242	1,090	242	100	17,666	17,666
	56	557–815	370	1,045	370	100	20,720	20,720
	46	816–1,193	493	1,034	493	100	22,678	22,678
	31	1,194–1,748	661	1,024	661	100	20,491	20,491
	30	1,749–2,560	793	872	793	100	23,790	23,790
	18	2,561–3,749	1,293	928	928	72	23,274	16,704
1 adult (not retired)	69	under 381	155	969	155	100	10,695	10,695
	19	381–556	223	650	223	100	4,237	4,237
	43	557–815	310	561	310	100	13,330	13,330
	63	816–1,193	400	413	400	100	25,200	25,200
	107	1,194–1,748	605	290	290	48	64,735	31,030
	118	1,749–2,560	863	147	147	17	101,834	17,346
	63	2,561–3,749	1,146	130	130	11	72,198	8,190

	29	3,750–5,489	1,747	79	79	4.5	50,663	2,291
	12	5,490+	3,116	95	95	3.0	37,392	1,140
2 adults (not retired)	27	under 381	309	1,105	309	100	8,343	8,343
	18	381–556	290	1,171	290	100	5,220	5,220
	42	557–815	310	983	310	100	13,020	13,020
	57	816–1,193	429	906	429	100	24,453	24,453
	138	1,194–1,748	583	551	551	95	80,454	76,038
	318	1,749–2,560	837	378	378	45	266,166	120,204
	445	2,561–3,749	1,184	292	292	25	526,880	129,940
	339	3,750–5,489	1,647	197	197	12	558,333	66,783
	120	5,490+	2,789	197	197	7	334,680	23,640
2 adults 1 child	11	816–1,193	332	1,000	332	100	3,652	3,652
	45	1,194–1,748	561	631	561	100	25,245	25,245
	177	1,749–2,560	784	461	461	59	138,768	81,597
	221	2,561–3,749	1,112	436	436	39	245,752	96,356
	114	3,750–5,489	1,550	388	388	25	176,700	44,232
	26	5,490+	3,330	322	322	10	86,580	8,372

Table F (continued)

Households		Original income	Average for each group of households				Total taxes	
			taxes paid	benefits received	taxes returned in benefits			
Composition	number	£	£	£	£	%	paid	returned
2 adults 2 children	49	1,194–1,748	540	871	540	100	26,460	26,460
	194	1,749–2,560	773	657	657	85	149,962	127,458
	320	2,561–3,749	1,071	641	641	60	342,720	205,120
	173	3,750–5,489	1,475	652	652	44	255,175	112,796
	51	5,490+	2,403	646	646	27	122,553	32,946
2 adults 3 children	12	under 381	430	2,320	430	100	5,160	5,160
	21	1,194–1,748	465	1,201	465	100	9,765	9,765
	63	1,749–2,560	746	983	746	100	46,998	46,998
	128	2,561–3,749	1,060	1,002	1,002	95	135,680	128,256
	70	3,750–5,489	1,406	1,009	1,009	72	98,420	70,630
	34	5,490+	2,499	853	853	34	84,966	29,002
2 adults 4 children	17	1,194–1,748	453	1,593	453	100	7,701	7,701
	26	1,749–2,560	663	1,459	663	100	17,238	17,238
	31	2,561–3,749	1,035	1,379	1,035	100	32,085	32,085
	26	3,750–5,489	1,406	1,313	1,313	93	36,556	34,138
	10	5,490+	2,493	1,253	1,253	50	24,930	12,530
3 adults	10	under 381	407	1,631	407	100	4,070	4,070
	19	1,446–1,748	716	1,104	716	100	13,604	13,604
	61	1,749–2,560	1,820	2,149	1,820	100	111,020	111,020
	141	2,561–3,749	2,503	1,306	1,306	52	352,923	184,146
	166	3,750–5,489	3,544	969	969	27	588,304	160,854

3 adults 1 child	18	2,116–2,560	841	1,012	841	100	15,138	15,138
	54	2,561–3,749	2,259	1,791	1,791	79	121,986	96,714
	69	3,750–5,489	3,188	1,744	1,744	55	219,972	120,336
	36	5,490+	2,677	876	876	33	96,372	31,536
3 adults 2 children	41	2,561–3,749	2,085	2,663	2,085	100	85,485	85,485
	41	3,750–5,489	3,134	2,259	2,259	72	128,494	92,619
	16	5,490+	2,308	1,122	1,122	49	36,928	17,952
4 adults	20	3,099–3,749	1,298	1,794	1,298	100	25,960	25,960
	51	3,750–5,489	3,381	1,633	1,633	48	172,431	83,283
	61	5,490+	2,703	693	693	26	164,883	42,273

Source: abstracted and calculated from Nissel, Muriel, and Perez, Jane, "Effects of Taxes and Benefits on Households," *Economic Trends*, February 1976, p. 220.

that, with "the social wage" around £1,000, families could be left with an average of about £500 a year to spend as they, rather than the politicians or officials, thought best. There would be some possible general requirements, such as health insurance to cover major medical risks and minimum educational standards; but even here families would have a choice of health insurer not confined to the state, and a choice of educational method not confined to state schools. There would be no need for compulsory school attendance at all, and certainly not a fixed minimum age for all children whatever their abilities or potentialities. And families would, of course, be able to take advice on how to spend their money from a wide range of advisers, public and private, official, charitable, secular, spiritual, voluntary or commercial.

Interest attaches not only to the number of households that might not be taxed at all, or not very much, but also to their income. For they are the poorest, or the near-poor—precisely those that advocates of compulsory government services say are least able to pay for services. Even retired couples (two adults) with original incomes up to £1,748 and receiving around £1,000 in benefits paid several hundred pounds in taxes.

What happens if we omit the "rich" and examine the effect on the others? The income group with £5,490 and over totals 449 households, or 7 per cent of the sample. If we take them as a fair approximation to "the rich," we are left arguing that the remainder, 93 per cent of households, must be supplied with free (or subsidised) services because they are too "poor" to pay. But the official statistics show that, except for 2,068 households with the lower incomes, the "poor" people pay *more* in taxes than they receive in benefits. The 2,068 form only 34 per cent of the households. So 59 per cent (93 per cent less 34 per cent) of households are *made* "poor" by the very state that says it must tax them to supply "free" services they are too poor to buy. Fifty-nine per cent of all households in the UK is over 10½ million—or, say, around 35 million people. So much for the poverty argument that the British people cannot pay for the private benefits in public services.

It must now be clear that there is enormous scope for leaving families with much or most of their taxes. And it must also be accepted that the "poverty" excuse for supplying them with free services is, for not far short of two-thirds of families, circular reasoning: their original (gross) incomes are high enough to pay if they were not taxed in the first place, or not as much as they are now.

What about the poor who receive more in benefits than they pay in taxes? They can be helped to pay in two ways: mainly by reverse taxes; possibly also by lower expenditure taxes on the sort of goods they tend to buy. Thus by reverse taxes for the real poor (with lower incomes) and returned (or rather abolished) taxes for the artificially state-created "poor," *all* could be made equal in status, dignity and consumer authority over the services they use. And they could all have the bonus of an enormous reduction in the bureaucracy and more efficient government with more attention to real public goods that are now neglected because of lack of tax funds.

These calculations must be regarded only as a first approximation because ideally they should be made for each household separately rather than for the groups; the figures given by the households in the sample cannot all be checked; and they may not strictly represent payments in and out during a single year. But they are the best figures we have. Let the government therefore do the more complete and refined calculations to provide a Twentieth Century Domesday Book from which each family can tell where it stands. We shall then know the full extent of abortive taxation. And until that day let the "poverty" argument for free public services be abandoned as based on lack of knowledge or on special pleading unsupported by reasoning, statistics or common sense.

Are the British irresponsible?

The third objection to charging is that some people who could pay would not pay. They would be short-sighted, inhuman, callous, self-indulgent, brutal. They would live in hovels, not send their children to school, not insure against ill-health, not have their refuse or sewage removed; mothers and fathers would abandon their young children while at work; they would not pay for water; their lives would be nasty, brutish, and probably short.

To list the spine-chilling examples is to show how unreal they are. I do not recognise, in this picture, the British in the second half of the twentieth century, regarded by visitors as the most considerate, helpful, tolerant and civilised people in the world, especially to strangers. There are some such people in every country: in the richest as well as the poorest; in Britain, in the United States, as well as in India and Russia. How many there are in Britain we do not know—2 per cent? 5 per cent? Advocates of state paternalism insist there would be many if people were left to themselves, and that those who are not must be treated as if they are until there are none.

How far we should run people's lives is itself a central question. People do not have to join in a free society with the burden of making choices in markets; they may drop out. Even where it may be desirable to prevent foolish or selfish people from neglecting themselves or their children, it is by no means clear that free government services are the best way. That method has been tried in Britain for a century without making everyone more responsible. It may, indeed, have the opposite effect: some people will not learn to take care of themselves—or their children—if they are taken care of by others. If social policy had been less paternalistic, years of practice in day-to-day responsibility would have taught more to be responsible. Yet in the name of equality it is argued by paternalists, more on the Left than on the Right, that social policies and government services should treat everyone alike so that the exceptional should not feel singled out or isolated. So if 5 per cent are irresponsible, the 95 per cent responsible must be treated as irresponsible. This is the argument that has maintained taxes at the high and rising levels to pay for services that more and more people could be buying for themselves.

Would charging destroy welfare?

The supporters of this irresponsible argument tend to claim that charging would create havoc by destroying the fabric of social services built up over a century. This argument is defective.

First, initially the charges are to be for services provided by government. If government can induce citizens to pay their taxes, increasingly against their inclinations, it can induce them to pay charges that will show them what they are paying for. There are apparent differences. In favour of taxes, paradoxically, is the lack of knowledge of tax-prices: knowing prices through charges may cause users to hesitate or wish to rebel when they know for the first time what services like education or fire-fighting cost. In favour of charges is this very knowledge, which might encourage users to pay more readily by economising elsewhere. But since government services are supplied for all citizens whether they pay for them by taxes or charges, the objection does not apply. Children will still be required to be educated, although not necessarily in state schools. Health insurance, not necessarily for all costs and risks but for major risks or catastrophic costs, could still be made obligatory, as is third-party motor insurance, though not necessarily with the government.

Second, the case for compulsion can hardly continue for ever. Fewer husbands would neglect their wives' health, or parents their children's health or education, or families their homes, than did so twenty-five, fifty or seventy-five years ago. If there are more, there must be something alarmingly wrong with government control of education and the social and moral environment it has built up over a century since 1870.

Third, if there is a minority, whether growing or declining, that refuses to pay for a service considered desirable for all to use, the argument for forcing them to use it by making them pay in taxes supposes that they are less likely to use it if they pay by charges. The opposite seems the more likely. People will make the most of a service if they know they are paying for it and know how much it costs, because they then appreciate what a sacrifice they are making of other things. State school parents have no idea of school costs. Fee-paying parents know it is more or less £250 a term in day schools. Truancy would be less common if parents paid school fees through cash or vouchers; it is less common in private than in state schools. And much the same attitude would appear elsewhere: "I am paying for this school (hospital, etc.) so I must make the best of it."

The unacceptable cost of exclusive tax-paid services

There is a more fundamental objection to all-embracing compulsion by taxation. *If the price of all-embracing participation in a service is that no other method of payment for a possible alternative can be allowed, the price—in sacrifice of services unknown—is too high to pay.* It is probably true that the comprehensive method of secondary education cannot be judged unless all children in the catchment area are channelled into it by suppressing all other methods. That is a logically defensible proposition. But it is not one that can be accepted by anyone in a civilised society. Its implications are fearful. This approach to policy could be catastrophic, for it requires that all other methods should be suppressed. The case, at best, is for temporary closure of other schools in the area until the comprehensive method is tested. This argument is seductive but must be rejected. In practice forces of inertia working for continuance of the comprehensive method, even if it was seen to fail (in education, health or anywhere else), would be all the stronger once the other methods that could draw off dissatisfied parents were not available.

The case for universalising a technique by suppressing existing or potential alternatives is defective because it overlooks the unknown and untold externality of improvement by experimentation and innovation that has sustained the progress of civilised life. It blocks the development of new and better techniques.

The case for making all pay for a universal, comprehensive, exclusive, "totalitarian" government service by taxes, because some would not pay charges or would try alternatives elsewhere, is similarly defective by circular reasoning. The apparently perfectionist technique is fatally *imperfect* because it requires suppression of alternatives—the only source of evidence by which its perfection can be proved.

Are the British gullible?

A fourth social objection to charging is that if it led some users to change between government suppliers (by moving between local authority areas) or from government to private suppliers, the chance of acquiring users would induce suppliers to attract them against their best interests.

The large unstated assumption is that users now receive the best possible services from their present government suppliers. Discussion of this aspect of government service is surprisingly naive in Britain, and much less sophisticated than in the USA. Perhaps complaints in recent years against the Post Office for its tardy letter post and inattentive telephone services, against unprompt government railways and road transport, indifferent quality of coal service, undependable refuse collection, inadequate police protection or corrupt Council building may have made the British public more critical. But there is still a lingering, though lately evaporating, faith in civil servants as sea-green incorruptibles, still a trust in British "public" men and officials, still a belief that any organisation described as "public" must be "in the public interest."

This attitude is surprising from the British mixture of common sense, humour and capacity to see through pretence. A man is not made a public benefactor by being made a public official. It is still the truest working assumptions that family man will maximise his private satisfactions, business man his private profit, official man his official influence, and political man his political power. What they do with their profit, influence or power is their affair: they can use it selfishly or unselfishly according to how they are taught by family, school or church. But much more understanding of public and political life is obtained by working from these realistic assumptions than by supposing that public men or government employees from town hall housing managers to Whitehall mandarins yearn to dispense nectar to all and sundry with never a thought for themselves or their families or concerns. American economists are ahead of British universities in their development of theories of public choice, democracy and politics,[10] although they

10. Buchanan, J. M., *The Inconsistencies of the N.H.S.*, IEA, 1965; *Public Finance in Democratic Process*, University of North Carolina Press, 1967; *Demand and Supply of Public Goods*, Rand McNally & Co. (USA), 1968; *The Limits of Liberty*, University of Chicago Press, 1975; and

are being closely followed.[11] There is no reason to suppose that government monopolies will safeguard their users better than suppliers (government or private) that have to satisfy their customers or lose them to competitors.

The objection that users will be at the mercy of persuasive suppliers is in any event at variance with the reaction of British consumers who *pay* for what they buy. If there is little prospect of alternative supply, as in wartime or local monopoly, they accept with good-humoured resignation what is offered. But if there are alternatives they are not supine or subservient: they expect good value or go elsewhere. The emergent wage-earner—and his wife—faced with the profusion of post-war labour-saving or leisure-serving products soon learned how to buy wisely. It is precisely in the "public" services supplied by government that they have been inured to passive acceptance because their faculties of judgement and discrimination have atrophied, because they have never, or at best rarely, been exercised. The demanding customer at the pub, butcher, hairdresser or airport often becomes a subdued supplicant in the state headmaster's study, the matron's ward or the Council housing manager's office; the minority who become aggressive to over-compensate for lack of bargaining power, demanding more than their due, distort the distribution. The result is arbitrary, the outcome of chance, not justice or "fairness."

What makes for social divisiveness?

A fifth objection to charging is that joint or collective payment by taxes for services shared by all without question of individual payment has the unique quality of creating a sense of social cohesion that unites everyone in the community. A public service that we use without payment makes us all feel at one with another. Something for which we pay separately divides us from our fellow beings. This sense of community, or fellowship, underlies the best of utopian Socialist teaching about men as brothers. It is also reflected in the Conservative feeling that, however the British may differ, they are basically members of One Nation. (The phrase was formulated to dramatise the contrast with the Conservative Benjamin Disraeli's characterisation of the nineteenth-century British as Two Nations, the rich and the poor.)

(with Tullock, G.) *The Calculus of Consent,* University of Michigan Press, 1962; Johnson, D. B., "The Charity Market: Theory and Practice," in *The Economics of Charity,* IEA, 1973.

11. Perlman, M., "The Economics of Politics," in *The Vote Motive,* IEA, 1976; and Rowley, C. K. (with Peacock, A. T.), *Welfare Economics: A Liberal Restatement,* Martin Robertson, 1974.

The importance of the public services in creating or strengthening the sense of social cohesion has been a repeated refrain in sociological writing since the war.

If this anxiety about social cohesion is to be urged against individual payment, it should be examined more closely. Charging would yield revenue for "public" services that government has not been able to raise in taxes. If "public" services strengthen social cohesion, as they may if they are *public* goods, charging is the only method available when other methods of financing them are exhausted because the limits of acceptable taxation have been reached.

If it is replied that charging may lead some people to prefer private services (which it might) that is a risk that the defenders of "public" services must take. The alternative is to extract still higher taxation from reluctant taxpayers by enforcement that becomes increasingly more stringent as the willing acceptance of taxation decreases and taxpayers resort increasingly to avoidance and evasion. Increasingly stringent enforcement can logically be argued by tax collectors, but it is hardly likely to create or promote the social cohesion between law-makers and citizens, tax-gatherers and taxpayers desired by the supporters of government expenditure. The dilemma is insoluble.

There is an even more fundamental doubt about the theory of social cohesion through public services. The theory is that shared public services create a sense of community. Each member of society says: "This train/coal mine/generating station/rubbish dump/library/telephone kiosk/beach/abattoir is owned in common by all my fellow citizens and me. I own part of it. It binds them to me, and me to them. I will therefore take care of it."

A noble conception. Or do we say: "They tell me this is mine, but it is also everybody else's. Only a tiny part of it is mine, so small I can hardly imagine it. And whatever my tiny nominal ownership I have no say in the way it is used, no real control over it at all. It is not really mine; it is theirs. And, no matter how much care I take, it will do me no good if everyone else does not."

Public services, especially as paying for them by taxes is increasingly resented, are seen not as everyone's property that all will protect and cherish, but as no one's property that is fair game for selfish use, abuse and exploitation. If each man's nominal ownership is tiny, public property is seen by each individual as owned by everyone else: the vast amorphous, anonymous "Them" that has become the description of the unknown outsiders with no names or recognisable faces who in the real world seem collectively to control the public property that only in theory, in political tracts, on paper, in

General Election manifestoes and speeches, belongs to everyman. It may be a bitter pill for the hopeful, generous-hearted advocates of public property who, for a century since the Fabians of the 1880s, have believed that all would own and share in mutual brotherly consideration. The truth is that ownership that is not individual, or possibly in very small groups, is ineffective. The environment is exploited, over-used, abused, ravaged and polluted because no one owns it. On paper it belongs to all of us, but in practice to none of us, so no one takes care of it, no one has an interest in preserving and protecting it.

That is a central economic truth that has not yet reached the environmentalists, perhaps because it is the opposite from the "public" property approach with which they typically set out. It is no less true of the whole range of public services and public property from telephone booths to swimming pools, trains to schools, buses to ante-natal clinics, fire-engines to police cars, allotments to libraries, docks and quays to deck chairs and beaches, public libraries to public lavatories.

There is a sense in which government expenditure in public services conduces to a sense of social cohesion. That is when there is a feeling that we have jointly paid in taxes for a service we share in common. These are the true public goods in which we benefit one another only because we share in a service we could not enjoy at all unless we did. But when we are forced to come together to pay for services that we regard as personal, and in which misuse by others can harm us, there is no social cohesion but social tension, mutual distrust, resentment and discord. A borrower who despoils a library book, a child who defaces a classroom, an adolescent who ravages a telephone booth or railway compartment, a Council tenant who neglects his house or garden, a nurse or patient who is careless with hospital equipment or crockery: these and many more do less for social cohesion than people who pay for what they want, benefit from their care of it, and suffer from their carelessness.

In the language of externalities, on which the advocates of public government services lean heavily (or too heavily), it is the user of public property who sheds external costs and damage on his unsuspecting fellow-citizens; and it is the man who pays for what he receives who bears them himself. For he internalises his externalities. And, in taking care of his own, he contributes to responsibility in the community.

Finally on this whole subject of poverty, inequality, deprivation, underprivilege and social divisiveness, I would address two questions to the many good people who still think the best solution is tax-financed free welfare and other public services.

I have argued that differences and deficiencies in income should be and can be corrected by a reverse income tax to enable all in time to pay.

First, do they deny that the tax-paid system throws up other kinds of differences and deficiencies that influence or decide access and distribution: in accent, social background, political influence, economic muscle?

Second, do they deny that these differences and deficiencies are more difficult to correct than are differences and deficiencies in income?

CHAPTER **11**

Administratively Impracticable

Charging for goods and services, many of which have been "free" for as long as we can remember, will seem strange, a nuisance, fussy, a new problem to think about. Prices would have to be fixed, methods of payment decided, recording and accounting organised. The fee for borrowing a book, for a term at school, for the services of a midwife, for advice on family planning, for a visit to or from a family doctor, or a week in hospital, the charge for emptying a dustbin, an hour on a tennis court, at a swimming pool, nine or eighteen holes on a golf course—all these and many more would have to be calculated. Isn't charging going to be administratively expensive, difficult, even impracticable? Shouldn't we take the word of officials who tell us that it will?

Obstruction from officials

Reluctance, resistance and obstruction may be expected from civil servants and local officials who run the existing system, and for three reasons, two bad and one (possibly) good. The first is that the present system is much easier for them. If users, customers, tenants, patients, parents pay someone in an office a long way off—the tax collector for income tax, the local authority finance officer for rates, someone even more remote and almost unidentifiable for VAT—there is no sense of obligation in taking their money, no exposure to their authority in laying down what they would like on every occasion they use a service, no physical handling of money or giving a receipt, no occasion even to say "Thank you." The public servant is clear of all these irksome encumbrances and can concentrate on the service he or she is "giving."

The second reason why we must expect resistance from public officials is that charging for private benefits will certainly disturb, probably disrupt and possibly cause upheaval in their working lives, if not sleepless nights. It could reduce their ranks by redundancy. For a change from taxing to charging would also change the very nature of their work, and require from them qualities they may not possess and will have to acquire, or change their jobs. Their relationship to the customers will have to change from that of *giver* to that of *seller.* And for that relationship they have not been trained. It is to require them to turn 180 degrees from facing colleagues who share their attitudes, hopes and lives to face their real paymasters who have a lot of other things on which to spend their money.

These two understandable reasons for obstructing charging throw doubt on the reliability of the third reason, which could conceivably be good but in practice is probably bad, or at least suspect. This objection is that charging would be unworkable, or would be so costly as to overwhelm its advantages, or cause such disturbance for such a long time as to damage the services themselves. The officials who administer the services now are, after all, the experts on the spot. No one knows more about running them than they do. Little wonder that Ministers in Whitehall and Councillors in town halls are guided as well as advised by their advisers—their permanent officials in town-planning, housing, medicine, education, amenities and facilities, protective and environmental services. And if they said that charging in its various forms was unworkable, too costly or disruptive we should listen to them with respect.

But there are several difficulties in the way of accepting and voting on their advice. The first I have indicated: their loyalties are in conflict. They are personally interested parties as well as expert witnesses. Their main duty may seem to be with the public they are paid to serve. But it is not easy to give advice that may shatter your daily routine and perhaps lose your job. So whatever advice they give must be checked from other sources: second opinions are as important in national policies as in personal health.

Secondly, the officials are authoritative, though not disinterested, in the running of the *existing* system of financing, but not on projected *new* systems. Their opinion on charging would be based not on experience but on conjecture—guesswork. Being human, good husbands (or wives) and parents, and not wishing to invite or encourage an unknown technique that, after all, might work even worse than they sincerely believe, they would unconsciously tend to under-rate its probable advantages and over-state its probable disadvantages. Above all, they could not claim the same authority in advising on a new method of financing that they can properly claim in advising on the system they know from experience.

Much the same is true of the specialists in government services—from teachers and doctors to refuse and sewage collectors (or the other way round: no order of importance is intended)—as is true of general officials and administrators. Insofar as they are in more direct personal contact with users, the effect on them might be even more cataclysmic. Their views must also, therefore, be regarded with scepticism and, where possible, double checked. Moreover they may reflect, even more than those of civil servants, local officials or general administrators, the value-judgement—which is an article of faith that does not call for logical proof—that public services are innately superior to private services because they enable the community to act together in caring for one another and especially for people in disadvantageous circumstances, in contrast to private services which create scope for individual self-seeking or profit-making at the expense of other members of society. We considered that belief in the last chapter, and the least that can be said is that it is not self-evidently true. Any official who believes that it is disbars himself to that extent from giving an authoritative and unbiased opinion.

Powers of officials in public monopolies

There is an even more disturbing tendency in the attitudes of general public officials or specialist operators that calls for early judgement by the public. If public officials and operators who regard themselves as more informed than their customers feel very strongly in favour of public services in principle, they may decide they must do what they can to dissuade or prevent the general public from adopting policies or methods they feel are not "in the public interest," whatever the public itself may think. As a motive, at least, this is praiseworthy.

At the other extreme, officials and operators have a strong incentive to do what they can to discourage policies that endanger their livelihoods. What they can do can be very effective. Since public services are usually protected from the competition of private services, the resulting degree of monopoly enables them to enforce their opinions by stopping the services altogether. In recent times they have refused, or have announced they would refuse, to carry out the policies of government: in Manchester (Tameside) to preserve grammar schools, in Kent County to study the feasibility of a voucher experiment, in National Health Service hospitals to tend patients in pay-beds. In all episodes they were of the view that their judgement should take precedence over the intentions of a newly-elected District Council (Tameside) and a County Council (Kent) acting within its powers (as well as over such tests of public opinion as the Ashford "referendum" and a large public meeting) as well as national policy under law.

It may be that if officials and operators carry their opposition to government policy from adverse but reasoned advice to high-handed obstruction, their authority as advisers will be further weakened. How far their opinion, or their personal interest in maintaining their livelihood, can take precedence over the opinion or interest of people who use public services without slowing down the economy until it seizes up and preventing the working of democratic institutions—how far, in other words, employees in state-protected monopolies can go in thwarting the sovereignty of the consumer in the economy and the elector in the polity—has hardly been discussed in much depth in Britain. But it must be clear that economic systems controlled by producers must deteriorate and decline, since they resist change.

Evidence on practicability from experiment

The only reliable source of evidence is experimentation. This is the method by which mankind has tried out new ideas or techniques down the ages. Trial and error, sampling, experience, pragmatism: there are various names, some more appropriate than others, for the principle. The British are supposed to be especially wise in applying it. It seems to embody the acme of common sense. Reason points to what sounds like a good idea, but there can be no certainty about how it will work in practice. So the sane course is to try it out, on a small scale, for a time; and then, if it seems to work, extend it gradually.

There are two difficulties in this approach. One is that if the idea is tried in an untypical area or for too short a time, it may fail, because people will not react as they would to a reform expected to be nationwide and long-term; and the main idea itself may be condemned and perhaps abandoned. Professor Milton Friedman has met this difficulty with the argument that the improvement would be so marked that even an imperfect experiment could dramatise the superiority of the new method.[1] Second, opponents of the idea in principle may try to discredit it by getting in on the experiment. The risk that the idea may be destroyed because its opponents will change their tactics to "If you can't beat 'em, join 'em" is an argument for eschewing an experiment and going for the whole hog. At its extreme this course is to introduce the idea overnight.

1. Friedman, M., *From Galbraith to Economic Freedom*, IEA, 1977.

Step-by-step or overnight?

The step-by-step approach has been adopted in the USA. A reverse income tax has been operated for three years in New Jersey (Trenton), an education voucher for five years in California (Alum Rock). Both devices facilitated charging: the reverse tax for purchases generally, the voucher for education. Research organisations and university departments have been working on an experiment in cash housing allowances, which would facilitate charging market rents. In Australia there is to be experimentation with a housing voucher and possibly an education voucher.

The brilliant example of overnight reform is that of Professor Ludwig Erhard who introduced the new German Mark on Sunday/Monday, 20/21 June 1949, and ushered in the German "economic miracle" that transformed desolation into affluence by liberalising and rewarding the individual will to work for self-improvement. On the other hand, the British overnight and nationwide reform, the National Health Service, has been in my view a disaster. This may sound strong language. The NHS replaced an emerging structure of charging by compulsory social insurance and taxing. It is a disaster not only because it was based on fallacious thinking: Bevan said it was "to generalise the best," which is deceptively easy but dishonest Utopianism; if taken seriously it could be accomplished only by fearful sacrifices in housing, education, pensions, etc. (Even wiping out all defence expenditure would not suffice; it would require more than the whole national income.) The NHS is a disaster in the severely economic sense that its price in alternatives we have sacrificed is inordinate because we are stuck with it whether it performs well or badly, because its supporters judge it not by its performance—the work of fallible beings with limited materials—but by its noble goal—"the best of everything for everyone free"—which it can never reach *and therefore never be judged as having failed.* And, in maintaining that it has not failed, its supporters keep going a system we can evidently never change by reasoned debate. ("The envy of the world," Mrs. Castle has repeated, but no country in the world has copied it.) So it will go on until it collapses. And in the meantime no one counts the cost—the opportunity foregone of channelling more money into medicine by charging. No one can be sure, but the trend in spending habits as incomes rise in Britain and the experience of comparable countries in Europe, America and Australasia indicate that the real cost of the NHS is the opportunity the British have lost for decades to put more resources into medical care by developing and refining the methods of charging by co-insurance, deductibles, etc., that were emerging spontaneously before they were suppressed by Aneurin Bevan, and, even more, by his followers who could see the consequences but refused to draw the lessons.

Whatever the drawbacks, the only way of demonstrating the advantages of charging would seem to be by experimentation. The irony is that even modest experiments are opposed and obstructed by supporters of holistic, nationwide policies like the National Health Service and comprehensive education that are not easy to reverse even when they do not reach their declared aims after decades of trial. Men of all schools, with the reverence for scholarship that has sustained the Western world through adversity, must insist that reasoned argument will not be dismissed as distracting attention from perfecting schemes that require the exclusion of every new idea. Room must be found for experimentation, however administratively distracting and intellectually disturbing.

Decentralised experimentation

How can experiments in charging for hitherto "free" public services be arranged? In Britain this task is more difficult than in other Western industrialised countries that are politically organised on a more decentralised, federal framework. In the USA, with its states, Canada, with its provinces, Germany, with its Länder, and Australia, also with its states, power is devolved to semi-sovereign regions that can initiate policies buttressed by power to raise local revenue. Regional initiative is more difficult in Britain where the counties raise local revenue to finance only a third of their expenditure, so that they have become increasingly the agents and executors of central government. Whatever they have said, or may say, in favour of decentralisation, both the Labour Party and the Conservative Party have accelerated the trend towards centralisation. In Chapter 12 I discuss the "winds of change" in all parties that may induce or compel them (or one of their wings) to look more kindly on charging as the ultimate form of decentralisation by enfranchising individuals in the marketplace and to see it as much more effective than the political decentralisation through electoral "representation" that is useless for personal services. In the meantime there is at least one British county that is using what powers it has to investigate new techniques in social policy.

If it persists with its readiness to abandon outdated ideas and apply new ones, Kent looks like emerging as the pioneering experimental county of the

1970s, as Birmingham was at the turn of the century, under Conservatives who call themselves Tories but who act like Whigs (as I define them). The influence of ideas on policy-making is not easy to trace: it may be long delayed, a prompter to action on long-held but subconscious intentions, or a spark that begins a new train of thought. Whatever the relationship of cause and effect in the Kent approach to experiment, it seems that a passage in *Choice in Welfare, 1970*[2] was followed by action. The passage said:

> scepticism about hypothetical social research can easily be met by experiments with a school voucher in, say, Lancashire for three years, or a health voucher in, say, Shropshire for four years, or a reverse income tax in, say, Kent (or on a smaller scale in Leeds) for three years, or a phasing out of national insurance in, say, Norfolk or Somerset for five years.

The action has been a series of experiments in Kent under John Grugeon, the "Prime Minister" (leader of the Council), Alistair Lawton and John Barnes, "Education Ministers" (Chairman and Vice-Chairman of the Education Committee), and Edward Moore, "Minister for Social Services" (Chairman of the Social Services Committee). (If Opposition MPs can describe themselves by unconstitutional labels like Shadow Environment Minister, my descriptions for local politicians running a British county with a budget larger than those of nearly half the UN countries are no more pretentious than for national politicians who run nothing. The Chief Executives of the States of Australia are called "Premier," a short form of Prime Minister, which is what they are, and their heads of departments are called Ministers. In the British tradition and unwritten constitution the form of titles is not unimportant in maintaining authority and power. In Australia the Commonwealth Prime Minister handles the state Premiers with more respect than Whitehall does County Council chairmen or party leaders.)

The Kent experiment that could most incorporate and apply the pricing (charging) principle is the education voucher, for which the Council voted nearly £10,000 for a feasibility study under academic guidance. If the voucher is regarded as earmarked purchasing power which can be used like cash to pay school fees at state or private schools, a new element of pricing will have been introduced into British education for the first time in history and the Grugeon "Cabinet" will have showered lasting beneficial external-

2. Harris, R. (with Seldon, A.), *Choice in Welfare 1970*, IEA, 1971.

ities over Kent and perhaps over the whole of England. The voucher can also be regarded as a certificate entitling the holder to a term's education (rather like a pensioner's free pass on a bus). As indicated briefly in Chapter 4, the voucher is a flexible instrument with the common purpose of giving the customer more authority by the new power of exit than he has in the free state system. If Kent falters, it cannot be long before the voucher is tried by another county or town urged by parents to strengthen their voice in education by the ultimate sanction of exit from unacceptable schools.

Privatisation

A second original use of pricing in Kent (as the economist sees it, though that is not how it may be regarded) is the Family Placement Project in which disturbed and sometimes delinquent adolescents of fourteen to seventeen years are placed in professional foster homes that can offer the environment of family life. Foster parents are paid around £40 a week, a contrast with the up to £100 a week of state institutions, of which the Kent County's Director of Social Services, Nicholas Stacey, said that they "too often only increase [the adolescents'] problems and set them on the wasteful (in human and monetary terms) road to Borstal, prison or psychiatric hospital." This scheme, thought "greatly encouraging" so far, could denationalise the care of young people from "public" institutions to private homes. The experiment began in March 1975 with financial help from the Gatsby Foundation for five years and with the advice and assistance of Nancy Hazel of the University of Kent at Canterbury. Four "public" (local government) children's homes were being closed and children put into real family homes as a result of this use of pricing.

A similar experiment in "denationalisation" (or "privatisation" in the jargon) is a three-year scheme for moving a hundred or more lonely or enfeebled old people from public institutions into the homes of professional "good neighbours" who are paid less than the £50–£60 it costs to keep them in an institution. Comparison with a similar area in which old (or mentally-handicapped) people are in institutions will indicate whether private family homes are better for the patient/"client" and more economic than institutional life. The scheme was estimated to cost around £200,000 including the pay of research staff, although it may in the end save even more. Financial help again came from a charity and assistance from the University of Kent. Two "public" old-age homes were closed and old people put into real family homes.

Such schemes—at once more humane and economic—could help the county bridge the gap between Whitehall requirements, reinforced by the rising standards expected in public services, and sluggish revenue from local rates and Whitehall taxes, further widened by the increasing longevity of old and mentally-handicapped people, the rising number of children placed "in care" (sociologese for "under the control of public officials"), the increasing number of family breakdowns reported for attention, earlier discharge from hospitals, and the increased number of battered wives, alcoholics and drug addicts publicised by pressure groups. Fostering, home helps and encouragement to voluntary bodies were the ways chosen by Kent to keep people in private family life, which in any event they preferred and which was much cheaper than public institutions. The 1976 government White Paper had indicated no growth in social expenditure for some years. The County was spending nearly £20 million on 1½ million people, but nearly £10 million went on institutions for the few thousand.

The philosophic reflections on these measures by Edward Moore in his 1975 annual report are significant as commentaries on the less-than-scrupulous way in which citizens' tax-money has been managed by the public authorities that ostensibly husband it on their behalf.

> We must ask ourselves whether we have relied upon residential care too much in the past as an "easy way out" to solve problems. It is expensive—it means a long-term commitment to a form of service which could become out-dated because of the many restrictions which bricks and mortar and built-in facilities bring with them. This can be seen all the time when we look at out-dated hospitals and housing which, because of design deficiencies, etc., are unsuitable for the needs of the elderly and the handicapped; old persons' homes which 10–20 or more years ago represented a satisfactory way of meeting the needs of the elderly for whom we then had to care; large children's community homes which can no longer meet changing philosophies of child care. Times of economic difficulty have the effect of making those of us responsible for growth services think much more clearly about our priorities.

For John Grugeon these innovations would encourage self-reliance and voluntary effort: "self-help, not help yourself." Like Nicholas Stacey, he spoke of difficult adjustments in thinking and staffing. Where Stacey was talking to the staff, Grugeon was talking to the electorate: there would have to be "very unpalatable decisions." And he made what must be for a politician a courageous judgement: ". . . we must not treat . . . police and fire . . .

in isolation. Law and order are prime points in our philosophy but not at the expense of our meagre resources." Here was a rare recognition by a politician of the overriding limitations of scarcity and the impossibility of doing everything desirable.

The City of Lincoln, run by a Social Democratic Council, and the City of Liverpool, under a Liberal Council, have courageously raised some charges. Councillor Peppiatt and some Conservative colleagues on Thanet Council have raised charges despite obstruction and resistance. Not least, there is the lone voice of Whig Councillor Margolis on Harrogate Borough Council and North Yorkshire County Council. His steady advocacy of charges for a wide range of services—Harrogate Royal Baths, the collection of derelict vehicles (previously the Council had paid the collectors), decorative lighting in shopping streets, tourist guides, colour TV aerials for Council tenants, courses for pot-holers (as Bernard Levin might say, stand there while I say it again: *free courses for pot-holers*), car-parking and entertainment facilities—has been resisted by Councillors, officials and local journalists with familiar unconvincing argument, but it has educated fellow Councillors, even where it has not yet inspired them to action, and earned increasing respect in the press. There may be more examples. But the scope is vast.

Everything is "impracticable" before it is done

In his writings in the 1950s Lord Robbins said that the Inland Revenue could be relied upon to produce conclusive administrative objections to every proposal for fiscal reform (he was discussing inheritance taxes to replace death duties).[3] When Keynes proposed PAYE in 1939 the head of the Inland Revenue rejected it as administratively impracticable; two years later it was introduced. When in the 1960s there were again murmurings about the administrative nightmares of various forms of reverse income taxes to make benefits more selective and therefore higher for people in most need, Lord Houghton retorted: "I am not put off by rude noises from government departments. I have seen too many impossibilities overcome to be discouraged by them."[4] (He should know: he was Secretary of the Inland Revenue Staff Federation from 1922 to 1960.)

If the opponents of charging insist that it is administratively impractical, let them subject their unsupported claim to the test of experience. I have ar-

3. Robbins, Lord, "Notes on Public Finance," *Lloyds Bank Review*, 1955.
4. Houghton, Lord, *Paying for the Social Services*, IEA, 1967, 1968.

gued the case for testing their claim that the education voucher is impracticable by erecting experiments to see whether they are right. Much the same is true of charging for other public services that are not public goods—even if some of them are supposed to be. (There is even a case for experimenting with methods of linking payment by taxation to the *total* financing of public goods in which the personal benefits are not separable.) The case for experimenting in the education voucher, therefore, applies in principle to experimenting with other methods of financing—and organising—a wide range of services from health and transport on a national scale to libraries and refuse collection on a local scale. If the objectors to charging object to experiments to see whether their objections are sustained, their objections may be seen as based more on mis-guided obstruction to reform or self-interested preservation of jobs than on arguments supported by evidence.

CHAPTER 12

Politically Impossible

"Politically impossible" is the instinctive retort of the sceptic—or perhaps cynic—who senses danger to his beliefs in a new approach but does not know enough to condemn it. He therefore damns it with faint praise: "It sounds a good idea but, of course, the people would not elect a government to act on it." A more recent version is that, if elected, the government would be prevented by opposition from organised interests, not least, the trade unions or at least their officials, whatever their rank and file think (or even know) about it.

The danger of this reaction is that it is plausible. There are always cranks with easy solutions: visionaries, utopians, millenarians who offer prescriptions based on the two untruths that have misled mankind down the ages: that men are saints and that manna can be laid on by Ministries. I am not arguing that every crank has an inalienable right to have his brain child, or brainstorm, tried, even for a short time, at the expense of the people. The argument is deeper-lying.

The imperative conditions: imperfect man, scarce resources

Some new ideas can be sieved out as obviously contrary to sense and experience. All notions, from communism to the National Health Service, that assume man to be selfless and resources to be superabundant, must be rejected. To be taken seriously a new idea must satisfy two criteria: that it is designed for man and woman as they are, with limited vision and interests, and that it can operate with scarce resources. This means that not everything desirable—like the best of health clinics, education, housing, car-parking or sports facilities—can be attained for everyone.

Yet some realistic new ideas are resisted on the spurious ground that, although desirable, they are "politically impossible." Charging is paying the price, paying your way, paying your penny and taking your choice; the archetypal idea that satisfies the two criteria: it recognises both human and material limitations but is designed to make the best of them. It is open, above board, does not encourage illusions, down to earth. When such a realistic and therefore practicable working idea is obstructed as "politically impossible" we must look to the scope in civilised society for new ideas of any sort, to the structure of power that enables them to be killed before they are born, and the motives, incentives or inducements of the obstructors.

The press was silent

At first blush, the objection contradicts itself. If a new idea is in the interest of the people, it can hardly be an objection that they would reject it. If they do, the reason must be that they do not know about it. In Britain, the "fifth estate," the press, can usually be relied on to give a sensible new idea a fair run, or even a fair wind. But here there is an odd episode in the recent press treatment of charging. There was, with a few honourable exceptions, little discussion of charging in the national press reports and comments while the world was "waiting for Layfield" from June 1974 when the Committee to investigate local government finance[1] was appointed to May 1976 when it reported. Even the Local Government Correspondents, who are presumably knowledgeable specialists in the subject, barely referred to charging.

The Layfield lacuna

The hope that the Layfield Report would accelerate the pace of public education in the relevance of charging was dashed. It recognised the case for charging, although it made too much of the external benefits of government services, and recommended "a review of policy and practice in charging for local services by the government and local authorities." This review may be postponed for years or decades. But the Committee confined its recommendation that local authorities consider raising charges to the existing services because it said it had not been asked to report on which services should or should not be provided by local government.

The Committee may have been technically or legally right in concluding it could not make a recommendation on charging that might affect the

1. Layfield Report, Committee of Inquiry into Local Government Finance, 1976.

structure of local services. But economically the two cannot be segregated. The Redcliffe-Maud Royal Commission reported in 1969 on the structure of local government and its services without considering its finances, which is like talking about supply and demand without considering the effect of price. The Layfield Committee in 1976 reported on financing local services without considering the effect on their scale, which is like talking about price without considering its effect on supply and demand. One more opportunity of encouraging public discussion has therefore been lost, and it will probably be at least five years before another committee of inquiry.

Fortunately, the Institute of Economic Affairs, which specialises in the micro-economic analysis of policy, has sponsored a series of studies going back to the early 1960s (listed in the References) that provide the best (or only) collection of succinct analyses as a scholarly background to a public discussion that I hope *Charge* will further stimulate. Appendix 1 briefly explains the method and results, discussed below.

The question remains: If a new idea is in the interest of the people, why should the people reject it? My reply is that what politicians (or academics or anyone else who claims to know public opinion) mean when they say charging is politically impossible is either that they themselves do not like charging or that they are incapable of showing the public to see it is for their benefit. At bottom the "politically impossible" objection conceals a failure of political education and a failure to resist pressure groups.

I base these conclusions on the emerging insights from the new theory of public choice which analyses politics in terms of "the vote motive"[2] and on the results of the four IEA surveys of public reaction to priced alternatives in state and private education, medicine, housing and pensions.[3] The theory of public choice is complemented by the theory of bureaucracy, also developed mostly by American economists. (Appendix 2 indicates the main sources.)

Public preferences unknown to politicians

The four IEA surveys have a significant origin. They were prompted by the very objection of "politically impossible" made by people of various political colours against the early IEA Papers on pensions, housing and medical care. It was said that, although their authors made cogent cases, there

2. Tullock, G., *The Vote Motive*, IEA, 1976.

3. Harris, R. (with Seldon, A.), *Choice in Welfare*, 1963, 1965, 1970, IEA, 1971; and Pennance, F. G. (with Gray, H.), *Choice in Housing*, IEA, 1968.

was no hope that their reasoning or conclusions would have any effect on policy because, the politicians thought, they were not politically *profitable*. Since IEA authors have always been asked to pursue their analysis wherever it led them without regard for what was politically expedient, this reaction was interpreted as a compliment, but with the danger that it would discourage academics from pursuing studies that might have important long-term results whatever their immediate prospects.

Moreover, it begged the question of what was possible politically. Scholars must, of course, be concerned with analysing what is right, not with what will produce immediate popularity for this or that party. But politicians are not a neutral part of the political process. They cannot reflect public wishes unless they also educate the public in the policies between which it can choose. Their competence is in question if they cannot apply good ideas that are in the public interest.

In the post-war economic climate of Keynesian macro-economic thinking (which Keynes, who died in 1946, might have rejected) politicians gave little time to micro-economic thinking, which they tend to pooh-pooh as rather old-fashioned. They did not recognise its explosive, revolutionary power as a critique of government in general and the size and structure of British government. They did not see its exciting potential for liberating policy, and in particular enfranchising the poor and the under-privileged in the second half of the twentieth century, who have been submerged and repressed in the developing structure of free services.

To test the politicians' hypothesis (or rationalisation of inaction) the IEA asked Mass Observation in 1962 to see how far it could discover opinion and potential reaction to alternative policies of higher taxes for better state benefits and lower taxes with charges for alternative private education, medical care and pensions. In the previous fifteen years or so since the creation of the post-war stage of the welfare state, polls and surveys had claimed to discover overwhelming general support for "free" tax-paid state welfare. The first Mass Observation survey in 1963 found otherwise; so did further surveys in 1965 and 1970 (Appendix 1). The reason was that it introduced realistic prices by using the micro-economic device of the voucher (for education and medicine) in discovering people's preferences and emphasised costs and taxes in a parallel series of macro-economic questions on government policy in general.

Essentially the micro-economic questions asked whether heads of families would take a voucher valued at one-third or two-thirds of state school fees and add to it to pay for education of their choice. A similar question covered vouchers to pay for health insurance. The three successive surveys found a gradually increasing proportion in every social class interested in or anxious for choice, even at the expense of dipping into their pockets. The macro-economic questions showed the same trend. A survey of reactions to housing policy led by the late Professor F. G. Pennance, on broadly comparable lines, found similar reactions.[4]

This was evidence—hypothetical and circumstantial, but nevertheless more scientific than any others—that reform in existing policies was, after all, *not* politically impossible. It came as no surprise to Ralph Harris and me. As economists with a strongly micro approach, we had always thought that the "price-less" surveys (still being used) were of no significance. What surprised us was the large proportion—a third, rising to two-fifths and a half—indicating a desire for something different from what the politicians had been giving them.

Disbelief

The instinctive reaction of some who did not welcome the findings was to question the technical accuracy of the surveys. The late Richard Crossman (badly advised) went further and suggested in the *Guardian* that pensioners and women had been omitted from the sample because they might not give the required replies. (He later publicly withdrew the insinuation.) Academics, mostly sociological, journalists and others to whom the findings were unexpected and unwelcome, found technical fault but did not disturb our general discovery that, *if investigated through charging*, the public was not as frozen in its attitudes as were politicians out of touch with its underlying preferences. The protesters may be judged to have resorted to the "politically impossible" objection in order to resist reform they disliked on philosophic grounds (Labour), or emotional grounds (Liberals), or traditional grounds (Conservatives). Not for the first time, political leaders were shown up as being a long way behind their followers. They were simply out of touch—because they did not understand the price system. What they asserted as "politically impossible" was not only politically desirable but—if they were not blinkered—could evidently be politically popular and politically profitable.

It was also now clear that the conventional method of discovering public opinion through the ballot box had concealed rather than revealed it. To

4. Pennance, *Choice in Housing.*

record mass votes in favour of free welfare from voters not told their costs proved nothing. Charging was the only way to discover preferences, as well as the way in which to finance the services the public wanted.

If the politicians are obstructing a reform that reason indicates is for the benefit of the public, and a reform, moreover, that the public shows it would welcome, the objection of politically impossible becomes a strange phenomenon. Economists have to examine the role of the politician more closely in the effort to see why he is reluctant to perform the task, for which he is elected and paid, of providing the people with the institutions they prefer. The new theory of public choice is shedding more light as it develops. The central insight that has emerged so far is that the politician is most fruitfully analysed in terms of his electoral interests. And if those interests do not necessarily conflict with the benefit of the public, neither do they necessarily coincide with them.

The entry of economists into the realm of what will seem to be politics is an aspect of their "imperialist" tendency in recent years to be concerned not only with buying and selling, but also with subjects not conventionally regarded as within their province: charity, government, tax avoidance and evasion, marriage, crime and others. In a sense, after being used or misused by politicians, economists are turning the tables on them by examining them more closely and critically. In the process much of the mystique of statesmanship and the self-importance of the politician may be blown away. I fancy he has been rumbled and, unless he enslaves us all first, will play a more humble role in the future. (Professor W. H. Hutt, another of the economists who have rebelled against early teaching that the solution to social problems lay in the state, has penetrating insights in a little book called *Politically Impossible . . . ?*[5])

Politically impassable?

But the road to that fair city will require skilful negotiating, not least because the politicians, and their acolytes and attendants, the officials, bureaucrats, employees, advisers and retainers, will put up a barrage of road blocks painted "Politically Imp*a*ssable." I have long been intrigued by the processes that decide whether new ideas are translated into policy or are ignored, neglected and forgotten. If it is permissible to think of ideas as contending with

5. Hutt, W. H., *Politically Impossible . . . ?*, IEA, 1971.

one another, they seem to require a range of techniques to achieve acceptance: they must influence thinkers and scholars fundamentally in the long run, politicians and public servants with power in the short run, and the communications media and the literati in the medium run. Ideas thus require intellectual long-range "artillery" and lobbying short-range "infantry." The academic case for charging in general, and for the voucher as a device for introducing it as one instrument in particular, has been made for fifteen years or more by the intellectual "artillery." But there was little interest from politicians until recently, when a company of "infantry" went into action in one sector of the field. Their activities are relevant in judging the objection of "political impossibility."

The "infantry" company of women

The possibility of translating ideas into policy is indicated by what may prove to be a significant chapter in education policy that has lessons for public policy in general. In April 1974 a resolution proposing experiments in the voucher was prepared for the conference of the National Council of Women (NCW) and in October received a majority vote in support but not enough for the two-thirds required to make it NCW policy. The motion was moved by Marjorie Seldon, daughter and niece of pertinacious social reformers, who had advocated vouchers in various writings,[6] and seconded by Margaret Jones, a teacher. It was opposed mainly by union representatives of teachers.

(I must declare a family connection. Marjorie Seldon is my wife. The difference between the success of independent schools in nurturing academic skills in pupils in the middle and lower range of intellect, and the unnecessarily low expectations of teacher, pupil and parent in the non-selective state schools, had developed her interest in the voucher. She wrote in the Liberal magazine *New Outlook* in 1966: "The problem is to extend choice to *all:* to the children of the bus driver, shop assistant and widow as well as of the stockbroker, University teacher, or politician . . . There is a danger that ability to pay is being replaced by ability to persuade. The best bargains in schooling may go to those with the "know how," the command of English, or of the political strings . . . The voucher would give buying power that speaks the same language irrespective of social class.")

In October 1974 the Kent County Council majority party (Conservative)

6. Seldon, M., "How Welfare Vouchers Work," *New Outlook,* June 1966.

said in an election manifesto that it was interested in the possibility of an experiment in the education voucher. In January 1975 a handful of NCW enthusiasts formed the Friends of the Education Voucher Experiment in Representative Regions (FEVER) with Marjorie Seldon as Chairman, Ruth Garwood Scott, a former headmistress, as her main aide, and a Committee of five women: a social worker, a teacher, a nurse, a lawyer and a social survey interviewer. Several months were spent on the familiar methods of gathering public support traditional in British social reform. FEVER made impressive progress, ultimately recognised by the BBC in a TV programme, educating the public and discovering wide support for experiments among parents of all classes, not least in working-class areas with little choice of school, and among educationists, religious leaders, teachers and MPs.

Academic examination of the voucher was continued in two further IEA Papers based on material prepared for the Layfield Committee, which had asked the IEA for evidence on charging and on the voucher as a means of raising revenue: one paper was based on the written evidence on types of voucher, economic effects, administrative aspects, etc., by Alan Maynard[7]: the other was based on oral evidence on charging for local government services in general and on vouchers in particular by Ralph Harris and me.[8] In February 1976 Kent County Council announced that it would conduct a feasibility study for an experiment.

The significant lessons of this pioneering in opening up, and persuading people in political power to consider, a radical new idea are mainly five:

(i) Academic analysis is a necessary prelude to consideration by authority, but it requires "activist" publicity and propaganda to stimulate public discussion in the press, which politicians too often regard as reflecting or making public opinion.

(ii) The voucher has been opposed, without any evidence at all, by the officials of teachers' unions on the general ground that it would damage education; yet all they could feel, or fear, was that it might disturb the system with which they identified their own, or their members', interests.

(iii) Such people have opposed the voucher not only in principle but also as an experiment that would reveal whether their objections

7. Maynard, A., *Experiment with Choice in Education*, IEA, 1975.
8. Harris, R. (with Seldon, A.), *Pricing or Taxing?*, IEA, 1976.

were well founded. This is a particularly reprehensible attitude from teachers trained to respect scholarship and the open mind.

(iv) The weight attached, even by Kent County Council Conservatives, to teachers' opinions indicates the weakness of the consumer in a price-less, "free" system vis-à-vis the supplier. Without charges to indicate costs, identify the paymaster and empower him to enforce his preferences, the piper does not call the tune: the consumer is thwarted by the employee he pays.

(v) The voucher was condemned, dismissed or ignored by journalists (Education Correspondents) caught up in reporting the existing system whatever its defects. Some evidently could not contemplate education financed in any other way than taxation. It is clear that a lot of effort must be put into educating those whom the public regards as the experts.

Pressure groups suppress individuals

The politician believes that some new ideas are politically impossible because he interprets public opinion at second remove through the newspapers and TV and the vocal activists in occupational organisations, political parties and pressure groups.

As long as services are organised and financed by government, it is administratively simplest to negotiate with the officials of organisations—unions of postmen and porters, teachers and doctors—since it cannot consult all their members, still less non-members. The convenience is clear. The danger—that the officials will act as a barrier between government and members rather than a link—is less clear. It is even clearer that government will pay more attention to the organised voice of the producer—in transport, fuel, schools, hospitals, refuse-collection, postal services, libraries—than of the consumer, who is usually not organised at all. The Patients' Association, Parent-Teacher Associations and other groups do what they can on general rules and procedures, but they cannot speak for individual patients or parents, most of whom, especially the self-effacing, do not join such bodies. Those who do are the more articulate who need them least. The Conservative solution of Parent-Governors reflects the middle-class failure to see that the voice of the working-class parent cannot be "represented"; it cannot be equalised with that of the articulate, well-connected, socially adroit, middle-class parent; it can be made effective only by the sanction of withdrawing purchasing power. The voice, even if equal, can be made effective only if it is supplemented by an exit. No one listens very hard to the man (or woman) who cannot escape.

There seems no way out of the "politically impossible" *impasse* except by organisations such as FEVER that set out not to "represent" individuals but to obtain reforms that will provide machinery—in this case the voucher—by which individuals of all kinds, most of all the least influential or articulate, *can represent themselves.*

The objection of "politically impossible" thus resolves itself into a damaging critique of the very institutions the objectors are trying to preserve by obstructing reform: the self-protective reaction of the vast structure of private interests locked in the public services. And financing these services by charging is the only way of rearranging them to suit the people for whom they are intended—ultimately by giving them the power of *exit* to make their voice heard, initially by empowering them with a more effective *voice* to require that the service for which they pay by taxes shall match their preferences, and not be misused to create or preserve jobs for public "servants."

The external damage of government expenditure

It is now time to turn the tables on the "politically impossible" obstructionists and consider whether it may not be the conventional policies of increasing government expenditure financed by rising taxation that are becoming politically impossible.

Even if it could be demonstrated that on all five secondary grounds—the pretexts of poverty, irresponsibility, externality, economy and monopoly—services should be provided by government whether they were public goods or not, the repercussions, the external damage on people and institutions, must be weighed in the decision. Here I discuss three main forms of damage; others are reviewed in other chapters.

The first is the increasing concentration of power in government that would spread from economic activity to political institutions, civil rights and freedom of expression. The general tendency is for the exclusion of independent activity in supplying public services to be followed by the restriction of independent activity in other spheres—political, literary, cultural.

So I would argue. But the advocates of increasing government authority over economic activity would deny it and nothing will convince them otherwise. There is a vast literature on both sides of the argument. For me the evidence is plain enough, in communist as well as capitalist societies from

Russia to Sweden. It is true that we in Britain have reached the point at which, although 60 per cent of the GNP (as calculated until recently) is disposed of by government, yet political and civil liberties largely remain. But there are two errors in the argument. First, we have not been here long. In 1970 the figure was 50 per cent and in 1960 40 per cent. An increase of 20 per cent in sixteen years will take time to work its way through political institutions. Second, the increase has mostly been not in cash benefits returned to individual citizens and spent by them (about 20 per cent of GNP), but in direct control over the production of goods and services. If the 40 per cent of direct control over men and machines and land continues to grow, the political repercussions cannot lie far behind. The avenues for *independent* activity in fuel, transport, education, medicine, postal services and elsewhere have been closed, or are closing. These are now wholly or largely state activities. People who could offer the public better services for private profit in competition with others have been regarded as disturbing public services. It may not be long before they are denounced as enemies of the state.

The second form of damage lies in the burgeoning bureaucracy. Here the growth is less steep but also relatively recent. The total labour force grew between 1959 and 1974 from 23.84 million to 25.11 million, by 5.7 per cent. Total government employees rose from 5.84 to 6.84 million. In 1959 the proportion was 25 per cent of the total labour force, in 1974 27 per cent. It is higher in 1977 than it was in 1974, and will be higher in 1980 if more industry is run by government, directly or through nominally independent public corporations, if all independent education, medicine and other services are outlawed, and if independence in the professions and trading is further repressed and its practitioners, from architects and actuaries to small business men and shopkeepers, take refuge in public employment.

Third, the repercussions of continued expansion in public services are so far most evident in the effects of the rising taxation required to finance them. The long-hallowed liberal tradition of the British is that the law is sacred and is to be obeyed. Anyone who does not like it must not break it but persuade his fellow-Britons to change it by constitutional procedure. In the last five or ten years it has become increasingly doubtful whether this is still the generally accepted British attitude to the law on taxes. Britain is nearer to lawlessness in public as well as private life than at any time I can recall. The readiness to pay taxes legislated by Parliament has been eroded by party-political acceptance (or encouragement) of resistance to, or open defiance of, law elsewhere—the law on rent in Clay Cross, the law on peaceful picketing by flying pickets, the law on unions by shop stewards, the law on property by sit-ins, the law on maintaining postal and other public services by a trade union, and others. Law is unenforceable unless it is generally accepted as just: fines or imprisonment cannot be imposed on thirty million taxpayers.

If several hundred trade union officials or several hundred thousand public servants or nationalised employees think the law threatens their jobs, the much larger number of taxpayers (that is, all earners and spenders) seem to be feeling increasingly that the tax laws threaten their livelihoods, their families, their ways of life and their values. They see government responding to the strike-threat of monopoly unions, not least in public employment. Ratepayers have protested. Taxpayers generally are reacting differently. Tax evasion is spreading in Britain, and it is not because the British are changing their moral standards from within; it is directly related to the continual increase in taxation required to provide unnecessary public services in recent years. And insofar as public services are not public goods, the politically-created deterioration in moral standards is another unnecessary but damaging externality of the failure to finance them by charging.

The high price of high taxes

The persistent effort to finance private benefits by taxes seems to be exacting a high price that the British have never been asked if they are prepared to pay—the weakening respect for law and the weakening confidence in representative political institutions. If, by raising taxes *unnecessarily,* politicians have forced the traditionally law-abiding British into breaking the law by tax evasion, then the law-makers can be judged no more moral than the taxpayers who break it. Politicians have not only created irresistible pressures to law-breaking; they also expect civil servants (tax collectors) to enforce an unenforceable law and they require citizens to inform on one another.

The will of the people?

The moral authority of the law rests on the consent of the people, normally interpreted in Britain as a simple electoral majority. The morality of even a majority is dubious. Legal coercion of a minority by a majority is unavoidable, we have seen, for public goods. But, we have also seen, some two-thirds of British public services are not public goods. To this extent the minority is coerced *unnecessarily.* Even so, Professor Gordon Tullock argues, a simple (50.1 per cent) majority is not efficient in indicating general assent where bargains have to be struck by groups in democratic systems ("log-rolling").[9] He argues that "reinforced majorities" of two-thirds should be used more widely. This rule would profoundly change British political institutions, though the reasoning underlying it is gradually finding its way into scholarly text-books. (We need hardly recall that the German people had given Hitler a majority in the 1933 Reichstag: Fascism, with all its works, was therefore "legal" and "democratic.")

But British governments have had their moral authority reduced in the thirty years since the war, when the vast expansion of non-public "public" services took place, because no government has had a majority of votes cast, still less of the electorate that could have voted. The highest percentage of votes cast was 49.74 per cent for the Conservatives in 1955; and that was 38.18 per cent of the electorate. At the last General Election, in October 1974, Labour attracted 39.29 per cent of the votes cast, or 28.62 per cent of the electorate (Table A). A party that attracts less than two in five of the votes cast, and not much more than one in four of all voters, can hardly speak with the moral authority of a government that attracts 60 or 70 per cent of voters in an election with a choice of parties.

A truer representation

Professor Tullock argues that in a multi-party system, which we have had since 1974 when the Liberals attracted nearly 20 per cent of votes cast, the wings of each party tend to diverge. If, instead of the barely distinguishable high-government-expenditure-for-state-welfare of both parties, the elector had been able to decide between the two philosophies of paternalism (with free services) and liberal individual responsibility (with charging), the votes in 1974 and the policies since then might have been very different. If the wings had been able to declare their policies openly, instead of suppressing them in internal party coalitions, the position might have been as in Table G to reflect more faithfully the underlying attitudes of the British people to state control, nationalisation, taxation, universal or selective welfare, bureaucracy, trade union power, independent initiative. There could have been a majority of 66 per cent for liberal individual responsibility and a minimal (lower taxes with charging) state and a minority of 27 per cent for paternalist collectivism (free services with higher taxes). The wings might then have

9. Tullock, *The Vote Motive.*

Table G. British Political Opinion — a Truer Result

	1974 (October) General Election vote for conventional party (% of votes cast)		Suggested vote for wing with identifiable philosophy
Conservative	36	Whig	22
		Tory	14
Labour	39	Social Democrat	34
		Socialist	5
Liberal	18	Libertarian	10
		Paternalist	8

formed a new coalition, outside the old party boundaries, perhaps temporarily until the state had been rolled back.

There is no technical difficulty in raising the state proportion of GNP from 40 per cent to 50, to 60, to 70, to 80. But I would say that beyond about 20 to 25 per cent it can be done only with increasing coercion in the face of intensifying resentment, resistance and defiance. That, broadly, is what seems to have happened since World War II, and especially since 1964. The two main parties may have believed sincerely that a "high-government-taxation-for-state-welfare" policy is what the British wanted; but they were misled by the defective electoral system based on price-less, 57-variety, full-line forcing of all-or-nothing political platforms that prevented voters from indicating opinion on single issues (from continued subsidies for relatively high-income Council tenants to price-indexed pensions for public servants). When they found by subsequent micro-economic reaction that the people did not want to pay high taxes, they should have stopped expanding public services long ago to discover where and why they had gone wrong. The electorate may have voted for state welfare because they did not know its price; they did not vote for a police state.

Supporters of the legalistic theory, or legal fiction, that whatever the state passes into law is moral and must be enforced, however high the cost, will probably have to meet increasing resistance based, perhaps unconsciously, on a sense of "natural justice" that there must be much more than 39 per cent (or 29 per cent) of voters in favour of high taxes to justify enforcing them on the majority of 61 per cent (or 71 per cent).

A numbered summary

Having completed the argument for charging and rejected the objections, I restate the main propositions.

1. Only about a third of British government expenditure is on public services necessarily financed by taxes because they are public goods.
2. Most public services yield separable private services that could be more efficiently financed by charges.
3. They have been brought into government production for five reasons that are largely or wholly insufficient.
   - i. Poverty: can be treated better on the demand side by a reverse income tax; only about half, probably less, of all taxes go to redistribute income; the rest is "abortive." Differences or deficiencies in income can be remedied more easily than differences in social background, political influence, or economic muscle in the access to free, tax-financed services. Moreover, the poor are not always the main users of the public services: higher education, sports amenities, etc. They would therefore be the gainers if public services that government did not have to provide were not provided by government at all.
   - ii. Irresponsibility: could be removed if "irresponsible" people were taught to exercise discretion and judgement by benefits in cash or voucher instead of being given "free" benefits in kind that do not teach choice but habituate them to passive acceptance.
   - iii. Economy: even where government services reduce cost by avoiding duplication, the better method is private organisation and management subject to minimal government regulation until technical innovation restores smaller-scale operation; but often state costs are higher than costs in competitive markets.
   - iv. Externality: the argument for government "free" provision of education, etc., is unsubstantiated and often nebulous; social benefits can often be ensured by cash grants or earmarked vouchers to consumers.
   - v. Monopoly: government control tends to perpetuate monopoly by exposing government to importunity from vested interests; again the better method is often private organisation and management subject to government regulation until technical innovation restores competition.

4. Charges would yield revenue for public services that could not be raised by government through taxation. Free services are sparser and inferior to paid-for services.

5. Charges would improve the efficiency of public services by subjecting them to consumer sovereignty and eventual producer competition.

6. Charges would increase the total resources channelled to services of which more were demanded than could be financed through taxation.

7. Taxation is the only method of financing true public goods, but it is still a second best because it does not indicate personal preferences.

8. Unnecessary taxation generates its own external costs:
   i. Progressive restriction of initiative independent of the state and, in time, of constitutional and civil liberties as the expansion in government expenditure works its way through political institutions.
   ii. Progressive expansion of non-productive bureaucracy at the expense of productive industry.
   iii. A weakening in the respect for law; deterioration of moral standards, social divisiveness between public servants and the public; corruption of bureaucracy.

9. The machinery of representative democracy has been extended from public goods, where it is unavoidable but defective, to private benefits, where it is avoidable and inefficient, and where it unnecessarily but irremediably prejudices lower-income people with little or no social connections, political influence or economic muscle.

10. New machinery has to be devised to decide the public will in public goods by referenda and in private benefits by markets.

11. The sectional and occupational resistances to charging could be overcome by public opinion.

12. The existing alignment of British political parties could be replaced by a realignment according to attitudes to "public" services and public goods and to the resulting policies on taxation, nationalisation, bureaucracy, consumer authority, choice, competition.

APPENDIXES

APPENDIX **1**

True and False Measures of Public Preferences

In Britain there are only two ways of measuring what the public wants: in the ballot box and the market. The ballot box records votes by crosses cast for this or that party, policy or politician. The market records votes by money paid for this or that commodity, service, brand, firm or business man.

The ballot box is crude compared with the market. The ballot box is used locally every three and nationally up to five years; the market is used every day or few days (for food, newspapers, transport, etc.), every few months (clothes, books, etc.) or years (furniture, homes, etc.).

The ballot box says: "This is my list of 57 varieties: take it or leave it." The market says: "This is my one item: pay for as much or as little as you want." (Motto, p. 96.)

The ballot box says: "This is what we promise." The market says: "What you see before your very eyes is what you take away if you pay."

The ballot box says: "Aren't our party slogans splendid!" The market says: "Judge us by your experience of our product."

The ballot box says: "We are saints, public-spirited, selfless and honest. The others are devils, in the pay of vested interests, selfish, dishonest." The market says: "We are the best. Compare our value, quality, price."

The ballot box says: "Look! Benefits galore! All Free!" The market says: "All our goods are priced; tax shown separately."

This contrast is over-simplified but basically right. Even if allowance is made for advertising, the persuasion of people to try this rather than that breakfast cereal, washing powder or newspaper is infinitely harmless contrasted with the persuasion to "buy" this or that political slogan, promise or policy. You can, with little loss, change from one cereal, powder or paper to another every few days. But you are stuck with the wrong political policy for years or a lifetime (no matter how bad it becomes, the NHS will go on and on and on).

Although the ballot box is very much a second best to the market, it must be used for public goods because opinion on, say, how much and what quality of defence, cannot easily be measured in the market by individuals voting with their money. But even where there are private benefits, the ballot box is still used because wrong thinking brought it into being and vested interests keep it going even where it is inferior to the market.

It has given wrong results because it has not used prices where it supplies private benefits that could be priced. Political elections (and private polls) have asked the electorate as a whole (or samples) to say whether they preferred this or that public service—say, state education, the NHS, Council housing. But to ask "Do you prefer A to B?" is *meaningless unless you know their prices.* You will prefer A if it costs much less than B, and B if it costs much less than A. General Elections ask for meaningless answers because political policies have no prices. They do not ask "How much more defence would you like at £100 more in taxes per family for each aircraft carrier or

Table H. Preferences Discovered by Education and Health Vouchers, 1970

(i) Proportions accepting £75 or £150 education voucher for each child (sample of people with children of school age under 19), expressed in percentages

	Socio-economic group			
	Highest	High-Medium	Low-Medium	Lowest
£75 voucher, requiring £150 in cash	38	29	26	21
£150 voucher, requiring £75 in cash	52	49	42	35

(ii) Proportions accepting £7 or £10 health voucher for each member of household, expressed in percentages

	Socio-economic group			
	Highest	High-Medium	Low-Medium	Lowest
£7 voucher, requiring £7 in cash	29	32	25	22
£10 voucher, requiring £5 in cash	36	38	29	26

air-to-ground missile?" And private polls that are price-less are similarly useless: not surprisingly they "found" large support for ("free") state this, that and the other.

The only attempts in Britain to discover preferences in the personal benefits in the so-called "public" services were made by the IEA in 1963, 1965 and 1970 for education, health and pensions and in 1968 for housing. Instead of the fruitless question "Do you prefer state or private education, health, pensions, housing?" the IEA questions put a price-tag on the alternatives by using the voucher as the way to show the cost of a choice between state and private services. Thus in 1970 it asked "If (instead of 'free' state education) the Government gave you £75 a year for each child aged 11 or more which could only be spent on education—and you would have to pay another £150 yourself to make up the fees—would you accept the offer or not?" It also asked what people would do if the offer was £150 to be topped up by £75. A comparable question was asked for health insurance premiums as for school fees: £7 for each person, to be topped up by £7; and £10 to be topped up by £5. The results were fascinating. Preferences (not surprisingly to the economist) were revealed as varying with price (the addition of money required to top them up).

This, although only approximate, is a fascinating glimpse into the preferences suppressed for many decades that lie below the layers of cotton wool of the welfare state. It showed, *for the first time since the welfare state was created*, the *true* state of public wishes that are ignored and frustrated by "free" welfare.

This method of discovering preferences was acknowledged as the right way, in principle, to investigate public demand for welfare services by the (Social Democratic) Professor Mark Blaug and (Liberal) Professor Jack Wiseman and the Conservative (Tory) Timothy Raison. But no political party has followed it through.

APPENDIX **2**

A Note on Further Readings

Readers who want to go into the subject more fully will find the following helpful on (i) public goods, (ii) charging and (iii) the economic debate generally.

(i) *The nature of public goods.*

The most systematic short analysis is Professor Maurice Peston's *Public Goods and the Public Sector.*[1] A somewhat longer, in parts more difficult, but more recent and rewarding discussion is Professor C. K. Rowley's and Professor Alan T. Peacock's *Welfare Economics: A Liberal Restatement.*[2] Readers will see that the position in *Charge* is nearer the latter.

An easier book is Professor Gordon Tullock's *Private Wants, Public Means,*[3] and a more difficult one Professor Mancur Olson's *The Logic of Collective Action,*[4] sub-titled "Public Goods and the Theory of Groups." A British book that discusses the externalities of economic growth, and is also a complement to *Private Wants, Public Means,* is Dr. E. J. Mishan's pioneering *The Costs of Economic Growth,*[5] a much more sophisticated analysis of social costs than that of the environmentalists who would lose the baby of economic growth with the bath water of externalities. (Since both Tullock and Mishan ascribe the origin of their books to me, I shall not take sides, but readers will see with which I agree more.)

1. Peston, M., *Public Goods and the Public Sector,* Macmillan, 1972.
2. Rowley, C. K. (with Peacock, A. T.), *Welfare Economics: A Liberal Restatement,* Martin Robertson, 1974.
3. Tullock, G., *Private Wants, Public Means,* Basic Books (NY), 1970.
4. Olson, M., *The Logic of Collective Action,* Harvard, 1971.
5. Mishan, E. J., *The Costs of Economic Growth,* Pelican, 1967.

Charity as a public good is discussed by Professor Thomas R. Ireland[6] and David B. Johnson[7] in *The Economics of Charity.*

The reader will be diverted by Professor Richard B. McKenzie's and Professor Gordon Tullock's *The New World of Economics,*[8] which discusses public goods in the course of applying economics to its new subjects of learning, politics, crime, the family, etc.

Most of the new thinking on the nature and implications of public goods is published in *Public Choice,* the journal of the Center for the Study of Public Choice at the Virginia Polytechnic Institute and State University, Blacksburg, Virginia, USA, whose Senior Editor is Professor Tullock.

(ii) *Charging.*

As a much-neglected subject, the literature is scattered and patchy. The References list a good source for each "public" service. The main sources are IEA Papers and US journals and books. British periodicals and publishers have been backward in seeing the potentialities of the subject.

(iii) *General.*

A good first entry to general economic policy on public goods is (liberal)* Professor Lord Robbins' latest book, *Political Economy Past and Present,*[9] accurately sub-titled "a review of leading theories of economic policy." It discusses the classical theory of "collective" goods with "indiscriminate" benefits. Readers might then dip into (Whig) Professor Hayek's *magnum opus, The Constitution of Liberty.*[10]

Two books for the general reader are by parents and son: (liberal) Professor Milton and Rose Friedman's readable *Capitalism and Freedom;*[11] (Adam Smith liberal) David Friedman's *The Machinery of Freedom,* sub-titled "Guide

* These philosophic labels are used by the authors about themselves.

6. Ireland, T. R., "The Calculus of Philanthropy," in *The Economics of Charity,* IEA, 1973.

7. Johnson, D. B., "The Charity Market: Theory and Practice," in *The Economics of Charity,* IEA, 1973.

8. McKenzie, R. B., and Tullock, G., *The New World of Economics,* Richard Irwin (USA), 1975.

9. Robbins, Lord, *Political Economy Past and Present,* Macmillan, 1976.

10. Hayek, F. A., *The Constitution of Liberty,* Routledge, 1960.

11. Friedman, M. (with Rose), *Capitalism and Freedom,* University of Chicago Press, 1962.

to a Radical Capitalism,"[12] discusses the nature of public goods incisively. Samuel Brittan's *Capitalism and the Permissive Society*[13] discusses public goods in a British setting. Professor J. E. Meade's *The Just Economy*[14] is the most recent discussion by a "liberal socialist" (Social Democrat).

The nature and indispensability of pricing is analysed by the Swedish (Social Democratic) economist Professor Assar Lindbeck in a short and easy book addressed to the "New Left" which thinks the world could dispense with prices and run on goodwill, *The Political Economy of the New Left.*[15]

The importance of charging in giving consumers an exit as well as a voice, or an exit to make voice effective, emerges from Professor Albert O. Hirschmann's *Exit, Voice and Loyalty.*[16]

Professor George J. Stigler's latest book, *The Citizen and the State,*[17] will illuminate thinking on the competence of the state in regulating what in Britain are called nationalised industries and "public" corporations that are not allowed to charge market rates for political reasons. He writes with his customary wit and lucidity.

The principles underlying the financing and organisation of the post office, education, justice, police, fire, roads and money are racily discussed by William C. Wooldridge in *Uncle Sam, the Monopoly Man.*[18]

Two more philosophic works that question the competence or relevance of the state in providing services are Professor Sir Karl Popper's *The Open Society and Its Enemies*[19] and Professor Robert Nozick's *Anarchy, State and Utopia.*[20]

Professor Harry G. Johnson's *On Economics and Society*[21] has illuminating passages and pages on public goods and the implications for policy.

Sweden is often quoted as the ideal society that controls essential services by government in the public interest. This impression is largely destroyed by Roland Huntford's *The New Totalitarians.*[22]

12. Friedman, D., *The Machinery of Freedom,* Harper & Row (NY), 1973.
13. Brittan, S., *Capitalism and the Permissive Society,* Macmillan, 1975.
14. Meade, J. E., *The Just Economy,* Allen & Unwin, 1975.
15. Lindbeck, A., *The Political Economy of the New Left,* Harper & Row, 1971.
16. Hirschmann, A. O., *Exit, Voice and Loyalty,* Harvard, 1970.
17. Stigler, G. J., *The Citizen and the State,* Chicago University Press, 1975.
18. Wooldridge, W. C., *Uncle Sam, the Monopoly Man,* Arlington House (NY) 1970.
19. Popper, Sir K., *The Open Society and Its Enemies,* Routledge, 1966.
20. Nozick, R., *Anarchy, State and Utopia,* Basic Books (NY), 1974.
21. Johnson, H. G., *On Economics and Society,* University of Chicago Press, 1975.
22. Huntford, R., *The New Totalitarians,* Allen Lane, 1975.

Readers who want a handwork of reference to economic concepts should have a dictionary of economics. I should be less than candid if I did not say that, although there are several on the British market with varying virtues, readers of this book would find most helpful the in-depth but still short essays in *Everyman's Dictionary of Economics.*[23]

Several US journals have in recent years vigorously reappraised the argument and evidence on the control and financing of "public" services:

The Public Interest, 10 East 53 Street, New York, 10022.
Publishes impressive rethinking of conventional attitudes and policies. (There is no British equivalent.)

Commentary, a comparable journal, 165 East 56 Street, New York, 10022.

Intercollegiate Review, 14 South Bryn Mawr Avenue, Bryn Mawr, Pennsylvania, 19010.
Published by the Intercollegiate Studies Institute; circulates mainly in American universities.

The Alternative, P.O. Box 877, Bloomington, Indiana 47401.
An "intellectual" journal published by students; maintains a high standard.

Reason, P.O. Box 6157, Santa Barbara, California 93111.
A monthly, intellectually stimulating.

Libertarian Review, 6737 Annapolis Road, P.O. Box 2599, Landover Hills, Maryland 20784.
A monthly, with one or two longish review-essays but mainly shorter reviews.

The Centre for Libertarian Studies, Suite 50, 200 West 58th Street, New York, NY 10019, publishes a news letter and the *Journal of Libertarian Studies.*

Laissez Faire Books, 208A Mercier Street, New York, NY 10012, regularly distributes a wide-ranging catalogue, covering history, economics and philosophy.

Postscript

After *Charge* was completed I learned of a book by Professor R. M. Bird of the University of Toronto on very much the same subject, *Charging for Public Services,* but couched in rather more economic/technical language. It

23. Seldon, A. (with Pennance, F. G.), *Everyman's Dictionary of Economics,* J. M. Dent, 1976.

was published in December 1976 by the Canadian Tax Foundation, Toronto. It seems a most sophisticated and persuasive discussion, set in the Canadian context, of the principles and their application to policy. Professor Bird's object is the same as mine: to inform public discussion because, like me, he thinks that the main obstacle to charging is not that the case is unsubstantiated but that there is not sufficient public understanding of it because vested interests will oppose it. I strongly recommend it to readers of *Charge* who want to go into the subject more fully.

April 1977

REFERENCES

Beckerman, W., *Pricing for Pollution*, IEA, 1975.
Bentham, J., *Manual of Political Economy*, 1825.
Bird, P. A., and Jackson, C. I., "Economic Charges for Water," in *The Theory and Practice of Pricing*, IEA, 1967.
Blake, Lord (with Patten, J.), Eds., *The Conservative Opportunity*, Macmillan, 1976.
Blaug, M., "The Economics of Education in English Classical Political Economy," in *Essays on Adam Smith*, University of Glasgow, 1976.
Brittan, S., *Left or Right: The Bogus Dilemma*, Secker & Warburg, 1968.
———, *Capitalism and the Permissive Society*, Macmillan, 1975.
Buchanan, J. M., *The Inconsistencies of the N.H.S.*, IEA, 1965.
———, *Public Finance in Democratic Process*, University of North Carolina Press, 1967.
———, *Demand and Supply of Public Goods*, Rand McNally & Co. (USA), 1968.
———, *The Limits of Liberty*, University of Chicago Press, 1975.
Buchanan, J. M. (with Tullock, G.), *The Calculus of Consent*, University of Michigan Press, 1962.
Burke, E., *An Appeal from the New to the Old Whigs* (1791), Bobbs, Merrill (USA), 1962.
Carmichael, J., *Vacant Possession*, IEA, 1964.
Carter, R. L., "Pricing and the Risk of Fire," in *The Theory and Practice of Pricing*, IEA, 1967.
———, *Theft in the Market*, IEA, 1974.
Coleraine, Lord, *For Conservatives Only*, Stacey, 1970.
Crosland, A., "The Long-term Future of Public Expenditure," Fabian Lecture, *Guardian*, 24 March 1976.
Crossman, R. H. S., *Inside View: Three Lectures on Prime Ministerial Government*, Jonathan Cape, 1972.
Diamond, Lord, *Public Expenditure in Practice*, Allen & Unwin, 1975.
Dolan, E. G., *TANSTAAFL (There Ain't No Such Thing As A Free Lunch)*, Holt, Rinehart & Winston (NY), 1971.
Freeman, Roland, *Municipal Review*, April 1976.
Friedman, D., *The Machinery of Freedom*, Harper & Row (NY), 1973.
Friedman, M. *From Galbraith to Economic Freedom*, IEA, 1977.

Friedman, M. (with others), *Verdict on Rent Control,* IEA, 1972.
Friedman, M. (with Rose), *Capitalism and Freedom,* University of Chicago Press, 1962.
Fulop, Christina, *Markets for Employment,* IEA, 1971.
Gray, H., *The Cost of Council Housing,* IEA, 1968.
Hailsham, Lord, *The Conservative Case,* Penguin, 1947, 1959.
Harris, R., in *Libraries: Free for All?,* IEA, 1962.
Harris, R. (with Seldon, A.), *Choice in Welfare,* 1963, 1965, 1970, IEA, 1971.
Harris, R. (with Seldon, A.), *Pricing or Taxing?,* IEA, 1976.
Hartwell, M., "The Consequences for the Poor of the Industrial Revolution," in *The Long Debate on Poverty,* IEA, 1972, 1974.
Hayek, F. A., *The Constitution of Liberty,* Routledge, 1960.
———, *Full Employment at Any Price?,* IEA, 1975.
———, *Choice in Currency,* IEA, 1976.
———, *Denationalisation of Money,* IEA, 1976.
Hibbs, J., *Transport for Passengers,* IEA, 1963.
Hicks, J. R., *After the Boom,* IEA, 1966.
Hirschmann, A. O., *Exit, Voice and Loyalty,* Harvard, 1970.
Holland, J., and Perry, N., *Aspects of Leisure in Two Industrial Cities,* Social Science Research Council, 1976.
Houghton, Lord, *Paying for the Social Services,* IEA, 1967, 1968.
Howell, D., "Instruments and Machinery for Control," in *Dilemmas of Government Expenditure,* IEA, 1976.
Huntford, R., *The New Totalitarians,* Allen Lane, 1975.
Hutt, W. H., *Politically Impossible . . . ?,* IEA, 1971.
Ireland, T. R., "The Calculus of Philanthropy," in *The Economics of Charity,* IEA, 1973.
Jefferson, M., "Industrialisation and Poverty: In Fact and Fiction," in *The Long Debate on Poverty,* IEA, 1972, 1974.
Jenkins, A., *The Case for Squash,* Jenkins, 1974.
———, "Leisure Amenities and Local Authorities" (Ms), IEA, 1975.
Johnson, D. B., "The Charity Market: Theory and Practice," in *The Economics of Charity,* IEA, 1973.
Johnson, H. G., *On Economics and Society,* University of Chicago Press, 1975.
Joseph, Sir K., *Reversing the Trend,* Barry Rose, 1975.
Keynes, J. M., *The End of Laissez Faire,* The Hogarth Press, 1926; *Collected Writings,* Macmillan, 1972.
———, *The General Theory of Employment, Interest and Money,* Macmillan, 1936.
———, "The Balance of Payments of the United States," *Economic Journal,* 1946.
Lange, O., "The Computer and the Market," in Feinstein, C., *Capitalism, Socialism, and Economic Growth,* C.U.P., 1967.
Lees, D. S., *Health through Choice,* IEA, 1961.
Lenin, V. I., *State and Revolution* (1919).
Lindbeck, A., *The Political Economy of the New Left,* Harper & Row, 1971.
Loughborough University, *The Swimming Pool Industry,* 1971.

Lynn, R., "How Effective Is Expenditure on Education?," in *The Dilemmas of Government Expenditure,* 1976.
McKenzie, R. B., and Tullock, G., *The New World of Economics,* Richard Irwin (USA), 1975.
Macrae, N., *To Let?,* IEA, 1960.
Marquand, D., "A Social Democratic View," in *The Dilemmas of Government Expenditure,* IEA, 1976.
Maynard, A., *Experiment with Choice in Education,* IEA, 1975.
Maynard, A. (with King, D.), *Rates or Prices?,* IEA, 1972.
Meade, J. E., *The Just Economy,* Allen & Unwin, 1975.
Miller, M., *Rise of the Russian Consumer,* IEA, 1965.
Mishan, E. J., *The Costs of Economic Growth,* Pelican, 1967.
Nozick, R., *Anarchy, State and Utopia,* Basic Books (NY), 1974.
Olson, M., *The Logic of Collective Action,* Harvard, 1971.
Paine, T., *The Rights of Man* (1789), J. M. Dent.
Pardoe, J., "Political Pressures and Democratic Institutions," in *The Dilemmas of Government Expenditure,* IEA, 1976.
Parker, R. A., "Charging for Social Services," *Journal of Social Policy,* October 1976.
Peacock, A. T. (with Shannon, R.), "The Welfare State and the Redistribution of Income," in *Westminster Bank Review,* 1968.
Peacock, A. T. (with Wiseman, J.), *Education for Democrats,* IEA, 1964.
Pennance, F. G., introduction to *Verdict on Rent Control,* IEA, 1972.
Pennance, F. G. (with Gray, H.), *Choice in Housing,* IEA, 1968.
Pennance, F. G. (with West, W. A.), *Housing Market Analysis and Policy,* IEA, 1969.
Peppiatt, W. D., "Pricing of Seaside Facilities," in *The Theory and Practice of Pricing,* IEA, 1967.
Perlman, M., "The Economics of Politics," in *The Vote Motive,* IEA, 1976.
Peston, M., *Public Goods and the Public Sector,* Macmillan, 1972.
Plant, Sir A., "The Economic Aspects of Copyright in Books," *Economica,* 1934.
———, "The Economic Theory concerning Patents for Inventions," *Economica,* 1934.
———, *The New Commerce in Ideas and Intellectual Property,* The Athlone Press, 1953.
Polanyi, G., *Comparative Returns from Investments in Nationalised Industries,* IEA, 1968.
———, *Contrasts in Nationalised Transport since 1947,* IEA, 1968.
Polanyi, G. (and others), *Policy for Poverty,* IEA, 1970.
Popper, Sir K., *The Open Society and Its Enemies,* Routledge, 1966.
Prest, A. R., *Financing University Education,* IEA, 1966.
Robbins, Lord, *The Nature and Significance of Economic Science,* Macmillan, 1932.
———, *The Theory of Economic Policy in English Classical Political Economy,* Macmillan, 1952.
———, "Notes on Public Finance," *Lloyds Bank Review,* 1955.
———, *Political Economy Past and Present,* Macmillan, 1976.
Roth, G. J., *Paying for Parking,* IEA, 1965.
———, *A Self-Financing Road System,* IEA, 1966.

Rothbard, M. N., *Man, Economy and State,* Van Nostrand (USA), 1962.
———, *Power and Market,* Institute for Human Studies (USA), 1970.
———, *For a New Liberty,* Collier-Macmillan (NY), 1973.
Rowley, C. K. (with Peacock, A. T.), *Welfare Economics: A Liberal Restatement,* Martin Robertson, 1974.
Savas, E. S., "Solid Waste Collection and Disposal," Graduate School of Business, of Columbia University, 1972.
Seldon, A., "Which Way to Welfare," *Lloyds Bank Review,* 1965.
———, *Taxation and Welfare,* IEA, 1967.
———, *After the NHS,* IEA, 1968.
———, "Taxing Social Benefits," *Daily Telegraph,* 1968.
Seldon, A. (with Gray, H.), *Universal or Selective Social Benefits,* IEA, 1967.
Seldon, A. (with Pennance, F. G.), *Everyman's Dictionary of Economics,* J. M. Dent, 1976.
Seldon, M., "How Welfare Vouchers Work," *New Outlook,* June 1966.
Shenoy, Sudha, "Pricing for Refuse Removal," in *The Theory and Practice of Pricing,* IEA, 1967.
Simey, M., *Municipal Review,* April, 1976.
Smith, A., *The Wealth of Nations* (1776), J. M. Dent.
Stigler, G. J., *The Citizen and the State,* Chicago University Press, 1975.
Tullock, G., *Private Wants, Public Means,* Basic Books (NY), 1970.
———, *The Vote Motive,* IEA, 1976.
Vaizey, Lord, "The Roulette of Public Spending," *New Statesman,* Feb. 1976.
West, E. G., *Education and the State,* IEA, 1965, 1970.
———, *Education and the Industrial Revolution,* Batsford, 1975.
West, E. G. (and others), *Regional Policy for Ever?,* IEA, 1973.
Wooldridge, W. C., *Uncle Sam, the Monopoly Man,* Arlington House (N.Y.) 1970.

Official Publications

Economic Trends, February 1976. "Effects of Taxes and Benefits on Households," Nissel, Muriel, and Perez, Jane.
Layfield Report, Committee of Inquiry into Local Government Finance, 1976.
Local Government Financial Statistics, England & Wales, 1973–4, HMSO, 1975.
Plowden Report, *Children and Their Primary Schools,* HMSO, 1967.
Provision for Sport, HMSO, 1972.
Road Pricing: The Economic and Technical Possibilities (Smeed Committee), HMSO, 1964.
Sports Council, *Sport in the Seventies,* 1971.

MICRO-ECONOMIC CONTROLS

DISCIPLINING THE STATE BY PRICING

Micro-economic Controls

I. Introduction

We are here to discuss the "taming" of government because it has become "wild"—out of control, undisciplined, inordinate.

We therefore think it can be cut down to size, be put in its place.

And if you think these descriptions are strong, I would draw your attention to a sober academic, Professor Richard Rose of the University of Strathclyde who has entitled his new book *Can Government Go Bankrupt?*[1]

Lord Robbins and Professor Littlechild have discussed what government should do and what it should not do. There is wide—and widening—agreement that it is doing much that it should not, and, as a result, not doing very well what it should.

Professor Tullock has indicated one large reason why it has grown too fast: bureaucracy is not only a result but also a cause of growing government that has grown too far.

The conceptually simplest, quickest way to take from Caesar what is not Caesar's is to "de-socialise" much of it: to transfer to the market fuel and transport, steel and motor-cars, much of education and medicine, all housebuilding, and many local services from water and ambulances, abattoirs and airports, to fire-fighting and refuse collection.

That would entail much tension and strife. It may be the ultimate solution, but if politicians shrink from the confrontation with public officials, trade unions and the advocates of big government, other methods may have to be used sooner or later. The one I would urge—replacing taxing by charging for public services wherever possible and economic—would have the same ultimate results but might possibly avoid the confrontations because it would transfer the decisions on cutting public services from politicians to the public itself.

1. Macmillan, 1979.

Professor Minford has reviewed one kind of discipline that would hold it in check: *macro*-economic controls. I now urge *micro*-controls, that is, disciplining government by subjecting it to market forces. I think we shall not be able to cut government down to size as much as is desirable *unless we put it into the market to justify itself* to the consumer—the taxpayer-citizen—in competition with any other supplier who can compete with it.

Before I do that I should say why I think macro-control, like patriotism, is not enough.

II. Macro-controls Not Enough

My main doubt about macro-controls is that they are operated by the very people, politicians and bureaucrats, who inflated and distended government in the first place. And I fear that they will find ways round conventional macro-controls and whatever new ones are devised, however sophisticated and subtle.

Consider the constitutional/legal macro-controls proposed in recent months to discipline local government councillors and their officials.

- councils asking for rates increases exceeding 20 per cent should have to be re-elected;
- a rates referendum to approve each year's rate increase;
- strengthening the legal powers of the District Auditor (who can surcharge councillors for "unreasonable" expenditure);
- taking councils to court for failing to provide services for which they have charged, as recently in the London borough of Haringey;
- stronger central government power to sanction loans for capital expenditure;
- rates strikes or delays;
- stricter cash limits—not only on central government grants but also on annual spending programmes and possibly rates increases;
- and, what the *Economist* calls "the best hope": direct election of mayors to represent the citizen who, it rightly implies, is not effectively championed by the councillors who are supposed to represent him.

No doubt each of these expedients would help. And together they might do a lot. But I doubt it. Even if cash limits set a ceiling to grants from central government and to payments by local government, they leave the local politicians and apparatchiks to decide which expenditure or service to cut down more and which less, and indeed which to increase within the general lower total. So we should probably end up with *less* spent on services the public wants *more*, say, police or roads, and *more* spent on services it wants *less*, perhaps overseas aid or housing subsidies. Macro-controls are clumsy, crude and indiscriminate: they are too much like a scythe that decapitates flowers as well as weeds.

[Examples were soon forthcoming. Following the cuts in expenditure ordered by the new Government, public officials, such as several Chief Education Officers, indicated they would use them to inconvenience the public in order to discredit the policy and generate opposition to it. A more extreme form of obstruction to macro-control was the refusal of an Area Health Authority in London to apply the policy. We can imagine the ingenuity public officials can apply in this process of manipulating government policy to serve their interests rather than the public. But we should be surprised: if there is criticism it is of those who expected public officials to put themselves second.—August 1979.]

III. How Much State Spending on Genuine Public Goods?

Unfortunately, macro-controls are probably the only ones available for some services, national or local—the so-called "public" goods proper—that government must supply because they cannot be refused to people who refuse to pay for them and hope to have "free rides." The obvious examples range from national defence to local street lighting. Taxing may therefore be the only way of paying for them, and government can control them in some fashion by cash ceilings and limits on tax revenue. Here government may be a necessary evil.

But such *jointly* consumed public goods account for only a third or so of total government expenditure. About two-thirds is spent on cash transfers and *separable* personal goods that can be refused to people who refuse to pay. Yet government goes on supplying them and taxing us to pay for them.

Table I shows the figures in a recent year. Public goods proper account for around 15 per cent of government expenditure (Group I). These are mainly external military defence, internal civil defence, Parliament itself, the law courts, public health. I must add that some American economists are examining methods of charging for even some in this category.

The rest I have divided into two groups: those which can *partly* be paid for separately by each user (Group II) and those that can *largely* or *wholly* be paid for separately (Group III). Group II, embracing mainly roads and

Table I. Government Expenditure on Public and Personal Goods

	Proportion of total government expenditure %	Proportion of gross national product %
I. Public goods with inseparable benefits (charging impracticable or uneconomic)		
Military defence	10	6
Civil defence	*	*
External relations (embassies, missions, EEC, etc.)	2	1
Parliament & law courts	1	*
Prisons	*	*
Public Health	*	*
Land drainage & coast protection	*	*
Finance & tax collection	1	1
Other government services	*	*
	15	8
II. Public goods with some separable benefits (charging partly practicable)		
Government (central & local) and "public" corporation current & capital expenditure	6	3
Roads and public lighting	3	2
Research	1	*
Parks, pleasure grounds, etc.	1	*
Local government services ("misc.")	2	1
Police	2	1
Fire services	*	*
Records, registration, surveys	*	*
	14	8
III. Substantially or wholly separable benefits (charging substantially practicable)		
Education	12	7
National Health Service	9	5
Personal social services	2	1
School meals, milk & welfare foods	1	*

Table I (continued)

	Proportion of total government expenditure %	Proportion of gross national product %
Employment service	1	*
Libraries, museums & art galleries	1	*
Housing	9	5
Water, sewage, refuse disposal	2	1
Transport & communications	5	3
	40	22
IV. Subsidies, grants, pensions and other (mostly) cash disbursements		
Agriculture, forestry, fishing, food	3	1
Cash benefits for social insurance, etc.	16	9
Misc. subsidies, grants, lending, etc., to private/personal sector	3	2
	22	13
V. Interest on National Debt	9	6
TOTAL GOVERNMENT EXPENDITURE	100	56

*Less than one per cent.

research, police and fire services, comprises 14 per cent of government expenditure, of which I imagine about 4 per cent could be paid for separately, leaving 10 per cent to be provided out of taxes. Group III comprises 40 per cent of government expenditure. It ranges from education, housing and medicine to employment offices ("job centres"), libraries, art galleries, museums, water, sewage, refuse collection, school meals, milk, welfare foods and the oddly-named "personal social services" like home helps and meals on wheels. Most of it can be paid for separately: the residue, I judge, would be perhaps 10 per cent to be provided by government.

Thus only 35 per cent of all government expenditure goes on public goods proper, and the rest on separable private benefits and cash payments. Since 70 per cent of government expenditure is on services and 30 per cent on cash payments, half of it is on private services that do not have to be supplied by government.

Where separate payment is possible it is the better way of disciplining government because the decision on where to control or reduce government is exercised by the individual consumer. It is therefore a more certain control or discipline on government than are macro-controls.

The mechanism is quite clear and simple: if you pay directly for something in the market you buy ("demand") less than if you pay indirectly to government through taxes, because you then think its price is nil—that it is "free."

There is no more effective discipline on over-spending than *knowing* the price and having to *pay* it. First, you *know* how much you pay if you pay by price; you do *not* know how much you pay if you pay in *taxes.* How many people—even in this exceptionally well-informed gathering—know the cost or price of:

- a year of state schooling
- a year of state university education
- a week in hospital
- the weekly cost of providing a council house
- the cost of supplying 1,000 gallons of water or removing 1,000 gallons of sewage
- borrowing a library book
- removing a bag of refuse?

Second, paying by price requires a conscious decision to buy or not to buy; paying by tax removes the consciousness of payment.

Third, paying by price teaches care in comparing values, forethought in using money, husbandry and economy. Paying by taxes teaches none of these virtues.

Fourth, price enables you to pay for each commodity or service separately. Paying by tax for 879 or 1,253 items removes from the individual consumer the power to decide differently for each purchase—whether to spend more on one, less on another, the same on a third.

IV. Controlling Expenditure by Pricing

Price is thus a more informed method of controlling expenditure and cutting government down to size: in separable personal services individuals know better than government where they want to spend their money. And where they want to spend it is largely different from where government spends it—as the results of field surveys reported in a forthcoming IEA book will indicate.[2]

V. Price Government Services

Moreover, putting government into the market by charging for its services would be more likely to cut it down to size because it is politically risky for politicians to set about cutting education, health or other ostensibly "desirable" services. Thus, although individuals would much rather spend less on state welfare (or other) services, and more on private services they can buy in the market with more choice,[3] which is what our researches over 15 years have found, politicians are virtually paralysed in their role of reflecting individual public preferences.

I conclude that the only effective way to discipline government in its supply of personal services is therefore to establish machinery for "do-it-yourself" cutting by each individual, or family or household. But, to do that, we must know costs and alternative prices. And that requires government services to be clearly marked with price-labels and to be charged for wherever possible.

VI. The Case for Charging

What kind of figures are likely to emerge?

Many of these personal services are provided through local government—shown for a recent year in Table II. You will see the large scope for charging—or higher charging—in the "rate-fund" services, which are supposed to be provided wholly or largely out of the rates. But even in the "trading services," which are supposed to pay for themselves more or less, there is wide scope for higher charging, especially for cemeteries, fishing harbours, markets, slaughterhouses and airports.

Take, for example, the London Borough of Ealing. School meals in 1977–78 cost 65p but have been charged at 25p, lately revised to 35p. School trans-

2. As far as I know evidence on this proposition is provided for the first time in Britain in Ralph (now Lord) Harris and Arthur Seldon, *Over-Ruled on Welfare,* Hobart Paperback 13, IEA, 1979, Chapter 6.

3. Evidence for this proposition has been provided since 1963 in the successive *Choice in Welfare* reports in 1963, 1965, and 1970, and finally in *Over-Ruled on Welfare.*

Table II. How Much We Pay for Local Government Services by Charges and by Taxes

	Charges etc. as % of expenditure	Remainder paid by taxes (%)
1. *"Rate Fund" Services (Current Expenditure)*		
Education:		
Nursery	*	100
Primary	1	99
Secondary	3	97
Special	11	89
Further:		
Polytechnics & Regional colleges	9	91
Colleges of art	8	92
Agricultural	18	82
Other major colleges, etc.	12	88
Evening institutes	19	81
Other	35	65
Teacher training	3	97
School health	1	99
Recreation & social & physical training:		
Youth	2	98
Adults, etc.	7	93
Other education services	6	94
School meals, milk, etc.	34	66
Libraries	6	94
Museums and art galleries	5	95
Health:		
Health centres	8	92
Mother/children clinics, etc.	6	94
Midwifery	1	99
Visitors	*	100
Home nursing	*	100
Vaccination & immunisation	*	100
Ambulance	2	98
Prevention of illness	3	97
Family planning	1	99
Personal social services:		
Residential care	26	74
Day care—day nurseries (incl. play groups)	12	88
Community care:		
Home helps (incl. laundry)	5	95
Meals in the home	18	82
Other	2	98
Police	4	96

Table II (continued)

	Charges etc. as % of expenditure	Remainder paid by taxes (%)
Fire	2	98
Justice (courts, petty sessions, probation)	2	98
Sewerage	6	94
Refuse	7	93
Baths (swimming & washing) & laundries	26	74
Land drainage, flood prevention	4	96
Smallholdings	12	88
Sea fisheries, pest control, etc.	27	63
Roads:		
Highways	3	97
Public lighting	2	96
Vehicle parking	60	40
Youth employment	*	100
Sheltered employment and workshops	41	59
Environment:		
Parks & open spaces	8	92
National & countryside parks	1	99
Town & country planning	4	96
Housing other than below—2)	6	94
Public conveniences	2	98
Air pollution prevention	*	100
Other health measures	6	95
River pollution prevention	*	100
Allotments	23	77
Private street, etc., works	51	49
Registration of births, etc.	35	65
Civil defence	1	99
Coast protection	*	100
2. *Housing (Current Expenditure "Revenue Account")*	60	100
3. *"Trading Services"*	60	40
Water	84	16
Passenger transport	84	16
Cemeteries & crematoria	35	65
Fishing harbours	61	39
Other ports & piers	88	12
Civic restaurants	88	12
Markets horticultural	39	61
Others	55	45
Slaughterhouses	55	45

Table II (continued)

	Charges etc. as % of expenditure	Remainder paid by taxes (%)
Aerodromes	63	37
Industrial estates	20	80
District heating schemes	83	17
Corporation estates	15	85

*Less than £1 million or 1 per cent.

port is "free"—or rather costs £1 million paid by rates and taxes—in a borough 4½ miles by 2½.

Nursery schools cost £170 per annum, primary schools £400, secondary schools about £450 up to fifth forms, around £600 for sixth forms. Parents could initially pay part of these costs by topping up vouchers worth, say, two-thirds of total costs. By giving parents choice between state and private schools, voucher-aided partial fees would make *all* schools more efficient, more cost-conscious and in the end cheaper.

In Ealing council housing repairs cost £100 a year each for 20,000 homes. A charge of £50 a year to start with would bring in revenue to reduce the subsidy and/or a spirited epidemic of do-it-yourself repairs. Car parking costs about 50p a day. Charges are nil. Thus motorists are subsidised by pedestrians they may knock down. Charging for refuse collection would encourage sorting of waste into the combustible, the re-usable and the residue of disposable to be collected.

And so in many other areas—for libraries, lavatories, sports centres, the police, art galleries, water, seaside beaches, even justice.

VII. The Case for Health Charges

Not least the apparently most difficult service of all—health. I have no doubt we should have better medical care if we withdrew some of the taxes we give the apparatchiks and make them sell their personal services to us for prices, charges and fees.

Prescriptions cost on average £2. Since 1969 we have paid 20p.[4] Visits to family doctors probably cost around £3–£5: we pay directly nothing. Hospitals can cost upward of £350 a week: we pay directly nothing.

4. Raised in June 1979 Budget to 45p—still less than one-quarter of the cost.

In spite of the view that doctors influence or control the demand for their services as well as the supply, and that price has lost its power to control demand, I have little doubt that charges for family doctors would prune submarginal calls on their services and time; higher charges for prescriptions would reduce the amount of pills poured down bathroom basins; and charges for hospitalisation would reduce the occupancy of hospital beds by discouraging premature entry and encouraging prompt discharge, and reduce expenditure on X-ray or other investigations. If there is no price doctors and patients tend to play safe and consume resources at the expense of other uses and users.

If, as a result of NHS charges, more people went to private doctors and more private hospitals were built, the state would have to sell off—desocialise—some hospitals. And that would cut out unnecessary government power.

VIII. Objections Refuted

Is it all practicable?

(1) Is it *administratively* workable?

The reply is that charging works in Europe, Australasia, North America, for health services through systems of insurance, private and governmental, voluntary and compulsory. They are by no means faultless but they are constantly studied and periodically refined.

(2) Is charging *socially* acceptable? What about the poor?

Even in health there is no insuperable difficulty. A reverse income tax in one form or other could provide the purchasing power for people with low incomes to pay charges. Their premiums could be paid for by government on a sliding scale—as has been done in Australia.

Health vouchers could enable them to shop around for health insurance that suited them, as the Secretary of State for Health, Education and Welfare in the USA has been urged to introduce.[5]

I would therefore not exempt pensioners or children as such. Many pensioners can pay and the others, except the mentally subnormal, could be enabled to pay. Many would prefer it that way. Many children have parents who could pay, and other parents could be enabled to pay. The same goes for nursing mothers. The criterion for paying charges or receiving free services is not age or physical or legal condition or anything else but income.

5. By Professor Alain C. Enthoven of Stanford University, California.

(3) Is charging *economically* realistic?

Yes—if there are large tax cuts, contracting out, reverse taxes and vouchers.

Whatever the outcome, the control of the state would decline either because the decisions to spend or not to spend on state services would lie with consumers rather than officials, or because the province of government would have been cut down.

Moreover consumer satisfaction—the efficiency of their expenditures—would increase because they would be exchanging unresponsive government services without choice for responsive private services with choice.

Not least, although demand for a service will fall as its price rises, people will willingly pay *more* for higher quality for themselves or their families. That is why people would spend more voluntarily on private education and medicine, etc., than they do compulsorily in taxes for state education and the NHS.

(4) Is charging *politically* possible?

In the absence of government attempts to discover public acceptability of charges as an alternative to paying for welfare by taxes, IEA surveys over 15 years have tried to discover the extent and trend of public attitudes and preferences. We have gone beyond simple opinion polling by introducing and emphasising price. We have asked national samples of heads of households of working age, who make these decisions, whether they would prefer to pay higher taxes for more state services or contract out, have lower taxes, but pay privately. We thus avoided the trap into which politicians and opinion-makers have fallen of asking merely if people would like lower taxes—to which the predictable reply is "Yes"; and of asking them if they want better public services, to which the again predictable reply is "Yes." The public have thus been misled into contradictory replies because they have not been supplied with the missing link—price. When price is introduced, the public indicates rational, consistent choices.[6]

Their preference for contracting out and paying by price or charges rather than by taxes has risen for education from 47 per cent in 1963 to 77 per cent in 1978 and for medical care from 57 per cent in 1963 to 72 per cent in 1978. That trend—with variations—goes through both sexes, all ages, all socio-economic groups and all party sympathies. And it is a measure of the degree to which the absence of the market enables government to ride roughshod over public preferences.

6. Harris and Seldon, *Over-Ruled on Welfare.*

IX. Opponents of Charging

There will be obstruction to the introduction of charging.

First, the demagogues will say price would damage the public services, dismantle the welfare state, weaken the fabric of government. I hope it eventually does all three. These reforms are long overdue. Government in Britain has passed out of public control; it has become wild, and it is high time it was tamed.

But charging would destroy only the so-called "public" services that government *should not supply at all* because they can be supplied in the market. It would dismantle *state* welfare but probably strengthen the welfare services as such by changing their suppliers from a public monopoly to state and private competitors. And it would weaken only *unnecessary* government. It would in time strengthen the residue of necessary government by leaving it supplying public goods proper.

Second, the trade unions will obstruct charging. Possibly only a change in the law will stop them.

Third, the bureaucrats will obstruct charging. We shall have to retire them early, transfer some to the industry market, buy them out, or ignore them.

Fourth, many academics will obstruct charging. Even good economists have neglected an instrument—the pricing system—their profession has spent two centuries refining and perfecting. I must say I am surprised how few economists indicate the relevance of pricing in all the discussion of government expenditure and how to control it.

X. Drawbacks of Charging

Charging has drawbacks, mainly four:

(i) It may be more costly to administer than a system of non-charging for free goods.

(ii) Supplying some goods free may be a simple way of equalising incomes.

(iii) Few goods are entirely private: most also have effects on others, so that if charging reduces demand the "external" good they do to others is also reduced.

(iv) There are sometimes technical difficulties in arriving at the right charge.

But there are other ways of dealing with these drawbacks, mainly by redistributing purchasing power. And even if charging is sometimes not as cheap or as certain as taxing, the drawbacks of not charging are even more damaging. These are the "externalities" of not charging that, here again, seem strangely to be ignored, even by some economists, and especially by economists who favour state provision of services and financing them by taxes. I list ten:

1. The strain in the body politic of trying to ration resources for private services without the assistance of pricing; the result is often not scientifically ideal but politically expedient.
2. Resources are used to satisfy articulate pressure groups rather than inarticulate individuals.
3. Neglect of the services that only government can perform—not least, defence and law and order.
4. Tax-financed services usually restrict choice.
5. Government services are normally not as good at innovation as private services.
6. The high taxation required to finance "free" goods weakens incentives to produce.
7. The tax-gatherers represent a waste of manpower.
8. High taxation incites tax avoidance and evasion, and a growing disrespect for law.
9. Government services supplied free interpose themselves between parents and children and weaken the family.
10. High taxes have lost Britain talent in science, technology, research, medicine, scholarship, engineering, the arts and sport.

I continue to wonder why economists who are technically sophisticated in identifying externalities that create market failure do not see externalities that go to the roots of the social order.

So to discipline and tame government I propose charging for everything wherever practicable as a necessary and urgent control—with large tax cuts to make it possible.

I think we are in for a very interesting, exciting, perhaps abrasive, but hopeful ten years.

THE RIDDLE OF THE VOUCHER

AN INQUIRY INTO THE OBSTACLES TO INTRODUCING CHOICE AND COMPETITION IN STATE SCHOOLS

To the millions of unorganised parents
locked into politicised education,
with unheeded votes and unproductive taxes;
and to the academics, educationists, politicians and
campaigners who have shown them the way to escape.

ACKNOWLEDGEMENTS

I have to thank the academics for allowing me to draw on their replies to the Department of Education. It had been intended to reproduce them in full but their wide variation in length (from 2,000 to 10,000 words), their confidentiality at many points, a degree of overlapping and the resulting inordinate length of the Paper made this course impracticable. But some of them will be published in early issues of the IEA's journal, *Economic Affairs.*

Professor Gordon Tullock's assessment of the exchange between the academics and the Department and Dr. Keith Hartley's short note on the latest state of the economics of bureaucracy were invaluable in helping me to judge the "status" of the Department's statement of December 1981.

I am grateful to the informed observers of government who made themselves available at short notice in September and October 1985 to reply to questions that seemed to me to be otherwise unanswered.

I have to thank the Chairman of FEVER for help in sifting through its voluminous records, reports and correspondence over the 10 years from 1975 to 1985. I wish I could have used them more fully to document in detail an episode in British public policy that reveals more of the working of government and the economics of democracy than I have been able to record here.

I am grateful to John Barnes and Professor Alan Peacock for reading a draft of the text to correct me on the numerous details I have tried to incorporate in order to illustrate the narrative and the argument. I have borne in mind the comments from them and other readers when making the final revisions, but they are in no way committed to my interpretations of events in the light of economic theories on which economists differ.

Not least, I thank Ruth Croxford for her conscientious co-operation in preparing the typescript at high speed.

A.S.
December 1985

A POLITICAL SEQUENCE

DECEMBER 1981

"I am intellectually attracted to the idea of education vouchers as a means of eventually extending parental choice and influence . . . and improving standards."

—Secretary of State for Education (*Letter to education lobbies*—Section I, p. 337)

OCTOBER 1982

"[W]e are concerned not only with the rich and the clever. We want to extend choice to every person. That is what a properly constructed voucher scheme could do."

—Secretary of State for Education (*Party Conference*)

OCTOBER 1983

"The voucher, at least in the foreseeable future, is dead."

—Secretary of State for Education (*Party Conference*)

JUNE 1984

". . . the idea of vouchers is no longer on the agenda."

—Secretary of State for Education (*House of Commons*)

JULY 1985

"I am very disappointed that we were not able to do the voucher scheme; I think I must have another go."

—Prime Minister (Secretary of State for Education 1970–74) (*TV Channel 4*)

JULY 1985

"[We must] re-examine any idea which gave purchasing power to parents."

—Parliamentary Under-Secretary, Dept. of Education (*Cambridge*)

NOVEMBER 1985

"Voucher schemes . . . are worth further study."

—Secretary of State for Transport (*Leamington Spa*)

NOVEMBER 1985

"[We should] re-examine some form of access scheme . . . purchasing power to give more clout to parental choice."

—Parliamentary Under-Secretary, Dept. of Education (*Harrow*)

NOVEMBER 1985

"Either we must go to a national system . . . or to a much deeper degree of decentralisation with directly-elected school boards and abundant facilities for individuals and groups to take the initiative in setting up schools of their own outside the state system."

—Adviser on Schools to Conservative Party at General Election 1983 (*Daily Telegraph*)

DECEMBER 1985

"The Assisted Places Scheme fulfils a need but works under economic constraints . . . I hope to see a greater variety and range of schools available to parents in all communities."

—Parliamentary Under-Secretary, Dept. of Education (*Dartford*)

FEBRUARY 1986

"There has been a change in the climate of opinion—parental power is now a real issue. We need to look to the future and re-examine options such as vouchers for extending effective parental choice."

—Parliamentary Under-Secretary of State, Minister for Industry and Education, Scottish Office (*Edinburgh*)

PREAMBLE

THE ECONOMICS OF POLITICS IN 1986

During 1984 two senior economists associated with the IEA, in separate discussions of its work in presenting general economic thinking and specific ideas and proposals over 25 years, expressed a degree of academic puzzlement about the failure of apparently fruitful economic stratagems to be reflected in public policy. The question was seen as timely especially since there had been a full term of office of a Government widely thought, rightly or wrongly, by hostile critics as well as sympathisers, to be receptive to market-creating reforms.

Both economists had in mind, as a prominent example of neglected ideas, proposals long discussed for reform in education, and both used the same words: "What happened to the voucher?" For over a century since the state began "free" schools in 1870 the natural market that had been developing and would have evolved further in education, with all its potential advantages of choice for consumers and competition between suppliers, has been largely suppressed. The voucher had been advocated by liberal economists and others because it would create choice and competition and so allow the market to resume its development.

The voucher is a highly flexible instrument, with many variations, that would replace the financing of schools through taxes under political control and bureaucratic supervision by payments direct from parents thus equipped with a new ability (for the 95 per cent with middle and lower incomes) to compare schools and move between them.[1]

In 1985 the relevance of a device that could end the political/producer monopoly in education had been dramatised by the prolonged disruption by

1. Its forms, working and effects are indicated in the text and discussed more fully in numerous writings, some listed in the Readings (p. 417).

teachers and the evident difficulty of the Government in persuading them to accept internal reforms designed to equip pupils better for a life of work.[2] Elementary economic analysis indicates that the ability of organised teachers to resist reforms was strengthened by the bargaining power residing in the suppliers' monopoly of education in the state system and the resulting inability of parents dissatisfied by the disruption of classroom teaching to ensure alternative schooling for their children. If they had been able to move out of disrupted schools, the teachers' unions, or individual teachers, could have been expected to modulate their claims, temper their resistance, and perhaps agree to acceptable compromises. The state system offers no such easy means of avoiding the consequences of disputes between teachers and their immediate employers, the local education authorities (but effectively central government, the Department of Education, since it holds the purse-strings). The adverse effects are suffered by their ultimate "employers," the parents, most of whom are locked in without avenues of escape.

It so happens that, in 1981 and 1982, the chief Minister, the Secretary of State for Education, had been considering precisely such a means of escape for the wider and long-term reasons of choice and competition persistently urged for decades by liberal economists, many in IEA Papers since the early 1960s. Elementary economic analysis again suggests that if a device such as the voucher for enabling dissatisfied parents to move their children had been introduced, or even provisionally announced, in 1983 or 1984 it would have strengthened the bargaining power of the Minister and improved the prospects of earlier settlement of the dispute. In the event, for reasons to be clarified, he was deprived of this bargaining re-inforcement. He has been left to bargain unaided with virtually dominant because "monopolistic" suppliers of teaching labour, at least in the initial stages when the largest union dominated the teachers' tactics. Omitting to alter the market structure of state education, which locks parent-consumers into the system, made the chief Minister's task more difficult: it lost potential allies—millions of par-

2. Two close observers of the early attempts to introduce vouchers in the USA conclude that a reason why they failed in some areas (New Hampshire, East Hartford, etc.) was that "Insiders and intellectuals saw vouchers as a solution to vague and abstract problems, such as monopoly power in education—not as the solution to the day-to-day problems of running a school system." (D. K. Cohen, Eleanor Farrar, "Power to the parents? the story of education vouchers," *The Public Interest*, New York, Summer 1977.) Teachers' pay in Britain is the largest constituent of school costs. The 1985–86 teachers' strike and its aftermath are a "shock" to the equilibrium of forces in the political market that Professor C. K. Rowley suggests (Section IV) could radically change political conceptions of the electoral feasibility of the voucher system.

ents, outnumbering teachers by about 30 to one[3]—who could have been mustered as reserves to encourage a more conciliatory approach from the teachers or their unions. The tactical weakness of parents facing a monopoly but with the ultimate power of parents as voters (or tax-rejectors) is discussed below (Section V).

It is true that the economic structure of the state labour market in the education industry is that of a bilateral monopoly: a dominant government buyer (proximately local government, ultimately central government) confronts a dominant supplier, the teachers organised in unions. Both can bring schooling to a dead stop, with little regard for the interests or anxieties of parents. But here economic analysis indicates that the outcome is indeterminate. Since there is no competitive market price (teachers' pay package), the settlement could end anywhere between the higher pay that teachers could expect in other occupations (or in private schools) and the lower cost to government of having pupils taught in other ways. In the short run, the outcome is likely to be decided by arbitrary conditions that have little to do with the well-being of pupils or the opinion of parents: not least the temperament and character of Ministers and the union leaders, their tactical skills and judgements of public reaction to the damage to pupils, the solidarity of the teachers' unions, and the timing of general or local elections.

How far the 1985–86 teachers' dispute has re-inforced the view—increasingly accepted by politicians and academics of all schools of thought—that consumer-beneficiaries of the welfare state, not least parents in education and patients in health care, have been out-manoeuvred by producers—politicians, officials, government employees in the political process—is the intriguing question that emerges in the pages of this IEA Hobart Paperback. What seems unexpected and significant is the early revival of interest in vouchers among Ministers—from the Prime Minister in July 1985 to middling and junior Ministers in early 1986, including two concerned specifically with education—so soon, hardly more than a year after it had been pronounced in June 1984 as no longer on the agenda. It was apparently very much alive in October 1982 but was politically "dead" some time before October 1983, perhaps by June 1983, the time of the General Election, when it surfaced briefly before it seems to have been silenced. The riddle of the voucher crystallised in the nine months from October 1982 to June 1983.

3. The number of pupils in England and Wales is around 7¼ million, with perhaps 12–13 million parents, approximately 30 times the total of 425,000 teachers. (The ratio of pupils to teachers is 17.5 to one.)

Whether the return of political interest in the voucher in 1985–86 is temporary or deep-rooted, whether prompted by anxiety about school standards or parental freedom (or both), it has never left the minds of academics intrigued to know why the artificial, politically-created monopoly, encouraged since its early decades by the officialdom,[4] persists in education when it is neither inevitable nor beneficial, and when it is coming under increasing criticism. The original question "What happened to the voucher?" can now be re-inforced by a second and third: "Why has it returned to political speeches?" and "What stops it from being introduced?" Are the reasons economic?,—political?,—technical?,—cultural? Do they lie in the political-monopoly nature of state education or in the interventionist-regulatory nature of government?

Especially in the 30 years that almost exactly cover the life of the IEA since the mid- and later-1950s, economists have become interested in the internal economics of government as well as in the economics of industry. In the course of this analysis they have come to abandon the notion, implicit in much of the writings of economists over 200 years,[5] that government is a neutral vehicle in judging proposals for policy primarily in the public interest, objectively and benevolently adopting the good and rejecting the bad.

This relatively new branch of economics is described by its mainly American founding fathers, generally recognised as Professors J. M. Buchanan and Gordon Tullock, as "public choice," to indicate the machinery by which preferences ("choices") made by citizens collectively in elections are assembled, processed and applied by government, in contrast to the machinery by which their personal preferences made individually are assembled, processed and applied in the market. Public choice is known more generally in Britain as the economics of politics. Although they acknowledge their origins in earlier work by the Scottish Duncan Black and the American Anthony Downs, Buchanan and Tullock must be accounted as two of the most

4. E. G. West, *Education and the State,* IEA, 1965; and *Education and the Industrial Revolution,* Batsford Books, 1975, argued that state education was enlarged by empire-building civil servants from its early years.

5. J. M. Keynes was one of the worst offenders, and some academics continue to neglect the pressures on government that *prevent* it from faithfully reflecting "the public interest." But some economists in the classical tradition like John Stuart Mill, Jeremy Bentham and D. H. Robertson saw the truth. Alfred Marshall used to ask: "Do you mean Government all wise, all just, all powerful, or Government as it now is?" (Quoted from Reminiscences by E. A. Benians in *Memorials of Alfred Marshall,* edited by A. C. Pigou, Macmillan, 1926, p. 80.)

fruitful minds among the economists of our times. They have provoked a new literature of economics, with by now numerous adherents and acolytes, chairs and faculties, books, articles and learned journals that carry the work of economists, political scientists, philosophers, historians and other scholars. Development, sometimes on independent lines, in Britain, notably by Professors Alan Peacock, Jack Wiseman and Charles Rowley, and in Europe, mainly by Professor Bruno Frey and his associates, have enriched, refined and further advanced the economics of politics. And in the USA the study of state regulation of industry by Professors R. H. Coase, George Stigler, Gary Becker and others[6] has re-inforced understanding of the economics of government.

There is now a burgeoning economic analysis of the political process that has spawned an economics of democracy, an economics of government, an economics of bureaucracy, and other specialist studies that analyse "the political market." Their importance was seen in the early years at the IEA, and their thinking incorporated into IEA Papers, as in Professor Buchanan's *The Inconsistencies of the National Health Service* in 1963 and Professor E. G. West's *Economics, Education and the Politician* in 1968. In 1973 Professor W. A. Niskanen wrote Hobart Paperback 5, *Bureaucracy: Servant or Master?* The Hobart Paperbacks were created as a series of studies into the reasons why promising ideas were lost in the political process; the first text, *Politically Impossible . . . ?*, was written by Professor W. H. Hutt in 1971. In 1976 Professor Gordon Tullock reviewed the elements of public choice in *The Vote Motive* (a title designed to crystallise the contrast with "the profit motive" of industry). In 1978 Professor Buchanan delivered the keynote address to an IEA Seminar, the proceedings of which were presented in *The Economics of Politics,* with notable contributions by Professors Albert Breton, Frey, Peacock, Rowley and Wiseman.

While sponsoring in Britain the study of public choice, some at the IEA had reservations about the name on the ground that the dominant finding of the new economics was paradoxically that government often or invariably *denied* the choice of the public. There were also aspects of government that did not seem to be covered by "public choice."[7] It was therefore thought that "the economics of politics" was a better general description than "public

6. A selection of Stigler's writings, salted with rare wit, are collected in *The Citizen and the State,* 1975; Becker's characteristic work is indicated in *The Economic Approach to Human Behaviour,* 1976; both published by the University of Chicago Press.

7. Some are indicated in F. Forte and A. T. Peacock (eds.), *Public Expenditure and Government Growth,* Blackwell, 1985.

choice" for the economic analysis of the motivations of government and the influences on it that *prevent* it from faithfully reflecting individual preferences and "the public interest."

There are thus two layers of frustration of public choices. First, government may not clearly discern and/or undeviatingly pursue public preferences. Second, it may be impeded by its servants because they too have private interests that may conflict with the interests of citizens. The economics of politics does not necessarily condemn politicians or bureaucrats but tries to analyse and explain the motivations that may bring them into conflict with, and prevent them serving, "the general interest"—comprising the individual interests of taxpayer/voters and, specifically in education, parents.

It is in this spirit of analysis and understanding that this Hobart Paperback studies the reasons why the education voucher, despite impressive intellectual lineage and distinguished academic advocacy, has so far failed to be applied in British public policy. The inquiry is necessarily couched in general terms, since the obstacles, the obstructors and the reasons for the failure in 1983 are hardly likely to be revealed in full so soon after the event; and the official papers will not be published for 30 years. Moreover, the political, official and professional individuals may be too near the events and too preoccupied with the immediate administrative or political pressures of the day to see the underlying longer-term influences at work. Their current explanations for the failure may understandably be coloured too much by immediate, surface causes and too little by less apparent but more powerful underlying forces. Ministers and officials preoccupied in "running" services may, indeed, not know or have time to study what is happening below the surface, nor whether their solutions to day-to-day problems remove the ultimate causes. Not least, they have no inducements to emphasise the opportunity costs or "external" effects elsewhere of *failing* to reform the institutions for which they are formally responsible: the effects of inadequate schooling on industry, exports, national income, living standards, resources for low-income people, etc.; these indirect sacrifices and losses do not appear in the short-term calculus of the political process.

Perhaps most fundamentally, as Austrian individualist market economics has long taught (notably in a tract by Eugen von Böhm-Bawerk,[8] a Min-

8. "*Macht oder ökonomisches Gesetz?*" (rendered "freely" as "political power or market forces?"), *Zeitschrift für Volkswirtschaft, Sozialpolitik und Verwaltung*, Vol. XXIII, 1914, pp. 205–271.

ister of Finance of Austria), government is not ultimately all-powerful in deciding the nature, course and speed of adaptation to the underlying market forces of supply and demand. Change in technology and social habits is ultimately uncontrollable and irrepressible. A politically-centralised society such as the USSR may be able to suppress market forces for decades, but a democratic society such as Britain, Canada, the USA or Australia, responsive to increasingly sophisticated public opinion and aspirations, cannot indefinitely repress technological or social change. If it persists in flouting individual preferences and opportunities, it will provoke defiance of the law and rejection of taxes that finance insensitive government which yields to organised producer interests. The intriguing question for liberal economists is how much longer government in Britain can maintain tax-financed, politically-controlled, producer-dominated education (and medical care) in denial of the increasing consumer sovereignty that is rapidly being asserted in other parts of the economy, where its benefits in raising quality and quantity of output are commonplace.

Academic interest in the voucher will therefore continue despite the comprehensible but not disinterested political/official reticence recounted in Section I. Economists will continue to ask not only "What happened to the education voucher?" but also what has happened to a score of other market-creating ideas, not least student loans, competitive health insurance, the abolition of rent restriction, portable housing subsidies,[9] reform of mortgage interest, privatisation of pensions, de-socialisation of coal and other fuels, rail and other transport, hospital grounds and other unwanted land, the ending of monopoly in professional services, charging instead of taxing for government services falsely presented as "social services" (the familiar confusion between public goods and merit goods[10]), and much else that remains neglected by post-war government. Ministers and officials have plausible tactical reasons that outsiders cannot judge or discover for putting some reforms before others, but their decisions are not to be accepted as disinterested. Government may have overriding, rational electoral interests—like the timing of four- or five-yearly General Elections—that it puts before

9. F. G. Pennance, *Choice in Housing*, IEA, 1968.

10. "Public goods" is an objective scientific description for those that cannot be supplied in the market because it is technically impossible or economically unprofitable to exclude "free riders" who will not pay. "Merit goods" are a more subjective and debatable category: those that self-appointed arbiters think people should have but cannot (or will not) pay for (Section V).

others, and that do not necessarily coincide with the generalised interests of citizens. Its familiar defences—"politically impossible," "electorally untimely," "administratively impracticable"—are especially contestable since it is judge and jury in its cause.[11] In yielding to the pressure of organised producers it may overlook the potential but unrealised allies, immediately among other producers, ultimately among consumers, that reform would create (Section VI). It may misjudge the popularity or unpopularity of proposals indicated by opinion-polling, since macro-economic responses based on uninformed general sentiment conceal individual preferences that can be revealed only by micro-economic, priced alternatives between state and private services or between more/better state services and lower taxes (Section II). Not least, it cannot be assumed that politicians or officials are necessarily the best judges of the technical/economic arguments for reform, or of the scope for its advantages in "the public interest": they may know the past, but not the effects of change in the future; they may not see the wood for the trees (Section VI).

Even, therefore, if the education voucher was abandoned in 1983 for pressing political reasons, or presumed administrative difficulties, or supposedly damaging disruption asserted by teachers who thought themselves endangered, academic interest that has grown over the decades cannot be suppressed by the momentary anxieties, real or imagined, of politicians, bureaucrats or state employees. Their doubts and opposition may be predictable, but they cannot expect academic curiosity to subside. Nor will parents troubled by inefficient, autocratic, irresponsible or unaccountable teaching accept for ever that it can all be left to earnest politicians or hard-working officials; or that there is no escape, as the Department of Education White Paper, *Better Schools,*[12] implies (Section V).

This Paper would thus be relevant even if present-day Education Ministers had decided there was no prospect for many years of creating a market in education by the voucher or by any other means of empowering consumers to control producers by the new power of exit to preferred competitors. But an inquiry into the likely causes of its abandonment is made

11. A recent example: "the mood [in 1980–81] was right for rather more legislation [on unions] than I thought politically acceptable." (James Prior, Secretary of State for Employment, 1979–81, TV Channel 4, 15 December 1985.) The politician's judgement of "politically possible" is inherently over-cautious: a better reform that requires more skill or endurance to implement is less preferable than a lesser reform that is politically easier or less exhausting.

12. Cmnd. 9469, HMSO, March 1985.

timely sooner than might have been expected because of the recent second thoughts by other Ministers, and their anxieties about the continuing deterioration in monopolistic state schooling. The dispute during 1985–86 on teachers' pay has been accompanied by a series of unexpected Ministerial suggestions or proposals (pp. 323–24) which have changed the title of this Paper. In its early stages it was provisionally *The Voucher Vanishes.* But the voucher, sometimes under other names, has clearly not vanished from political as well as academic minds. It has been politically disinterred no more than a year after it was politically buried. Apart from its overriding inherent virtues of restoring choice for parents, other powerful reasons for its restoration to public notice that may be counting with political minds will be reviewed in Section VI.

The purpose is not to rehearse the arguments for making state education more responsive to parental opinion (that ground has been covered in IEA and other writings—Readings, p. 417), but to review the obstacles, in faulty ideas and vested interests, that obstructed it in 1981–83 in Britain, and so to continue the academic debate and better understand the obstacles that remain.

The Paper is based on three main sources of raw material. The first are documents that passed in 1981–82 between the Department of Education and 14 academics—economists, political scientists and sociologists—or written by them in 1983–84, who can be named. The second source is confidential conversations in the summer and autumn of 1985 with knowledgeable individuals in the political process who are not named. I have also drawn on FEVER records and documents, including transcripts of radio and video cassettes of TV broadcasts on the voucher.[13] Full use of these sources would have produced a much larger text than is attempted here. It should be written one day by an historian of contemporary government. My purpose in this interim appraisal, written mainly as *rapporteur,* is to identify the main features of an intellectual debate that will continue as long as there are independent academics who study, research and think, and politicians or officials who make judgements that history sometimes falsifies.

13. *You the Jury,* BBC Radio 4, November 1982; *Open Door,* BBC 2, September 1982; "Decision-making in Britain," The Open University, BBC 2, first broadcast March 1983; Diverse Reports, TV Channel 4, May 1984.

A Summary Narrative, 1944–86

The 1944 Butler Education Act and post-war political settlement or consensus on education was, like the rest of the welfare state, essentially paternalistic. Improvement was to come from above—from well-intentioned politicians and able officials, rather than from below—from uninformed and perhaps uninterested parents. The 1870 approach, that the market could not supply the desired quantity or quality of schooling for all, was continued unquestioned.

The recently published official papers for 1955 indicate[1] that, 10 years after the war, the settlement continued undisturbed. In 1955 the Minister of Education advised the Eden Cabinet that the Opposition proposals for turning all secondary schools into "comprehensives" would succeed if the Government did not produce an alternative to assuage the resentment of parents whose children had failed to pass the 11-plus examination (for entry into grammar schools). They would demand "selection" (into three types of secondary schools) either for none or for all. Selection for none would be ensured by comprehensive schools for all, with parental choice virtually abolished and grammar schools eventually closed. Selection for all, he advised, could be ensured by enabling (some) secondary schools to develop specialisms and more vocational courses to construct "an alternative route" to grammar schools that would take pupils at secondary modern and technical schools to well-paid jobs via colleges of technology. He rejected the principle of "assisted places," to enable state school pupils to move to public schools, as politically difficult (the theme of this IEA series), though he advised that public schools be brought closer to the state system by changing their entrance requirements to give easier access to pupils from state primary schools. ("Assisted places" to provide exits for poor but bright children to public schools were enacted by his party in 1980.)

1. David Walker, *The Times*, 4 January 1986.

In the 30 years since 1955, most of the grammar schools have been closed by local authorities run by both the major political parties. If the 1955 Minister had been advised by his officials, scouring the world for new thinking in education, that an idea to transfer influence in schools from the top to the bottom of the political pyramid had been launched that very year by a relatively little-known economist at the University of Chicago (below), Britain's grammar schools would have been saved, parents would have learned to choose schools and insist on rising standards, numeracy and literacy among the school population would now be higher than ever, taxation would be much lower, the officialdom smaller, the state would not have encroached on civil life to the point at which it is now difficult to roll back.

As late as 1974, the (Conservative) Opposition "Shadow Education Minister" promised a Parents' Charter to strengthen their voice but without a new power to leave schools that dissatisfied them. That new note came in 1976 (below, pp. 336–37).

The use of "exits"[2] from state schools to break the monopoly of control by central and local government appeared in early IEA studies. People with higher incomes or prepared to sacrifice other purchases can exit by paying fees to private schools or the higher housing costs of districts with the better state schools. The idea of universal exits for *all* parents by distributing earmarked purchasing power in place of providing nil-priced schooling had been advocated by Professor Milton Friedman in 1955.[3] It could be traced back to Cardinal Bourne in 1926[4] and in tenuous embryo to Tom Paine in 1792.[5] In 1963 the first of four field studies designed at the IEA used the voucher as a device to discover individual micro-preferences between state and private schooling.[6] In 1964 Professors Alan Peacock and Jack Wiseman

2. The terms "voice" and "exit" were used by Professor A. O. Hirschmann in an original study of methods of disciplining and correcting inefficiency in states, firms and other organisations: "exit" to a competitor in a market, generally favoured, he said, by economists, and protest to the management, or "voice," generally favoured by political scientists. "Loyalty" is a secondary device used by the stronger "voices" where exit is difficult or costly. (*Exit, Voice and Loyalty,* Harvard University Press, 1970.)

3. "The Role of Government in Education," in Robert Solo (ed.), *Economics and the Public Interest,* Rutgers University Press, 1955.

4. Quoted by A. C. F. Beales, *Education: A Framework for Choice,* IEA Readings No. 1, IEA, 1967 (2nd Edn., 1970), p. 6 ff.

5. *The Rights of Man,* 1792, quoted in E. G. West, *Education and the State,* IEA, 1965 (2nd Edn., 1970) and in more detail in his essay in *Education: A Framework for Choice, ibid.,* pp. 63–64.

6. R. Harris, A. Seldon, *Choice in Welfare,* 1963.

were the first economists in Britain to examine the separation of the supply of schools, by (private or public) self-supporting institutions, from its financing by the state, with parents enabled by vouchers, grants or loans to shop around in a free market.[7] In 1965 Professor E. G. West's now classic *Education and the State* demonstrated from neglected historical evidence that a market had been emerging in the 19th century long before 1870, since when it has been almost annihilated by successive expansions of state-financed and government-supplied schools paid for by taxes in place of prices. In 1967 four authors, including Professors West and Mark Blaug, compiled *Education: A Framework for Choice,* for which the Foreword to the Second Edition was written by an economic historian, then a headmaster, Dr. Rhodes Boyson, later a junior Minister of Education. (He was the first considerable Conservative politician who understood that "exit" was indispensable.)

This intellectual groundwork in honing ideas in the 1960s was, as Keynes might have expected (Section VI), the forerunner of public lobbying and political interest in the 1970s. The first (and so far only) lobby to promote parent-power through the voucher began with a motion in favour of experimental vouchers at the September 1974 Conference of the National Council of Women. The support it received (a majority of delegate votes) encouraged the sponsors to establish the Friends of the Education Voucher Experiment in Representative Regions (FEVER) in December 1974. Five years of vigorous campaigning confirmed Professor Gordon Tullock's emphasis on the ultimate power of voters (Section IV). Public meetings (a school hall packed with 500 parents caused a local Member of Parliament to declare instant support for the voucher), a local "referendum" in Ashford, Kent, radio and television broadcasts, press publicity and approaches to Party and religious leaders (Section V) led to a deputation in December 1979 to the Secretary of State for Education to present a national petition in favour of vouchers for all schools, state and private. And in December 1981 the new Secretary of State responded to an approach from FEVER with a Departmental statement of difficulties seen in a voucher scheme,[8] which initiated the debate with academics examined in this Paper.

The political reaction to the academic analysis and public advocacy of the voucher led in 1976 to a motion by the Conservative Opposition in the House of Commons, initiated by Dr. Boyson, in favour of local experiments with school vouchers. It was supported (on a three-line Whip) by all Conserva-

7. *Education for Democrats,* Hobart Paper 25, IEA, 1964.
8. Appendix 1 to Section II, pp. 357–64.

tive MPs (including a former Prime Minister, later a critic), with one abstention. Henceforth experiments with vouchers became official Conservative education policy.

In 1978, a Kent County public survey, based on Ashford, revealed strong parental desire for choice and indicated that the number who would switch schools would not be unmanageable.

The prospect of political action on the voucher quickened with the election of the Conservative Government in May 1979. In December 1979 the deputation of the FEVER lobby to the then Secretary of State included the economist Professor C. K. Rowley and the political scientist John Barnes (whose replies to the Department are also reviewed below), and a further academic experienced in local government, Gordon Richards.[9]

The first overt step came in November 1981 when the new Secretary of State invited two education lobbies[10] to comment on the difficulties or problems the Department (or its officials—below) saw in the introduction of a voucher system. Its 2,250-word statement followed in December (Section II, Appendix 1). In response, FEVER invited observations from 11 economists, political scientists and lawyers, several with direct experience of running schools, which it embodied in its refutation[11] of the Department's difficulties and problems. Three academics responded through other channels. In all 14 replies are reviewed below. In alphabetical order they were made by:

John Barnes, London School of Economics
Professor Mark Blaug, University of London Institute of Education
Professor John Coons, University of California, Berkeley
Professor S. R. Dennison, former Vice-Chancellor, University of Hull
Professor Malcolm Fisher, University of New South Wales, Australia, formerly University of Cambridge, England
Professor Antony Flew, University of Reading
Professor Milton Friedman, formerly University of Chicago
Lord Harris of High Cross, Institute of Economic Affairs
Michael McCrum, Master of Corpus Christi College, Cambridge

9. The others were the Chairman and Vice-Chairman of FEVER and the writer of this Paper.

10. The second was the National Council for Educational Standards, which largely concentrated on internal reforms in state education, notably by strengthening parental "voice." It did not submit a formal response to the Department.

11. Signed by its Chairman and Vice-Chairman, Marjorie Seldon and the late Ruth Garwood-Scott.

Professor Alan Peacock, University of Buckingham
Professor C. K. Rowley, University of Newcastle upon Tyne
Professor Stephen Sugarman, University of California
Professor E. G. West, Carleton University, Canada, formerly at the University of Kent
Professor Jack Wiseman, University of York

(Notes on the academics appear in Section II, Appendix 2.)

FEVER organised replies to the Department of Education in early 1982. The further three appeared later in 1982 or early 1983. It was understood that the officials would be asked to respond to the academics' refutations. No reply was made during 1982 or 1983. In October 1983 the Secretary of State announced (at the Conservative Party Conference) that the voucher was "dead."

Since the middle of 1985 the growing re-consideration of the fate of the voucher (pp. 323–24) indicates that the principle of the voucher would not, after all, be abandoned but would perhaps be incorporated, possibly under a different name, into education policy.

The possible reasons for this early re-appraisal are discussed in Section VI. They range widely from political philosophy and vision to political self-interest; from the realisation that teachers could not be expected to respond to the Government's anxiety to emphasise "industrial skills" as long as they commanded a monopoly service, to the view that a new power for parents to exert influence over state schools could be electorally popular. For opinion *has* been moving. Apart from the persistent academic interest in a new method of financing education, more reflective teachers will wonder why their spokesmen feared it, students of government have an intriguing episode to study for its lessons in the working of democracy, and parents, taxpayers and voters will want to know why a new idea that promised more choice of school, lower taxes and more political respect for the ballot box was abandoned after shallow consideration and without trial.

In 1985–86, with its industrial dispute, even more than in earlier years, the relevance of the voucher could above all lie in the intensifying realisation that raising school standards could be sought more securely by market forces through parent power than by Ministerial ukase, on which the Secretary of State still appears to rely.

This is the stage that the 30-year and recently intensifying debate on the control of education—whether by producers or consumers, teachers or parents—has now reached in early 1986. Had the century-old developing state control of education worked? Why were new methods being urged? The exchange between the Department of Education and the academics in 1981–82 raised the main economic and administrative issues. It was indeed a rare development for a Department of State to indicate its doubts about a reform and to have them discussed openly in public at an early stage by independent academics. Even though the immediate political outcome was for the Department's doubts to prevail over the academics' rebuttals, the chief Minister is to be complimented on allowing the issues to be debated in public. Since no political decision is final, not least because no Minister can bind his successors nor a Government its successors, the exchange will have clarified the difficulties, at least as seen inside government, as a guide to thinking and policy in the future.

SECTION II

Official Objections, 1981, and Academic Refutations, 1982

The difficulties anticipated by the politicians and/or the officials at the Department of Education in 1981 seemed to derive essentially from presuppositions about the existing structure of the education industry, the prevailing law, especially as determined by the wartime-consensus 1944 Act but also more recent legislation in the 1980s, and the state of the market in education—its conditions of supply and demand. The structure of the industry, it was objected, would be disturbed by a reform that moved initiative and influence in schools from producers (politicians, officials, teachers) to consumers (parents). The law, which laid obligations on government, such as providing schools without charge, would be breached in changing the financing of schools from government revenue to parental prices (fees, etc.). And the market in education could not, physically or economically, change the number of places supplied by individual schools or in total to meet the increase or decrease in demand resulting from the new power of parents to move their children from unsatisfying to preferred schools.

The economic reasoning in the objections implied that the established structure of education should determine whether reform was acceptable, that the law would be difficult to change, and that the market in education was inert and could not be revived.[1] Underlying the implication or assumption that the supply of school facilities would be inelastic in responding to new demands—for places at individual schools or for the content of school

1. A parallel opinion was implied about housing in D. V. Donnison, *The Government of Housing*, Pelican Original, Penguin Books, 1967. In the six years since 1979 a million families, never before owner-occupiers, have bought their homes at sub-market prices but with restrictions on resale and with the financial risks and costs of ownership. The market in home-hiring has been suppressed by distorted municipal rents for 70 years, the market for schooling by nil or politicised pricing for 115 years. With flexibility in pricing both would re-emerge from not far below the surface.

education or for methods of teaching in general—was the concentration on the income-effect of voucher-financing on "rich" and "poor" parents to the virtual exclusion of its price-effect. For in creating price-incentives, the voucher would produce new courses, new forms of teaching and, not least, new entrepreneurs who would create new schools and kinds of schools to meet new demands from newly-enfranchised parents which they have hitherto been unable to express. And there was no recognition of the "feed-back" effect on schools of the potential resort to exit in stimulating inquiry by Governors or Heads into the reasons for loss of pupils. The neglect of the effects of pricing also led the document to over-rate the "problems" of shortage of (mathematics or other) teachers, which can be cured by paying them more, and of transport, which is minor if parents pay fares to cover costs.[2] School pricing would hardly be a shock to parents who pay for nursery schools and universities.

Discussions in the second half of 1985 indicated that not all the 1981 administrative and other difficulties would be retained in detail but that in principle the continuing objections to a voucher system centred on four anxieties: the obligation to supply free education, to make it compulsory, to maintain standards and to minimise costs. Yet these four supposed immutables do not comprise definitive obstacles to allowing the natural market in education to re-emerge.

It also seemed in 1985 that the decisive objections to adopting the voucher in 1983 were *not* ultimately administrative, as suggested in 1981, but essentially political, as emerged later in 1982 and 1983, and emphasised in 1985.

Since the administrative objections are now seen to be secondary, implausible or unconvincing, they can be disposed of by a brief review of the academic refutations in 1982 and later. But their importance remains for students of the history of government reaction to proposals for reform in general and to change in the political control of education in particular. And for economists studying the analytical power of public choice, the episode reveals the quality of argument and the influence on policy of the officialdom, concerned properly with the administrative rather than the political aspects of reform in public policy.[3]

Specifically, the main objections were 10. The refutations reflect the aca-

2. I am obliged to Robert Miller for a timely reminder.

3. In the Open University programme, Professor Antony Flew said the Department's 1981 document was not researched, was complacent about state education and biassed in favour of the suppliers.

demics' replies, FEVER's additional arguments, and my conclusions based on developments since 1982. I incorporate only rejoinders to the economic and public choice arguments, not observations on the relevance, quality or internal consistency of the Department's statement.

1. *Costs would increase by the extension of vouchers to private schools not now financed by government. The saving in state school (marginal) costs avoided by the shift of pupils to private schools would be much less than the value of the voucher at average cost.*

Refutation: The Department's statement shows no awareness of the wide range of vouchers—and their combinations of characteristics—to suit specific purposes. There is an especially deep difference, emphasised by Professor Blaug, between vouchers of fixed value that cannot be supplemented and open-value vouchers that can be supplemented. If confined to state schools with little else (teachers' pay scales, local authority control, etc.) changed, fixed-value vouchers would merely remove zoning, already arranged by the 1980 Act. If extended, he argued, they would create a subsidy to private schools. The voucher that has "truly excited" economists, because it would restructure the school system, is the open-value voucher tenable at all schools charging fees reflecting their costs. In the middle run, state costs would rise to facilitate expansion in some state schools and contraction in others. But it would disturb the power of local education authorities and teachers:

> Open-value, supplementable vouchers are a radical idea that would overturn the education system. . . . Freedom of access and greater educational efficiency cannot be achieved on the cheap. [*Professor Blaug*]

Marginal costs would, even with some shifts of pupils, rise nearer to average costs as some school classes could be closed and some buildings transferred to private school educationists and teacher entrepreneurs. In time all costs become marginal: blackboards and chalk are not replaced, equipment not renewed, buildings not retained. State disinvestment can be speeded by sales or renting of buildings and equipment without waiting for physical exhaustion (*Professor Fisher,* p. 351).

In the early years the value of the voucher could be varied in numerous ways to keep total costs unchanged: it could be related to parental income; it could be treated as taxable income; it could be reduced to a percentage of school costs (Lord Harris suggested 80 per cent, Professor Friedman 75 per cent, in which event, he argued, total costs would *fall*) to offset the additional cost of the voucher for the 5–6 per cent of children whose private fees would be lost; and so on. Moreover, in the long run, costs would be *reduced* by turning each school into an entrepreneurial cost-conscious centre. There is no comparable inducement to contain costs in tax-financed schools without the necessity to attract or retain pupils.[4]

The argument on costs is indeed ironic. Professor West has lately argued that tax-finance for education is inherently unreliable, and he has envisaged "the demise of 'free' education."[5] Tax-financing implies an assumption about the buoyancy of tax revenue that is unconvincing. Competing claims, not least from services that cannot be financed by consumer payments, notably public goods (defence) and re-distribution (pensions, income-supplementation), will reduce the ability of government to finance services that can increasingly be paid for in the market, not least education, particularly where government cannot provide the rising standards that taxpayer/consumers have come to expect from price-paid schools. Even where national economic growth creates increasing taxable capacity, tax rejection will restrict the expansion in tax revenue. The inadequacy of tax-finance for education will then in time have to be remedied by increasing payments by parents. The tax system cannot raise enough funds for improved schooling, yet the egalitarian ethos of tax-financed education obstinately discourages or prevents parents from adding voluntary payments to finance improvement in staffing or equipment apart from ancillaries. The voucher, or a similar device, would become indispensable to encourage additional voluntary payments by parents. In time, voluntary payment, aided by reduced taxation, could replace the voucher.

The argument on cost is essentially short run. The change to voucher financing would, before too long, *not* raise the costs of education but *reduce* them by improving its efficiency. US evidence from Professor James Coleman and others suggests that private schools can be run at half the cost of comparable government schools.[6] In a larger private sector in Britain, similar results could be expected. (The defence that the political process can em-

4. The Deputy-Director of Education of the State of Victoria, Australia, remarked to the author when the Director had left the room: "We know it is the private schools that turn out the lights." This everyday example dramatises a world of waste-avoidance, cost-consciousness and provision for uncertainty in private schools.

5. E. G. West, "The Demise of 'Free' Education," *Challenge* (published by M. E. Sharpe Inc., White Plains, NY), January–February 1985.

6. J. S. Coleman, T. Hoffer, S. Kilgore, *High School Achievements; Public, Catholic and Private Schools Compared,* Basic Books, 1982. (The American "public school" is the British state school, described in official jargon as "maintained.")

brace no reform that requires a short-term cost for long-term advantage is considered below, p. 386.)

In the developing private sector the voucher would add a new inducement to cost reduction by offering an incentive to parents to shop around for schools that were run economically as well as efficiently in producing good results. Costs in an expanding market would be lower than in a monopoly because schools competing for voucher-pupils would offer required standards of teaching at the lowest possible costs, especially when parents could retain the difference between voucher values and school fees and put it to educational or other purposes.

Even with the existing small private sector, private school costs are often no higher and sometimes lower than state costs. Official statistics (£730 per primary pupil, £1,015 per secondary pupil in 1983–84) probably understate the total value of resources consumed in state schools, and are strictly not comparable with private school fees. State school expenditure varies widely; averages conceal the important differences. A former Government adviser reports[7] that the Inner London Education Authority spends £1,750 per secondary pupil p.a., contrasted with £1,250 at "an independent school like Bedales" (and about £1,000 by Leicestershire County). A Government anxious to reduce avoidable public expenditure could look to a voucher-induced competitive market as a fruitful source of improved administrative efficiency and tax reduction as well as higher-quality schooling. Private costs of Youth Training Scheme courses indicate what could be possible (Section VI).

Finally, the argument on cost obscures the difference on quality. The purpose of the voucher is to make schools *different.* Even if private schools were more costly, parents might prefer to spend more on education for *better* schooling.

2. *The cost could not be cut by reducing the value of vouchers or taxing them because "under present education law" and "the 1944 legislation which precludes charging" the voucher would have to entitle parents to free education at state schools.*

Refutation: The 1944, 1980 or other Education Acts are not Holy Writ (*Professor Dennison*). Observance or enforcement of "the existing law" is an illogical and ironic objection to be raised by government departments that are

7. Oliver Letwin, *The Spectator,* 25 January 1986.

continually engaged in reforming or repealing, as well as supervising the administration of, the law. If the 42-year-old 1944 Education Act is adduced as the decisive obstruction to reform, the education system it created will increasingly fail to reflect changing economic, social and technical conditions. Not even its main architect, R. A. Butler, claimed that it set the optimum educational scene for all time in the unforeseeable future of unceasing industrial, technical and social change.

3. *Choice of school would be restricted by "the availability of willing sellers." Private schools would limit increases in numbers. Opening a new (private) school is "a slow, expensive and risky business."*

Refutation: This unsupported assertion of inelasticity of supply creates an unsubstantiated pre-judgement that would preclude *any* attempts to open up opportunities for new ideas or investment in monopoly services long debilitated by captive markets. There is no reason to suppose that all existing employee-teachers prefer paid employment to the opportunity to establish or work in schools serving pupils whose parents chose and paid for them in open competition. That the existing private sector is small is not evidence of teachers' preference for salaried employment: only competition between state and private schools *on comparable pricing terms* would reveal the preferences of teachers. A voucher-based system of financing would create such a test by unifying the system of payment for all schools. Middle- and lower-income parents are now forced into the state system, and held there, because they cannot pay both taxes for the state schools they have to use and fees for the private schools they might prefer.

The voucher-like grant to young people in the Youth Training Scheme of the Manpower Services Commission suggests that the supply of educational facilities is very elastic in response to new demands. Mr. John Pardoe reports[8] that in a short time 4,000 managing agents appeared "from nowhere" to supply new courses. In primary and secondary education supply would be made elastic because buildings surplus to falling requirements would be taken over and run by entrepreneurially-minded teachers newly motivated by the voucher. The "supply" comprises the effectiveness of the schools, not the bricks and mortar.

The Youth Training Scheme is being expanded from one to two years in 1986. The potential expansion in the market is doubly emphasised by Mr. Pardoe.

8. *Economic Affairs*, October–November 1985, Supplement, p. viii.

> . . . if anyone had suggested that within four years there would be 4,000 managing agents able and willing to deliver a two-year Youth Training Scheme, he or she would have been greeted with raucous scepticism. Some of us, however, are not at all surprised. We always believed that, if it was ever possible to allow the providers and consumers of education and training a relatively free market in which to meet each other, there would be a huge expansion in both supply and demand.
>
> The barrier to this expansion was the apparently insuperable virtual monopoly of state provision and state funding of education and training.
>
> The only way to create such a free market would be for the Government to issue an education voucher or bond . . . [to] entitle the holder to purchase the bond's face value of education from any approved supplier.[9]

4. *"Fluid" parental preferences could not be satisfied because of legislative obstacles to the creation of "spare capacity" where required by parents armed with the new purchasing power. The 1981 Regulations restrict the number of children at "popular" schools* (sic): *mobile classrooms require authority under the 1980 Education Act if they "significantly enlarge" schools.*

Refutation: State schools can be expanded or contracted to a degree under the law as it stands. Shifts between schools with a voucher system would not be massive. Acts of Parliament can be amended or repealed by Parliament. Mobile classrooms are relatively inexpensive and easy to erect. If they changed the character of schools to the point at which pupils were removed, voucher-financed schools would not use them. State schools financed by taxes have no comparable incentives to satisfy parents.

5. *The "ebb-and-flow" of pupils "at will" could create "difficult management and organisational problems for schools, at least in the short term."*

Refutation: This is the characteristically corporatist view—that consumers should be subservient to producers. It illustrates the contrast between civil servants who run schools with assured markets and the required entrepreneurial mentality that learns to adjust supply to demand. It emphasises the wide gulf between the relatively rigid, brittle conduct of state schools and the flexible organisation of private schools accustomed to (and strengthened by) variation in pupil numbers. It overlooks the day-to-day experience of 2,500 private schools that contend with a competitive market in which they have learned by everyday

9. *Training and Development*, December 1985.

(in practice term-by-term) experience what rate of "ebb-and-flow" between schools is to be expected and to prepare accordingly with flexibility and contingency reserves of equipment, space and even staff by adding part-timers or "temporaries" to full-timers and "permanents." And it ignores the information "feed-back" of the school market and the provision for probable "ebb-and-flow" that it encourages which enables private schools to anticipate, and thus remove the causes of, dissatisfaction and so reduce the amplitude or periodicity of "ebb-and-flow." Such adjustments have been forced on state schools by changing birth-rates and especially severe scarcities of some teachers, but they are made relatively reluctantly in contrast to their systematic incorporation into the management "chemistry" of private schools.

Although the Department of Education has a section dealing with private schools, the "ebb-and-flow" objection suggests that their characteristics have not been learned in the effort to remove the organisational weaknesses of the state schools. But, again, there is no comparable inducement to flexibility in the state sector. The market-oriented schools coping with uncertainty are evidently regarded as the exception rather than the desirable norm to which all schools should gravitate.

6. *The 1980 Education Act created a new power for parents to shop around for state schools with a prescribed timetable and within the limitation that their preferred school would not be offered if it resulted in "inefficient" use of resources or conflicted with selection according to ability.*

Refutation: This new ability to shop around is a very inadequate step compared to the full consumer sovereignty of a voucher that enables a dissatisfied parent to withdraw his apportionment of purchasing power. It is a common fallacy to confuse objective technical efficiency, such as in the full use of existing plant or space, with economic efficiency in the sense of consumers' subjective satisfaction.[10]

7. *The new power in voucher-financed schools for Boards of Governors to recruit and dismiss teachers would conflict with national salary scales; it would incur*

10. The Chief Education Officer of a Home County near Oxford told the Chairman of FEVER: "We do not require the voucher to tell us which schools pupils would leave: we know the bad schools in . . . shire; but we have to fill them." His purpose was technical efficiency, not consumer satisfaction. The voucher, as Professor Dennison has remarked (below, p. 389), is resisted precisely because it would *publicly* reveal which schools were rejected. In the state system they can be discreetly concealed and the embarrassment of Governors, Heads and teachers avoided.

"frictional costs," risk "employee resistance," and undermine "professional morale."

Refutation: The unacceptable assumption that reform must accommodate itself to existing corporatist institutions (collective bargaining between a monopolist and a monopsonist) is again evident. National salary scales are precisely a rigidity that weakens education by standardising employee costs between very different schools and teachers. "Plant bargaining" at each school would more effectively reward the better teachers and caution the rest. (Private schools usually pay more than the national scales.) Trade union bargaining by enjoining standardised pricing has thrown the unavoidable adjustments onto other conditions of service. More variable *pay* would permit more uniform *conditions* of service. Frictional costs would fall rather than rise when teachers had rearranged themselves into the posts and schools where they fitted best. "Employee resistance" is a symptom of the nationwide state monopoly. "Professional morale" would improve when teachers were recognised in the schools where they teach, and valued and paid for their individual talents and application.

8. *Parental preferences might conflict with "the needs" of pupils or employers.*

Refutation:

(i) *Parents and children:* The implication that teachers, officials or politicians are better equipped or more strongly motivated to serve children than are their parents reverses the neglected truth about the effect on the family of the welfare state, not least state education. Parents live with the consequences: they have a strong incentive to choose schools wisely; social workers and others do not suffer: they "walk away." Instead of strengthening the family by enabling parents, with information and advice, and purchasing power if their incomes are low, to learn the arts of judging teaching and schooling, it has usurped the role of parents, thus impairing their ability to serve their children and re-directing the expectations of children from their parents to outsiders. If state education denies choice on the ground that parents do not choose well, it condemns itself for failing to make parents good choosers. The implication is a moral libel on working-class parents who have learned to choose food, clothing and shelter.

(ii) *Parents and employers:* Without the interposition of political influence, parents would over the decades have developed judgement in seeking schooling that would best equip their children for adulthood and a life of work. It is inconceivable that numerical and literary skills would have degenerated in parent-oriented schools as far as they have done in producer-oriented schools from which parental influence has been discouraged. Employers want high standards in local schools; too often they have to repair their deficiencies by remedial classes at places of work.

The view repeated here that state schooling has been deteriorating in quality draws on four elements. First, there is the public perception of aspects—indiscipline, assault on teachers, truancy, vandalism—that seem increasingly common. Second, there is the absence of a public sense that state schools are keeping pace with expectations of secular improvement familiar in market-supplied services. Third, there is increasing recognition on what is called the "Left" (as by Professor Stuart Hall and Frances Morrell, Leader of the Inner London Education Authority, *New Socialist,* February 1986) that it has grievously neglected working-class concern with numeracy and literacy. (". . . The pragmatic critique that parents make of the public education service—pragmatic because it relates to their own children—is . . . borne out very comprehensively by research": Frances Morrell. "We . . . have to take the question of quality more seriously": Professor Hall.) Fourth, there is the growing desire for a choice outside the state system, revealed by the IEA surveys, that would not have accompanied substantive improvement in state schools. The official statistics of O and A level passes cannot be quoted as evidence of improvement: they are open to differences of interpretation that make them unsuitable as unambiguous indicators of performance.

9. *If vouchers provided the sole income of state schools, the 1944 Education Act requirement that every child should receive "adequate and appropriate education" would require local government to prop up some schools since costs vary with size, curricula, age of premises, etc.*

Refutation: Standards can be maintained by "propping up" (the income of) individual parents as well as schools. This is the essential difference between the supplier-support of the century-old state system and the consumer-support of a voucher system. Supplier-support destroys choice between schools; consumer-support creates it. School-propping suppresses the market; parent-propping creates it.

This was one of the several seminal distinctions between producer-oriented and consumer-oriented school systems missing from the Department of Education statement. Another was the distinction between state-required and market-ensured standards. State standards can in theory rectify low standards produced by imperfect competition, but they are politicised; they are difficult to vary with economic change; and, not least, they can be too high (in the sense of restricting expenditure on other desirable services such as health) and so restrict the competition from new schools that would raise them to the optimum level. The high standards of most private schools are maintained not by the state but by competition in the market (*Michael McCrum*, p. 353). It is no objection to choice that it entails the risk of poor choices or "low" standards. "High standards" are one objective; so are choice, accountability, influence, the power to improve—which are not available or not encouraged in state schools. When private school standards are for a time low, parents can escape; they cannot, especially if their incomes are low, escape from low standards in state schools because they are not allowed to take their money with them. That is why low standards persist longer in state than in private schools. It is precisely the defect the voucher is designed to remove.

10. *A voucher system might undermine the power of local government to manage education.*

Refutation: There is no decisive economic or other reason why education should be "managed" by politicians or their employees in local or central government. The reason why they have come to do so goes back to the original *political* misjudgement in 1870, amply documented by Professor West,[11] to fill the diminishing gaps in private education by tax-financed, politically-controlled schools (instead of by money grants to low-income parents).

One of the five practical proposals reviewed in Section III is John Barnes's re-channelling of the central government Rate Support Grant away from local government direct to parents, rather than remain in central government if control of curricula passes to the Department (Section VI). Both central and local government would thereby lose the political control of education.

11. E. G. West, *Education and the State*, IEA, 1965 (2nd Edn., 1970).

Specific refutations

Apart from these general refutations, the 14 academics offered further observations on specific issues.

Static approach v. dynamic approach. The Department's approach was "entirely static . . . with no recognition of the changes now going on, still less of those desirable in the interests of education." New schools would be established, some taking over the premises of state schools closed down. Many of the supposed administrative problems were imaginary—as in the age-break between schools in new types of sixth-form colleges. The Department was also confused in its reading of consumer-parental pressure, which was both praised for bringing improvement yet condemned as a cause of disturbance. (*Professor Dennison,* author of *Choice in Education,* Hobart Paperback 19, IEA, 1984.)

Transition not disruptive. The displacement effect on teachers of fewer posts in declining schools would probably be *less* disruptive than in the long-run switch in demand for other services, because the labour skills deployed in education could be more readily re-trained for other professions. (*Professor Fisher.*)

Capital retained in unpopular areas. The more difficult problems, in the short run, of surplus capital in school plant and buildings would be *more* readily overcome because vouchers would attract staff to schools in unpopular areas that teachers tended to avoid in the state system. Moreover, since the newly-released demands would soon settle down, plant and buildings would not be radically re-arranged to meet purely temporary shifts. (*Professor Fisher.*)

Adjustments become acceptable. The problems of speed of adjustment to new conditions of demand were over-dramatised. Once the new incentives introduced by the voucher to adapt supply to varying demand began to demonstrate their effects in the state sector, confidence in the system by administrators and politicians would grow: "the rest of the journey would be less hazardous." (*Professor Fisher.*)

Bureaucracy on bureaucracy.

Every large bureaucracy, government or private, is certain that the way it conducts its affairs is the only way they can be conducted. That is precisely

> what the Department of Education is saying about vouchers . . . in its perfunctory examination of the issues . . . (*Professor Friedman.*)

"Ebb and flow" in monopoly and competition. The "ebb-and-flow" problem was essentially a characteristic of government-operated monopolies, as seen in Russia or Poland, or in British Railways, not of private institutions such as hotels, restaurants or department stores. (*Professor Friedman.*)

The nationalised industries in Britain hardly suggest that the costs of the private sector would fall where it was taken over by government: "Yet implicit in this document is precisely such a claim." (*Professor Friedman.*)

Long-lived voucher would increase supply. The notion that private schools would not expand in response to increased demand supposes that the voucher scheme would be short-lived: "If it were widely expected to be permanent, independent schools would be created to meet the demand." (*Professor Friedman.*)

This reaction opens up the question whether local experiments limited to five years, as in the 1973–78 scheme in Alum Rock, California, would yield realistic information on which voucher policy could be based. Academic and other advocates of voucher systems are accordingly re-considering experimentation in favour of long-lasting national systems.

Voucher restores producer/consumer link. A defect of state education is that it lacks a direct link between producer and consumer, other than arbitrary and unsystematic invasion of the bureaucratic machine (by consumers) to influence producers. The nexus of price, and its financial power, is missing. The voucher would restore it. (*Professor Rowley.*)

Parents who pay a little more to escape from "distasteful" schools where their children are physically or spiritually abused cannot do so unless they pay twice. Even where zoning is relaxed, they may face hostile bureaucrats opposed to movement of pupils. The middle classes can protect their children better than can the less educated or the unemployed. (*Professor Rowley.*)

> . . . if bright children are to be given a more intensive education, the voucher value could vary according to scholastic record. (*Professor Rowley.*)

Effects on supply and demand. A voucher is a highly flexible device: if it were tenable ("trade-able") at private as well as state schools, had a lower value in private schools to encourage contributions to their fees, and its value varied with age and scholastic record to encourage work at school, it would increase the influence of parents, encourage simple but effective teaching methods rather than fashionable but disproportionately costly devices, close down schools that failed the market test and enable low-income parents to buy their way out of the worst state schools. (*Professor Rowley.*)

Avoidance of excessive shifting. The anxiety about periodic shifting of pupils between schools was unrealistic. The voucher would not produce more *voluntary* movement than the *compulsory* movement by age increasingly common between the four-fold division of state schools—infant, primary, secondary, sixth-form college. Parents would soon learn the adverse effect of, and avoid, excessive switching. (*Professor Rowley.*)

Teachers' "rents." The opposition of teachers to vouchers derived essentially from their fear of the loss of the "rents" (excessive income produced by political pressure) they extracted from the Department of Education, from local government or from individuals by virtue of the bargaining power derived from their monopoly. The "rents" would fall as the voucher replaced monopoly by competition. (*Professor Rowley.*)

Voucher not revolutionary. The voucher idea strongly resisted by the Department is not a revolutionary radical reform; in essence it is contained in the 1980 Education Act. (*Professor West;* he amplified his argument into one of the practical proposals briefly presented in Section III.)

Competition and standards/quality. The limited choice created by the 1980 Act "does not go nearly far enough." The new power of the voucher "would make an enormous psychological difference." The effect on standards was not clear to the Department of Education but "most of us who have worked in independent schools know competition works wonders." (*Michael McCrum.*)

Choice and competition possible. Education is not unique. If food-shops had been run by government in wartime to ensure "fair" distribution, the resulting bureaucracies and shopkeepers' union would have been held to demonstrate the impossibility of choice and competition in food. (*Lord Harris.*)

State system shortcomings.

A well-informed critic could produce an equally formidable list of shortcomings in the state system: the widest conceivable discrepancies between

> schools in cost, standards, facilities, locations and, not least, achievements. (Lord Harris.)

> *Inducements to improvement.*
> The distinctive merit of the voucher is that it offers a mechanism by which poor schools would have a compelling incentive to raise standards in order to avoid a progressive flight of customers, with dwindling job prospects for the headmaster and staff. (*Lord Harris.*)

> The aim is not perfection but a less intolerable system—with a built-in improvement mechanism, the absence of which is the worst deficiency of the present system. (*Lord Harris.*)

Vouchers to raise standards in state schools. The voucher had been studied by independent academics as a means of raising quality because of the fall in standards in state schools. The Department's statement paradoxically both dismissed occasional over-subscribed schools as exceptions or inflated them as a danger to the stability of the state system. Its reluctance to welcome reform was reflected in the absence of reference to innovations such as the use of private school equipment in two-shift systems. (*Professor Flew.*)

Education not unique. The Department's reservation about voucher and consumer choice in education could also be made against market solutions in the supply of bread, banking or motor cars. (*Professor Sugarman.*)

Small movement would alert state schools. Movement of voucher-financed pupils would not disrupt schooling: small movements would alert school authorities to take early action. The 1978 Kent survey found that, although there was overwhelming support for parents' right to change schools, only 10 per cent said they would switch at the time. (*FEVER.*)

Voucher would adjust supply of teachers to demand. An argument that anticipated the NUT-led teachers' disruption in 1985–86 was that the Department of Education misunderstood the price-effect of teachers' pay. The Department's anxiety that "adjustments of expenditure on teachers . . . would bite directly on numbers [of teachers]" was precisely the desired effect of the voucher both on individual schools that lost pupils and generally on the national supply of teachers in less desired subjects. (*FEVER.*)

Department unaware of voucher literature? The Department's statement seemed to show no knowledge of the extensive literature on the economics of the voucher system or awareness of the relevance of the falling standards in the state schools and of the abuses in the state system as a whole.

> There is a deal of useless, or harmful, fat to be cut, especially in the administrative, advisory and training establishments, local and national. (*Professor Flew.*)

On the economics of politics, Professor Flew added:

> It is one thing to talk about irresponsible, ill-informed working-class parents . . . quite another to say anything of the sort on the doorstep canvassing for [their] votes. . . .

Finally, on the Department's argument on equality:

> How could one justify a situation in which a voucher did less to satisfy some parents than others?,

Professor Flew remarked:

> . . . parents in a few areas so thinly populated as to be served by one school might gain no direct benefit . . . or suffer no disadvantage. So the stringent conditions of Pareto optimality[12] are satisfied. But the Department of Education authors go for a dog-in-the-manger principle.

And an anonymous Australian professorial colleague of Professor Fisher observed on the Department's proposition on equality:

> Absolute nonsense. How can one justify a [state] system in which, purely by accident, some parents are perfectly satisfied and some entirely dissatisfied?

Advantages of the voucher

The Department's statement invited additions to its list of four advantages for the voucher system: parity of choice between state and private schools, parental choice between state schools, making schools accountable to parents, raising school standards. The numerous additions included:

- removal of social divisiveness by extension to the ordinary parent-consumer of the dignity of choice and personal responsibility now reserved to the wealthy or the articulate and aggressive;

12. A proposition in economic theorising, named after the Italian economist, Vilfredo Pareto (1848–1923), which envisaged a situation where no individual can move to a more pre-

- the prospect of raising teachers' pay by reducing the number of non-teaching functionaries;
- it would benefit the ordinary consumer *more* than the wealthy because "social science discloses that it is choice that makes for good education and upward mobility."

This condensed review of the exchange between the Department and the academics conveys something of the quality of the defensive official approach to reform and its complete rejection by the academics, somewhat surprised at the indifferent quality of the argument.

It has been questioned whether academics are qualified to present practical proposals for reform. It so happens that many of the academics who had reservations about the 1981 statement had direct experience of managing or regulating schools (Section III). But in opposition to the doubt about academics there is the at least equally considerable doubt whether the political process and its inhabitants are equipped to adapt British state schools to the tests and opportunities of the market that is emerging with economic and social change. The 1981 statement and subsequent Departmental verbal reactions displayed little of the entrepreneurial ethos required in an increasingly competitive service. Education, like every other activity, uses precious scarce resources. What the Department regards as disadvantages of the voucher—its penalties for failed teachers and schools—are its essential advantages. Professor Niskanen has indicated three reforms that could help to make the bureaucratic response more entrepreneurial: quasi-profit incentives to cost-consciousness, market alternatives to government agencies, and reorganisation to make bureaucrats more sensitive to the ultimate taxpayer/consumer. These are not criticisms of officials but conclusions from their protected environment.[13] The ultimate solution may be to take education out of the Department of Education.

At bottom, the authorities were saying that, for economic, political and administrative reasons, the people could not have freedom to choose schools.

---

ferred position except by causing another to move to a less preferred position. In a rural area with one school every parent has his child in his "best" school.

13. It is arguable that government officials have to be exceptional to overcome the disadvantage of the lack of competitive stimulus. If exceptional bureaucrats are required to achieve ordinary objects in government, ordinary individuals in private industry are stimulated by the competitive market process to achieve extraordinary objects. I am indebted to Professor Harold Rose for discussion on this proposition.

The academics were replying that the reasons offered, or implied, were unconvincing.

But, it was asked, were the academics equipped to judge the official objections?

Appendix 1 to Section II

DEPARTMENT OF EDUCATION AND SCIENCE
ELIZABETH HOUSE YORK ROAD LONDON SE1 7PH
TELEPHONE 01-928 9222
FROM THE SECRETARY OF STATE

Chairman
The Friends of the Education Voucher
Experiment in Representative Regions
Sevenoaks
Kent

16 December 1981

Thank you for your letter of 18 November asking for details of the practical difficulties which would need to be overcome before the idea of education vouchers could be considered further.

This Government is committed to the extension of parental choice and involvement in education. The Education Act 1980 takes us a long way in the right direction, giving primacy to parental preferences; requiring the publication of detailed information, including examination results, about individual schools; and establishing the Assisted Places Scheme to improve the access to good independent schools for children from poorer families. This sets the scene for the foreseeable future.

I am intellectually attracted to the idea of education vouchers as a means of eventually extending parental choice and influence yet further and improving educational standards. I therefore welcome your interest in exploring the difficulties in the way of any voucher scheme to see whether a scheme can be developed which genuinely copes with them.

The main difficulties so far identified are set out in the enclosed note. These, together with others that may emerge as a detailed study progresses, need to be rigorously considered and met or resolved in an acceptable way if a workable scheme is to be devised. Only if it is clearly possible to formulate a scheme which could deliver, in a way which could be commended, more benefits than are obtainable under the 1980 Act would it be worth considering whether to facilitate an experiment.

I look forward to receiving your considered findings in due course.

In view of the widespread interest in this topic, I am releasing copies of this letter and note to Parliament and the Press; and I shall make the note freely available on request to others interested in the problems to be overcome in pursuing the voucher concept.

Yours sincerely,
Keith Joseph

DEPARTMENT OF EDUCATION MEMORANDUM
ON EDUCATION VOUCHERS

The Nature of this Paper

1. This Paper is written in response to the requests from the National Council for Educational Standards and the Friends of the Education Voucher Experiment in Representative Regions (FEVER) for an account of the problems that would need to be resolved before an education voucher scheme could be defined, and its implications assessed, for the purposes of educational policy. The Secretary of State for Education and Science has made it clear that he has no plans for the general introduction of a voucher scheme. He thinks that a voucher scheme could—if the difficulties were resolved—give parents a wider choice even than the 1980 Education Act will provide and could tend to raise educational standards. But he wishes the discussion of the possibility of such a scheme to be properly focussed on the complex issues which would be involved. To that end he considers that it is for the proponents of education vouchers, after explaining what the purposes of such a scheme would be, to describe how it would operate, how the practical difficulties would be tackled and what changes in present arrangements would be involved.

2. The points made below are those which, for the present, the Department of Education and Science has identified as likely to be significant. But further significant issues needing resolution may be identified as thinking develops.

The Purposes of Education Vouchers

3. Several, and to some extent inter-related, purposes appear to be in the proponents' mind. It seems possible to distinguish at least four:

i. vouchers might be a means of providing parity of parental choice for all schools whether maintained or independent;
ii. vouchers might be a means of increasing parental choice of school within the maintained sector only;
iii. vouchers might be a means of making schools more accountable to parents;
iv. the increase of choice and accountability should tend to raise educational standards.

Are there other possible purposes?

Choice across the Maintained and Independent Sectors

4. Any voucher scheme which extends to independent schools as well as maintained schools would entail additional costs. There would be an immediate and substantial "dead weight" addition to total costs as the voucher would have to be available to those parents (about 5 per cent) who already, or who would in the future, send their children to independent schools, entirely at their own expense. Further substantial additional costs would accrue because the marginal cost saving in the maintained sector would be only a fraction of the average cost value of vouchers spent in the independent sector by parents who would otherwise have used the maintained sector.

5. These costs could be reduced by setting a lower value on a voucher used in the independent sector (although the voucher would still need to entitle parents to a free education for their children at the maintained school of their choice, as long as section 61 of the Education Act 1944, which precludes charging, remains in force). But to the extent that the "top-up" required from parents increased, the value of the voucher as an agent of choice would diminish, and at a certain point the vouchers would become little more than straight subsidy for parents currently using the independent system. Since under present education law vouchers could not put the money in the hands of parents it would not be possible to reduce the net costs of the scheme by taxing vouchers. If it were possible, any tax revenue would have to be returned to the maintained education sector.

6. The extent to which a voucher scheme would in practice extend choice is limited, because the extent of choice depends on the availability of willing sellers. "Open enrolment" could not be imposed on

existing independent schools, which could be expected to wish to retain final control over the total number to be admitted and over individual admissions, at least on academic grounds. The scope and often the desire for existing schools to expand is limited. Starting a new independent school is a slow, expensive and risky business even without the inhibiting background provided by party political differences. Because of the limitations on the ability of the independent sector to respond to substantially increased demand (other than through the price mechanism), the likely effect of a voucher scheme on educational standards in either the maintained or the independent sector is also unclear—particularly as experience in the present independent school market, with its very wide range of educational standards, suggests that a parent's choice of school is influenced by a variety of considerations of which educational quality, even as perceived by the decision makers, is only one.

Choice within the Maintained Sector

7. A voucher scheme limited to the maintained sector only would, as far as parents were concerned, be simply a system of open enrolment. The usefulness of vouchers as an agent of choice and openness in the maintained sector has been to some extent overtaken by the Education Act 1980. In respect of admissions in September 1982 and subsequently parents will be able to shop around for schools within a prescribed timetable and with the benefit of extensive common information about the available schools. The Act then requires those choices to be met unless they would lead to inefficient use of resources or be incompatible with selection by reference to ability or the special rights of aided and special agreement schools over admissions.

8. The ability to satisfy fluid parental preferences depends crucially on the existence of spare capacity in the system. How could a voucher scheme increase parental satisfaction by comparison with present arrangements given the obstacles now in the way of maintaining or creating this spare capacity in the right places and at the level demanded? How would one deal with the following?
   i. Voluntary aided and special agreement schools would presumably wish to retain control over their own admission arrangements.

ii. Whilst there is nothing in the Education Act 1980 to prevent an LEA admitting to its county and voluntary controlled schools all those who apply (the Act's admission targets are management tools rather than inflexible measures), there are significant practical limitations on an LEA's ability to admit all comers. The Education (School Premises) Regulations 1981 place an upper limit on the number of children which may be accommodated at popular schools. Those Regulations' requirements for site and central facilities may also constrain the possibility of extending capacity by the addition of mobile classrooms; and such extension would, in any case, require prior formal action under sections 12 and 13 of the Education Act 1980 where this would amount to a "significant enlargement" of the school.

iii. The ebb and flow of children at will could create difficult management and organisational problems for schools, at least in the short term. The level of disturbance introduced by a voucher system could be significantly larger than the 10 per cent suggested by the Kent feasibility study in 1978. This was the average proportion of parents who would choose a school different from the one their child was already attending. Departmental experience with choice of school cases shows that many parents disappointed with their original choice of school are subsequently satisfied with their second choice. While the movement of *existing* pupils may well be limited to 10 per cent, *initial* choices may show a much greater concentration on popular schools; some already have as many as three applicants for each available place. Even on the Kent study basis, however, the fluctuations in the rolls and intakes of individual schools could range as wide as plus or minus 20 per cent. The consequent problems for both more and less popular schools (particularly secondary schools) could lead to rapid changes in the staffing and general character of the schools which had attracted parents in the first place. This could also weaken attempts to achieve continuity between different phases of education through the development of close links between primary and secondary schools.

iv. Where a selective system continues to operate, admission to selective schools would need to be limited according to ability. The use of "guided parental choice" as a means of selection might reduce the practical implications but does not eliminate the difficulties.

v. The maintenance and creation of the necessary spare capacity in both accommodation and staff also has significant cost implications. To this must be added the possibly substantial additional cost that, consequent on the philosophy of complete freedom of access, would flow from the provision of free transport to any school at which a parent obtained a place for his child.

9. These practical limitations could mean significant numbers of parents being unable to secure a place at their chosen school. Subject to the appeals procedures of the Education Act 1980, their children would need to be educated in less popular schools. How could one justify a situation in which a voucher did less to satisfy some parents than others? Overall, it may be that few schools' rolls would directly reflect their market attraction.

Greater Accountability of Schools to Parents

10. If the voucher were the sole source of finance for a school which would then have complete freedom of the way in which it disposed of its own resources, a voucher system could lead to a situation in which parental choices and decisions determined the character of the maintained school system. This—as voucher proponents recognise—would be a very far-reaching change, raising many issues.

11. First, each school would need freedom to decide how its resources should be divided between teaching and other costs and then which teachers it should employ and dismiss to match its own assessment of what its paymasters, the parents, wanted. The school would, in effect, have to become the employer of teachers and other staff. Would this be compatible with present arrangements for national salary scales for maintained schools, which imply that any adjustment of expenditure on teachers in those schools would bite directly on numbers?[1] The concept of national scales is of course not sacrosanct, but local variations would be dependent on both changes in the present legal position and the outcome of negotiations. Dismissing teachers entails substantial frictional costs and, if this is simply in response to demand at a particular school, raises difficult questions

1. [The question-mark has been inserted editorially; the original document as issued by the Department incorrectly employed a full stop here.—ED.]

about the identification of candidates for dismissal as well as important issues of employee resistance and professional morale. The extra costs would fall mainly on contracting schools, creating a spiral of falling standards and further enforced contraction. A system of re-deployment could solve some of these problems, but this presupposes the existence of an employer at a higher level than individual schools and pre-empting their management decisions. Experience shows that successful re-deployment is difficult even in large LEA areas; these difficulties increase disproportionately for smaller units.

12. Secondly, would the greater adaptability of the schools be compatible with efficient staffing, with present methods of supplying and training teachers and with government oversight over teacher supply and training? What would be the impact if it were not compatible? Would there not still be problems over subjects in which there was a shortage of qualified teachers and over minority subjects? More generally the quality and scope of the school curriculum is a matter of great national importance and its improvement is very much the concern of all those affected by it. How far would parental preference for what schools offered coincide with the needs of employers, and indeed of the pupils themselves? These questions have large implications for both the school curriculum and the present balance of responsibilities for it.

13. Thirdly, if vouchers represented the totality of each school's income, how could this be reconciled with sections 7 and 8 of the 1944 Act under which LEAs must ensure that each child receives adequate and appropriate education? For example the LEA would be obliged under present law to prop up very badly resourced schools. Account needs to be taken of the fact that unit costs vary significantly between different schools, both within the area of an individual local education authority and between one authority and another. This is partly a function of size, partly a matter of organisation in relation to the curriculum offered, partly related to such factors as the age and general state of repairs of the premises, and partly, in the case of inter-authority differences, a function of different policy decisions on the funding of the education service as a whole. (Average unit costs in some authorities are at least 50 per cent higher than in others and it seems likely that there are comparable differences between schools

within an authority as well.) A voucher pitched at the average unit cost in an individual local authority's area would thus provide, to a significant degree, differently for the different conditions and management of different schools.

14. Inevitably, the LEA would need on account of the implications of paragraphs 13 and 15 to subsidise the staffing and other resources of some schools. The corollary of this is a reduction of the pressure which can be exerted by parental preference on such schools to improve their provision to attract greater resources.

15. The above considerations raise large questions about what the function of the LEA would be and how education would be organised and run under a voucher system. Among others, the following points arise:

    i. Would a voucher system be compatible with individual LEA's management of the education service in its area? How would it fit in relation to an LEA's responsibilities to determine general policies in response to demographic change and in respect of the pattern of schooling (e.g. whether it should be selective or non-selective, where the age break between schools should occur, etc.)?
    ii. In view of the substantial differences in inter-authority average unit costs, how would movement across LEA boundaries (currently covered by automatic recoupment under the Education Act 1980) be facilitated?
    iii. How should education outside the compulsory period be organised and financed? In particular, if vouchers are available for school sixth forms, should 16–19 education provided within the FE sector be financed similarly or differently?
    iv. What changes in the present law would all the above considerations entail? More specifically, what changes would be needed so that the voucher would in effect be a means of giving cash to parents which they would only be free to spend on their children's schooling?

DEPARTMENT OF EDUCATION AND SCIENCE

December 1981

Appendix 2 to Section II

The Academics

JOHN BARNES is a political scientist and a local government politician. He is a Lecturer in Government at the London School of Economics and author/co-author of studies on the governments of Baldwin and Macmillan. He has been "Minister of Education" of Kent County Council (Chairman of its Education Committee). He has advised his Party (Conservative) on reform in the structure of government.

Professor MARK BLAUG teaches economics at the University of London Institute of Education and at the University of Buckingham. He is an historian of economic thought. He has written extensively on the economics of education, has been a student rather than an enthusiastic advocate of vouchers, and advised Kent County on its 1978 Feasibility Study.

Professor JOHN COONS teaches law at the University of California, Berkeley. With Professor Stephen Sugarman (below) he has actively promoted the voucher in California, most recently in a constitutional initiative designed to add to the Constitution of the State of California a section empowering private and public (government) schools to redeem education vouchers.

Professor S. R. DENNISON has encompassed almost the whole range of education as Examiner in Economics from A-level to post-graduate degrees, Chairman of the Board of Governors of the Royal Grammar School, Newcastle upon Tyne, Professor of Economics at the Universities of Manchester, Cambridge, Belfast, Swansea and Newcastle, a member of the University Grants Committee, and Vice-Chancellor of the University of Hull. He has sat on government committees and Wages Councils.

Professor MALCOLM FISHER taught economics at the University of Cambridge before returning to Australasia as Professor of Economics at the Graduate School of Management, University of New South Wales. His observations are mainly on the economic aspects of the transition of education from state to market.

Professor ANTONY FLEW has taught philosophy at the University of Reading and at the University of York in Canada. He is a combative advocate of the voucher as an essential ingredient in freeing education from state control.

Professor MILTON FRIEDMAN, world-distinguished economist and Nobel Laureate, has urged a voucher system since 1955. He has also been active in the American lobby, the Education Voucher Institute.

LORD HARRIS OF HIGH CROSS is interested in the promotion of freedom in education from primary and secondary schooling to higher education: he played a leading part in the establishment of the University of Buckingham.

MICHAEL MCCRUM, now Master of Corpus Christi College, Cambridge, knows school education from the inside as Headmaster of Tonbridge and of Eton.

Professor ALAN PEACOCK began, with Professor Jack Wiseman (below), the discussion of education vouchers in Britain in 1964. He has been Professor of Economics at the Universities of Edinburgh, York and Buckingham, and Vice-Chancellor of the University of Buckingham. He is now Research Professor of Public Finance at the Heriot-Watt University, Scotland. He is Chairman of the Committee inquiring into the financing of the BBC, another vehicle for the education of children, students and adults.

Professor C. K. ROWLEY is a public choice economist who wrote an early article on vouchers in "The Political Economy of British Education," *Scottish Journal of Political Economy,* in 1969. In a book with Professor Peacock in 1975 he identified the voucher as "the most attractive means of education support" (Section VI).

Professor STEPHEN SUGARMAN is Professor of Law at the University of California, Berkeley, and has been associated with Professor Coons in promoting the voucher in California.

Professor E. G. WEST, now at Carleton University, Canada, re-wrote the history of British education to reveal that a market in schooling had been evolving long before the 1870 Education Act, conventionally considered by historians and educationists to have established a "national" system of education. In later writing he has refined the history of private education and argued that the expansion of state education was encouraged by the bureaucracy.

Professor JACK WISEMAN wrote on vouchers with Professor Peacock in 1964. He is Chairman of the Public Choice Group (the American description is retained) of the Institute of Social and Economic Research at the University of York.

Professors Peacock, Rowley and Wiseman are Patrons of FEVER.

SECTION III

Approaches to Practical Proposals, 1981–85

The criticism emerged more recently in 1985 that it was not sufficient for academics to emphasise general principles or hypothetical advantages; they should be ready to propose practical solutions. During 1981–83, four schemes emerged from the academics for the Department to consider, one was evolved elsewhere.

1. Bypass local government

The most radical proposal was made in 1981 by John Barnes, the political scientist who had also been the "Minister of Education" of Kent County.[1] Barnes is one of several academics who knows school administration from the inside of local government.

He proposed that the Department of Education pay for schools not through local government but direct to parents—in the form of vouchers. By chance about half (on average) of all local government revenue comes from central government in the Rate Support Grant (a payment made to support the local revenue derived from the "rate" levied on property), and (again on average) a half or more of the total revenue is also spent on local education. The Rate Support Grant could thus by-pass local authorities and be paid to schools by parents instead of via local Councillors and officials.

The task in practice would remain to re-distribute the Rate Support Grant between parents in different areas since at the extremes some local authorities are much more, and others much less, if at all, dependent on central government finance.

This procedure would incidentally remove the perennial risk that central government finance would be misused by local party politicians. Liverpool is the best-known example, but there are probably many more; and there is

1. The proposal was briefly sketched in *Economic Affairs*, October 1981.

no foolproof way to avoid it by setting "cash" limits on local expenditure or limits on local rates ("rate-capping"), both of which are also objectionable in centralising the control of local government. The only ultimate method of minimising the political risk of abuse is to remove from local government the services that are not "public goods"[2] and that it therefore does not have to provide; they have been broadly estimated by Professor C. D. Foster and two colleagues, Richard Jackman and Morris Perlman,[3] as accounting for nine-tenths of local expenditure. John Barnes's proposal would remove at a stroke a half of local expenditure, leaving most of the remainder to be removed politically by "privatisation" (de-socialisation), or more gradually but more sensitively by charging market prices and leaving the decisions to consumers. The Barnes proposal would broadly both halve the extent of local government (and the scope for political abuse) and also de-socialise education.

2. Local experimentation

The second proposal also came from John Barnes.[4] The scheme was to be operated as a pilot by Kent County and was to be supported by several other local authorities. The scheme is of special interest since the Kent County politicians (Councillors) and officials had done more preparatory work on vouchers, including field research, than any others in Britain.

The law would require to be amended to permit government finance to cover the "start-up" costs. Vouchers for state schools would be financed by local rates and a central government grant, and for private schools wholly by central government. In view of the administrative difficulties foreshadowed in the Department of Education statement, it is relevant that the Kent County local authority did not see the administrative problems as insuperable. They were thought no more unmanageable than those of the Open Enrolment Scheme devised by the Kent officials and piloted in December 1981 to enable more parents to indicate preferences but without parental control of purchasing power as in a voucher system. It had been found that Open Enrolment schools had been able, without disruption, to revise their admissions, staffing and accommodation within six months by May 1982 in good time for the September term.

2. "Preamble," page 331, footnote 10.
3. *Local Government Finance in a Unitary State,* Geo. Allen & Unwin, 1980.
4. *The Times Educational Supplement,* 1 October 1982.

Kent County found that the opposition came mainly from the teachers' unions which, it thought, could "complicate the operation" of the scheme. The proposed scheme was to be initially for 26 state schools. The vouchers (looking like cheques) would be issued annually to all pupils at the state schools and could be claimed by the parents of children at private schools in Kent "or within travelling distance." They would be presented as payment term by term, thus giving parents the sense of consumer sovereignty. Falling birth-rates in the 1960s and 1970s and the lower numbers of new entrants in the 1980s would ease the task of accommodating additional pupils in the more popular schools. Too rapid expansion that could change the character of schools would be avoided. The scheme would last initially for four years. A school that failed to attract pupils to fill a stated proportion of its capacity would be considered for closure. Kent County consultation with parents would initially be through Boards of Governors (an administrative convenience but a third best). In time, individual schools were to be allowed increasing control of their budgets, incomes and expenditures. A separate pilot was proposed to see how much expenditure could be devolved to individual schools to make them independently entrepreneurial.

The 1978 Kent Feasibility Study had found that 72 per cent of parents had said they should be allowed a voucher for private schools, although only 10 per cent thought they would move their children initially.

> "Ultimately," the Kent proposal concluded, "it seemed probable that there would be savings dependent on the precise volume of transfer to the independent sector. But the non-quantifiable benefits for the education of our children would in themselves have justified the scheme."

This voucher proposal was not the work of academics in ivory castles but of practical local politicians very much aware of public reaction and sensitive to the probable repercussions on local government by-elections.

3. A "half-way house," 1982

The third scheme was submitted by Professor Alan Peacock to the Department of Education in April 1982 after the "bombardment" of replies from the FEVER academics. He had been Economic Adviser and a Deputy Secretary at the Department of Trade and Industry from 1973 to 1976, during which period he had to advise no fewer than seven Secretaries of State. He is Chairman of the Committee of Inquiry into the financing of the British Broadcasting Corporation.

His proposal was for parents who contract out of the state system to receive a (taxable) voucher to help pay fees at a preferred private school.[5] He labelled it a "half-way house" scheme that fell far short of a voucher available to all parents irrespective of income or ability of children. Initially, the "timid" version would require parents to "contract in" to the scheme by applying to the Department of Education for a voucher, which could be "spent" in "accredited" private schools: the central cash grant to the local authority would be reduced accordingly. In time the "ambitious" version would require all parents to "contract out" and receive a voucher to be added to their taxable income and to be tenable at state or private schools. If they stayed in the state system they would surrender it to the local authority and it would become a vote for entry to a preferred state school. If they preferred a private school the voucher would pay (part of) fees. Professor Peacock claimed three advantages: choice would be enlarged, although not as fully as with a voucher proper; parents, teachers and administrators would be acclimatised to a régime of wider choice, and (unlike a short-lived experiment) it might make possible a more radical reform in the longer run; and local authorities would remain in control of state schools, with the power to make major decisions in allocating finance, including the method of paying teachers.

Professor Peacock offered the "half-way house" as a *politically* more acceptable stage on the way to more radical changes than an early transformation of all state schools into self-contained cost- or profit-centres exposed to competition from private schools to which parents armed with vouchers could escape.

This tactically persuasive proposal should be read in the light of Peacock's explanation of the 1983 political rejection of the voucher (Section IV). A reservation would be that, as with the Alum Rock voucher, which was emasculated by limitations that prevented it from establishing the maximum of choice, the "half-way" voucher might enable hostile teachers and politically-motivated officials to discredit the essential principle of the voucher in the early "contracting out" stage and so prevent its potential power to create a market from being established for all to see in everyday practice. The economics of politics suggests that, if public opinion is moving strongly in

5. Alan T. Peacock, "Education Voucher Schemes—Strong or Weak?" *Economic Affairs*, Vol. 3, No. 2, January 1983.

favour of choice of school, and a political party or coalition can see votes in yielding a degree of choice by a "half-way" voucher, the opponents will seize and "capture" an attenuated voucher in the hope of warding off further inroads into their political monopoly to the long-term disadvantage of the consumer-parent. The principle is familiar: "If you can't beat 'em, join 'em." The good might then not lead to the better; and it could be the enemy of the best. In principle there is no reason why parents should be satisfied with anything less than the voucher, the whole voucher, and nothing but the voucher. The argument is on political tactics and short-term expediency.

The interest in Professor Peacock's proposal is that it is the product of an economist who knows the government machine from the inside and who has attempted a scheme that aims at the optimum compromise between the public interest and the capacity of the political/administrative establishment to absorb reform. (It bears a similarity to the fifth scheme, p. 373.) It may be the best that the political process can yield, at least in the short run. The question is whether the political process and its compromise "bargains" can produce better education than a more fundamental, whole-hearted voucher reform which parents would prefer but which is inhibited by political apprehension in overcoming vested interests—including the opposition of people in all parties who rejoice in the power and prestige of running schools as Councillors, politically-elected governors, administrators or bureaucrats (Section VI).

Despite official silence or discouragement, Professor Peacock continued to develop his thinking on ways to widen choice in education. He re-emphasised his proposal as recently as December 1984, in a wide-ranging analysis of the scope and forms of privatisation in general,[6] in which (unlike economists who think of privatisation as applying only to industry) he properly included state welfare services—universities as well as schools, pensions and medical care as well as education. If government "fought shy" of privatising education and health in the strict sense of transferring their assets to private ownership and the market, more competitive conditions could be created by de-regulating them to facilitate entry of private suppliers. Here he urged vouchers for school education, student loans for higher education, and for pensions a subvention to the individual national insurance contribution—in all three replacing collective by personal financing.

6. "Privatisation in Perspective," *The Three Banks Review,* December 1984.

4. Extend the Assisted Places Scheme, 1982

The fourth proposal was made by Professor West in his response to the 1981 Departmental statement.[7] Although he wrote from Canada, he is a British economist who had taught at the Oxford Polytechnic and the Universities of Newcastle and Kent from 1956 to 1970 and knew the contemporary British scene in education, as well as its history since the early 19th century.

Professor West saw a way to the voucher by evolution from the current law without the revolutionary disruption feared by the Department of Education. The 1980 Education Act required state schools to publish information on their services and on examination results. And it established the Assisted Places Scheme with financial aid "for children from poorer families" to attend "good independent schools." Professor West argued that, with minor modifications, both reforms could be used to create a voucher scheme, in effect if not in name. (A comparable proposal was made recently by Oliver Letwin.[8])

The essence of the voucher scheme is that (earmarked) purchasing power follows a pupil from a rejected to a preferred school. The Assisted Places Scheme directs funds to schools (as agents for parents) rather than direct to parents, to suppliers rather than to consumers. But Professor West argued that the effect would be the same, not least in two essential ingredients. The parent of an Assisted pupil may top up the grant by paying additions required by the chosen school, as would a parent receiving the supplementable voucher recommended by Professor Blaug. And schools taking Assisted pupils have to compete for the available candidates.

Professor West showed that such grant-to-school schemes had been gaining ground in several Canadian provinces, especially British Columbia (and they have been used for generations in Vermont). But the Assisted Places Scheme is essentially confined to the brighter children of lower-income parents and therefore covers only a very small number (21,500 in 1985–6). He now proposed that the Scheme be developed into a full "voucher" system by applying it (a) to children in a wider range of ability, (b) to parents of a wider range of income and (c) to a wider variety of schools. The principle of paying government grants to private schools in England began in 1833. It was formally ended in 1976 when grants direct to British private schools (thus

7. The central proposal was outlined in *Economic Affairs,* October 1982; the objections to the principle are rebutted in *Economic Affairs,* April–May 1986.

8. "Good Schools for All at Minimum Cost," *The Times,* 6 February 1986.

dubbed direct-grant schools) ceased. (The two systems are not precisely the same: the Assisted Places Scheme provides a grant for the parent and is not at a flat rate but is assessed for each pupil each year according to parental income and the Department of Education scales of income. In 1984 only 40 per cent of the parents received grants that covered full fees; the remainder paid part fees.)

5. Voucher in four logical stages

A fifth scheme was devised during 1982–83. It was still-born and, like the others, was set aside in deciding government policy on education in the period approaching the General Election of June 1983. It paid especial attention in its details and timing to the probable obstruction from local authorities and teachers and to the projected political advantages.

It proposed a three- or four-stage introduction of the voucher. The purpose was to gain increasing public acceptance by making improvements in the financing of education at each stage, thus bringing home to parents the common sense of moving on to the next stage.

In Stage 1 the central government education grant to each local education authority (LEA) area would be based on a grant for each child at a *state* school. This approach avoids the possible or probable abuses of the area grant that it can be ignored in deciding expenditure on education (LEAs may now spend less or more), it is open to manipulation by central government, and it is said to be mistrusted by local Councillors and the general public. A grant per state school pupil, such as £500 from age 5 to 11, £1,000 in the age range 11 to 16, £1,500 beyond 16, would be recognisable and understood. This stage could run for two years: parents would become accustomed to the order of magnitude of education costs; LEAs hitherto under-spending on schooling would spend more, and those over-spending would be induced to reduce their costs.

In Stage 2, the central grant to LEAs for *state* school children might be extended to *all* children. Parents would thus be able, for the first time, to "bypass" the local authorities and receive the value of the grant (although not yet in a voucher) instead of a "free" place at a state school. The additional cost of the grant for the 5–6 per cent of children at private schools could be accommodated either by reducing the individual grant, so that the total central grant remained unchanged; or it could be absorbed in Stage 3 when total education expenditure and costs declined as numbers fell, efficiency improved, and more parents put private money into schools by topping up the central grant. Parents would now have the new right and power to opt out of the state system. Stages 1 and 2 would thus begin to liberate the market forces. The independent schools would respond to the new choice by expanding as necessary; the state schools would have to respond by providing what the parents wanted under threat of their moving away. There could be envisaged the beginning of a process of self-improvement of the state schools, with the ultimate transfer of some from Governors and teachers unable or unwilling to respond to parental preference and financial pressure to others willing and able.

In Stage 3 the central lump-sum grant to each *area* is replaced by grants for each child to *parents*. Opting *out* of state schools would thus be replaced by opting *into* any school, state or private. The voucher proper—an entitlement in earmarked cash—would emerge at this stage, perhaps like an airline ticket booklet with three tickets, one for each term in a year.

In Stage 4, which could develop without further legislative action from Stage 3, the number of state schools would have fallen, of independent schools expanded, and some LEAs would have become superfluous where all state schools had lost their pupils and changed themselves into independent schools. State schools would survive if they could attract pupils by parental preference rather than locked in by zoning.

Economists will recognise three elements in the restoration of a market in education. First, the change from macro-grants to micro-vouchers is the essential that enables parents as taxpayers to know the cost of the services they are paying for, or are supplied with. Much of the macro-"information" now supplied by central and local government is useless: a total figure of national expenditure on defence or roads or housing or education is meaningless: only micro-grants, or individual expenditure, costs or prices convey the micro-information on which parents can act to remain in the state system or move to private schools. Second, there is the change from a benefit in kind to a benefit in cash—from a "free" school place to money, which creates choice and enables a market to be established by evoking supply. Third, and not least, the influence on schools by parents would change from the exercise of "voice" by representation on Boards of Governors or individual discussion with teachers or Heads, which is inherently inequitable since parents differ in the capacity to persuade, to the power to "exit," which makes "voice" effective or unnecessary: schools, staff and Governors can ignore voices that are locked in without avenues of escape.

This outline proposal can be seen as a phased approach to ease the transition from a virtual state monopoly, from which only a small number of mostly upper-income parents can move, to a variegated structure in which *all* parents can move with a choice. Existing suppliers would adapt their service—curricula, staffing, atmosphere, and so on—to parental opinion, which in turn would be guided by advice that would emerge ("from nowhere," to echo John Pardoe) when parents are newly equipped both by *legal* power and by *purchasing* power to pay for a competing choice.

It is not difficult to imagine that such a scheme would be dismissed *à l'outrance* on technical administrative grounds as disturbing the existing system of financing education. As John Barnes remarked, the technical "snags" would count with officials more than the prospect of liberating the inducements and impulses to improve school education beyond the present expectations of parents and the vision of administrators.

This scheme envisaged introduction by stages in order progressively to demonstrate the advantages for parental choice, school standards and pupil performance and so offset the obstruction of teachers by the 30-fold potential support of parents. In the ideal scheme all parents would ultimately have the maximum choice allowed by urban or rural geography (which is itself a choice); all schools would be competing, in towns more so than in rural areas; the worst would have been shut or their physical assets acquired by entrepreneurially-minded teachers; most schools looking to parents rather than to officials for their revenue would have changed to private ownership; education would have been effectively de-socialised and de-politicised; the teachers' monopoly would no longer be able to obstruct reform; local authorities would have been denied power over their largest service and have been reduced to around half of their empires. The political, bureaucratic and pedagogic exploiters of the exploited taxpaying parent would, to echo Marx, have been expropriated.

For reasons presumably judged politically decisive by the Government's advisers in 1983, the opportunity to initiate all these boons was then abandoned.

No full account of the deliberations within the Department has been published. The Minister's short informal statement on television in May 1984 was followed by a short formal statement in Parliament in June 1984. Before examining the arguments in them, and considering the probable role of the officials, I review briefly in Section IV the explanations from the academics, who were invited to help in the preparation of this Paper by offering their interpretations as independent observers of the unexpected early change from the "intellectual attraction" of December 1981 and the apparent promise of October 1982 to the uncompromising dismissal of October 1983.

SECTION **IV**

Political Rejection, 1983: Independent Theories and Official Reasons

In 1984 the IEA invited the academics' opinions on the change from the "intellectual interest" of 1981 to the "death" in 1983.

The general tenor of their responses indicates explanations—"theories"—for the political decision to abandon the voucher, the lessons to be learned, and the prospects for the voucher in the coming years.

Seven reasons that emerged for the rejection of the voucher in 1983 and the replies follow.

Independent theories

1. *Government must supply free education.* The voucher does not conflict with the statutory obligation to provide free education (p. 382).

2. *Costs.* The voucher would conflict with the government aim of reducing public expenditure. (The objection of "cost" was one of the four that have emerged as the difficulties officially thought to be finally decisive—Section II.)

This was the view of Professor Blaug; in an essay published in 1984 he wrote:

> Even if the full value of the vouchers were added to taxable income, the additional cost to the Exchequer of a national voucher scheme might be as much as half a billion pounds . . . this is clearly what took the steam out of the voucher movement in Britain.[1]

This order of magnitude was emphasised by opponents, like *The Times Educational Supplement* (July 1982) and earlier by Mrs. Shirley Williams. The arguments on cost are reviewed in Section II.

1. Mark Blaug, *Privatisation and the Welfare State,* Geo. Allen & Unwin, 1984.

3. *Opposition of vested interests.* Professor Fisher wrote:

> It is hard to believe that production or administrative costs were decisive . . . More likely resistance to interference with the *status quo* proved overwhelming, especially fears of sectional interest or media criticism.

4. *Lack of entrepreneurship in the public sector.*

> The electors will demand more efficiency and entrepreneurship from the public sector; or privatisation will make further inroads. Inertia irritates the advocates of reform and the community. But it enables administrators to enjoy a more peaceful path to retirement. [*Professor Fisher;* Sections V, VI.]

5. *Inadequate public support.* I argue below (p. 382) that politicians are misled by faulty opinion polling in assessing public preferences.

The view of the Secretary of State (below, p. 384) that not enough British parents saw the advantages of the voucher was apparently supported by one of the American academics, Professor Sugarman. He suggested that opinion polls during 1982–83 which indicated returning Opposition popularity might have weakened Government support. A General Election seemed probable in 1983 and there might have been inadequate time to explain the benefits of the voucher, still less for the public to see them demonstrated in practice. The element of time was also emphasised by the Secretary of State in May 1984 (below, p. 386).

But Professor Sugarman added an indication of a change in American public opinion as a result of the continuing deterioration in government schools. In 1970 less than 40 per cent in the USA favoured vouchers; in 1983 nearly 60 per cent said the state should pay for the school of the family's choice (and 40 per cent said they personally would opt for private schools with a voucher). (The parallel shift in British opinion from state to private schools is discussed in p. 383.)

6. *Parliamentary resistance.* There was evidently a lack of will to "embark on the long political struggle to get the required legislation through Parliament." (*Michael McCrum.*)

The question is why, or whether, the 1976 support (Section I) had evaporated; only one Conservative MP had failed to support the Parliamentary motion calling for experiments. The riddle runs through the whole decade from 1975 to 1985.

7. *Public choice: the economics of politics.* Probable reasons under this heading were suggested by John Barnes and Professors Peacock, Rowley, West and Wiseman.

Professor Peacock (July 1984) doubted whether the opposition of senior bureaucrats would have deterred a sufficiently determined Minister. Earlier, in April 1982,[2] he had submitted, in response to a request from the Secretary of State after the concerted academic replies, his "half-way house" proposal to minimise the opposition of bureaucrats and teachers.

> Some senior officials of the Department of Education are bound to be opposed in principle to vouchers. Their patrician stance—"we know what is right for others"—may be well-intentioned, if misguided, but as the Government's advisers they are in a strong position to protect their interests.

His explanation was rather that vouchers were probably "crowded out" by other proposals with more immediate philosophic or political appeal, like the privatisation of "public" corporations. His conclusion was the most sympathetic to the politicians: "I am impressed by how far Ministers managed to travel in political promotion of the voucher."

Professor Rowley's diagnosis indicated hope: ". . . Politicians . . . are the brokers of the political process." In the state of equilibrium between the forces of supply (politicians, officials, administrators, teachers) and demand (parent/voters) in the political process "the politician is the oil that eases the transition (to equilibrium) or the grit that delays it." The equilibrium of forces had hitherto obstructed the voucher. A "shock" from outside the political market-place, by acting on the supply side or the demand side, could dislodge the equilibrium in favour of the voucher. Politicians would then scramble to implement it, declaiming irrelevant justifications.

So the voucher, concluded Professor Rowley, is not "dead," but dormant. (Several possible shocks, both on the side of supply and of demand, unexpected, or perhaps under-estimated, by politicians in 1983, are reviewed in Section VI.)

Professor Wiseman argued that the British education system illustrated the dominance of a "positive" right of pressure groups to coerce parents in education over a "negative" right of families to reject coercion. Parents who want "negative" rights are more difficult to organise than groups like teachers wanting "positive" rights to coerce them. And groups that achieve posi-

2. Alan T. Peacock, "Education Voucher Schemes—Strong or Weak?" *Economic Affairs,* Vol. 3, No. 2, January 1983.

tive rights to coerce acquire "property rights" and resist change in them. Coercive groups cannot be swayed solely by reason, and they carry political clout. A Minister may rationally not act on intellectual conviction about a proposal that will attract political opposition and seems never likely to be implemented. Reform will come rather from changing minds and institutions, so that political inaction loses more votes than hitherto. The lesson is to work by private effort and example: the University of Buckingham could be followed by establishing schools in "deprived" areas and asking voucher-type support from selected local authorities. Professor Wiseman concluded: ". . . if this Government will not act, the only way to shift opinion must be by acting without them."

Professor West concluded that the producer interests had prevailed over the consumers in the political decision to take the voucher off the agenda, but he offered a hopeful, if gradual, long-term outcome. As the British population aged, the pensioner lobbies would induce a squeeze on the education budget. As local authority funds fell away, they would have to call for more direct financial aid from parents—to spread from ancillary library and sports facilities to teachers' costs and teaching equipment (as has happened in the USA and Canada). As these voluntary but expected contributions to state schools increased, however, the additional cost of moving to a private school, with its advantages of choice and influence, would fall. Money would increasingly tend to follow the pupil. Competition with the state system would intensify, and at least some results of the voucher—choice of school, more influence on curricula, and so on—would be accomplished without waiting for government. He concluded, in a memorable phrase, "Parents in the end can, and will, be their own Ministers of Education."

The academic who had been the most administratively and politically active in education, John Barnes, listed four likely reasons: inadequate support in the governing Party; the difficulty of exerting parental influence through representatives or through a government department; the hostility of collectivist-inclined teacher union leaders and teachers to "commercialism" in education; and the occupational tendency among civil servants to search for "snags" rather than to solve problems.

> The power of departmental civil servants opposed to an idea or, just as dangerous, simply sceptical, lies in their propinquity and in their ability to return to the attack as long as they are permitted . . .
>
> Official secrecy is their ally. Outsiders remain ignorant of what is going on . . .

(The bureaucratic monopoly of information has been emphasised by public choice economists.)

In view of the agitated debate in the mid-1980s over local government finance (rates v. local income tax v. a poll tax v. charges), a national reform, Barnes thought, urged as a solution to local government financing, might have had a better chance than the advocacy of local voucher experiments centred on the specific issue of choice in education. Like Professor West, he indicated a fundamental development that could change the equilibrium of influences in the political market: the many teachers who would like more education revenue to come from the central government did not yet see that this shift in financing could carry with it also the central control of school curricula. Many teachers might therefore have been "educated" to see that channelling the finance through parents (by the voucher) would have safeguarded their professional independence. In other words, teachers' support for the voucher could have been mustered for what they would come to see as the lesser of two "evils." Since they must eventually accept more influence to ensure the higher standards required for the good of pupils and industry, they might prefer it to come from parents than from politicians. But without a device such as the voucher to strengthen parental interest by the power to "exit" as well as a stronger "voice" in school management, more control by politicians at the centre is the alternative teachers are virtually making inevitable by the instinctive resistance of their union leaders to a more parent-oriented school system.

Temporary Ministers, permanent officials, precarious advisers

In the absence of a full official statement of the reasons for the 1983 abandonment of the fundamental reform in state education, independent academics and other observers can do no better than reason from general principles. As analytical onlookers personally disinterested they may indeed see more of the game than officials and politicians nearer to the details but also personally affected by the outcome. The relative influence and role of the transient politicians, the permanent civil servants and, more lately, under both Labour and Conservative Governments, the short-term political advisers, are in particular difficult to disentangle. The December 1981 statement of difficulties came directly from the Department, and therefore with political approval. But it is plausible to believe that it was substantially the work of the officials, perhaps altered here and there, modulated or even strengthened, but largely accepted by the Ministers as a document on which to seek "second opinions" from outsiders.

The recorded experience of Ministers of both the hitherto major parties, the late Richard Crossman, Mrs. Barbara Castle, Mr. Gerald Kaufman, Sir Frederick Corfield, Mr. Teddy Taylor (Sections V, VI) and Mr. Nicholas Ridley,[3] as well as the recent views of Sir John Hoskyns and other Government advisers, indicate that the influence of the permanent officials has often been more substantial than is commonly known and less disinterested than their reputation for austere independence (or the testimony of generous-minded and loyal Ministers) would suggest. This conclusion, to repeat, is not a criticism of civil servants but a realistic recognition that, because of the structure of incentives and influence in government employment, their interests do not necessarily coincide with those of Ministers or of the general public.

The economics of bureaucracy has long been the subject of examination by social scientists from Max Weber to C. Northcote Parkinson. Apart from Ludwig von Mises's *Bureaucracy* in 1944, the activities and motivations of bureaucracy have been examined by Professor Tullock's *The Politics of Bureaucracy* in 1965 and Professor Downs's *Inside Bureaucracy* in 1967. The examination has lately become more intense, especially in Professor Niskanen's *Bureaucracy and Representative Government* in 1971, the essence of which was refined in the 1973 IEA Paper, *Bureaucracy: Servant or Master?*[4] Before the economics of bureaucracy is applied to the official handling of the voucher in 1981–83 (Section V), the Minister's reasons for the outcome in 1983 are reviewed here.

The purely political reasons for the abandonment of the voucher in 1983 were indicated by the Secretary of State in a television interview in May 1984 and a House of Commons statement in June 1984. These are the two main public government statements available to independent analysts.

The television interview led the Minister, in a mood of regretful resignation in the face of supposedly ineluctable political imperatives, to emphasise three of the main advantages of the voucher: it would give all parents the choice of school hitherto enjoyed only by the better-off; it would give parents dignity in a personal aspect of parental decision; and it would raise the quality of schooling by giving parents an escape from bad schools that did not satisfy them. He followed with four reasons why it had nevertheless been abandoned.

3. Below, p. 392, for a reaction from a former Department of Education official to the IEA Paper by Professor Niskanen on the economics of bureaucracy.

4. Hobart Paperback No. 5.

1. *Government had a statutory obligation "that all children should be given education free."*

Observation: This is a very general statement in a popular television interview. Yet "free" education is not a bar against a voucher system. The 1944 Act did not require education to be supplied solely by the state (even if it did, it can be amended). It required government to ensure that it was supplied. The formula was by the state "*or otherwise.*" The voucher can be used either as a "passport" to a state school or to pay the costs of "education otherwise" at private schools.

The adjective "free" is ambiguous. It has long been used, especially by sociologists, to necessitate government-provided, tax-financed, bureaucratically-controlled monopoly. The ambiguity lies at the root of the misdirection of social policy for a century in "free" education (and in "free" medical care, subsidised housing . . . for 50–60 years). The argument was that, since people with low incomes could not pay for the "essentials" of education, medicine, housing or other services, they had to be supplied without cost to the customer at the point of supply. The error was to ignore the alternative method of supplying the purchasing power to pay the price. This method would equally have secured the service "free" to the consumer because without cost. But its vast superiority has eluded the dominant sociologists. It would have avoided the impersonal, bureaucratic, politicised and inherently inequitable structure of government benefits in kind of which they now, belatedly, complain. But that is a subject covered in other IEA Papers. The ambiguity of "free" arose from the confusion between the income-effect of nil-prices, which is, of course, to ensure access, and the price-effect which, with income supplementation, could have ensured access without losing the information, decentralisation and de-politicisation of the price system. That distinction did not appear in the Department of Education's statement of December 1981.

2. *"So deeply has the habit of looking to the state bitten into the public awareness that only a minority of parents appreciate the improvement that vouchers might have brought."*

Observation: It is not easy to discover public reaction to an idea of which the public have had no personal experience in everyday life and little political explanation. What evidence has been assembled by the "second-best" techniques of field studies inviting preferences between hypothetical alternatives, since real-life choices have been removed, does not indicate that potential support for the voucher and the new choices it would make possible is confined to "a minority." The Kent County 1978 Feasibility Study (which was based on advice from Professor Blaug) found that 72 per cent of a sample of Kent parents said they should be allowed a voucher to enable them to transfer their children to private schools, and gave as their main reason falling standards in state schools. John Barnes's conclusion was that "the [voucher] scheme would be very popular with parents." In the same year, the fourth IEA "choice in welfare" study based on a quota national sample[5] found that the proportion favouring freedom for individual parents to contract out (with a return of taxes) from state to private education had doubled from 27 per cent in 1963 to 60 per cent in 1978. (The proportion favouring higher taxes to pay for better universal state education had collapsed from 44 to 15 per cent.) This emphatic finding was re-inforced by the 81 per cent who rejected the state monopoly in education by affirming their opposition to the view (put into the question to avoid bias) that parents should not be allowed to pay "extra" for their children at fee-paid schools. Whether British parents as individuals wish to transfer their children from state to private schools or not, they overwhelmingly believe that other parents should be allowed to do so. (Recent opinion polls amply confirm this early IEA field finding.) Their individual decisions not to avail themselves of a right at the time did not conflict with their support for the general proposition that the right should be upheld for others—or for themselves if circumstances changed and they wished to exercise it.

In view of the limitations of "macro" opinion-polling that asks individuals what *others* or people generally should be allowed to do, without reference to the costs of the alternatives, the four field studies since 1963 have incorporated micro-questions asking what individuals *themselves* would do if faced with a choice between state and private education *with full knowledge of their comparative costs.* After inquiry of academics in Europe and America, we discovered no other students of public preferences in education who had conducted such *priced* researches. Yet they are the only method recognised in economic analysis as yielding significant results in the form of a demand curve derived from a schedule relating demand to price, which Professor Blaug was the first economist-reviewer to recognise.[6] A general opinion-poll sentiment in favour of "free" education means little. First-year economics teaches that preference, want, "demand" varies with price. The findings of a "price-less" survey are, in this sense, meaningless and valueless as a guide to public policy.

The main finding based on *priced* alternatives in state and private education

5. R. Harris, A. Seldon, *Over-Ruled on Welfare,* Hobart Paperback 13, 1979.

6. M. Blaug: "Economists will recognise immediately that the inquiry in effect elicited information about the slope of the demand schedule." (*Education: A Framework for Choice,* IEA Readings No. 1, 1967.)

is that the proportion of a sample of male heads of households with children of school age who would add a third of day-school fees to a voucher valued at two-thirds of day-school fees rose from 30 per cent in 1963 to 51 per cent in 1978 (women indicated 52 per cent). If the voucher had been given a higher value at 75 or 80 per cent, or 100 per cent to cover full fees, the proportions would have been higher. And if the principle of the Assisted Places Scheme of varying a grant with parental income had been added, the preferences would logically have been still higher. The Minister's supposition that only a minority of parents understood choice would thus seem to have been unjustifiably pessimistic.

This technique of estimating probable "demand" for a voucher was refined with each IEA survey in 1963, 1965, 1970 and 1978. The methodology of the research has not been refuted by academics. Professor Gordon Forsyth of the University of Manchester has questioned details.[7] Nicholas Bosanquet of the University of York has doubts about the conclusions[8] but sees that general attitude questions ("satisfied," "dissatisfied") are futile without introducing cost and price: "The IEA has done a service in gently pointing out the inanity of this kind of exercise." More recently, Peter Taylor-Gooby of the University of Kent has also contested the conclusions for policy drawn from it.[9] But no critic has faulted the micro-economic technique. Indeed, there has been increased interest in it among academics in all schools of thought characteristically sensitive to criticisms of state education and of the welfare state in general. Although the last IEA field survey is now nearly eight years old, the attention of critics has recently been renewed by the increasing urgency of finding a solution to the continuing deterioration of the state schools, which now equip 40 per cent of their pupils with no significant standard of achievement.

The findings in favour of choice continue to be ignored by politicians in all parties, on the mistaken ground that only a minority understand, or could understand, the simple idea of earmarked purchasing power in a school voucher. Yet this is a technique with which millions of manual and office workers are familiar in the ubiquitous luncheon voucher, and the commonplace record voucher or book token.

If the findings are doubted, three remedies lie with government. First, it can organise larger, more refined surveys beyond the resources of a privately-financed institute. Second, it can elicit opinion by a single-subject "referendum"—which, as Switzerland has shown, is a device not limited to constitu-

7. G. Forsyth, *Doctors and State Medicine,* Pitman, 1966.

8. N. Bosanquet, *After the New Right,* Heinemann, 1983.

9. *Public Opinion, Ideology and State Welfare,* Routledge and Kegan Paul, 1985, in the Radical Social Policy Series, "a forum for democratic socialist debates in social welfare."

tional questions. Third, and best of all, it can see how the people decide in day-to-day practice by returning taxes to them and seeing how they are spent. This last method would best satisfy the politician who, confronted by the 1970 findings, said he was impressed by them but wondered whether they indicated how people would behave if they had to "dig into their pockets" (to top up the voucher). The simple reply is "Fill their pockets with taxes and let them dig." Yet for the public choice reasons discussed in these pages, a well-disposed Government has pursued none of these three ways to discover voters' preferences as parents with children at state schools.

3. *"There would have been a great deal of controversy in our own Party, as well as across party lines."*

Observation: It is probable that controversy could be expected from a range of obstructors, from a former Prime Minister who had indicated his opposition to vouchers, to the National Union of Teachers, the leaders of which had hinted at a local strike. This is hardly a decisive objection. Its main significance is that it graphically illustrates the inappropriateness of the political process for the conduct of education. If the people's preferences—and the advantages of better education for pupils, parents and industry—can be thwarted, *inter alia*, by a formerly leading politician and a trade union leader, the conclusion must be that a voucher scheme or other reform to take education as far as possible outside the state monopoly should be pursued with all speed. We are here at the heart of the public choice critique of democracy: that it does not necessarily—indeed, probably cannot—reflect the will of society, still less a majority, but that it tends to yield to pressure of organised producer interests. The essential, simple but sobering truth is that it does not pay individuals or consumers in a democracy (like school parents) to organise, but it pays producer pressure groups (like teachers). And that dispiriting conclusion raises a host of troublesome questions for democrats. *Over-Ruled on Welfare* concluded in 1979:

> Representative government which can reflect a limited range of voters' preferences for public goods has become increasingly unrepresentative government . . . The inevitable disturbance of vested interests from which politicians now shrink can only be intensified by further delay in arresting and reversing the drift of unlimited government to unlimited disaster.

The disagreeable truth for democrats is that what Professor Buchanan calls "majoritarian" democracy does not easily tolerate minority (from 49 per cent to one person) preferences. Only the market can satisfy individuals and minority groups (at a cost) as well as majorities.

British education has fallen to a new low ebb since 1979. The incumbent Government has made some moves towards giving parents more say—"voice"—in state schooling. But the method of "voice" is essentially ineffective and inherently inequitable since voices differ: middle-class activists grind their axes because parents properly put their children first. Nothing less than the new power of "exit" will move the established education authorities to yield to the sovereignty of the consumer. Disembodied voices that cannot vote with their feet can be ignored or placated; they do not have to be heeded.

4. *"I would not have flinched from putting it to my colleagues if it had been proved to be possible in time to have brought a harvest quickly enough to reward the political slog."*

Observation: That candid observation from an exceptionally upright politician reveals the central weakness of democracy as we have known it. If he was advised that the voucher was not worth its trouble since its benefits would not appear before the General Election (and would then be vulnerable to a change in government), on what was the advice based? Public choice again points to the failure of democratic government to reflect the democrats' preferences. The urgency of removing education as far as possible away from the pressures of periodic elections is re-emphasised. If no reform can be introduced that does not reveal its benefits in time for the succeeding General Election in a five- (or four-) yearly cycle, Parliamentary government must exclude many desirable reforms. And the exceptional politicians who take risks with reforms that reveal their advantages only over seven years or longer are forced into subterfuges to conceal that they are doing good by stealth. Yet the gradually rising degree of public understanding that not all reforms can show their results overnight, the general trend to *embourgeoisement,* and the instinctive liberal impulse that infuses Western society offer the prospect that the short-run political view enforced by interest-group pressure will not always prevail.

Constitutional reform to deny transient majority (or minority) government the power to abrogate fundamental liberties is hopefully urged by liberal economists. Yet legal rules can be avoided or evaded. Legal limits on the power of government would be most effective if *embourgeoisement* was re-inforced by technical advance that broke up coagulations of pressure groups, which Professor Mancur Olson[10] has argued grow in countries that fail to modernise their institutions with changing market conditions. Market forces are making the state monopoly in education out of date (Section VI). The case for the voucher is that

10. *The Rise and Decline of Nations,* Yale University Press, 1982.

it would liberate education from its outworn local government, trade union, professional and fiscal institutions as no other reform would, certainly not cosmetic improvements in the government of schools.

Further reasons for abandonment of the voucher were offered in the Minister's statement in Parliament in June 1984:

> In the course of my examination . . . it became clear that there would be great practical difficulties in making any voucher scheme compatible with the requirements that schooling should be available to all without charge, compulsory and of an acceptable standard.
>
> These requirements . . . were seen . . . to entail an involvement on the part of the state which would be both financial and regulatory and on a scale likely to necessitate an administrative effort as great as under the present system.

Observation: The meaning of "examination" is not clear. The Ministerial "examination" was not based on practical experience of parental choice between competing schools in real everyday life over the years but on an exchange of opinion over several months between politicians, permanent officials and temporary advisers, none of whom could know how a voucher system would work in practice. *The Times,* which for 18 months has asked periodically, like the academics, what happened to the voucher, said in its most recent critique of government policy:

> The Government, having abandoned without much examination, ways of devolving management of schools by, for example, voucher schemes and their analogues, has adopted a centralising stance.[11]

"Examination" did not include experimentation. The "great practical difficulties" were not verified in practice. Opinions were presumably passed between officials and politicians but they were about the past, not the future. The rejection of the voucher was based not on knowledge but on surmise.

It is true that the unbiased opinions of academics were sought (Sections II and III), but they were ignored. If it is objected that they were couched in general terms and did not offer specific detailed solutions, the *tu quoque* must be two-fold. First, the Department's statement of December 1981 was in speculative,

11. *The Times,* Leading article, 16 December 1985.

conjectural, defensive terms that invited solutions to difficulties that are either improbable or are routinely solved by 2,500 private schools. It betokened an attitude that would immobilise all new industrial enterprise if it shied from ventures until every uncertainty had been foreseen and resolved. And, second, the academics offered four proposals based on knowledge of government (Professor Peacock) or of current law and practice (Professor West) and on practical experience of controlling schools (John Barnes), supported in principle by academics with knowledge of running schools (Michael McCrum, Professor Dennison).

The four "requirements"—education free, compulsory, of an "acceptable standard" and at lowest cost—have been discussed elsewhere in these pages. The view that they require state *supply* is unhistorical. Ultimately they do not require even state *financing*, except in a general re-distribution of purchasing power to top up low incomes. Schooling in Britain (as in North America) was becoming universal without being made either compulsory by law or "free" (a euphemism for politically-controlled money) long before the state stepped in to fill the gaps, and ended by almost destroying the private gap-fillers.

The "involvement" by the state in a structure of education comprising entrepreneurial schools paid for by parents would clearly be much less than in a system in which schools were owned, managed, and financed by government. The state "involvement" in returning, or redistributing, taxes in vouchers can hardly be compared with the large education structure in which the buildings and equipment are owned and the teaching and non-teaching staff are employed by government. Most of the buildings and equipment would become privately owned and the staff privately employed. The "administrative effort," and the number of bureaucrats required—from senior Whitehall civil servants to local clerks—would be comparatively diminutive.

The economics of bureaucracy suggests, on the contrary, that this very *reduction* in administrative involvement is a clue to the "problems" alleged by the officials as well as by the politicians.

The administrative objections raised initially in 1981, even if unintentionally, have obscured the anxieties of the authorities that a reform as fundamental as the voucher would disturb, or disrupt, a system that, as they saw it, whatever its faults, was working and trying to cope with its "problems." The academically-inspired proposal for the voucher was a distraction from pressing tasks: training teachers, controlling curricula, re-shaping Boards of Governors, influencing negotiations with trade unions, contending with importunate local authorities.

The voucher was plainly an implied criticism of the educational policy, planning and law of a century since 1870. It is not surprising that it was resisted, perhaps for reasons that the authorities were temperamentally not disposed, or ready, to recognise. Professor Dennison remarked that the Department's objections were to parents' choice *per se* rather than to the voucher as a means of creating it:

> Many of the problems attributed to vouchers are with us now—they will become *more* urgent the longer they are unrecognised; vouchers would not only bring the problems more into the open (which will thus not commend vouchers to the Department of Education) but make them easier to deal with.

In short, the voucher was a challenge to the formidable fortress of paternalism, professional corporatism, monopoly and political authority that had long ruled British education. That the ramparts did not fall to the first intellectual assault was almost predictable.

If the administrative anxieties were fundamentally unfounded, the remaining difficulties were, then, political. The voucher was judged to be too slow in revealing its benefits. It was likely to arouse damaging opposition, especially in the final 12 to 18 months of a Parliament, when opposing politicians could misrepresent it as a *douceur* to the rich and their schools. (This view is the direct opposite of the truth: the voucher is essentially an egalitarian measure that would remove social divisiveness because all parents would be consumers who pay; it would emancipate the working classes from their subjection to schools from which they cannot escape.) Or it might offend the middle class who do well out of state education: as local authority controllers, employees or consumers who can work the system to the advantage of their children or incur the higher housing costs of moving to districts with the better state schools.

What, then, are the "politics," or rather the economics of the politics, of the voucher? What interests are ranged for and against it? How do they influence government? How can the general interest prevail over the organised special interests?

This is precisely the province of public choice analysis, the branch of economics that has replaced the romantic notion of government as a benevolent instrument established by the people, of the people, for the people.

It is the subject of Section V.

SECTION V

The Forces Ranged Against the Voucher

If the 1983 abandonment of the voucher was ultimately political, its advocates may have to make more allowance for the economics of politics and the rigidity of the machinery of government if their next essay is not to end in a second failure.

In recent years the working of government has been anticipated much more realistically and accurately by economists who use public choice analysis than by conventional economists or political scientists who have analysed government as a vehicle for implementing public wishes and serving the public interest. The pursuit of the voucher will require an understanding of government that discards the prevailing notions of influential inter-war economists like Beveridge and Keynes, who believed that if government were equipped with the right ideas it would put them into effect. Beveridge believed that the wartime coalition and the post-war Labour Government would incorporate his proposals for social security into post-war reforms. He was soon disillusioned when for "political" reasons the 1945–50 Government abandoned his notion of a 20-year build-up for the national pension. Keynes, Hayek has emphasised, was arrogant in his belief that if his proposals for budget deficit financing were abused by governments that found inflation politically rewarding, he would work on public opinion and so indirectly induce politicians to resist their political temptations.[1] Professor Buchanan has been especially critical of Keynes not merely because he was intellectually vulnerable but even more because he was politically unrealistic to suppose that government could operate a symmetrical policy of electorally popular budget deficits to inflate the economy and electorally unpopular budget surpluses to deflate it.[2] Keynes had electorally "turned the politicians loose." Economists who see glittering prizes in the voucher must

1. F. A. Hayek, *A Tiger by the Tail*, Hobart Paperback 4, IEA, 1972 (2nd Edn., 1978), p. 103.
2. J. M. Buchanan, John Burton, R. E. Wagner, *The Consequences of Mr. Keynes*, Hobart

now accept that it will not come to pass simply because a Government of sympathetic politicians is furnished with the intellectual argument.

The conventional view has misled both the Keynesians and most political scientists. A leading Keynesian, Professor Paul Samuelson, has taught unprotected students that "sensible men of goodwill [can] be expected to invoke the authority and creative activity of government to civilise the unbridled market place."[3] And political scientists have taught that the competition of interests will tame, civilise, control and limit power to "decent human purposes" and reduce coercion, "the most evil form of power," to a minimum (Professor Robert Dahl of Yale).

Political decision-makers in government are by nature no more nor less rational or self-interested than people in the market: the difference is that the disciplines on them to serve the populace are less effective than those in the market. They are spending other people's money and do not suffer the consequences of their failures; their opposite numbers in the market spend their own money and normally suffer if they fail to satisfy the people who pay them. "Public" officials are not disciplined by their customers as closely as producers in the market. Anthony Downs originally emphasised[4] that an individual voter is rationally apathetic: the time-cost in learning how best to vote far outweighs the small prospect of widely-dispersed gain or of a single vote helping to promote the "right" policy. Voters plump for images, slogans. In the market the individual gains personally, directly and substantially by deserting unsatisfying suppliers (like slack or inefficient schools) and taking his vote/money to preferred suppliers. Hence the 30 to 60 per cent abstentions in the political market (elections) and the 100 per cent voting (using every penny) in the market for goods or services. Hence the dominance of group interests (teachers) in the political market and the sovereignty of the individual consumer (parent) in the private market.

Public choice analysis also better explains the working of bureaucracy than the conventional view that it is essentially an instrument at the service of Abraham Lincoln–like governments. Again, officials are essentially no different from other men and women, but the incentives that influence them are very different. There is no reason in logic or common sense for an offi-

---

Paper 78, IEA, 1978, refined and applied to Britain the Buchanan-Wagner argument in *Democracy in Deficit: The Political Legacy of Mr. Keynes,* Academic Press, 1977.

3. *Economics,* McGraw-Hill, 1958 Edition, his celebrated, best-selling and influential (especially with students) but dangerous textbook.

4. *An Economic Theory of Democracy,* Harper & Row, 1957.

cial to exert himself in furthering the introduction of a reform that would disturb his daily round and, moreover, diminish his authority. And the penalty for *failure* to promote a reform that would serve the public is virtually inoperative. On the contrary, officials, as Professor Stigler has argued in his theory of "capture," tend to satisfy the interests they are supposed to regulate rather than those of the remote and unorganised consumers who are supposed to be served by the regulating authority. And the interest groups are not the contending competitors seen by the political scientists but joint raiders of the public purse. Special interests compete less with one another than jointly against the public.[5] And as the interest groups become entrenched, the political process weakens in its service of the general interest. Professor Olson has therefore seen the recovery of Germany and Japan after 1945 as facilitated by the destruction of their special interests by defeat in war.

Dissection of the working of bureaucracy is apt to be resisted, in Britain more than in the USA, as an assault on reputable "public servants," sea-green incorruptibles. Yet sceptical criticism has been growing in recent years. Professor Niskanen's general conclusion in his 1973 Paper was that bureaucrats aim to maximise their budgets and end with twice the optimum size of departments. A former Department of Education civil servant, Maurice Kogan (below), rejected Professor Niskanen's assessment of the bureaucracy,[6] but Nicholas Ridley, who held office in the early 1970s, and is (January 1986) Secretary of State for Transport, broadly agreed with it. He said:

> All decisions, actions and inactions are laid at the door of Ministers . . . the obvious truth [is] that all but a tithe of policy decisions and almost the whole of administration never comes near them. With 700,000 bureaucrats [there are now fewer] and 70 Ministers [there are now more] it could hardly be otherwise.
>
> Select Committees . . . are a new twist in the age-old political struggle between the Executive and the Legislature.

5. Party politicians compete against one another but in the same business of using power over the public to further their interests. As with all statements of general tendencies, there are notable exceptions, but democrats have suffered by regarding politicians as a race apart from ordinary men and women.

6. ". . . welfare state institutions are run by people who believe in what they are doing rather than in expanding budgets . . ." (M. Kogan's Commentary, "An Over-simplified Model," in Niskanen, *Bureaucracy: Servant or Master?*, IEA Hobart Paperback No. 5, p. 83.)

> We cannot know . . . what bureaucrats do, and how efficiently . . . while they are organised in one colossal monolithic secret bureau, sheltering under the cloaks of the Official Secrets Acts and the doctrine of Ministerial responsibility.[7]

No outsider can know how far the Department of Education officials resisted the voucher as a danger to their interests or welcomed it as a possible new solution to stubborn old problems. One view could be that, once it became plain that Ministers were determined to have a practicable scheme to consider, the civil servants buckled down to the task, worked hard and honourably, and produced coherent and practicable methods that could have been embodied in legislation—and would have been consistent both with the Ministers' philosophy and with compulsory and free education for all. (But no such scheme has been published.) Another view could be that, since Ministers were not agreed (as the Secretary of State has indicated[8]), the officials were tactically reluctant, tacitly unco-operative, unconsciously resentful and in effect obstructive, doing as little as they had to, not as much as they could to further the scheme until determined Ministers replaced lukewarm predecessors. The Ministers must have depended considerably on essentially sceptical officials for information, interpretation, advice and drafting of documents, including the 1981 statement.

Reference to trends and episodes in recent years supports this judgement. The influence of civil servants can be seen in the continuity of the policies pursued by Ministers of different governments. One of the most able of recent times, Maurice Kogan, later Professor of Government and Social Administration at Brunel University, served Conservative and Labour Ministers (Sir Edward Boyle and the late C. A. R. Crosland); it would have been surprising if their similar views on developments in the 1960s, especially the argument for comprehensive secondary schooling, owed nothing to their persuasive advisers.[9] When FEVER requested interviews with two Labour Secretaries of State for Education in 1975 (one later Conservative) and with the Prime Minister in 1977, the letters of refusal deployed defensive prejudgements that were echoed in the Department's statement of 1981 under a Conservative Secretary of State (Appendix to Section V, pp. 400–402). At the FEVER deputation of six to the Secretary of State in 1980 he was accompa-

7. N. Ridley's Commentary, "Efficiency Begins at Home," in Niskanen, *Bureaucracy: Servant or Master?*, quotations from pp. 87–8 and p. 89 respectively.

8. Channel 4, Diverse Reports, May 1984.

9. *The Politics of Education*, Penguin, 1971.

nied by five, intent, officials. The senior officials at the Department, moreover, are regarded by academic observers as persuasively pre-eminent in their influence on Ministers and policy in the last two decades (below).

"An ambitious bureaucracy"

Two close academic observers of the "politics" of education over 20 years[10] discerned in 1985 "a bureaucratic dynamic located primarily in the central apparatus, the Department of Education and Science." They categorised it as "an ambitious bureaucracy," with a sustained resolve to maintain "managerial continuity" through the alternation of Ministers of opposing parties and a long-term design to wrest control of school curricula from local authorities, the teachers and their unions, and from the examination boards.[11]

These academics wondered how the Department viewed "the erosion of its traditional responsibilities" by the Assisted Places Scheme and its "regeneration" of the private sector. Since the voucher would in time lead to a much more fundamental "erosion of its traditional responsibilities," it is unrealistic to suppose that its reaction in 1981 could have been other than sceptical. On the fate of "innovations with vouchers, open enrolment and student loans," the two academics said the Departmental officials "no doubt strongly emphasised . . . costs and administrative problems." The officials' reaction to market-creating reforms was, it seems, predictable from their known attitudes and interests. The 1981 document, in short, could have been foreseen. The view that informed, able, influential men and women, conscious of their careers, put the interests of others first, and worked with might and main in 1982–83 to promote parental influence through the voucher, is difficult to credit.

10. Dr. Brian Salter, Senior Research Fellow in Education Studies at the University of Surrey; Ted Tapper, Reader in Politics at the University of Sussex. They have written on the changing "dynamics of the educational state" in Britain since the 1960s in three detailed books researched in depth: *Education and the Political Order,* Macmillan, 1978; *Education, Politics and the State,* Grant McIntyre, 1981; and *Power and Policy in Education,* Falmer Press, 1985.

11. Salter and Tapper are not the only observers to detect "a continuity of purpose which reflects the abiding and deep-seated problems affecting our education system." They quote the editor of the leading school education periodical: "Every new Minister means a new set of pet projects to look at—loans, vouchers, assisted places . . . The long-term policy of DES goes underground, to re-emerge when Ministers have been taken patiently through the old arguments." (Salter and Tapper, *Power and Policy in Education,* p. 213.) The reference is to *The Times Educational Supplement* edited by Mr. Stuart Maclure.

In view, therefore, of what seems to have been a prominent role of the permanent officials *vis-à-vis* the transient politicians, the IEA invited Dr. Keith Hartley[12] of the University of York to prepare a short statement on the economic characteristics of bureaucracy to update the analysis of Professor Niskanen in 1973[13] (which Niskanen's then membership of the President's Council of Economic Advisers precluded him from doing), and Professor Gordon Tullock[14] to judge the Department of Education exchange with the academics.

Dr. Hartley argued that government bureaucracies have property rights in the control of activities measured roughly by their budgets; promotion prospects increase with number of staff. In naturally seeking to grow, to expand their budgets, bureaucracies—like the rest of mankind—will tend to exaggerate the demand for, and under-state the costs of, their projects and policies. Hence they will predictably (as in the Report, *Better Schools,* of March 1985 if it reflects their advice)[15] urge policies that ostensibly increase the "voice" of parents in running existing schools rather than those that enable them to influence state schools by the power to take their money to schools outside the system over which officials have much less control. Vouchers in particular are dangerous to the bureaucracy since they would transfer the influence on or control of education from central and local government to individual parents.

Policies that can be expanded within the state system will, moreover, be emphasised because the costs will be borne by large numbers of unsuspect-

12. Dr. Hartley is the Director of the Institute of Social and Economic Research, University of York, and author of *Problems of Economic Policy; Micro-economic Policy; NATO Arms Co-operation: A Study in Economics and Politics.*

13. *Bureaucracy: Servant or Master?*

14. Professor Tullock is the Holbert R. Harris University Professor of Economics, Center for Study of Public Choice, George Mason University, Fairfax, Virginia, USA. Author, *inter alia,* of *The Calculus of Consent* (with J. M. Buchanan); *The Politics of Bureaucracy; Towards a Mathematics of Politics; Private Wants, Public Means; The Economics of Income Redistribution; The Vote Motive.*

15. Cmnd. 9469. Of its four "initiatives" proposed for new directions in education policy, the only one on parents was "harnessing [their] energies in a reformed system of school government." School "government" reproduces the imperfections of political government, chiefly that it yields to pressure from the articulate and the organised. That is why parents, like political voters, are rationally indifferent, and the activity of Parent-Governors and Parent-Teachers Associations is largely left to the politically skilled and experienced.

ing, widely-dispersed parent-taxpayers most of whom have no control, or knowledge, of how their money is being spent. Government bureaucracies, unintentionally or otherwise, are, in short, engaged in a vast exercise of "divide-and-rule."

The economic characteristics of "bureaus" do not predispose them to side with parent/taxpayers. First, there are no inducements to economise in spending the taxpayers' money, since savings are likely to go to another Department. Second, there is no inducement to replace expensive teachers with relatively less expensive auxiliaries or equipment. Third, officials are more likely to consume potential savings by on-the-job leisure (what economists call X-inefficiency), indulgence in the latest prestige-conferring high-technology equipment, or, with complaisant politicians, commission research that supports the official approach. Fourth, Departments will be motivated to collusion by support for one another's projects, just as politicians trade support—"log-roll"—for their favoured projects. And, finally, high (and rising) standards without end will tend to be urged by politicians regardless of costs.

Hence the common fallacy that government is essential to maintain standards that might otherwise fall (as in private schools) in the market. Government standards are probably too low in state schools because their financing is limited to taxation. In other activities they can be too high, but no official suffers since the cost is borne by the taxpayer. There is no support for the assumption that government standards will be set at the optimum point. Parents will want rising standards and will pay for them. Government standards are arbitrary because government is irresponsible and unaccountable. It does not always know what it is doing: it measures output efficiency by inputs (like expenditure per pupil), a procedure which would bankrupt a private school in the competitive market.

State activities will be protected to safeguard the officials' property rights. "Fighting their corner" has become a familiar description of Ministers' duties that officials expect them to pursue in the annual round of apportioning public expenditure to Departments. Officials will complain if the Minister does not maintain or increase the Department's budgets. And they have no incentive to co-operate in advancing efficiency. They cannot be expected to further schemes, such as vouchers, that would deplete their province unless offered compensating benefits. And they can retaliate if threatened—as by reluctance to draft a difficult document to urge a proposal to the Cabinet that the Minister favours but they oppose.

So much for the general economic characteristics of bureaucracy. Professor Tullock's view of the exchange between the Department and the academics was that bureaucratic objection was predictable and their catalogue of "problems" could be broadly anticipated from first principles. They could be expected to argue that tax costs of voucher-financed education would rise because people (especially the wealthy) who had hitherto paid the full cost for private education would now pay only part. They would tend to overestimate the difficulties of "planning" the organisation of education by the state managers when parents could move to other suppliers. They would suggest anxiety that there might not be suppliers to satisfy parents who wished to move. They would insinuate that parents would buy poor quality schooling once state supervision or inspection were removed. And there would be a host of minor "problems": who would establish the new supplies?; where would they be?; how could consumers' access be made equal?; how would they be regulated? And so on. In short, the whole idea was futile, and no informed educationist could be expected to support it.

Tullock posed two questions. Why do civil servants obstruct such reforms? And why do their political masters tolerate the obstruction? The analysis of bureaucrats' motivations is re-inforced by experience.

The answer to the first question seems clear. The voucher would undermine the officials' authority and cause them additional exertion. They see no reason to help reformers in this demolition. They believe the proposal is based on ignorance, and would probably help the rich rather than the poor. It would disturb the *status quo* without certainty of improvement. (They would have few or fewer such qualms if the proposals seemed likely to *extend* their authority.) The voucher would, for the first time, establish a test of their efficiency. Large-scale movement out of state schools prompted by the voucher would visibly condemn them. (The US teachers' union declaims "No report cards." The British National Union of Teachers has similarly resisted measurements of efficiency.)

These tactics, said Professor Tullock, are "the standard civil service techniques used in ten thousand internal squabbles." He concluded: "The only real mystery is why anybody pays any attention to them."

On the tolerance of obstruction by Ministers, Professor Tullock pointed to the limited powers in controlling officials. They can collude with officials in other Departments, undermine Ministers' authority by leaking embarrassing confidences to the press, by creating bad news by sabotage, by spreading disaffection among junior staff, by tolerating a proposal they think will work badly or by other forms of "guerrilla war."

Three examples of bureaucratic unhelpfulness follow:

(i) In the Open University course "Decision-making in Britain," a programme televised in March 1983 (and subsequently), a Minister responsible for education in Scotland in 1970–71 and in 1974 (Mr. Teddy Taylor) replied, to the question "How far would civil servants go in persuading a Minister?":

> There's every device under the sun that can be used . . . if a Minister is too active in pursuing a policy they don't like, they keep him very busy in other directions.
>
> . . . When I was pushing one line, I was presented with 10 thousand conferences all over Scotland which, they said, it was absolutely vital for me to speak at . . . I found myself travelling around gatherings of social workers and psychiatrists at Ballachulish and elsewhere.

(ii) The Shadow Education Minister (Norman St. John Stevas), asked in 1974 whether he could carry out his policy, replied:

> When you are in Government you have 100 civil servants whispering in your ear that you can't say this or that and giving you very good reasons why you can't. But I am making these commitments and . . . shall do my best to fulfil them. (*Sunday Telegraph*, 4 August 1974.)

(iii) Most recently, Mr. Michael Heseltine, a Minister for 13 years to early 1986, said (like the Scottish Education Minister) in a BBC 2 broadcast, on 15 January 1986:

> Civil servants conspire to keep Ministers too busy to ask embarrassing questions. You can never empty the in-tray because very rapidly a highly-sophisticated civil service gets used to the speed at which you will work. If you can clear a foot of paperwork each day, there will always be a foot of paperwork to clear. If two feet, two feet.

The Minister's defences are minimal: generally he cannot fire. In practice he may have to settle for diluted reforms that provoke least resistance from the officials, or even abandon a favoured proposal in order to avoid disrupting a more immediate objective.

This suggestion might explain the seemingly determined obstruction to vouchers in 1985. Indication of a Government intention to revive the idea would have antagonised the teachers' unions and confused the delicate negotiations on teachers' pay. Furthermore, the political desire to raise school standards by central government influence on curricula made allies among civil servants whose collaboration, even if problematic, would be further risked.

Yet, ultimately, Professor Tullock concluded, the politicians' weakness was that they knew they could be fired by the voters. Public pressure could in time prevail.

The economics of bureaucracy analysis of the interests ranged against the voucher led Professor Dwight Lee, another American public choice economist, to a provisionally pessimistic conclusion in a Paper for an international conference of economists on "Freedom in Education" in 1985.[16] Essentially, producers and consumers prevail in different kinds of markets. In education, the producers (teachers, etc.) are strong in the political market, where they are organised, concentrated and vocal, but would be relatively weak in the economic market, where they would be more dispersed and more likely to bargain with individual schools that can assess their individual performance. Consumer-parents, in contrast, are weak in the political market, where they cannot vote for or against particular teachers or schools, or even the state system as a whole because political elections do not isolate single issues, but would be strong in the economic market, where they can desert bad teachers or schools for better competitors.

Although parents would gain from a device like the voucher, individual parents cannot do much to introduce it. They are "rationally" ignorant and apathetic. Although a market with choice between competing schools would benefit them, they cannot obtain it easily through the political process. Even if advocacy by a small number of academics, and perhaps a small parents' lobby, induces a handful of politicians to instal an experiment, it is likely to be hobbled by spanners-in-the-works thrown by teachers, as at Alum Rock;[17] so it will not show the results which could be produced by a "clean" voucher that maximised choice and competition. The interests will "allow" a voucher to be tested only in emasculated form that will discredit the principle, because a "clean" voucher would deprive them of their monopoly, property rights or rents (gains made by political pressure).

16. Liberty Fund Conference, Baden-Baden, May 1985.

17. A small local experiment in Alum Rock, a township near San Francisco: the teachers' unions co-operated only if schools could not expand or contract in response to demand, no teacher lost his job if found unwanted, and so on.

Hence Professor Lee's pessimistic conclusion. The best hope of improving education might be, he regretted, to forget about vouchers, leave the state schools to the special interests, and resign ourselves to a continued decline in the quality of state education, in the expectation that parents will transfer their children to higher-quality private schools. Later, in a private paper, he concluded that the cloud over competitive choice had a silver lining. The suppliers were vulnerable: the teachers hid their special pleading behind a façade of "public interest" rhetoric. The solution was to penetrate the façade and reveal their real purpose: private gain at public expense. In short, the 30-to-one parent/voter to teacher/voter predominance could in the end prevail.

What are the prospects in Britain?

Appendix to Section V

The Official Resistance to Vouchers, 1975–1981

(The Department of Education replies to FEVER requests for interviews)

12 March 1975
(in reply to request to the Secretary of State, Reginald Prentice)

Mr. Prentice . . . sees serious objections to the voucher schemes propounded in this country during the past 20 years.

Mr. Prentice would be opposed to any scheme which would . . . provide a general subsidy to parents . . . outside the maintained sector [i.e. private schools].

Within the maintained sector the results would also be unacceptable. A voucher scheme would introduce an undesirable element of competition in place of co-operation.

The inevitable imbalance in the use of resources between schemes, some over-burdened, others under-used, would be wasteful in teachers and in physical and financial resources.

Your argument that "the voucher would do more for working class people . . .": Mr. Prentice takes a different view. He believes the outcome would be socially divisive, accentuating the differences between the standards of education available to relatively well-off, articulate and enterprising families, and to children from poor, educationally apathetic and ill-informed families.

. . . the Secretary of State does not feel that a meeting would be helpful.

N. J. Sanders
Private Secretary

15 May 1975

Mr. Prentice believes the disadvantages of a voucher system preclude its introduction on even an experimental basis within the maintained sector.

An education voucher could not guarantee admission to the school of the parents' choice.

. . . it is unrealistic to expect school provision to adjust rapidly to meet the demands of parents.

Unpopular schools cannot simply be dispensed with . . .

Even if the popular schools could be expanded at will . . . there would be large-scale redundancies of buildings and teachers at great public expense.

Mr. Prentice finds it hard to believe that the open-market principle would not favour the more articulate, more enterprising . . .

. . . the 1944 Act expressly forbids tuition fees . . . thus a proposal to furnish . . . a voucher for each child . . . would require new legislation . . .

N. J. Sanders

25 June 1975
(to Secretary of State, Fred Mulley)

. . . the capacity of any school is limited and the popular schools tend to be filled to capacity . . .

. . . their expansion would be slow and uncertain . . . admission would have to be restricted for a long time if not indefinitely . . .

. . . no voucher scheme could guarantee admission to any school a parent chose; many parents would find they were no better off . . .

. . . many would find they were worse off because a rational system of allocation had been replaced by . . . a scramble or a queue.

Even if there could be quick enlargement of more popular schools, this could only happen in most places at the cost of under-use of less popular schools and under-employment of teachers.

If [vouchers] did not cover the cost at a maintained school (unit costs vary between areas and schools) any charge to parents . . . would contravene the Education Act 1944.

. . . local authorities' power to pay fees at independent schools is restricted . . . By regulations under the 1944 Act they may help with fees, means-tested, to avoid hardship; and by the 1953 Education Act they may arrange free places at independent schools if there is a shortage at maintained schools. Vouchers which offered places without regard to parental means or to a shortage of maintained places would be outside the law.

N. J. Sanders

5 December 1977
(in reply to request to Prime Minister, James Callaghan)

The idea of a voucher scheme . . . raises tremendous problems, especially in connection with the massive public investment in the maintained schools.

It would be impossible to re-deploy this investment so flexibly as to meet all the changing demands that parents might have to make . . .

Unless parents were to be frustrated and disillusioned, there would have to be a great waste and duplication of resources.

On choice of school, parents . . . have the right to make their wishes known . . . and the local education authority must have regard to such wishes . . . if the school chosen is suitable to . . . the child and the authority are not involved in unreasonable expenditure . . .

(Miss) C. E. Sullivan
Schools Branch I
Department of Education

SECTION **VI**

Prospects: State and Market

The final Section draws the argument together and indicates personal conclusions on the lessons from the events of 1981–85 and the prospects ahead.

British education faces the basic alternatives of increasing politicisation or an adventure in commercialism. The third alternative is derived from the charitable urge; it has established many schools and could grow with widening affluence, but will not be sufficiently potent or all-embracing to contend with the political interests that resist reform. Parents will also voluntarily raise more funds to supplement deficient tax-finances, but the main thrust will have to come from educationists, entrepreneurial administrators and high-flyer teachers who gain financially or otherwise by responding to the developing demand for effective education. Good schools must prosper, bad schools must founder. The essential is entrepreneurship. The commercial market will have to supplement the charity market in order to redeem the failure of the political market.

The voucher initiative has failed so far because it has lacked the support of an organised pressure group of producers as entrepreneurs who would gain financially from its introduction. Apart from rare educationists, like Michael McCrum (and Alan Barker, former Headmaster of The Leys School), the suppliers of private education do not actively lobby for an expansion of choice and competition in a market for education because they are not motivated by the prospect of earning profit. Most are non-profit-earning charitable institutions that are not only indifferent to prospects of profit but sometimes even culturally hostile to the "commercialism" of which they are the residuary beneficiaries. They regard themselves, not very differently from state suppliers, as "giving" a service, not "selling" it to consumers who must be persuaded by superior performance to pay for it. Many who wish to serve others are enabled by non-profit education (or medicine) to express their inclination to give their services for a good cause. And they contribute substantially to the national economic and cultural life. But the politico-economic limitation of the charitable urge cannot be ignored. The non-profit instinct is a contribution, possibly growing, but not the solution to the task of creating choice for all parents. Charity is blessed; but it is not enough.

The scope for expansion in private education that is sensitive and responsive to consumer-parental inclination is, moreover, not visible but for most parents potential. The politicians and civil servants are right to emphasise the unknown magnitude of the eventual reconstruction of education from virtual monopoly to general competition that would follow the voucher. What they do not emphasise is that far-sighted educationists, many of the best teachers, the vast majority of parents and industry in general would welcome and benefit from the reconstruction. The authorities cannot emphasise the prospect too strongly since, if the outcome were indeed different from the present condition, it would demonstrate that state education had departed far from the real but repressed preferences of parents, the interests of pupils and the requirements of industry. The evidence from the Kent Feasibility Study is that the movement out of state to private schools would be of the order of 10 per cent. But even that requires an exercise of the imagination that may be too much to expect from civil servants who would not gain financially but who would lose in authority and opportunities of personal advancement. The impetus to reform therefore requires a strong finance-oriented commercial process, which in turn will require political removal of obstacles to take advantage of technical change.

Primary and secondary (as well as higher and further) education require an injection of the kind of motivation, expansion-mindedness and cost-consciousness that has led Sight and Sound Education Ltd. to expand its youth training schemes. And it has been enabled to do so by what its moving spirit (John Pardoe, the former Liberal parliamentarian who in private enterprise bears the description Managing Director) has called a voucher in effect if not in form.[1] His firm, with many others, has responded to the new demands from 350,000 young people, armed with an earmarked money grant ("voucher") of £2,000 from the Youth Training Scheme of the Manpower Services Commission, for courses in office skills and technology that will equip them for well-paid posts in industry. The result has been a remarkable increase in the number of new suppliers. With strong market incentives, the supply of educators (*pace* the Department of Education) is elastic (Section II).

1. *Economic Affairs*, October–November 1985.

The courses supplied by John Pardoe (and other managing agents) have had to deal with young people who, he says,[2]

> have for the most part left school with precious little to show for it. A minority may have genuine learning difficulties. But most of them have suffered from a school system that appears to believe that learning is easy. . . .
>
> Many of them were "turned off" by school in their early days . . . For the majority of people [existing] education is a "turn-off."

This view was supported by a spokesman for the National Association of Head Teachers:

> The vast majority of my 1,250 boys spend the day sitting with a pen in their hands doing something that is going to be totally different from the way they are going to earn their living for the rest of their lives.[3]

John Pardoe goes further to a view that most critics of state education have not yet reached, although they may have to do so before long:

> The Youth Training Scheme is not an extension of school. Rather it is an essential part of de-schooling society . . . Ivan Illich has written what ought to be the slogan of the Youth Training Scheme: "For most men and women the right to learn is curtailed by the obligation to attend school."[4] The less like school the Youth Training Scheme is, the better it is likely to be.

A comparable expansion could be expected in primary and secondary education. When this prospect was put to a government adviser the reaction confirmed the characteristic failure of the educationist's mind to understand the market process, with the familiar confusion between the technical and the economic. It was doubted whether the supply of schools would react to a voucher because there was no shortage of schools but an adequate number, even possibly a surplus. The reply is that the market would respond to vouchers by producing new entrepreneurial school enterprises run and staffed by the more alert educationists, Heads, and teachers. They would offer schooling in existing physical structures or new ones.[5] Supply would

2. *Training and Development,* December 1985.
3. *The Times,* 5 February 1986.
4. *De-schooling Society,* Penguin Books, 1973.
5. A recent example is a primary school in Surrey for ages 4 to 12/13 to introduce the

not be limited to existing bricks and mortar or blackboards and chalk, but would grow in response to new requirements from parents. For the first time in their lives 95 per cent of them would be able to influence or discipline the schools by their power to move if dissatisfied, and so call into being new suppliers. The technical number or the condition of buildings called "schools" is not a decisive limitation on the supply of entrepreneurs.

The century-old attempt to run school education by the political process has failed to satisfy pupils, parents and industry. The change from politicisation to commercialisation will be disturbing in the early years, although not as much as the educational establishment fears or asserts. But it will also be invigorating, liberating, innovative and, above all, creative. The new educators will be avid to embrace the new technologies and to satisfy the consumers in families and industry.

The objection that education, even in its junior forms, is not only vocational but also cultural—a "merit good" that pupils should have even if their parents do not understand why they should pay for it—does not create a decisive case for state/local *government* ownership of the assets or employment of the staff. Even if the "experts" agreed on which subjects have most "merit," there is only a presumptive argument for money subvention to the requisite subjects, though even then with the risk that the grants themselves will become politicised, as has some or much of the money channelled to further and higher education through the University Grants Committee, the Economic and Social Research Council, and other government agencies or departments. The "merit good" argument starts as paternalistic benevolence and can end as uncontrollable autocracy.

There must be considerable doubt whether the Department of Education can take British schools into preparations for the 21st century. It carries too large a load of inherited "continuity" to embrace the opportunities created by market forces. Its characteristic attitudes are revealed by the ruminations of a recent Permanent Secretary (1970 to 1976) on the ethos of the Depart-

elements of technology at an earlier age than in state schools. Its modest initial funding will be mainly by gifts, with costs covered by fees in the early years and bursaries for children of lower-income parents. The target is a network of primary and secondary schools to produce applied scientists, engineers and technologists as a parallel to the grammar schools that produced leading figures in academia, pure science and the "liberal" professions.

ment, on the voucher, on the competence of parents and on the impartiality of civil servants:[6]

On the ethos of the Department:

> . . . it's inevitable that any bureaucracy will always have the sort of weight of its own prejudices on its back. You can't help that. And there are good reasons why you should have a centre that at least maintains the continuity. Politicians come and go. The system goes on for ever. Stability is important. It's important that past experience and errors are built into the race memory. That is what the civil service does.

On the voucher:

> . . . the voucher scheme could be very attractive to the bright parents of bright children; it wouldn't do much for the . . . dull parents of bright children; I think it would do nothing, it could in fact disadvantage, the dull parents of the dull children. The [voucher] proposition [is] not in the national interest but in a sectional interest.

On the competence of parents:

> You can't substitute for accountable elected bodies like local authorities and the Secretary of State, on whom you have devolved statutory powers and duties. You can't abolish those and transfer them to an undifferentiated—admirable but undifferentiated—body of persons simply called parents.

And, not least, on the impartiality of civil servants:

> I don't think civil servants really do obstruct Ministers. I don't think they generally would die on their convictions. They are bred on the principle that at the end of the day they must do the Minister's bidding. We are political eunuchs; if we weren't, we would be politicians.

Among the reflections provoked by these *obiter dicta* of a senior civil servant, one must be that the notion of bureaucrats as eunuchs has long been discarded by academic students of bureaucracy. If the conclusion is that they are indeed politicians, they wield power without the authority of the electorate.

But Salter and Tapper suggested in 1985 that the "bureaucratic dynamic" of the Department may not continue. They said it is now vulnerable both to

6. Open University telecast, "Decision-making in Britain," March 1983.

competition from the Manpower Services Commission, which could invade its territory, and to criticism from what they called "the New Right" (in which they included the liberal market critique reflected in this IEA Paper). The "pet projects,"[7] they said, could this time constitute "a substantial shift in policy." As a result, "the balance of education power has shifted." This development could, in short, create the "shock" to the political equilibrium of supply and demand that Professor Rowley said could radically change the prospects for a fundamental reform such as the voucher.

It is now time to consider how, and how soon, education can be moved from the culturally conservative Department of Education to an enterprise-oriented agency such as the Manpower Services Commission. Its direction could also be changed from a philosophic politician trying to run an inherited state monopoly more efficiently by strengthening central direction and parental "voice" to an industry-minded entrepreneur uninhibited by political hesitancy and monopolistic trade unions and ready to use all available efficient suppliers, private as well as public, that are disciplined by "exit" to raise standards in teaching and training to the requirements of British industry. Sooner or later it will be discovered that the task of preparing young people for a life of work is made unnecessarily difficult by requiring them to spend 12 years in primary and secondary schooling ultimately dominated by party-political decisions, not least in finance.

The expansion of the Manpower Services Commission as a competitor to the Department of Education could take place if it showed itself better at promoting the skills required in industry. John Pardoe told a conference of school teachers and educationists in Cambridge that their monopoly of education had ended.[8] His argument for a free market "was received with unexpected enthusiasm." The new development is that their pupils could in time switch to courses provided (in return for earmarked purchasing power or quasi-voucher) by the Manpower Services Commission in the Youth Training Scheme. Such schemes could be expanded in duration and down the age-scale to cover pupils of 14 and over. The Youth Training Scheme for the 16+ group is being extended from one to two years. The Technical and Vocational Education Initiative (TVEI) has since September 1983 aimed to reach pupils in secondary schools from the age of 14. Schools could still in-

7. Section V, p. 394, note 11.
8. *Economic Affairs*, October–November 1985.

fect younger children jesuitically with anti-industry prejudice. But they no longer have a monopoly. The new network of technology-oriented primary and secondary schools (above, pp. 405–6) could teach the romance as well as the arts of industry. The private schools are shedding their anti-industry ethos,[9] but the state schools will retain a bias against commercial society as long as parents cannot easily desert their anti-capitalist teachers.

State school classes could be gradually depleted if unfavourable comparisons were made, by parents, educationists and industry, between the Department of Education's "free" schools and the Manpower Services Commission's "voucher"-financed courses. High performance at lower costs could be expected from the voucher-financed courses precisely because they incorporate the market ingredient of choice between competing suppliers. John Pardoe's company supplies such courses at a half to a third of the costs of similar courses provided by local government Colleges of Further Education.

In this transition from politicisation to commercialism some such device as the voucher, under this or another name, which shifts the power of initiative from suppliers to consumers, will be indispensable. The burden of advocacy has so far fallen on long-sighted liberal economists, most associated with the IEA, a handful of educationists, a dozen politicians, and the meagrely-financed parents' lobby FEVER. The task now is to identify and organise the *potential* educational interests that would invest new resources in existing or new buildings and in the more gifted teachers to resume the market in education that has for too long been interrupted by the political century of state education.

Although the interests identified by public choice analysis have so far been ranged against choice in education, in favour of tax-financed government schools and on the side of teacher control, there are forces on the side of both the supply of and the demand for education that are working against politicised education. *First,* Professor West has argued that the rising numbers of pensioners would squeeze expenditure on education, induce schools to invite and depend on parental contributions, and thus reduce the cost of transfer to fee-paid schools.

Second, John Barnes has argued that, since the urgency of raising school

9. G. C. Allen, *The British Disease,* Hobart Paper 67, IEA, 1976 (2nd Edition, 1979).

standards is being accepted on all sides, even if grudgingly by teachers, they are less likely to prefer the alternative of more control of curricula by politicians at the centre than by parents at the periphery. If family doctors, as Barnes emphasised, are self-employed rather than salaried by the state, teachers could see some comparable advantages in contracts directly with parents, as an economist-teacher has also recently argued (below, p. 411).

Third, British local government, far from coming under more popular control by local voting than central government (a familiar theme of conventional political science), has been seen by political activists as an easy way to control billions of the ratepayers' money to spend on bizarre projects that have brought local government into disrepute and ridicule. Any means that would cut off the supply of spendable funds at the source, like the voucher that by-passed local government, as again proposed by John Barnes, could be seen to have unique political attraction and voter-appeal.

Fourth, the worst excesses of trade unions have been in the public sector, especially in local government, where they can be particularly intransigent because the cost of their monopoly "rents" can be spread among large numbers of innocent and unsuspecting ratepayers. Here is yet one more reason to roll back the frontiers of government.

Fifth, in time local industry could be enlisted to support methods of inducing higher standards in state education so that employers do not have to instal remedial classes to repair the deficiencies of the schools for which their corporation taxes and local rates have paid.

Sixth, parents with lower incomes or with "domestic" rather than political life-styles could be shown that the voucher or a similar device is the only practicable means in the foreseeable future by which they can escape from the worst state schools. Strengthening "voices" requires every man and woman to be a politician.[10]

Seventh, parents of all income groups, who heavily outnumber teachers, and who are apprehensive of the secularisation of state schools by a relative handful of opinionated educationists, could see the voucher as the best way to escape to schools that reflect their religious beliefs.

10. Mrs. Shirley Williams's book *Politics Is for People* (Penguin, 1981) reveals the failure of the political mind to understand that politics is the world of political animals who frequent committee-rooms and conferences. Politics is for political people, not for those who prefer to go home after work. Mr. Ian Mikardo once argued that the political people should have more votes than the domestic people.

Apart from these existing or potential interest groups and lobbies with long-term anxieties that could see the voucher as their remedy, there are two secular developments, one on the side of supply, the other on the side of demand, that are tending to weaken the state monopoly in education. Together with the interest groups and lobbies in favour of choice and competition, they justify the hopeful note on which this Paper ends.

On the side of demand there is the overwhelming effect of rising incomes and the *embourgeoisement* of what is still called the working class. It is difficult to believe that the sharpening contrast between consumer sovereignty in everyday or household purchases, in amenities, comforts and leisure pleasures—food, clothing, furnishings, motoring, holidays—and the demeaning subservience, for any but the angry and the bully, to officials and teachers in primary and secondary schooling will be borne with equanimity for many more years by the owner-occupying children of Council house tenants. When the shopper and her husband are accustomed to receiving their "money back" from Marks and Spencer if dissatisfied, it will occur to them, or to a shrewd politician interested in their votes, to show that they could demand their "money back" from the state if dissatisfied with its schools. And when enough of them do so, the power of the National Union of Teachers and the Department of Education to obstruct reform will finally be broken.

And on the side of supply, the convenience of supplying education in large buildings called schools is evaporating: teachers will instruct pupils in small groups at their homes. The economies of large-scale teaching will remain, though not as far as the over-large schools for 1,000 pupils created by the state,[11] but computerisation is facilitating teaching at a distance; individual tutoring will prove more efficient than mass teaching in large classrooms. The difficulty of measuring the output of, and rewarding, outstanding teachers will encourage decentralisation and entrepreneurship in the classroom, as Simon Harding has persuasively argued.[12] Other changes in the conditions of supply will alienate the populace from British state schools: the weakness of comprehensive mixed-ability teaching in which the slow learners rather than the fast learners set the class pace; the anti-enterprise culture which has spread from the British aristocracy[13] to the disaffected

11. A better guide to the optimum size is the market, which has produced schools bunching at 650 to 750, as indicated by most private secondary ("public") schools; and even they are usually decentralised into federal houses of about 50 pupils for domestic self-government.

12. "Adam Smith and the Classroom," *Economic Affairs*, October–November 1985.

13. Wiener, *English Culture and the Decline of the Industrial Spirit, 1850–1980*, Cambridge University Press, 1981.

British teacher; the growing anxiety to escape from schools in which not all parents are equipped with the qualities required for effective participation in school management—now accentuated by the 1985–86 teachers' disruption.

People who see the importance of choice and competition in schooling may conclude they need not abandon the quest for the voucher, leave state schools to the producer interests, and resign themselves to the prospect that the continued decline in the quality of state education will gradually provoke public opinion into demanding reform. The obstacles that government sees in the way seem too formidable to expect political initiative to end the state monopoly in the near future. The maturation of benefits for pupils and parents seems too slow for four- to five-year Parliaments; a government that sows the seed may see its opponents reap the electoral fruit in the succeeding Parliament. Yet analysis of the potential rather than the existing group interests, the underlying and unawakened rather than the surface and superficial anxieties, suggest that the market forces that are working on the side of choice and competition could be anticipated by forethought, explanation and education on the general merits of the free society based on a market order. A distinguished academic who was a senior adviser of the Government at the 1983 General Election when the voucher was silenced has, two years later, urged "abundant facilities for individuals and groups to take the initiative in setting up schools of their own outside the state system";[14] so it is plausible to see a new readiness to return to neglected expedients. There was no overt reference to the voucher but, as Professors Rowley and Peacock have argued, it "dominates the field as the most attractive means of education support."[15]

This process has barely begun. We are witnessing an intellectual revolution. Until the 1970s, the supposed advantages of state control or regulation of industry, welfare and almost everything else were widely accepted in all schools of thought and all political parties. In the past five or ten years, faith in the state has been replaced by doubt, agonising re-appraisal, suspicion, hostility and finally rejection. Academics who favoured the statist solution are openly acknowledging they were wrong. The earnest literature of what is called the Left in British (and world-wide) intellectual life is filled with self-

14. *Daily Telegraph*, 27 November 1985.
15. *Welfare Economics: A Liberal Restatement*, Martin Robertson, 1975.

doubt, turmoil and disarray. Paradoxically, the Marxist academics are blaming the supposedly innocuous Fabians for tying socialism to the chariot of the state. The *New Left Review* anxiously concludes that even Marx was wrong:[16] markets are essential; the derision of "market forces" is stilled. There is a fervent search for "socialism without the state"[17] and a return to an earlier socialist tradition of local, voluntary, self-help organisation. The state is again seen as the oppressor, not as the safeguard, of liberty.[18] The state is the new enemy, on the Left as well as on the Right. But the alternative to the state is the market. Its former critics, even the Labour Party Deputy Leader, are having to discuss it, though they have yet to grasp its power and its populism.[19]

The power of the market is also being expressed in graphic language. A former trade union leader who had resisted the voucher finally saw it in picturesque language: "You mean, put the frighteners on them?" He had understood competition, though it works by emulation as much as anxiety to keep customers.

The effect of the continuing deterioration in state education and the widening understanding of the power of the market is seen in America. Ten years after the disappointing failure of the emasculated voucher in Alum Rock, the US Secretary of Education proposed in November 1985 the introduction of $600-a-year vouchers to enable low-income parents of 5 million children to escape from state schools by paying for private schools. And in 1986 a ballot in California will propose certificates (vouchers) of $2,000. After 20 years and billions of dollars directed to the suppliers with little effect on the schooling of poor children, the lesson has perhaps at last been learned. Money is being re-directed away from schools to parents. More money will not raise standards unless it creates comparison by competition and the power to desert the lesser schools for the better.

In this new intellectual world, former philosophic opponents who had sought liberty by what seemed conflicting routes could learn from experience. A century of state initiative has taught that it does not yield the hoped-

16. Alec Nove, "Soviet Economic Prospects," January/February 1980; Wlodzimierz Brus, "Socialism—Feasible and Viable?" September/October 1985.

17. The title of a book by Evan Luard, a former Labour MP, Macmillan, 1979.

18. David Green, "From Socialism to the New Liberalism," in *The "New Right" Enlightenment,* Economic and Literary Books, 1985.

19. Roy Hattersley, *Socialism and Markets,* Second Fabian Lecture, 19 November 1985.

for results. The merits of the market are now more widely recognised than ever before,[20] not least in welfare—medical care and housing as well as education.[21] The essence of the market is not "voice"—argument with a monopoly supplier—but "exit"—the reserve ability to desert it. In the task of allowing the market in education to re-emerge, the voucher by any name will be indispensable.

The final reversal of the balance of power from producers to consumers will require a change in ideas, emphasised by Keynes as the dominant influence on events, and a re-assertion of interest, the decisive factor identified by Marx. Keynes was the more right since interests cannot dominate without ideas. But John Stuart Mill anticipated both Keynes and Marx with more subtle insight when he saw that ideas required "circumstances" to "conspire" to make them effective. The circumstances of long-run *embourgeoisement* and fortuitous technological advance are "conspiring" to make politicised state education inadequate for the requirements and aspirations of the late 20th century. Only an open market in school education can allow free rein for the consumers and producers, the demanders and suppliers, to meet in voluntary exchange of information and experience to discover the optimum quantity and quality of schooling. To allow the market to re-emerge, the price of education must be restored as the link between supply and demand. And the way to restore price is through the voucher, in essence, even if another name is politically more expedient.

20. Among the numerous re-appraisals on the Left that have appeared in recent months, the most incisive are by Professor Stuart Hall of the Open University, Andrew Gamble of Sheffield University, and P. J. Dunleavy of the London School of Economics in *Marxism Today* and *New Socialist.*

21. Ellie Scrivens, "Creating Choice through Markets: Housing and Care for the Elderly," *Public Money,* December 1984. Nicholas Bosanquet, now a sceptic rather than an opponent of the market in welfare, proposes "service credits" (another variant for vouchers) for disabled people to use at private nursing homes: *After the New Right,* Heinemann, 1983, and in *Economic Affairs,* February–March 1986.

SECTION VII

Summary and Conclusions

1. "What happened to the voucher?" The solution to the riddle is not administrative impracticability but official feet-dragging and political underestimation of potential popular acclaim (and its "harvest" of votes).

On the bureaucracy's approach to the voucher and its "death," it may not be unkind to adapt Arthur Hugh Clough's couplet:

> Though shalt not kill; but needst not strive,
> [Officially], to keep alive.

On the political judgement of the voucher's potential "harvest" of votes (Secretary of State, Section IV), the early second thoughts on the "death" suggest that more political information and advocacy directed at parents and less sensitivity to the special pleading of the suppliers could induce the "harvest." The unique, irrefutable IEA researches over 15 years discovered growing desire for choice that could be adduced as evidence to re-inforce a more resolute political initiative in 1986. The material reviewed in this Paper clearly points to the conclusion that "the bureaucrats, if told to do so, would produce a perfectly workable scheme. There is no difficulty that cannot be overcome with ingenuity. But it requires political will."[1]

2. The task in the arena of ideas is to dramatise the power of exit as the ultimate control that could be put into the grasp of parents. Notions of power, accountability, participation are still too dominated by the concepts of political science and government, in which control is exercised by the voice of the voter respected by elected representative politicians. This system, though it must be tolerated in public goods, is a poor second-best to the economist's notion of control by the power of exit in the market. The political process has

1. FEVER Chairman, Open University telecast, "Decision-making in Britain," BBC 2, March 1983.

failed in education because it is distorted by organised producer groups and by the arbitrary cultural power of the higher-income groups and of the politically adroit in all income groups.

3. The imbalance in political advocacy has prejudiced choice and competition in education. The politicians who favour choice and competition cannot condemn *à l'outrance* the principle of the political process by which they live; but politicians who condemn choice and competition have no difficulty in extolling the political process which is the source of their power.

4. To redress the political imbalance, market forces should be given full scope in both supply and demand by removing obstacles to the exertion of parental preferences and entrepreneurship in schooling.

5. The voucher *affaire* goes to the roots of British democracy. The politicisation of education has transferred power from *demos* to public "demos" in which the dispersed parent cannot match the marching, banner-carrying teacher. A British newspaper not noted for revolutionary sentiments spoke recently of

> . . . measures dear to [the Prime Minister] which fell by the wayside include education vouchers, student loans, repeal of rent control . . . though her aspirations reflect popular feeling, they run counter to those of the political classes . . . the establishment, by now accustomed to rule whomever *demos* elects.[2]

This verdict on recent events was anticipated in March 1983 by the former Scottish Education Minister:

> You have to have a determination on the part of the whole Government from the Prime Minister downwards, if you want to bring forward a revolution in education.[3]

2. *Daily Telegraph*, 13 January 1986.
3. See note 1 above.

SELECTED READINGS

Background references in addition to sources cited in the text

Barnes, John, "Take Education Off the Rates," *Economic Affairs,* Vol. 2, No. 1, October 1981.

Blaug, Mark, *Readings in the Economics of Education,* Penguin Books, 1969.

Blaug, Mark, and Dennison, Stanley, "Can Independent Education Be Suppressed?—Two Views," *Economic Affairs,* Vol. 2, No. 1, October 1981.

Dawson, Graham, "No Merit in State Education," *Economic Affairs,* Vol. 5, No. 4, July–September 1985.

Dennison, S. R., *Choice in Education,* Hobart Paperback 19, IEA, 1984.

Hannan, Audrey, "The State School Straitjacket," *Economic Affairs,* Vol. 2, No. 3, April 1982.

Hutchison, T. W., *Markets and the Franchise,* Occasional Paper 10, IEA, 1966.

Illich, Ivan, *De-schooling Society,* Penguin Books, 1973.

Maynard, Alan, *Experiment with Choice in Education,* Hobart Paper 64, IEA, 1975.

McKenzie, R., and Tullock, G., *The New World of Economics,* Irwin, Illinois, 1975.

Olson, Mancur, *The Logic of Collective Choice,* Harvard University Press, 1965.

Peacock, Alan T., "Education Voucher Schemes—Strong or Weak?" *Economic Affairs,* Vol. 3, No. 2, January 1983.

Seldon, A., "West on Vouchers," *Economic Affairs,* Vol. 3, No. 1, October 1982.

———, *Taxation and Welfare,* Research Monograph 14, IEA, 1967.

Tullock, G., *Toward a Mathematics of Politics,* University of Michigan Press, 1967.

West, E. G., "Education Vouchers: Evolution or Revolution?" *Economic Affairs,* Vol. 3, No. 1, October 1982.

Wiseman, J., "The Economics of Education," *Scottish Journal of Political Economy,* 1959.

INDEX

The text for this book is set in Minion; the display type is Meta Plus Book. Both are relatively new faces, chosen to reflect Seldon's influence on and activity in contemporary social and economic thought. Minion was designed by Robert Slimbach for Adobe in 1990. In spirit and intent it derives from the Garamond tradition. Meta, designed by Erik Spiekermann in 1993, with open spacing for legibility at small sizes, has grown into an extended family and is now widely used.

Printed on paper that is acid-free and meets the requirements of the American National Standard for Permanence of Paper for Printed Library Materials, z39.48-1992. ♾

Book design by Barbara Williams, BW&A Books, Inc., Durham, North Carolina
Typography by Graphic Composition, Inc., Athens, Georgia
Printed and bound by Edwards Brothers, Inc., Ann Arbor, Michigan